D1455610

Master Scheduling

A Practical Guide to Competitive Manufacturing

John F. Proud

THE OLIVER WIGHT COMPANIES

Oliver Wight®

Oliver Wight Publications, Inc.
85 Allen Martin Drive
Essex Junction, VT 05452

Oliver Wight Publications books may be purchased for educational,
business, or sales promotional use. For information, please call
or write: Special Sales Department, Oliver Wight Publications, Inc.,
85 Allen Martin Drive, Essex Junction, VT 05452.
Telephone: (800) 343-0625 or (802) 878-8161; Fax: (802) 878-3384.

Library of Congress Catalog Card Number: 93-060667

ISBN: 0-939246-36-8

Designed by Irving Perkins Associates.

Printed on acid-free paper.

Manufactured in the United States of America.
2 4 6 8 10 9 7 5 3 1

This book is dedicated to manufacturing professionals worldwide, especially those who have chosen master scheduling as a career.

Acknowledgments

I am deeply grateful to a number of people who have shaped as well as enhanced my professional career through education and idea sharing. Many of these people are current and past members of the American Production and Inventory Control Society (APICS), which I have been a member of for twenty years (and I look forward to continuing that association for another twenty years). However, two people have had more influence in that career than the many others:

Dick Ling, former Oliver Wight associate and former president of Arista Education and Consulting, exposed me to the profession of master scheduling. If I had not crossed paths with Dick Ling and several other Oliver Wight associates, I would not have been able to write this book. I learned my master scheduling skills from the best in the industry—Dick Ling, Oliver Wight associates, and professional master schedulers working in Class A companies worldwide.

Dick Pugliese, while serving as general manager of a Xerox plant, gave me the opportunity to be part of a Class A manufacturing resource planning system implementation. It was during this time that I learned how a manufacturing company should work if it is to be successful and achieve Class A results.

Other colleagues and associates have also taught me much about this complex subject. John Dougherty literally spent hours with me discussing and developing concepts that we hope furthered the industry's understanding of how important master scheduling is to the manufacturing environment. Walt Goddard, John Sari, and Al Stevens also developed numerous master scheduling concepts over the years and were kind enough to share them with me. Oliver Wight associates Tom Gillen, who helped me with the engineering issues, and George Palmatier, who made sure I did justice to the demand side of the business, also deserve recognition.

Several other people whom I would like to thank and acknowledge are: Dick Leucke and Steve Bennett, who were instrumental in taking my thoughts and structuring them into sentences and phrases that actually make sense; Lori Stacey, who spent hours upon hours typing, correcting, re-typing, and re-correcting the lengthy manuscript; the Oliver Wight Publications staff, who have been effective, cooperative, patient, and understanding throughout this book's entire process.

Once the manuscript draft was available, Mike Bales, manufacturing manager, Joslyn Manufacturing Company; Dick Pugliese, retired executive; John Sari and Larry Wilson, Oliver Wight Associates; worked their way through the many pages, challenging my thoughts and recommending changes as appropriate. Without their critical input, this book would be less than the book that it is today. My "severest and best critic" was Oliver Wight associate Darryl Landvater, who challenged not only content but organization. A special thank you goes to Darryl for his effort, time, and patience.

Another special thanks goes to my editor and publisher, Jim Childs, whom I am sure I caused great grief when I missed several milestones along the way—what, the person who wrote the book on valid master schedules was "past due"? If you ever doubt how important it is for a manufacturing company to create valid schedules and then perform to these schedules in order to satisfy its customers, just give my publisher a call. In addition to Jim Childs, Dana Scannell was the first to give me the chance to write this book and encouraged me to keep going when my frustrations were high and my stamina was low.

My final thank you goes to my lovely wife, Darlene, who gave me the time necessary and seldom complained about being left alone while I worked in the office. Darlene is truly my best friend, and without her understanding and encouragement, I would never have found myself in a position to write these acknowledgments for what I believe is the first definitive book covering the subject of master scheduling.

Contents

11. Finishing Schedules 309

12. Sales and Operations Planning 335

13. Rough Cut Capacity Planning 353

Foreword

It took someone with knowledge, understanding, breadth of experience, and passion for the subject to write this book.

A book that fills a gap in the literature of manufacturing.

A book that took tremendous effort to produce.

I have known John Proud for more than fifteen years. I have worked with him, taught with him, and debated concepts with him, developing a respect that he deserves both personally and professionally.

John has accomplished a monumental task in writing the definitive work on Master Scheduling. There are very few people who have the combination of user experience, software understanding, and consulting and teaching experience in a variety of industries that would enable them to present Master Scheduling in both an understandable and readable format.

This is not a theoretical book. John has taken great pains to help the reader to thoroughly understand the application of the principles of Master Scheduling, describing what works in great detail. When first reading the book, the reader could become mired in the technical detail of an environment that is different from his or her own company. My suggestion is to concentrate on those areas that apply to your environment and, at a later time, return to those areas that have no direct bearing on your experience for further understanding.

The manufacturing community, academia, and professional organizations will need to look very seriously at this work. It has the characteristics to make it the standard text for any course on Master Scheduling and the standard resource for all manufacturing companies who desire to do Master Scheduling well.

John, my sincere congratulations for writing such a definitive book on Master Scheduling.

Richard C. Ling
President, Richard C. Ling, Inc.

Introduction

The Master of All Schedules

***I seek not to know all the answers,
but to understand the questions.***

The 1960s were times of radical change in America; the youth of the country challenged almost every traditional value, rebelling in ways unheard of in previous generations. In manufacturing, a much quieter, though no less dramatic, revolution also was taking place. Traditional means of production and inventory control went by the boards as companies like Twin Disc and J. I. Case made effective use of Material Requirements Planning (MRP) a reality. Though crude by today's standards, these early attempts at MRP gave manufacturing professionals their first real weapons in the war on production inefficiencies.

When companies first began using MRP, they drove it with a forecast and/or customer orders (demand). In other words, to calculate material requirements, computers multiplied the latest demand numbers by the quantities required in the bills-of-material (BOM). The problem with this approach was that it blindly assumed that the resources would be available to manufacture a product in sufficient quantities just as it was sold. Unfortunately, manufacturing rarely produced each product as it was sold. And as demand numbers inevitably changed over time, material requirements changed with them. With computer-driven tools, it was very possible to generate overwhelming change to schedules that plants and suppliers could not handle. This meant that the information in the system was often in chaos. And so was the production line. The frequent result was an overloaded schedule, underutilized resources, or both.

Some of the MRP pioneers quickly realized that their formal systems were of little value if they failed to predict and control the resources needed to support the way production was actually scheduled. They also realized that they had left the computer too much decision-making power; nowhere in the process was there a human being who ensured a true balance between supply (factory and supplier resources) and demand (customers). These insights led to the development of a "master schedule" that controlled all other schedules: factory, purchase orders, and so forth. Equally important, a new position was created: that of the master scheduler. These developments really marked the birth of Master Production Scheduling (MPS), or to use the term favored in this book, Master Scheduling. (The acronym MPS will be used throughout the book when referring to master scheduling.)

Master scheduling is the pivotal point in a manufacturing business when demand from the marketplace is balanced with the capabilities of the company and its suppliers in real-time terms. As the modern manufacturing environment has grown more complex in terms of products and product options, and more demanding in terms of the competitive requirements for quality, fast delivery, and low prices, this balancing mechanism has been a vital tool for management at many levels. At the top-management level, sales and operations planning has become the integrator of all other plans: sales, marketing, quality, engineering, financial, and production. At middle-management levels, and on the factory floor, master scheduling spells out in detail what needs to be produced so that the company can ensure that capacity will be available, that materials will be on hand when needed, and that customer requirements will be satisfied on dates specified by the customers.

MPS as Part of the Overall Business Planning System

Like all other business planning systems, MPS is geared to market demand. It coordinates that demand with resources in the company to schedule optimal production rates. To help management make decisions about aggregate production rates, companies developed a process called Sales and Operations Planning (S&OP). In the S&OP process, the heads of each function meet at least once a month and develop a company plan that synchronizes planned output with marketplace demand.

The sales and operations planning team considers products by aggregate families, and it is the job of the master scheduler to break down those aggregate build rates into detailed, weekly production schedules for each item. In this way, S&OP drives and guides the master schedule.[1]

The expansion of the original material requirements planning technique into a set of functions encompassing demand management, sales and operations planning, master scheduling, material requirements planning, capacity planning and control, and supplier and factory scheduling has become known as Manufacturing Resource Planning (MRP II).[2] It's fair to say that the addition of MPS was a key ingredient in the evolution of MRP to MRP II (see chapter 2 for a schematic of the MRP II process).

[1] For a complete discussion of sales and operations planning, see Richard C. Ling and Walter E. Goddard, *Orchestrating Success* (Essex Junction, VT: Oliver Wight Publications, 1988), pp 125–33.

[2] For a complete discussion of manufacturing resource planning, see Darryl V. Landvater, *World Class Production and Inventory Management* (Essex Junction, VT: Oliver Wight Publications, 1993), and *Manufacturing Resource Planning: MRP II, Unlocking America's Productivity Potential* (Essex Junction, VT: Oliver Wight Publications, 1981), Appendix 1, pp 403–17.

Just having a master schedule does not ensure success. As with all tools, the MPS must be managed. Failure to manage the MPS results in the company's manufacturing and supplier resources being poorly deployed. This in turn means that the company may be unresponsive to customer needs or wasteful in its use of resources. Ultimately, the company risks losing its competitive position. Moreover, if the MPS is improperly managed, many of the benefits from the sales and operations planning process will be lost.

Managed well, the MPS provides the basis for good customer order promising and good resource utilization. By maintaining an up-to-date picture of the balance between supply and demand, master scheduling allows each customer to get the best service possible within the constraints of inventory, resources, and time. And by providing updated information about the current status of company schedules and their ability to support customer commitments, the MPS focuses management's attention where it is needed. In short, MPS plays a major role in helping companies stay responsive, competitive, and profitable.

Who Should Understand Master Scheduling?

This book is not intended solely for master schedulers, but also for those who should participate in designing their company's approach to master scheduling. For master schedulers—both new to the job and those who have been doing it for years—this book can help them to do their jobs more effectively. Beginners will find a complete framework for understanding the MPS process and how it connects with the rest of the business. Seasoned professionals will be challenged into rethinking master scheduling at their companies. And all readers will benefit from numerous tricks of the trade, drawn from years of management, consulting, and teaching experience.

Managers in sales, marketing, manufacturing, materials, design, engineering, systems, and finance will also benefit from knowledge of MPS, which is, after all, the integration point for other planning, analysis, prioritizing, and performance measurement. They will find the chapters that cover the general principles of the MPS process useful reading.

Senior managers should familiarize themselves with the basic concepts of this book and should understand the later chapters, which cover sales and operations planning, rough cut capacity planning, demand management, and effective implementation. This is because master scheduling balances resource utilization and customer satisfaction while supporting the strategic as well as tactical directions determined in the sales and operations planning process. As one manufacturing manager put it, "No one ever got to Class A without doing MPS well."[3] It therefore behooves everyone of authority in the company to understand what goes into and comes out of the master schedule.

The master scheduler and people in special environments will benefit from the middle chapters, which cover specific environments and advanced techniques. Overall, the book has been designed to have something for just about everyone connected with competitive manufacturing.

How This Book Is Organized

Master scheduling involves many functions of business and crosses most departmental lines. This is the first book designed to pull together a comprehensive body of knowledge about master scheduling

[3] The term "Class A" refers to the top rating a manufacturing company can achieve, based on the Oliver Wight ABCD Checklist for Operational Excellence. The original checklist was developed by Oliver Wight in 1977 and has been updated since to reflect the evolving standards of performance achieved by world-class manufacturing companies. (See the Appendix, page 485.)

and to discuss the MPS process within the context of various manufacturing environments. It not only paints a broad perspective across the whole canvas of manufacturing but provides the fine details needed to understand MPS in specific types of businesses. Whether you make finished goods to stock, assemble or finish to customer order, or design and build products to customer specifications, you will find information and tools relevant to your business.

Chapters 1 through 6 of *Master Scheduling: A Practical Guide to Competitive Manufacturing* define the MPS process by explaining why and what to master schedule, the basic terminology, calculations, formats, and mechanics, and how to manage change using MPS. Chapters 7 through 11 cover specific tools and techniques used in various manufacturing environments (make-to-stock, make-to-order, engineer-to-order, make-to-contract). Chapters 12 through 14 describe the supporting functions of MPS, such as sales and operations planning, rough cut capacity planning, and demand management. The book's chapters conclude with chapter 15—guidelines for implementing and operating a successful master scheduling process across the boards.

Master Scheduling is not intended to be read cover to cover in one sitting. Rather, the general sections should be covered first, followed by those chapters that address the reader's manufacturing environment.

This book is intended to impart a thorough understanding of the master scheduling process, how it interfaces with other manufacturing systems and processes, and the role various people play in it. It aims to arm the reader with the knowledge required to fine-tune the master schedule process to the needs of his or her own company with the goal of improving customer satisfaction and enhancing competitiveness.

No company ever gets to Class A without managing MPS well, nor does anyone ever perform master scheduling well without having a firm grasp of the basic concepts and principles underlying the process. In the manufacturing arena, knowledge is truly power. Use that knowledge well, and your company will prosper.

Master Scheduling

1

Chaos on the Manufacturing Floor

Don't mistake activity for accomplishment.

The Place: A typical North American manufacturing company
The Time: 10:00 A.M.
The Date: Friday, the last day of the month

What had been a quiet and sporadically busy area three weeks ago has turned into a three-ring circus. Lift trucks careen through the stockrooms at full tilt, barely avoiding head-on collisions. Every inch of the shipping department is piled with partially completed products waiting for missing components. Normally neat and orderly work areas now resemble obstacle courses as excess materials clog the aisles.

Outside the supervisor's office an angry manager berates an expediter, demanding to know why the night shift had run the wrong size product. The expediter shifts his weight from foot to foot as he explains that the required product had been at the top of the "hot list"—and maybe the night supervisor did not get that revision of this week's list (of which there had been three).

Over in one of the assembly areas a worker complains that she has gone as far as she can without the next skid from the processing department. A supervisor moves from worker to worker, asking people to sign up for weekend overtime. A chart on the wall shows that 30 percent of the month's shipments still need to be made.

The cost variance reports that were the burning issue of the manufacturing meetings just two short weeks ago are now buried under a stack of quality control reject reports. Management has temporarily waived the rejects so that needed materials can be used to meet this month's numbers.

Off in a corner by the coffee machine, a gray-haired foreman shakes his head and mumbles: "So this is the factory of the future that the guys in corporate promised. It looks like the factory of the past to me."

This scene plays itself out in many manufacturing companies today. Worse, like a recurring nightmare it returns to haunt companies month after month. It happens, in part, because many companies still operate in a reactive mode, in which all decisions, priorities, and schedules are driven by the day-to-day fluctuations of the marketplace, momentary changes on the factory floor, and the performance of individual suppliers. It is a cycle of action and reaction, and until companies break the cycle, they will never rid themselves of the end-of-the-month nightmare.

Breaking the cycle entails four steps:

1. Admitting that serious problems exist, and that the current situation is not healthy for the company or the people who work in it

2. Identifying the specific problems—not just the symptoms

3. Determining the cause of the problems

4. Creating and acting on effective solutions

Problems on the Factory Floor

Consider again the scenario above, this time through the eyes of the plant manager, who sees that although everyone is attempting to do a conscientious job, the efforts are often misdirected. The use of hot lists to set priorities in getting products out the door causes major disruptions and confusion on the shop floor. Schedule changes prompted by these hot lists satisfy some short-term requirements but throw a monkey wrench into others. Shipment dates are missed, the customers complain to the sales force, and the sales manager vents his anger onto the production manager.

Although there appears to be much work-in-process, the reality is that most of the work is sitting in queues. In addition, a staggering amount of unplanned overtime and quality problems are mounting.

Symptoms of Master Scheduling Problems

Uncontrollable costs	Hot lists
Disruptions on the shop floor	Frequent schedule changes
Late deliveries to customers	Many full-time expediters
Late deliveries from suppliers	Customer complaints
Unplanned overtime/off-loading	High "past dues"
High work-in-process	Long queues
Mismatched inventories	End-of-month crunch
Over-/under-utilized resources	Finger pointing/low morale

After inventorying the problems, the plant manager begins to look for their underlying causes. The hot lists, he finds, are used because of frequent part shortages, some of which result from late deliveries from suppliers, late ordering by the company, and the poor quality of parts actually delivered. Other part shortages result from inaccurate bills-of-material and inventory record inaccuracies that report parts in stock when they are not.

Schedule change problems often stem from the lack of a priority mechanism, or from following the wrong priorities—such as keeping a machine busy rather than satisfying a customer. (It is not unusual for a company that has just purchased a new piece of expensive equipment to believe that its first priority is to keep the machine running, even if there are no customer orders for the machine's output.)

Missed shipment dates may result from part shortages or problems with capacity. Some companies are not ever sure what their capacity is nor do they have a mechanism to measure it. In other companies, measuring mechanisms may be available, but they may not be accurate.

Additionally, material can sit in queues on the manufacturing floor because of part shortages, because of the capacity issues just described, or because factory priorities and work flows are driven by an overly optimistic sales forecast that is used to communicate priorities to people on the shop floor.

Still other problems on the factory floor have their source in inaccurate forecasts of demand—forecasts that instruct the plant to build either too much or too little.

THE INACCURATE FORECAST

It seems to happen all the time. The marketing department forecasts customer demand at one level, while actual demand turns out to be something different—sometimes more, but often less.

The difficulty of scheduling production in the face of forecast inaccuracies should be obvious: Materials and capacities are planned for one level of demand, but the demand that actually finds its way to the production facility is something different. Consider the simple case on the facing page.

Periods	April	May	June	Quarterly Total
Forecast	100	100	100	300
Demand	140	65	120	325
Variance	+40	−35	+20	+25

This company's quarterly forecast was off the mark by 25 units (about 8 percent). Not bad. Its forecast for individual production periods, however, was greatly off target. This is typical, as forecasting aggregate demand is always easier and tends to be more accurate than forecasting for shorter periods.

Unfortunately, production is scheduled in these (or even smaller) periods, where grousing about inaccurate forecasts is commonplace but does little to alter the fact that forecasting the future will never have the precision of rocket science. Forecasts may be improved, but never guaranteed. Besides, any forecaster who could really see the future clearly would be in the next limo headed toward Wall Street, where rewards for accurate forecasting are mind-boggling!

Management Issues

People in the day-to-day business of manufacturing must learn to live with the variances between forecasted and actual demand, and with the problems they create. For managers, forecast inaccuracies create a number of important issues. First among these is the fact that when someone creates a forecast, real things happen: Materials and components are ordered. If current capacity isn't up to the forecast, people start thinking about increasing it with new equipment and new personnel. In other words, forecasting demand is not an intellectual exercise done for its own sake, but an activity that triggers a number of other costly actions within the company.

Unfortunately, forecasts are not always taken seriously. Salespeople are tempted to overstate the forecast as insurance against possible stockouts. The forecast itself is generally uncritical of the estimates submitted by each salesperson and contains no rewards and penalties for accuracy. The task of management is getting all parties to the forecast to work together and have a vested interest in its accuracy. Production and finance need to understand the concern of sales personnel about stockouts and lost commissions. Sales and marketing need to understand the cost of excess inventory to the profitability and survival of the company.

There is now a large body of knowledge and experience indicating the heights of customer service and profitability that result when teamwork replaces hostility among production, finance, marketing, and sales personnel. Management can and should act as the catalyst in team-building efforts.

While the team-building activity may be the greatest contribution of senior management, other issues merit its concern:

- *What about inventory?* If a plant is scheduled to build 100 units and orders for 140 appear, is there enough inventory to satisfy the unexpected demand? In the reverse case, when demand fails to appear, should the plant keep running and building inventory?

- *What alternatives exist on the factory floor?* When forecasted orders fail to appear, equipment and trained people are idled—unless alternative work is found. Moving up an order might keep some hands busy; maintenance or training might occupy others. When demand exceeds scheduled supply, can more supply be created through overtime or outsourcing of part of the workload?

- *What are the real costs of forecast inaccuracy?* An overloaded schedule creates overtime expenses. The production floor and its personnel are stressed and, perhaps, made less productive. Overforecasted demand creates idle hands and capacity, and inventories of unused materials.

- *How are customers affected?* When actual demand is underestimated, management becomes a traffic cop, directing the company's limited output to certain customers and withholding it from others. How should product be allocated when there isn't enough to go around? Which customers have priority?

As management ponders these issues, the fallout of forecast inaccuracies has other minds working. Marketing observes the discrepancies between its forecasts and actual demand and wonders if these mark a trend. If the forecast is usually on the high side, manufacturing thinks about discounting the forecast as a matter of policy. The corporate controller jokes about just tossing the manufacturing budget out the window. Out in the field, the individual salesperson grows apprehensive about guaranteeing delivery on firm orders; when push comes to shove, another sales representative's customer may have priority.

Knowing that forecasts will never match actual demand, except on rare occasions, experienced master schedulers understand that they must be flexible in shifting capacity and materials from one period to another. They must know whom to call about splitting a customer's delivery over two or more periods. And they must have the courage to look beyond the forecasted numbers as they plan production. Indeed, many top managers would be stunned to know that the solution to many of their production headaches is in the hands of the master scheduler, who either solves them with skill and ingenuity, or allows them to fester out of inexperience or indifference.

And the Solutions

The search for solutions to these problems should begin with a fundamental question: Why is this company in business? And the answer should be: To make a profit and satisfy customers. This answer entails ensuring an adequate product supply to meet the expected demand for the company's products. If a product is not on hand to satisfy demand, the company must have the material, labor, equipment, capital, and time to produce it. This is where master scheduling and manufacturing resource planning (MRP II) play such a critical role in the purpose of the business.

Manufacturing resource planning is a demand-driven process. This demand can consist of a forecast, customer orders (which may or may not be part of that forecast), contracts or long-term agreements, branch warehouse requirements (i.e., replenishing a distribution center), or orders from another division within the company if the product in question is, in turn, a component of that division's products. Demand can also originate in the need for service parts or spares, safety stocks, and lot sizes.

To satisfy these demands, the master scheduler needs to consider the available supply of materials and capacity resources. These materials include those being produced internally as well as those being procured from outside sources. Besides the item itself, quantities, dates, and lead times must be taken into account. Capacity involves people and equipment—both of one's own company and of its suppliers. Again, time is an important factor.

As mentioned in the introduction, the job of the master scheduler is to effectively balance product supply with product demand. One way to envision the situation is to imagine a seesaw like the one shown in Figure 1.1. In a perfect world, the seesaw is parallel with the ground; supply is always an equal counterweight to demand. When demand

Figure 1.1 Balancing Supply and Demand

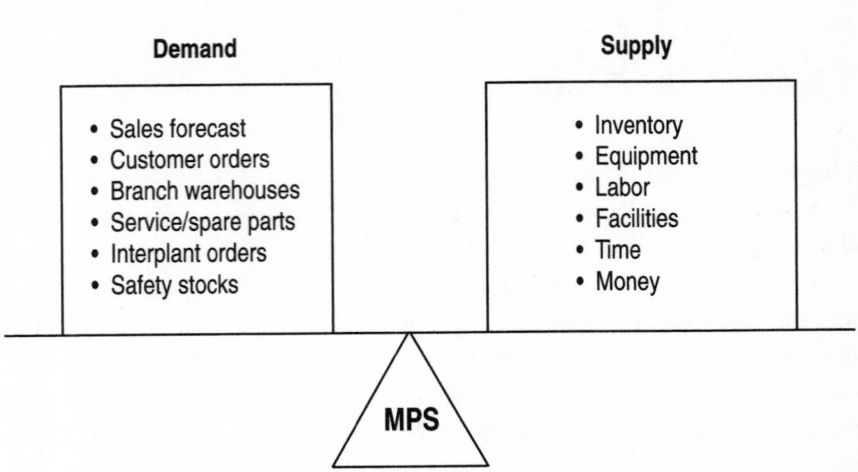

changes, supply instantly adjusts in a way that keeps the system in perfect balance. In the real world, however, demand rises or falls in unpredictable ways, and imbalances occur. These occasions require a master scheduler to make adjustments to the system of demand and supply.

When a company has more demand for its products than it has supply, it has two options for returning to a balanced situation:

1. Increase the supply of product—get more material and resources
2. Decrease the demand—turn away or reschedule some demand orders

The situation in which there is more supply of the product than demand also suggests two choices:

1. Generate greater demand—energize the sales force, run a promotion, discount the price, etc.
2. Decrease the supply of the product or the material/capacity needed to produce it—cut back on production, people, and equipment

Even though these situations can be solved only by the choices described above, some companies nevertheless believe that if they ignore the situation it will go away—an approach to problem solving called "ostrich management."

The periodic imbalances between demand and supply are represented in Figure 1.2 on the following page, which shows inventory's constant fluctuations over time between high, medium, and low demand as well as high, medium, and low supply, resulting in a "sawtooth curve." In manufacturing, the goal is generally to stabilize production by level-loading the plant while smoothing out the demand. The situation shown—stockouts as well as excess inventory—is not the objective; the objective is to have just enough inventory to satisfy demand, thereby satisfying customers.

Figure 1.2 The Sawtooth Curve

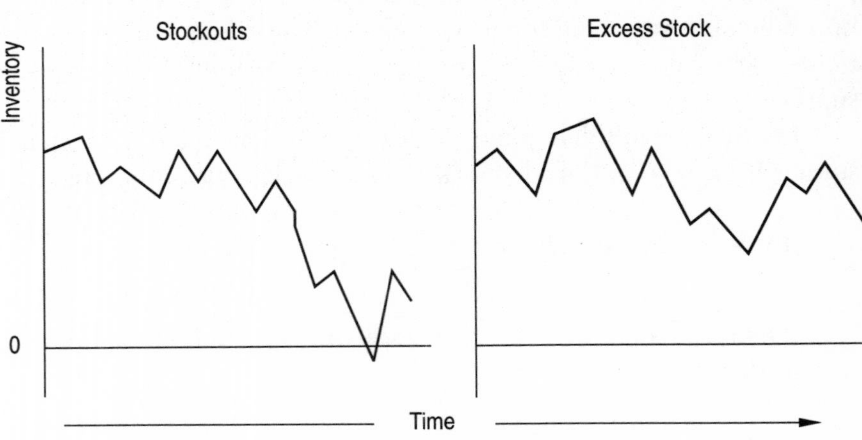

In the presence of sawtooth demand, the factory will be a seesaw in constant motion, with all the stockouts, hot lists, and confusion that characterize the company profiled at the beginning of this chapter. If the company is not experiencing stockouts, it is experiencing excess inventories. What is known for sure about this environment is that it continually goes back and forth. Companies that try to smooth out sawtooth demand through artificial contrivances usually fail. Tactics like schedule freezes and placing limits on the volume of orders salespeople can take cause more problems than they solve. Telling a sales force to limit its sales for a particular period, for example, is a sure way to torpedo the important relationship that must exist between sales and manufacturing if a company is to grow and prosper. Using these types of approaches is like installing welded struts onto the bottom of the seesaw: nothing moves. A better approach is to install "shock absorbers" under the seesaw, to dampen expected fluctuations in supply and demand (see Figure 1.3).

Inventory, in the form of finished goods, is one traditional type of shock absorber. Inventory helps the company to accommodate changes in both supply and demand. Another type of shock absorber is flexibility in the manufacturing chain, which allows the company to

Figure 1.3 Dampening Supply and Demand Fluctuations

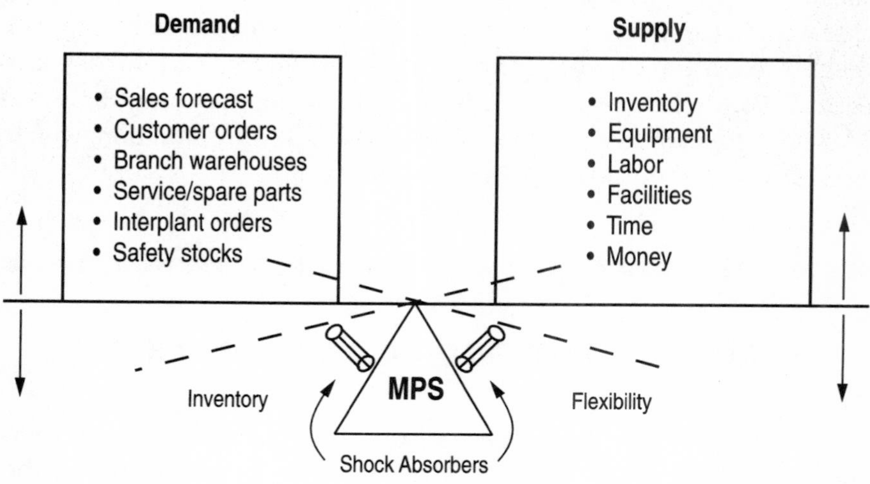

alter the activity rate on the factory floor in order to satisfy demand fluctuations without severe disruption. Flexibility can also be extended to sales and marketing. If the customer orders a red item, will a blue one work? If the customer orders the product for a next month delivery, would that delivery better suit the customer's business purpose if it arrives in this month or in two months? If the customer cannot be so swayed, discounts or other sales inducements may give him reasons to cooperate with your demand-balancing problem. The point is, don't be afraid to ask. In any case, the company should identify whether it wants its flexibility in sales and marketing or manufacturing. It should decide whether it wants to "sell the products manufacturing makes" or "build the products that sales sells." Once that determination is made, the company can move on to the task of balancing product supply with market demand. This is done in demand management, sales and operations planning, and master scheduling.

It's this effort to balance supply and demand that drives a company to improve its master scheduling process and capability. The job ahead certainly is not an easy one. However, Class A and world-class companies face uncertain demand and supply in a controlled and managed way. The next chapter addresses the issue of why companies that wish to formally establish planning and control processes elect to tackle the master scheduling function right from the start. Most Class A and world-class companies believe it's never too early to start. However, before we move on, consider the following situation, which is all too typical of today's manufacturers.

THE CASE OF THE OVERLOADED MASTER SCHEDULE

Some companies are always behind schedule on production and shipment. If Friday afternoons are a hellish race to whittle down the mountain of late manufacturing orders, Monday mornings are even worse. On Monday morning, the manufacturing manager and master scheduler face the dismal prospect of starting the new week under a load of past-due orders. It is tough enough to run a smooth operation when each week begins with a clean slate; but when you are faced with the normal scheduled orders *plus* all the work that failed to get done the previous week, the outlook is far from rosy. Yet this is how some companies operate—many on a continuing basis. Like a football team that starts the second half three touchdowns behind its opponent, the manufacturer that carries past-due orders into the next period plays a desperate game of "catch up."

Here is a typical scenario. Spectrumatic Paint Company, which has a weekly capacity of 300 units, begins the current week with 500 units to produce—the result of inept scheduling, arm twisting by salespeople to accept orders, and so forth. To compound its current problem, Spectrumatic ended the previous week sitting on past-due orders totaling 200 units.

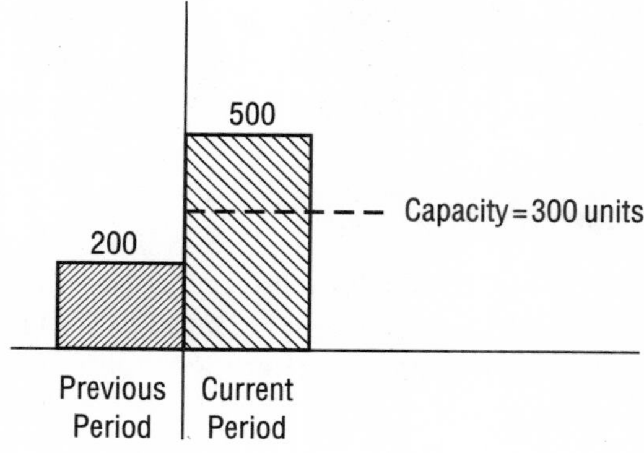

There is one unfortunate principle about past work periods, however, and this is *inalterable:* Time that passes is gone forever. Once a current production period expires, there is no retrieving it, and any orders left undone must either be done in a future period or dropped entirely. Many companies simply move them into the current period. In the case of Spectrumatic Paint Company, its inexperienced scheduler simply piled the 200 past-due units on top of the 500 units currently scheduled, resulting in a total burden of 700 units in a period with 300 units of capacity. As the next figure shows, this is what the company was faced with on Monday morning.

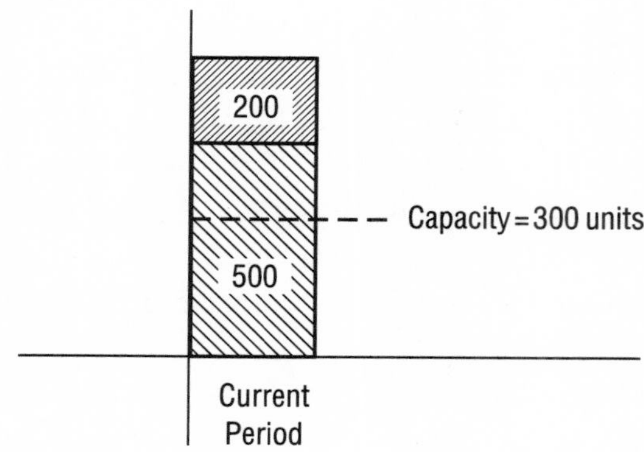

This is like packing your family station wagon to the rain gutters for a summer vacation, only to find that—*oops!*—you forgot the bicycles, fishing gear, and canoe. Chances are that with all this new stuff loading down the wagon, you and your passengers are destined for an uncomfortable ride. Therefore, this scenario suggests an ironclad law for master schedulers to obey: The master schedule cannot be past due.

Issues for Management

Past-due MPS orders and overscheduling current work periods are two major sources of the overloaded master schedules that plague so many companies. And these overloaded schedules create a host of *internal* problems for management.

- *Production efficiency decreases.* "Drop what you're doing and start order 0247. We have to get this customer taken care of or we'll lose their whole account!" Poorly timed line changeovers, downtime due to material shortages, and stress take a toll on efficiency on the floor. Floor supervisors also get mixed signals as to real priorities.
- *Products do not get shipped.* An overloaded master schedule results in material stockouts; partially built products are taken off-line, where they sit as work-in-process until missing materials are received. Products not shipped and billed reduce current revenues, thereby creating financing problems for the entire company.
- *Costs go up or out of control.* As production efficiency decreases, financial managers see costs rising. Dependence on overtime, expedited material purchases, air freight charges on late orders, concessions to irate customers, and other compensations drive up unit costs and cause havoc with cost planning and budgets.
- *Widespread confusion makes it difficult for management to identify the real problems.* Why are products not being shipped? Lack of coordination of materials and production scheduling? Capacity problems? Credit holds?
- *Product quality suffers.* Production is pressured to work faster and faster to complete work in less than planned lead time, causing quality to drop.

Given all of these negatives, we have to ask: Why would anyone allow the master schedule to be overloaded? Very often, the answer comes down to some basic human behaviors in situations where trust and confidence are absent.

Consider the sales representative who must ensure delivery of 100 units of Model 5B3 refrigerators to an appliance distributor on the 15th of October. If the company's history is such that production is *always* late, or *always* short, or the stockroom *never* has enough components to complete an order, this sales representative has every incentive to inflate the size of the order and to ask that the order be moved up in the schedule. "One hundred twenty units delivered to the customer on the first of October," becomes his entry to the order book. Discounting production's capabilities is a natural response to past lack of performance, and deliberately overloading the schedule is seen as a way of ensuring that enough materials will be on hand and that enough units will be built. Naturally, production schedulers learn to play this game and begin discounting orders as they appear. In no time at all, no one can trust anyone else's numbers.

The unfortunate part of this dysfunctional charade is that all the players are motivated to do the right thing: for the sales representative, to fill the customer order with the right quantity at the right time; for the purchasing department, to have just enough materials on hand; for the production facility, to meet *real* demand in an efficient and timely manner.

The net result of all these fine intentions in an atmosphere of distrust, however, is an overloaded master schedule and profit- and energy-sapping people problems, the most deadly being the "blame game." Marketing blames manufacturing for lost orders due to shipment delays. Manufacturing points the finger at the sales representatives, who "promise anything to get an order." Everything is a crisis. Finance yells that "costs are out of control" because of overtime and air freight. In this atmosphere, the refusal to recognize the seriousness of the problem naturally becomes a survival trait. Why admit that there *is* a problem? You can only be blamed for it and, maybe, fired ("If you can't get the job done, we'll find someone who can!"). Avoidance or denial of the problem becomes the course of least resistance. Sweep it under the rug. Park it at someone else's door.

Ultimately, all the people problems come to rest at the doorstep of management. Management must create an environment in which all concerned can be honest about their numbers. Sales and production must be motivated to be frank with one another and to operate in a mutually beneficial partnership. Very often, the key to developing this environment of cooperation is, as W. Edward Deming noted, to "drive out fear."[1] Management must end the blame game and create a climate in which people can admit to problems and past mistakes without fear of blame or retribution. Lacking this climate, problems will simply continue being swept under the carpet.

With fear driven from the workplace, the next step toward dealing with an overloaded master schedule is a top-down analysis that

- lists sales and production priorities;
- seeks practical remedies to production constraints;
- prioritizes and allocates production to customer demands; and
- establishes a strategy to get out of—and stay out of—the over-scheduled condition.

The ultimate goal of this analysis, or course, is to give management the knowledge and the tools to shake off the oppressive burden of the overloaded master schedule and to reschedule production with completion dates that are both realistic and that satisfy customer needs to the company's best ability.

Getting Out of the Overloaded MPS

One of the primary responsibilities of the master scheduler is to create a valid master schedule. A valid master schedule is one in which the material due dates equal the material need dates, and the

[1] From Deming's "Fourteen Points," W. Edward Deming, *Out of Crisis* (Cambridge: Massachusetts Institute of Technology/Center for Advanced Engineering Study, 1982), p. 23.

Figure 1.4 Past-Due Master Schedule

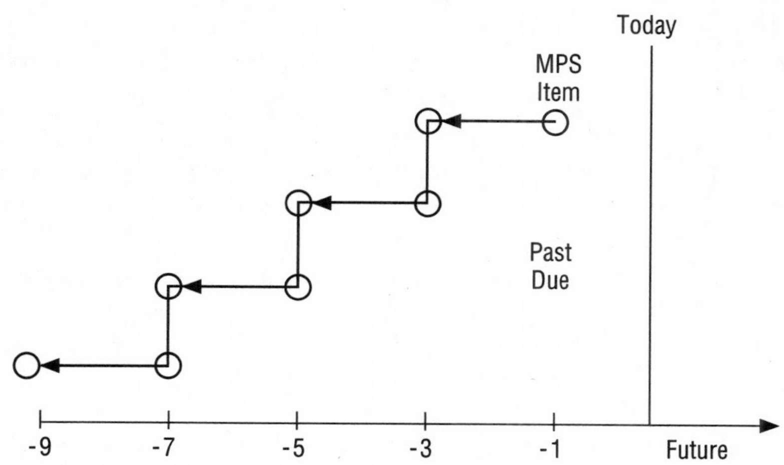

planned capacity equals the required capacity. Look at Figure 1.4. As you can see, a master schedule item has gone past due. This MPS item is used to drive the material requirements for all lower-level items as well as the capacity requirements for the entire manufacturing and engineering resource data base. If the MPS item is past due, what does that say about all the material that still needs to become part of the scheduled item? All this material is also past due. If we start with a past-due date, all the material and capacity still required, by definition, is past due. And how valid is a past-due date? How do you answer manufacturing or engineering when they ask, "Which past due do you want me to work on today?"

The job of creating a valid master schedule is not an easy one. It certainly is harder to do than to create an invalid schedule. In fact, it is not difficult at all to create an invalid schedule! Just about anyone can do that! The real challenge is to create a schedule that balances supply of resources and products with the demand for those resources and products. So, when in an overloaded condition, how does a master scheduler successfully orchestrate getting out of this inevitable situation?

The first step is to admit that the master schedule is overloaded. With the question answered, an assessment of the situation and identifying the constraints facing the company become necessary. Can overtime be used? Can work be subcontracted? Can more people be hired? Can material be expedited? Can premium air or ground freight be used? Knowing these opportunities and constraints, a rescheduling strategy needs to be identified. Other approaches to the rescheduling strategy have been tried, most of which have been unsuccessful. Look at the example presented in Figure 1.5, which illustrates a situation where forty-two orders have been scheduled over a seven-period (current plus six-period) horizon. As the figure shows, six of these scheduled orders are past due, while five others have been committed over the planned capacity. Clearly, this represents an overloaded master schedule. Over the years, three

Figure 1.5 Overloaded Master Schedule

Today

Capacity

−2	−1	Current	+1	+2	+3	+4	+5	+6	+7
		14	22						
		13	21	29					
		12	20	28	35				
		11	19	27	34				
	6	10	18	26	33	39			
	5	9	17	25	32	38			
2	4	8	16	24	31	37	41		
1	3	7	15	23	30	36	40	42	

Past Due

approaches have been tried to correct this situation. The first might be "ostrich management"—ignore the situation and it will simply go away. History has shown that this approach has never worked and probably never will.

The second approach is to "freeze" the schedule; no more orders are taken until a period well into the horizon; this will allow the company to work its way out of the overloaded condition. Refer to Figure 1.6 for a visual of this approach. What the master scheduler has done in this example is to inform everyone that no orders can be committed for delivery inside of seven periods. By doing this, the master scheduler expects to use the unconsumed capacity in periods current plus 4 through current plus 6 (see Figures 1.5 and 1.6) to work off the overload. In other words, the orders keep their same priority and just shift to the right as seen in Figure 1.6.

Figure 1.6 Correcting the Overloaded Master Schedule by Freezing Incoming Orders

Today

Capacity

	6	12	18	24	30	36	42	
	5	11	17	23	29	35	41	
Past Due	4	10	16	22	28	34	40	
	3	9	15	21	27	33	39	First New Order Placed Here
	2	8	14	20	26	32	38	
	1	7	13	19	25	31	37	*
	Current	+1	+2	+3	+4	+5	+6	+7

How long do you think the directive will last? Maybe about seventeen seconds—or until the next customer order that must be committed within the seven-period freeze zone! Another issue with this approach is to recognize that these orders are not shipping because of some problem; it could be material, capacity, quality, credit hold, missing engineering specification, etc. This approach somewhat ignores the fact that these problems may exist, and the product cannot be completed as scheduled, or cannot be completed even in the first or second periods, no matter how much pressure is put on the facility. A better approach, although requiring more work, is to reschedule.

Using the reschedule strategy requires that the right mix of people—the people who have the authority to make decisions—participate in an exercise to put achievable and realistic dates on all orders needing rescheduling. This process may require properly scheduled products to be moved out (or in some cases in) due to another product's being rescheduled into its committed time slot. Using Figures 1.5 and 1.7, let's review how this rescheduling process takes place.

Before beginning the actual rescheduling process, the company should be sure to identify a more realistic approach to booking customer orders in the future. This is important so that when the rescheduling exercise is complete, the company will not find itself right back in the same overloaded condition. Not only does the company need to identify how it will book orders in the future (using available-to-promise and realistic lead times), it must also implement the changes necessary to ensure that this more realistic approach is followed.

To start the rescheduling effort, a few key people must be available. The first and probably most important players are sales and marketing. In fact, when it comes to determining new dates, sales and marketing, working with the facts known as well as within the identified constraints, must have the final say. Manufacturing and materials management must be included in the session to answer questions on capacities, capabilities, and key materials. Other interested parties may include finance, quality, engineering, and general management. For obvious reasons the general manager should speak last: it's called

Figure 1.7 Correcting the Overloaded Master Schedule by Rescheduling Commitments

Today

Capacity

	Current	+1	+2	+3	+4	+5	+6	+7
	13	22	29	35	38	41	40	
	9	17	25	34	28	19	42	
Past Due	7	14	24	33	36	11	20	
	6	5	23	30	32	39	37	
	2	8	21	18	31	27	16	
	1	4	15	12	3	26	10	

"people empowerment" and getting the people close to the situation to solve the problem. Of course, general management may want to have the final call. The general manager is also responsible for breaking ties when sales, marketing, manufacturing, and finance cannot agree.

Figure 1.5 on page 18 identifies an overloaded condition. Before starting the exercise, the status of each order (why it is past due or scheduled beyond the capacity limits) needs to be known. Once this data is on the table, the painful process of deciding a realistic promise date begins. Looking at order number one and reviewing the problems associated with it, the group determines the new, realistic date. In the example, order numbers one and two remain as the highest priority. Order number three has been rescheduled into the current period plus four, while order numbers four and five have been rescheduled for a period 2 (current plus one) delivery. Order number six is designated as the number-three priority and rescheduled into the current period. This process continues until all orders have new expected delivery dates.

The next step in the process is to secure approval for the new plan from sales, marketing, materials, manufacturing, engineering, finance, and general management. Once this is done, it is time to implement and make it happen. This is when the sales and marketing functions really earn their money. Someone (with sales and marketing responsibility) must notify the customer of the anticipated delay and reschedule. It's generally not a pleasant task. Remember, many of these orders may already be late and the customer is now being told that the expected delivery has been pushed out further. No, it's not a pleasant task, but someone needs to do it. The challenge now is to ensure that the new delivery dates are met. Although implementing a rescheduling strategy is difficult, it works and the benefits are many.

As you can see in the scenario, guarding against an overloaded master schedule is one reason why companies need to pay attention to how they master schedule. The next chapter discusses the whys of master scheduling and the framework into which this master scheduling process must fit.

2

Why Master Scheduling?

Success in business is easy if you do two things well: plan your work and work your plan.

All manufacturing entities have a set of "cornerstones"—markers that define who they are, whom they serve, and the resources they draw upon. If they have been in operation for any length of time, they have customers, products, internal resources, and a set of suppliers. These are their cornerstones, and getting these cornerstones to fit together profitably is one of the challenges of manufacturing.

This view of the manufacturing business is represented in Figure 2.1 on page 24. Here, each of the cornerstones is disconnected, and in the center are the two qualities that must bring them together: vision and competence. Vision is the creative element that sees new and effective ways to combine the resources of the organization (human, material, equipment, and financial) with those provided by suppliers to create products that serve customer needs. Competence is the sum total of organizational and technical skills that transform the intangible vision into tangible plans and the activities that make the vision a reality. These competencies include innovation, sales and marketing, design and engineering, manufacturing, and so forth.

Figure 2.1 The Four Cornerstones of Manufacturing

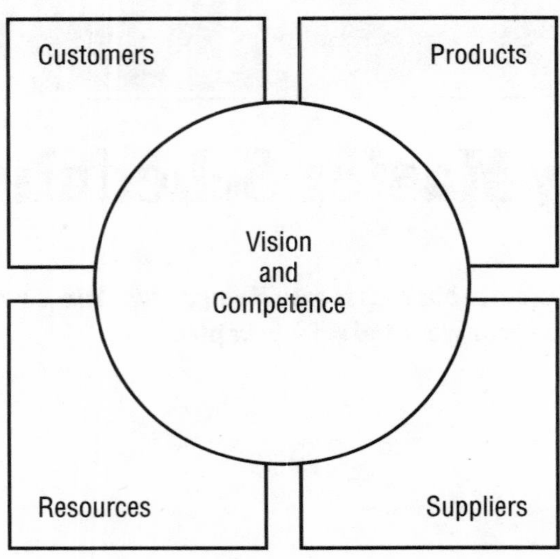

Both the vision and the competencies that exist to fulfill the vision express themselves through plans. All businesses have plans. Planning is first among the four essential functions of management, along with organizing, motivating, and controlling. Without a plan there will be no control. Vision expresses itself through strategic plans determined by top management, painted in broad strokes, and addressed to the fundamental goals of the company. Strategic plans inevitably speak in the language of finance: "Revenues of $24 million"; "Pre-tax earnings of $3.5 million"; "A return on shareholders equity of 14 percent." At other times they present a market share goal.

But strategic plans cannot, by themselves, accomplish anything. To be fulfilled, they must be broken down into tactical operating plans—*plans that define what must be done.* These focus on business problems at operational levels and include:

- *The sales plan.* The number of units the sales representatives will sell

- *The marketing plan.* Markets to target; product, pricing, promotion, and distribution schemes that will be used
- *The engineering plan.* Programs and projects on the drawing board
- *The financial plan.* Target revenues, expense budgets, and profit margins
- *The manufacturing plan.* How much will the factory make, when will it be made, and at what rate

These operating plans must be linked with one another and with the strategic plans of the company. The financial plan, for example, establishes target revenues, but this target is meaningful only when plans to make and sell the product are considered. Likewise, manufacturing cannot independently determine what it will make and in what quantities: manufacturing quantities must be determined in consultation with sales, which has its thumb on market demand; with engineering, which knows what is on the drawing boards; and with the financial department, which must pay for materials, labor, and inventory.

Between Strategy and Execution

The broad area between strategic plans and their execution at the tactical level is the domain of middle management. Middle managers are charged with the development of lower-level plans and their execution. In this sense, middle management "decouples" the broad strategies of the company from the details of execution. However, as detail execution takes place, middle management is also responsible to ensure "linkage" of the detail work to top management's

Figure 2.2 Middle Management as a Decoupler

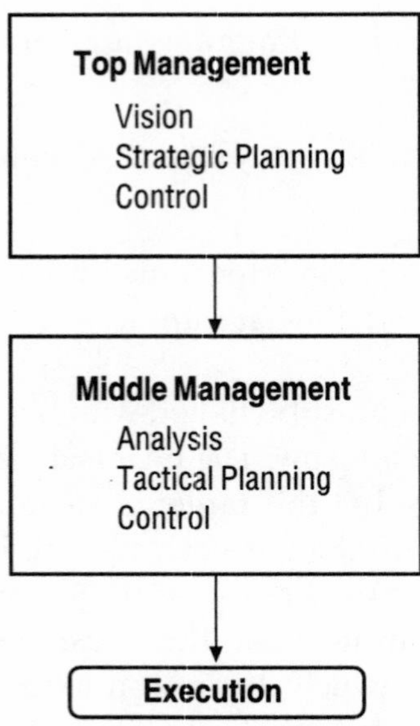

aggregate plans. Figure 2.2 represents the integration between top-management plans and execution.

The master scheduler is one of these important midlevel management decouplers. This individual (or individuals) operates as a buffer between one set of activities in the company—sales—and another—manufacturing. Customer demand for the company's products can vary from period to period, and that variation is difficult to forecast with anything resembling certainty. Suffice it to say here that variation can be greater than manufacturing's ability to respond. Nor is it in the company's best interest to have production vary in lockstep to incoming sales. The frequent result of direct linkage between demand from customers and supply from the production floor is the kind of manufacturing chaos and the sawtooth production rates described in the preceding chapter. The decoupling capability in master scheduling—its ability to balance supply and demand—gives the company an opportunity to avoid both chaos on the floor and uneven production rates.

Figure 2.3 shows two companies. Company A, on the left, has no middle-management buffer between its sales forecast and the production floor. Its sales forecast drives production directly; there is no intermediate gearing, no decoupler, to keep the forecast from causing gyrations in production. Company B, on the right, has interposed a master scheduling function between the sales forecast and production. This function has the intelligence and experience to interpret the signals it gets from sales and the forecast, to think of alternative means of satisfying customer needs, and to make the adjustments in capacity, inventories, and so forth that allow the company to serve the customer without causing supply and demand imbalance. In so doing, it helps the company avoid manufacturing chaos and fulfills the overarching strategy of profitably satisfying customers.

Figure 2.3 Master Scheduling as Buffer Between Sales Forecast and Production

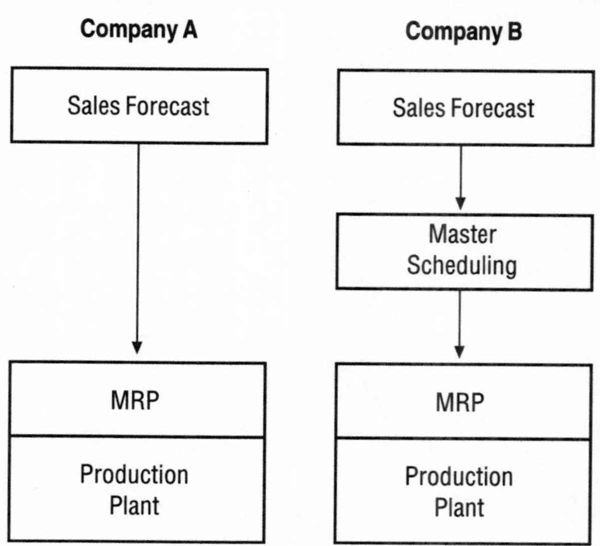

Both sides of Figure 2.3 show MRP perched atop the production function. Material requirements planning is shown here for a simple reason: without the buffer provided by master scheduling, MRP takes the full shock of every fluctuation in the sales forecast. It, in turn, causes production fluctuations, sometimes two, three, even ten times faster than the initial change in the sales forecast. Figure 2.4 presents an analogy to this situation. Here, a big wheel makes a half turn; its movements cause the small wheel geared below it to make a full turn in the opposite direction. The still smaller wheel attached to it makes two full turns . . . and so it goes, in escalating fashion down to the very smallest wheel, which spins at high speed in response to the slightest movement of the first, largest wheel.

Figure 2.4 Big Wheel – Little Wheel Analogy

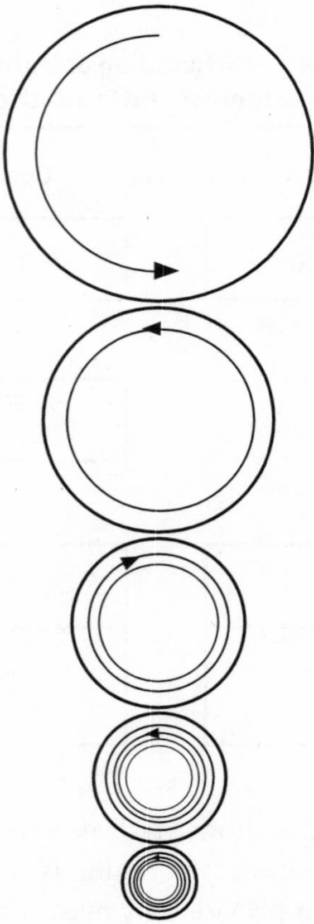

Early practitioners of MRP discovered how disastrous the unbuffered linkage between production and the sales forecast could be, and developed master scheduling as the solution. This development allowed MRP to work effectively. In fact, it was not until the advent of master scheduling computer software in the mid-1970s and the practical implementation of master scheduling that MRP achieved its full potential.[1] MRP users in the early 1970s were unsuccessful because of the missing link of the master schedule.

What Is the Master Schedule?

The master schedule is an operational plan, a subset of the larger production plan. And like any plan, it is integral to the plans of other functional areas within the company. It must be linked to sales, marketing, engineering, finance, and manufacturing, and in some sense it is in a pivotal position between these and other important functions. According to the American Production and Inventory Control Society (APICS) Dictionary, 7th Edition (1992), the master schedule is (for selected items):

> a statement of what the company expects to manufacture. It is the anticipated build schedule of those items assigned to the master scheduler. The master scheduler maintains this schedule and in turn, it becomes a set of planning numbers that drives material requirements planning. It represents what the company plans to produce expressed in specific configurations, quantities, and dates. The master production schedule is not a sales forecast that represents a statement of demand. The master production schedule must take into account the forecast, the production plan, and other important considerations such as backlog, availability of material, availability of capacity, management policy and goals, etc. It is the result of the master scheduling process. The

[1] Oliver Wight could not have defined Class A performance (which first appeared in 1977) without the master scheduling function.

master schedule is a presentation of demand, forecast, backlog, the MPS, the projected on-hand inventory, and the available-to-promise quantity. *Syn:* master scheduling.

The key words in this definition are *anticipated build schedule*. The master schedule is a statement of planning numbers that drive the detailed material and capacity systems, and that statement is based upon expectations of demand—present and future—and of the company's own estimated resources.

Other key points are *specific configurations, quantities*, and *dates*, all of which are specified in the master schedule. Finally, the master schedule is not a sales forecast; rather, it takes the forecast into account, along with the production plan, backlog position, and availability of material and capacity.

Maximizing, Minimizing, and Optimizing

Many books tell us that manufacturing companies should have these objectives: maximize customer service, minimize inventories, and maximize the utilization of company resources. Ideally, this means running the plant at or near capacity at all times. Inventory should be at or near zero. When the customer calls to order a product, that product should be just coming off the line for shipment.

Practical considerations of the real world, however, tend to obscure this perfect world of manufacturing. Fast customer response usually requires some inventory, and plants cannot be run at constant, level rates when demand for the product goes up and down on an irregular basis. So instead of being "maximizers" on service and plant utilization, and "minimizers" on inventory and other costs, master schedulers must be "optimizers"—finding the best middle course, the one that best satisfies conflicting goals and the strategy of the company.

Ultimately, master scheduling is an important part of the competence that, along with vision, unifies the four cornerstones of the manufacturing business. Taking its cue from customer demand, master scheduling sets the pace at which internal and supplier resources are drawn upon. Master scheduling touches all cornerstones.

The Challenge for the Master Scheduler

Ask someone in the sales department what the demand for Product A is and the likely answer will be something like "forty-eight hundred units per year—about four hundred each month." This way of thinking about sales—in broad terms—suits the sales department just fine. Its planning is most likely done in monthly, quarterly, and annual terms; sales forecasts, commission structures, and sales quotas are usually expressed in monthly, quarterly, and annual figures; marketing budgets are expressed in annual spending. If sales in some months are 300 and others are 500, this may be just fine for the sales department, as they average out to 400 a month, or 4,800 a year.

Down on the production floor, demand painted in broad, *average* strokes will not do. The production floor needs disaggregated information: How many should we build today? . . . This month? . . . This week? In this sense, the production floor is more on the customer's wavelength than is the sales department. The customer does not want 1,000 *this year*. The customer wants 100 this week, 125 the next week, 90 the following week. Take a look at Figure 2.5 on page 32. Customer demand is just as the sales department would likely express it: 4,800 per year, an *average* of 400 per period. On a period-by-period basis, however, the production department sees volatile demand: 400 in period 1, 500 in period 2, 200 in period 3, and so forth. This kind of volatility is difficult to manage in the factory.

For the master scheduler, the challenge is to arrange production to approximate the stable master schedule shown at the bottom of

Figure 2.5 Unstable Demand Versus Stable Supply

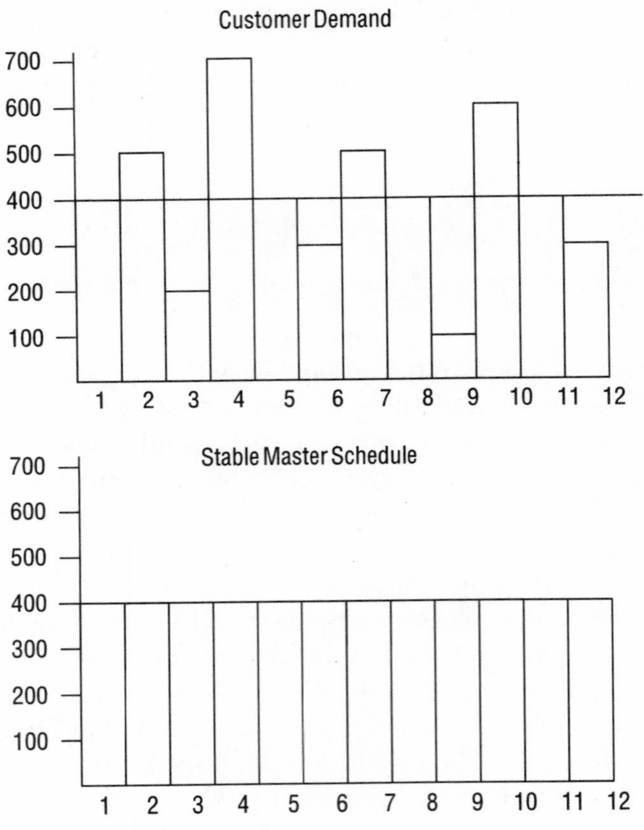

Figure 2.5. In a nutshell, this is what the master scheduler must do to take the chaos out of manufacturing.

But how does a company smooth out the peaks and valleys of demand while stabilizing the master schedule? Here are number of available choices:

- Use of inventory and safety stock strategies
- Managing the supply through the use of overtime, off-loading work to other facilities, adding a shift, etc.

- Managing demand by running promotions, offering extras for customers who take early delivery, price breaks for customers willing to delay delivery, etc.
- Varying the lead time when quoting delivery dates to customers or varying internal lead times by prioritizing orders
- A combination of the above—managing supply, demand, and lead time
- A modern heresy: turning away customer orders that cannot be delivered as requested; put another way: "choosing the business you want"
- Design for manufacturability—a long-term method for coping with supply/demand imbalances

Master Scheduling and MRP II

In essence, four important functions must be fulfilled if the company expects to operate effectively:

1. Planning priorities (quantities and dates)
2. Planning capacity (internal and external resources)
3. Controlling priorities (execution of function number 1)
4. Controlling capacity (execution of function number 2)

To help manufacturing companies perform these functions, a formal process, generally supported by computer software, is available. Some readers may recognize that process and software as manufacturing resource planning (MRP II). Master scheduling is an important element of that process and the system that supports it. To understand just where it fits in, see Figure 2.6. Here master scheduling is one of the four central boxes—along with sales and operations planning, demand management, and rough cut capacity planning—which, collectively, form the basic content of this book. Within the "closed loop" of MRP II, master scheduling is a vital link to these and the rest of the process.

For those who are not familiar with an MRP II system, it is useful here to discuss some of its main parts.[3]

Business Planning

Business planning acts as the brains of this system. As a function of top-level strategic and financial plans of the company, it is the driver of all other activities. Business planning communicates through both annual and monthly financial budgets that project revenues and expenses for all major elements of the business. Being a top-level function, business planning is done by the president and other senior officers of the company and their staffs.

Sales and Operations Planning (S&OP)

S&OP is concerned with sales, production, inventories, backlog, and shipments. It is a tactical plan designed to execute the strategic objectives represented in the business plan. It expresses itself in nonmonetary terms: units, tons, hours, and similar quantitative measures. S&OP is conducted within the broad framework of product families.

S&OP is an important link between the top and middle levels of management. It is typically conducted by means of formal meetings that bring together the company president and various vice presidents and/or managers. In these forums, they thrash out conflicting expectations about demand and manufacturing's capability and capacity to meet that demand.

[3] Here we rely heavily on the very fine description of the MRP II loop provided by Thomas F. Wallace in *Customer-Driven Strategy* (Essex Junction, VT: Oliver Wight Publications, Inc., 1993), pp. 131–35.

Figure 2.6 Manufacturing Resource Planning (MRP II)

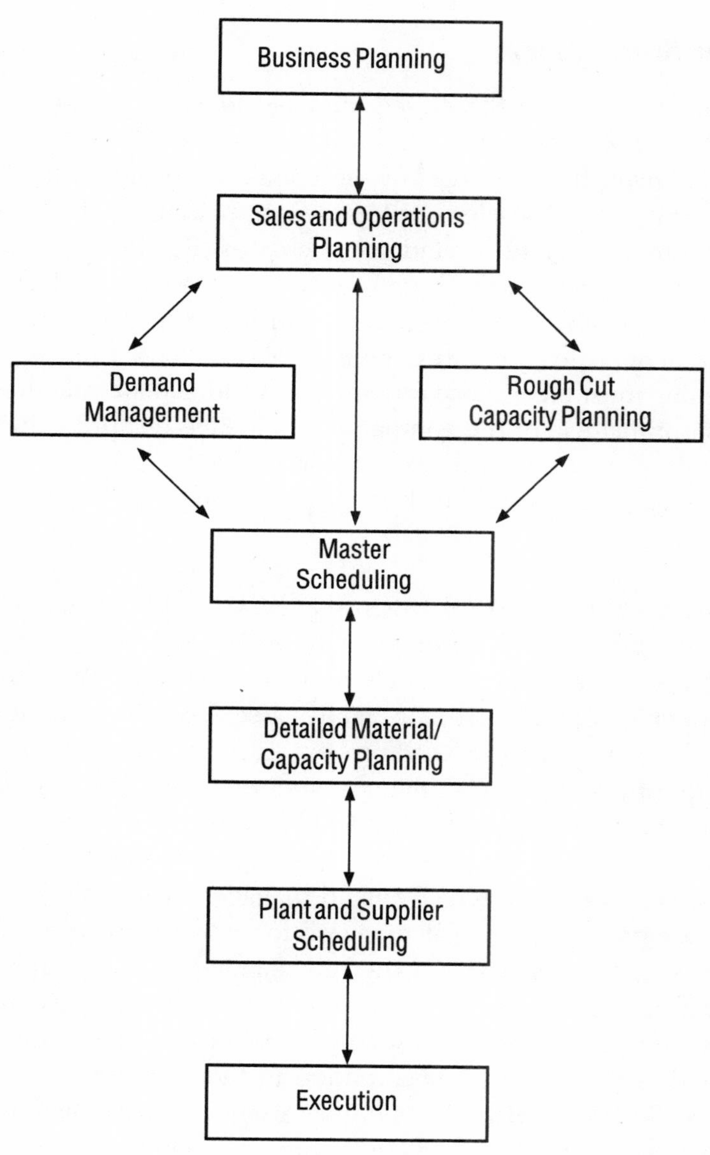

Master Scheduling

Master scheduling in the closed-loop system has already been discussed. The master scheduler must develop a plan that makes it possible, given the resources of the company, to meet the requirements articulated by sales and operations planning. This takes the form of items, quantities, and specific dates. But here, the level of planning is not within the broad context of product families, but of individual product family members; and here the dates are not expressed in quarters or months, but in weeks and days. Further, master scheduling must meet those requirements with a plan (schedule) that makes optimal use of the company's productive resources and time. This is the balancing act described earlier.

In developing that schedule, two other disciplines are brought to bear:

Rough Cut Capacity Planning (RCCP). Rough cut capacity planning address the question: "Do we have enough equipment, enough people, enough materials, and enough time to meet the sales and operations plans?" It is a "sanity check" on the quantities and dates developed by the S&OP process. If the answer is no to any of those questions, some rethinking is required. RCCP is also used to validate the quantities and dates developed by the master scheduler.

Demand Management. Demand management is the function of recognizing and managing all demands for products to ensure that the master scheduler is aware of them. It encompasses the activities of forecasting, order entry, order promising, branch warehouse requirements, interplant orders, and service parts requirements. Many companies do not pay sufficient attention to this important part of the process. That's a mistake! Manufacturing resource planning is a demand-driven process and, therefore, the demand aspect of the process needs full attention.

The remainder of the closed loop, *Detailed Material/Capacity Planning*, and *Plant and Supplier Scheduling*, is very much a part of the MRP II system. Full discussion of these important interfaces with master scheduling is, however, beyond the scope of this book. Suffice it to say that once the master schedule is created by item, quantity, and time, its items are "exploded" using bills-of-material to determine the gross requirements for all lower items. MRP II, coupled with detailed capacity planning, plant scheduling, and supplier scheduling, ensure that the materials and the capacity to build all of the items planned by the master scheduler are available at the right time and in the right quantities.

Not shown in Figure 2.6 (page 35) are other important functions that make master scheduling, and MRP II, possible. For example, inventory records with a high degree of accuracy (95 percent minimum) are required to support the master scheduler's most basic decisions; and bills-of-material that define the contents of products in detail must be at least 98 percent accurate. The routings that identify the sequences of events that a product goes through must be at least 95 percent accurate in regard to structure, sequence, manufacturing centers, and also must contain a realistic standard for setup and run times. Besides the routing data, a manufacturing center data base identifying demonstrated and planned capacities must be available to support the overall MRP II process.

Master scheduling occupies a critical point in the MRP II process—midway between the planning functions of top management and the detailed tactical level that turns those plans into products that satisfy customers. To better appreciate *why* master scheduling is so important a part of the entire process, consider the following scenario.

WHERE HAVE ALL THE ORDERS GONE?

"We really missed it this time," the marketing vice president sighed as the CEO and other managers stared glumly at his revised forecast. "Frankly, we were as surprised as everybody else that interest rates would spike upwards as they have. And that single fact accounts for the dismal outlook for orders over the next few periods. The financing costs for the customers are just too unfavorable right now."

"So when do you expect things to pick up again?" the manufacturing vice president asked.

"When interest rates come back to earth—and please don't ask me when that will happen. I don't know, and I doubt that any of the so-called experts know either."

Original Forecast	10	10	10	10
Actual Demand	7	4	3	1
Master Schedule	10	10	10	10

Indeed, the current outlook for the next four periods was dreadful. Almost as bad was the uncertainty. As a producer of expensive machine tool equipment, sales were extremely sensitive to interest rates, and uncertainty as to future rates created a puzzle for production planners and schedulers. If rates came back down, demand for the company's products would quickly bounce back. As for correctly forecasting those rates, the firm's treasurer liked to say that "those who tell don't know, and those who know don't tell."

The current master schedule has undoubtedly already triggered the purchase of materials and components and building of other components of various lead times. These are either in the stockroom or somewhere in the pipeline. The production capacity is there; the skilled personnel are there; the fixed costs of the plant are there. All that's missing are the customer orders. What to do?

Lots of head scratching takes place in times like these. The marketing people wonder: "Why was our forecast so far off target?" The sales department beat the bushes for opportunities to fill the gaping hole in its revenue forecast. Manufacturing evaluates other ways to utilize unused capacity, fearing layoffs of experienced people who might never come back when business improves. The people in finance start having nightmares in which production keeps humming along, and keeps piling up expensive and unsold inventory.

Management Issues

The situation just described raises a number of management issues—both with respect to the current situation and with respect to a company's whole approach to the problem of operating in environments of unstable demand. In terms of the immediate situation, some would advocate pulling up 3 of the orders from the second period into the first. Perhaps some customers could be induced to take early delivery. This would keep all activities on course through the first period but would create a worse situation for the second.

An optimist would hope that a sudden "uptick" in demand would rescue the master schedule and might build inventory in the expectation of an order turnaround. Someone once said that the definition of an optimist is "a person who has no experience." A pessimist would begin reducing capacity and laying off labor. Someone also once said, "I'd be a pessimist, but it wouldn't work anyway." A pragmatist would think through alternatives for preserving the company's financial, productive, and human resources through a hostile period: building common parts for use in a variety of company products; rescheduling material purchase to later dates; redeploying personnel to other useful work.

What Kind of Company Are We?

The situation of slack demand provokes a larger question introduced earlier about a company's sense of itself: Are we in business to sell what we make or to make what we sell? A production-oriented company sells what it makes; it usually listens more closely to technical capabilities than to the voice of the customer and relies heavily on sales and marketing to move its steady output. In the face of slack demand, it may slow down, but it rarely stops. Instead, it invests heavily in a tool set that sales and marketing can use to clear its inventory: price flexibility; attractive financing terms; warrantee extensions; and so forth. A sales-and-marketing-oriented company makes what it sells. When sales are brisk, production responds; when order volume withers, its production responds accordingly—it is not in the business of just pushing product.

Which orientation is best? It probably depends on the product and the industry. But one thing is certain: both require flexibility. The company that sells what it makes needs flexibility in the ability to move finished goods. The company that makes what it sells needs greater flexibility in production; for it, the new model of "lean production"—the capability to produce at low cost in small batches, and to economically switch production to other items—may be an important key to getting through periods of slack demand like that in our example.

The Four Cornerstones of Manufacturing Revisited

The first part of this chapter conceptualized the manufacturing business as four cornerstones—customers, products, resources, and suppliers—integrated by the unifying power of vision and competence. As the following chapters will make clear, master scheduling is a competency like engineering, financial management, and logistics. It represents a capability to get the job done, and to fulfill the larger vision and mission of the company. To see the core of vision and competence in more tangible terms, refer to Figure 2.7. Here the core of the company is represented by five people-based technologies that, when linked together, integrate the four cornerstones of the business. Starting at the top and moving clockwise, these pieces are:

- Customer-Driven Strategy
- New-Product Development
- Total Quality Management
- People and Teams
- Planning and Control

Figure 2.7 Integrating Elements of the Manufacturing Business

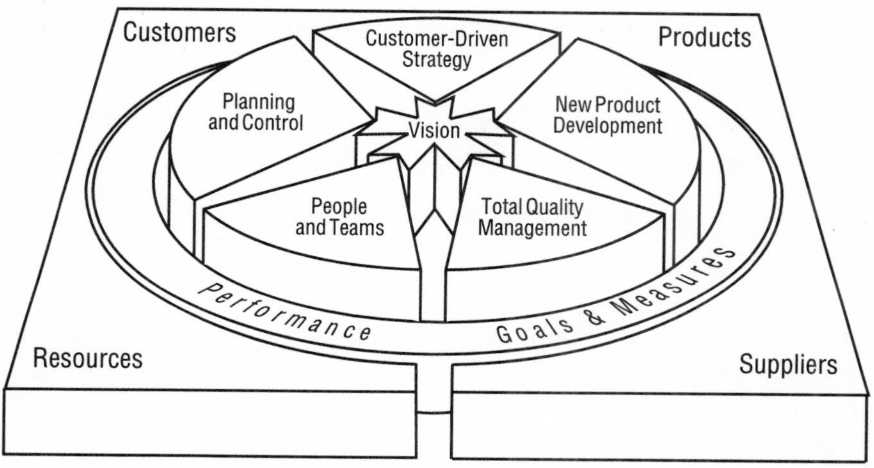

Each of these people-based technologies is critical to the success of a manufacturing company, and each is worthy of study. It is also a matter of convenience that each is represented separately, as if there were no links between them, or that somehow one piece—new product development, for example—did not have its own requirements for planning and control, or total quality management in the development process, etc. Master scheduling, the subject of this book, resides in the planning and control wedge of the figure.

So, Why Master Scheduling?

At this point we can summarize a response to the question: Why master scheduling? This is answered as follows:

1. To ensure integration and implementation of the business, sales, marketing, engineering, finance, and manufacturing plans
2. To manage inventory and backlog to a position desired by top management
3. To create a foundation for accountability within the company to customers, to suppliers, and to ourselves
4. To drive detail material and capacity requirements
5. To plan and commit resources to satisfy customer demands

The details of how a company goes about master scheduling are treated in the following chapters. There the reader will learn the basic mechanics of the process. Initially, this will appear to be a process better relegated to a computer than to a human operator. Computers have proven to be excellent helpmates in the business of storing, displaying, predicting, calculating, and underscoring the numerical data that is essential to master scheduling. Indeed, the availability of master scheduling software since the mid-1970s has done much to advance the implementation of master scheduling in the ranks of manufacturing, and in so doing has helped make MRP II the powerful process that it is today.

As a moderate-level "expert system" with built-in decision rules, modern master scheduling software can detect potential supply/demand imbalances and alert the master scheduler to their presence; the software can even recommend what action should be taken. As time passes, the diagnostic abilities of master scheduling software are bound to increase.

None of this computing power, however, does anything to eliminate the need for the human judgments, or the insights and decision-making capabilities that a master scheduler brings to the job. Master scheduling is no cut-and-dried numbers game. The numbers are there in abundance, but understanding the assumptions behind them, how to use those numbers, and making decisions in an atmosphere of uncertainty is at least 75 percent of the master scheduler's job. No one said that this job was easy!

* * *

This chapter has explained the "why" of master scheduling. The following chapter explains the "how," or the mechanics, of the subject. Once the mechanics of basic master scheduling are understood, discussion will move on to what the master scheduler does with the numbers and information available.

3

The Mechanics of Master Scheduling

You can definitely make mistakes, but you can't make mistakes indefinitely.

The objective of master scheduling is to plan the impact of demand on materials and capacity. This is a vital function because every company must deploy its people, equipment, material, and capital in the most efficient way possible. Master scheduling does this by ensuring that enough product is available for customers, while costly and unneeded inventories are avoided. This is the business of balancing supply and demand.

In addition, master scheduling lays out detailed build schedules in support of the aggregate plans developed during the sales and operations planning process. By ensuring that the detail plans are within the constraints of the overall aggregate plans, MPS implements management's directives. Finally, the master schedule is used to establish some degree of control and accountability: Who is accountable for the different inventory levels the company maintains? Who is accountable for managing capacity? Who is accountable for bringing the materials in-house? Who is accountable for managing the lead times that are used to buy and produce the product? Accountability is very important if a company is to successfully use MRP II and master scheduling.

The MPS Matrix

One of the bottom-line goals of the master schedule is to balance supply and demand *by time period*. That means looking at all demand—from all sources—in discrete time segments and understanding the resources that will be necessary to satisfy that demand—again, in terms of time segments. This business of matching up supply and demand in time segments creates the need for a matrix that immediately reveals when supply and demand are in or out of balance. There are several different MPS matrix formats available, and the actual design is a matter of software choice. For purposes of illustration, this book uses the one shown in Figure 3.1.

The MPS matrix is a series of columns and rows that defines scheduled activities in terms of time and type (supply or demand). The time elements are arrayed across the top, and the activities are listed along the side. Each column contains all the master scheduling

Figure 3.1 The Master Schedule Matrix

	Past Due	1	2	3	4	5	6	7	8
Item Forecast									
Option Forecast									
Actual Demand									
Total Demand									
Projected Available Balance									
Available-to-Promise									
Master Schedule									

activity expected to take place within a specific time period (typically a week or day). The nature of the activity—either supply or demand—is determined by the row in which it appears.

Time Segments

The matrix displayed in Figure 3.1 shows time periods 1 through 8 across the top. The number of periods is dependent upon the software and the company's choice of planning horizon. Each period could represent a day, a few days, or a week. In practice, the array is usually dated: for example, period starting 10/1, 10/8, 10/15, and so forth.

By convention, period 1 is the "current" period—the present—and remains so as time passes. Thus, one week period 1 would read 10/1; a week later it would read 10/8. The data in each column shifts to the left as time passes. The column just to the left of the current period is labeled "past due" (an explanation of this will come later). The columns to the right represent future time periods and are used to display data by identified activities. The cells in the master schedule matrix are for convenience of display when using a horizontal MPS format. Inside the computer, the quantities are stored by real dates—i.e., October 15, April 11—and, therefore, can be displayed using any time period arrangement that the master scheduler requires.

Demand Section

The top four rows of the MPS matrix show the components of demand for a master scheduled item: the "Item Forecast" of independent demand, the "Option Forecast" or dependent demand, the "Actual Demand," and the "Total Demand."

Item Forecast. The forecast row identifies the "independent demand" for the master scheduled item. An example of this would be an item such as a table saw motor sold directly to the customer. Besides selling the table saw to the customer, the motor used in the table saw could be sold by itself and would appear on the motor's independent forecast line if the motor is an MPS item. Generally, demand of this type is to satisfy a service or spare part requirement. An item can, of course, have both independent demand and dependent demand (the motor is also required to build table saws). This situation explains why we have the "option forecast" line in the MPS matrix.

Option Forecast. The option forecast row reflects the anticipated demand for an item that will be sold as part of something else. For example, suppose that the production of electric motors is master scheduled. Sale of the motor outright, as a service or spare part, would constitute independent demand. The same motor may also be used as a component in other products produced by the company, such as drill presses. Demand for these motors will therefore be "dependent" upon the volume of drill presses the company expects to sell as well as the demand for motors to be used as service parts. Consequently, demand for these motors will appear in both the service or item forecast and option forecast rows.[1]

Actual Demand. Actual demand is concerned with customer orders that are booked or sold, but not yet shipped. A customer has placed an order for a quantity of motors. Because of company strategies, current schedules, material availability, plant capacities, or customer desires, these motors might not be ready for shipment for several weeks. These motors constitute actual demand and the master scheduler must keep track of each order by customer, quantity, and promised delivery dates to ensure that the customer will receive the desired products as promised.

Total Demand. This row in the MPS matrix reflects the combined demand for the item by time period. Total demand is calculated in various ways. Normally, it is the sum of the item forecast, option

[1] The scheduling literature has for years used the term "production forecast" for what is here called "option forecast." The former is not an appropriate term in that the forecast is not of production, but of demand. The master scheduling line represents production. Thus, the term "option forecast" is used in place of the more familiar production forecast term throughout this book and, hopefully, it will become the standard term over time.

Naturally, when scheduling products that contain no option element, this line of the MPS matrix remains blank. Sometimes in a make-to-stock business (one that produces products to inventory in anticipation of customer orders), the option forecast line is used to display the requested inventory replenishment by time period.

forecast, and actual demand. If the respective forecast row is reduced whenever orders are booked, then the total demand remains unchanged as demand is recorded. If, however, the forecast is not replaced with booked customer orders, then the logic used in the master scheduling system must take this into account when calculating the total demand. The process we are talking about is called "forecast consumption," which is addressed in chapter 14. For the purposes of this chapter, as demand orders are received, the forecasted quantity will be reduced by the quantity ordered. On the surface, this seems logical. Since the forecast is really an expectation of future demand orders, customer orders that are booked by the sales force may be seen as the fulfillment of that earlier demand forecast. However, what if the customer order was *not* thought of when the forecast was created? In this case the customer order would not be part of the forecast and should be treated as incremental demand. This type of demand is known as "abnormal demand" and will be covered later in the book. Until then, all demand in the examples will be treated as normal or expected demand.

Supply Section

Look again at Figure 3.1 on page 46. The rows in the matrix that indicate the level of demand for each time period have already been explained. It now remains to interpret the rows within which the supply and balancing of the two will appear. First, look at the bottom line, the "Master Schedule" row, or the total supply line.

Master Schedule (MPS). This is the row in which the master scheduler and the computer place supply orders to meet the demand for each period. Each quantity on the MPS row represents a defined amount of the ordered item by due date.

Master schedule supply orders appear in the matrix in three different forms: released orders, firm planned orders, and computer planned orders. These various replenishment orders are identified on the MPS row by period. The sequence in which we would expect to see these orders as we move further out on the time line would be released orders first, firm planned orders second, and computer planned orders last. The nature of these orders, explained below, will make it clear why that sequence makes sense.

Released Orders. These orders initiate the production process by authorizing material, labor, and equipment to be used to manufacture a specific item. A released order has many aliases. Some of the names used are scheduled receipt, campaign, batch, manufacturing order, production order, shop order, work order, purchasing order (if the item is purchased, not made), and run rate.

Firm Planned Orders (FPO). An FPO is an order that the master scheduler places to take control away from the computer. It is a "place holder" that allows the master scheduler to firm a computer planned order in quantity and time. The computer software is restricted from changing an FPO; it is the responsibility of the master scheduler to change it. This technique can aid schedulers in planning materials and capacity by firming selected computer planned orders. Firm planned orders are the normal way of stating the master schedule. In effect, the master scheduler says, "I'm going to produce so many units of this product, which will be due on this date, but I am not yet ready to release the work or issue a released order."

Generally, firm planned orders explode through the MRP system to plan materials and other resources. This explosion process is the same as the one used on computer planned orders. Released orders are not exploded via MRP because these orders create lower-level allocations for materials when they are placed, which are then treated as demand until the material is issued in accordance with the build plan.

Computer Planned Orders (CPO). A CPO is an order created by the computer software rather than by the master scheduler. It is not a green light to manufacturing, but serves as a suggestion to the person doing the scheduling that a firm planned order of the indicated size will be needed if supply and demand are to balance. Generally, for a computer planned order to have a lasting effect on a master scheduled item, the master scheduler must convert the computer planned order into either a released order or a firm planned order. As stated above, the firm planned order takes control of the order away from the computer and firms the date and quantity. Chapters 4 and 5 discuss in detail when this action needs to take place.

The computer bases its creation of CPOs on demand need dates, predetermined lot sizes, and lead times to ensure that the release and production or procurement of material will satisfy the demand need date. Computer planned order creation rules are generally built into the MPS system's software and controlled by a "planning time fence" (a more detailed explanation of the planning time fence and how it is used in master scheduling is presented later in this chapter). This date-related boundary allows the computer to only generate CPOs with due dates *after* predefined dates, and not before. Inside the planning time fence, the master scheduler must control all the supply orders. By operating within the boundaries of the planning time fence, the computer software "knows" when it may or may not generate a CPO.

Each type of supply order plays a unique role in the master scheduling process. A released order is a manufacturing order against which material, labor, overhead, and other resources can be charged. Firm planned orders are also essential; without them, the computer software logic would assume responsibility for balancing demand with supply, and would then attempt to rectify the situation by launching CPOs where needed, regardless of the actual material or capacity availability. Computer planned orders in effect represent the computer software's own version of a firm planned order. Once the master scheduler creates firm planned orders and balances supply to demand, the computer software will not attempt to create additional supply orders because they will not be needed.

Note that there can be many variations on the preceding supply order scheme; the movement from computer planned to firm planned to released order is only a generic approach. In fact, it is possible for the master scheduler to take a computer planned order and convert it directly into a released order without ever going through the firm planned order phase. Regardless of how supply orders are used, each contributes to the MPS row in the computer format, which is the underpinning for an "anticipated build plan"—what we intend to produce.

PROJECTED AVAILABLE BALANCE. This row predicts what will be in inventory at a specific point in time. It is also the basis for the computer's critique of supply-and-demand balance. The outcome of the critique determines what action will be recommended. Action recommendations are sent to the master scheduler by the software in the form of "action" or "exception" messages.[2] Unless a company uses safety stock, the perfect supply-and-demand balance will be a projected inventory balance of zero (the supply of the product perfectly matches the demand for the product so that there is no projected inventory remaining). If a company uses safety stock, e.g., 100 items, then the perfect balance is 100 units.

Rarely do we have a perfect balance in the imperfect world of manufacturing. Assuming that a company is not using any safety stock, a positive balance for any period of time in the projected available balance row suggests a potential surplus or excess stock condition. If there is a negative balance, the system is projecting a potential shortage. In the case of a potential surplus, the computer system may recommend that the master scheduler move orders out or even cancel orders altogether. In the case of a potential shortfall, the master scheduler will receive recommendations from the system to release new orders or move future orders in to cover the projected deficit.

AVAILABLE-TO-PROMISE (ATP). This row is used for customer order promising and displays the projected supply of product less the actual demand. The result of this calculation informs the sales and marketing departments of the products that still can be sold without modifying the master schedule. This is an extremely useful piece of information because it identifies what can honestly be promised to a customer in terms of delivery. If available-to-promise indicates a total of 10 units by a particular period and we promise a customer 12 by that period, then we have made a bad promise. Anyone who books orders

[2] Action or exception messages are notes to the master scheduler made by the computer based upon data in the system. These typically appear beneath the formatted supply-and-demand information. Chapter 4 explains action and exception messages in detail.

should be aware of ATP, how the system calculations are done, and what the company's policy is regarding the commitment of product to customers. Available-to-promise is discussed in depth in chapters 8, 9, and 14.

Master Scheduling in Action

Now that the matrix for organizing master scheduling data has been presented, we need to understand how to use it as a scheduling tool for a simple product.

The product we will be looking at is a standard flashlight, with a bill-of-material consisting of the following: one head subassembly, one light subassembly, and one body subassembly (see Figure 3.2). While each of these subassemblies might in reality contain other subassemblies, for simplicity's sake, we will ignore any secondary product structure.

Figure 3.2 Flashlight Product Product Structure

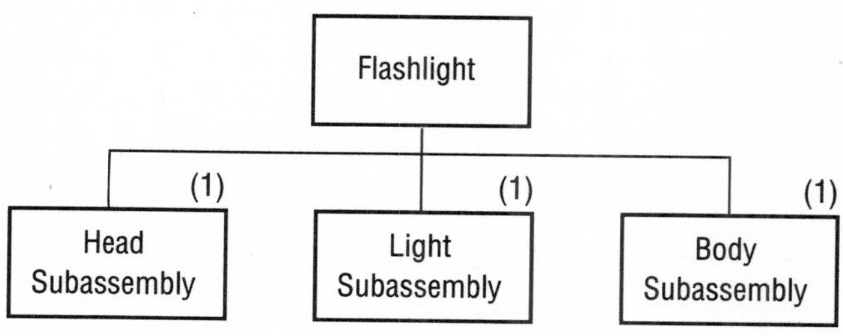

In Figure 3.2, it is important to note that the numbers in parentheses indicate the number of items needed to build the "parent" part, the finished flashlight. In addition to knowledge of the specific product structure, several other pieces of information regarding the flashlight must be known before master scheduling can begin. We make the assumption here that the flashlight is being made-to-stock—i.e., completed flashlights are placed in a finished-goods inventory. With that assumption in mind, consider the current status of flashlights:

On-hand balance: 12

Lead time: 1 period

Order quantity: 20 units
(Lot size)

Thus, 12 units already exist in inventory. A lead time of one period is required to complete the final assembly process. And the company has determined that flashlights should be built in order quantities, or lots sizes, of 20 units; this means that whenever the decision is made to build more flashlights, the *minimum* order quantity should be 20 units. In Figure 3.3 we see how this data finds its way into the master scheduling matrix.

Figure 3.3 The Master Schedule Matrix Example

	Past Due	1	2	3	4	5	6	7	8
Item Forecast		10	10	10	10	10	10	10	10
Option Forecast									
Actual Demand									
Total Demand		10	10	10	10	10	10	10	10
Projected Available Balance	12	2	12	2	12	2	12	2	-8
Available-to-Promise									
Master Schedule			20		20		20		

Computing the Projected Available Balance

For the purpose of this example, we assume a forecast of 10 units every period, and these appear in the forecast cells in each of the eight periods considered. No actual demand is present because the flashlights are being built to stock using the forecast of independent demand as the only demand input. Therefore, the total demand for each period is 10 units.

Notice that the column labeled "past due" of the forecast row is blank—this indicates that there is no past due, or unconsumed forecast. A past due forecast is a forecast that was not consumed or satisfied. Any unconsumed forecast should either be rolled forward or dropped, depending upon company policy and the forecast consumption logic being used. Besides the demand, we know we have 12 units on hand, which has been placed where the past-due column and the projected available balance row intersect. This does not imply that the on-hand balance is past due; it is merely a convenient place to put the on-hand balance so that the MPS software can begin its calculation of the projected available balance line. Knowing the on-hand quantity (12), the forecasted quantities in the future, and the expected supply orders (20 in periods 2, 4, and 6), the MPS system can project the expected quantity on hand for future time periods. Once this is done, the MPS system will be in a position to critique the balance of supply and demand.

PERIOD 1. There are no supply orders (MPS row) due in period 1, so we have 12 units available to satisfy period 1's demand of 10 units. Therefore our projected available balance at the end of period 1 will be 2 units (12 − 10), a surplus reflected as projected available balance. This becomes, in effect, the projected on-hand balance for the next period.

PERIOD 2. Again, demand exists for 10 units. What about supply? There is a supply order or scheduled receipt of 20 units due in period 2. This scheduled receipt is a result of the master scheduler's having placed a supply order for flashlights prior to now. If this scheduled receipt is received as scheduled (MPS quantities are shown by due date), the 20 units can be added to the 2 already projected to be on hand and will equal 22 units available to satisfy period 2's demand. Since the total demand for period 2 is 10, a projected available balance of 12 units will be left at the end of period 2 (2 + 20 − 10).

Period 3 through Period 7. The master scheduling system has projected a positive balance of 12 units at the end of period 2. Demand again stands at 10 units in period 3, and no scheduled receipts are identified in the MPS row. In case the reader has not recognized this situation, it is the exact duplicate of period 1. Looking ahead, we can see that the same pattern of demand, projected available balance, and anticipated scheduled receipts repeats every other period through period 7. The reader may want to work through each period in turn to gain added practice in the projected available balance calculation, going back to the beginning on-hand-balance column and period 1 if he or she gets stuck.

Period 8. In period 8 the situation changes. Period 7 ended with a projected available balance of 2 units. Again, this constitutes a projected on-hand balance for the next period. Demand in period 8 is again at 10 units. No additional units are scheduled for receipt in period 8 (see MPS row, period 8 cell). Given this situation, the system will correctly project a negative balance of 8 units (2 − 10) in period 8 if the master scheduler does not take corrective action and the demand occurs as planned.

Nature abhors a vacuum, cats hate water, and master scheduling software cannot stand the sight of a negative projected available balance. The computer will spot the potential shortage in period 8 and will automatically place a computer planned order to be received in period 8 to restore the projected available balance to zero or a positive number. Its order will be for 20 units (the minimum lot size or order quantity). If in the future the master scheduler chooses to accept the computer's recommendation, the computer planned order will be converted into a firm planned order or a released order and the projected negative available balance of 8 units will shift to a positive 12 units (the 2 units available from period 7 added to the expected receipt of 20 units less the total demand of 10). The result of the adjustment produces the MPS matrix in Figure 3.4.

Figure 3.4 Flashlight Master Schedule Matrix

	Past Due	1	2	3	4	5	6	7	8
Service Forecast		10	10	10	10	10	10	10	10
Option Forecast									
Actual Demand									
Total Demand		10	10	10	10	10	10	10	10
Projected Available Balance	12	2	12	2	12	2	12	2	−8 12
Available-to-Promise									
Master Schedule			20		20		20		(20)
Released Order									
Firm Planned Order			*		*		*		
Computer Planned Order									*

(For purposes of illustration, the entries in the master schedule line have been specified as to the "types" of order they are. Thus, the orders in periods 2, 4, and 6 are firm planned orders, and the final order in period 8, the one circled, is a computer planned order.)

In addition to determining where and for what quantity CPOs should be generated, the system also critiques the timing of the receipts in periods 2, 4, and 6, provided they are scheduled releases or firm planned orders, to determine if the orders are scheduled properly. The system will start its critique by going back to period 2 and asking,

"Is this MPS order of 20 units scheduled properly?" In this case, the answer is yes. This is so because without the 20 units arriving as scheduled, the projected available balance will be negative (2 − 10).

The same logic is used in testing the orders on the MPS row in periods 4 and 6. The answer to the question will be yes in both cases since each MPS lot of 20 is properly scheduled and needed in the defined periods.

Analysis

This example not only illustrates how the projected available balance is calculated but underscores the fact that the computer's recommendations are just that—recommendations. The master scheduler ultimately determines whether the computer's recommendations are valid for the particular situation at hand. There is a universal principle in both master scheduling and MRP II: Machines make recommendations; people make decisions.

The software system supports the master scheduler in creating a realistic master schedule based on the availability of material and capacity. With respect to the availability of material, the issue is whether or not material *due* dates (dates placed by the master scheduler) match true *need* dates (dates calculated by the computer). With respect to capacity, it must be available in sufficient quantities to satisfy the resource requirements by specific time periods. This is a balancing job, and how well or how poorly a master scheduler does that job determines the real worth of the scheduler and the particular MPS system. The question now is what to do with period 8's computer planned order. To balance the supply and demand at the MPS level, this order for 20 flashlights is necessary. (Actually, only 8 are needed, but 20 is the minimum order quantity.) Therefore, the system will assume that the master scheduler will convert this computer planned order into a firm planned order when it is necessary (based on the lead time of the product). The next step in the process is to communicate this expected build plan to lower levels to ensure that materials and capacities will be available when needed. Let's look at the integration between master scheduling and material requirements planning.

How MPS Drives MRP

The basics of the MPS matrix, and how the software system and master scheduler together ensure a balance between demand and supply, should now be clear for the simple case just given. So far we have been dealing at the level of completed flashlights, ignoring the flashlight's underlying components. Yet we know that another set of scheduling problems lies beneath the surface of the master scheduled item, one for each of the components that makes up the final flashlight. The need to deal with the underlying components—and the materials, capacity, and build-time issues that each entails—requires an interface between master scheduling and material requirements planning (MRP). That interface is made via the flashlight's bill-of-material. To fully understand that interface, let us follow the flashlight example a bit further.

Given that it takes one period (specified lead time) to build the flashlight once the head, light, and body subassemblies are available, and since some flashlights are scheduled for completion in period 2, then there must be sufficient head, light, and body subassemblies on hand in period 1 to start building the flashlights required for completion in period 2. If the master scheduler expects to have 20 flashlights as scheduled receipts in period 2, then 20 head subassemblies, 20 light subassemblies, and 20 body subassemblies had better be available in period 1. Therefore, a "gross requirement" for 20 of each of these subassemblies exists in period 1. In other words, the master schedule row is what drives requirements down to the MRP level. Using the same logic, 20 head, light, and body subassemblies are needed in period 3 coming from the MPS lot in period 4, and 20 more in period 5 coming from the MPS lot in period 6. The computer planned order in period 8 generates a gross requirement for 20 head, light, and body subassemblies in period 7. Each of these subassemblies, then, needs its own MRP plan and schedule. Figure 3.5 represents the linkage of these schedules graphically.

To understand how MRP accommodates each of these subassemblies (and *their* various subassemblies, manufactured parts, components, and raw materials if they exist) and links them to the master schedule, we will follow just one of those subassemblies—the light subassembly—from the master schedule down to its own MRP matrix.

Figure 3.5 Master Schedule Linked to the MRP System

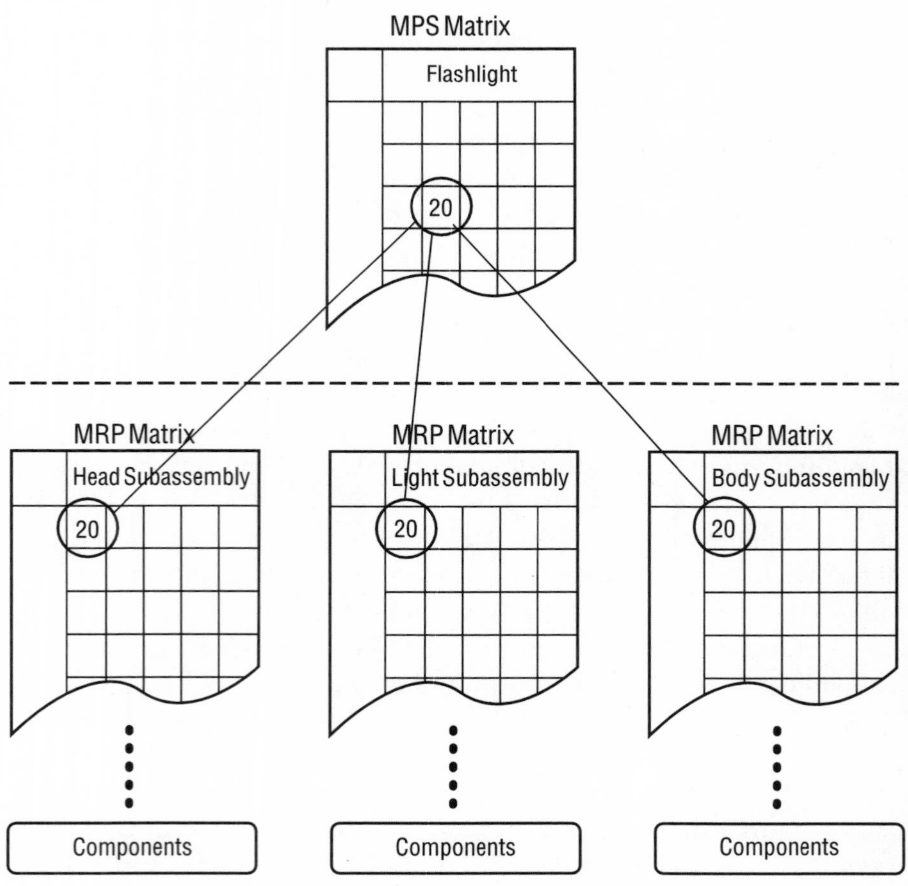

Material Requirements Planning

To get started on planning the light subassembly, some basic information about the subassembly is required.

On-hand balance: 3

Lead time: 2 periods

Order quantity: 25 units
(Lot size)

For illustration purpose and to show just how the MPS and MRP matrices are linked via the computer software, the bottom row of the MPS matrix is shown in Figure 3.6 on page 62. The various orders for 20 completed flashlights in periods 2, 4, 6, and 8 of the master schedule line are shown to trigger respective gross requirements for the same quantity one period earlier in the MRP matrix.

The projected gross requirements row of the MRP matrix represents demand for the identified item, not from the final customer, but from the master schedule—specifically, from the MPS row. For instance, when the master scheduler placed an order for 20 completed flashlights in period 2 on the master schedule, that translated into a projected gross requirement of 20 light subassemblies in period 1 on the MRP matrix. Taking the lead time into account, the computer software system places the requirement of 20 units in period 1 of the MRP matrix.[3] The same process repeats itself whenever an order appears on the MPS row of the master schedule.

Projected gross requirements are the sum of all the demands over time for this item. In our simple example, the light subassembly is used only in the flashlight. In a more complex environment, that same light subassembly might be used in other products manufactured by the company, in which case the demand for the light subassembly

[3] Remember, the stated lead time to take the head, light, and body subassemblies and produce a flashlight is one period, which is not to be confused with the lead time of two periods that it takes to build the light subassembly itself.

from many different master schedules would accumulate in the various projected gross requirements time periods of the light subassembly's MRP matrix.

Figure 3.6 The MRP Matrix—Light Subassemblies

MPS Matrix	Past Due	1	2	3	4	5	6	7	8
Other rows of MPS Matrix not shown									
Master Schedule			20		20		20		(20)
MRP Matrix	Past Due	1	2	3	4	5	6	7	8
Projected Gross Requirements		20		20		20		20	
Scheduled Receipts		25		25					
Projected Available Balance	3	8	8	13	13	−7 18	−7 18	−27 23	−27 23
Planned Order Release				(25)		(25)			

(Circled values are computer planned orders).

The scheduled receipts shown in the MRP matrix are orders that either MRP planners or schedulers have placed. (There are no computer planned orders here.) These scheduled receipts can go by many possible names: work orders, shop orders, production orders, manufacturing orders, campaigns, or run rates, and are used for parts that the company builds or produces. Purchase orders or confirmed supplier schedules are used for parts or items that the company buys. It is important to understand that a scheduled receipt is expected to be received in the period shown and will be used in calculating the projected available balance, the next row in the matrix.

Just as in the MPS matrix row of the same name, the projected available balance is where the projected inventory balance is reflected. The past-due column in this row contains the starting on-hand balance, but from that point forward, the projected available balance is the sum of on-hand balance for the prior period and scheduled receipts for the period being calculated less the projected gross requirements for that period. That figure, in effect, becomes the projected on-hand balance for the next period. For example, in Figure 3.6 we see an on-hand balance of 3 light subassemblies; added to the 25 scheduled to be received in period 1; this represents an available supply of 28 in period 1; since demand in that period (projected gross requirements) is 20, the projected available balance for the period is 8 (3 + 25 − 20).

The MRP system calculates the projected available balance quantity in much the same way as does the MPS system. The basic calculation in both systems is to take the projected available balance from the prior period and add scheduled receipts from the period being evaluated, then subtract the demand for that period. This yields the projected available balance for the period being calculated.

The planned order release row contains the equivalents of the computer planned orders found in the master schedule. It is the row in which the computer attempts to deal with any potential supply shortages that appear in the projected available balance row. For example, the MRP matrix for the light subassembly projects a negative available balance (the top row of numbers in periods 5 through 8) unless some action is taken. Demand from the master schedule outstrips the expected supply of light assemblies by a cumulative of 7 units in periods 5 and 6, and by a cumulative of 27 units in periods 7 and 8.

To avoid a deficit situation from developing in period 5, a computer planned order is needed to arrive in period 5, and therefore must be released in period 3 (remember, the lead time for light subassemblies is two periods). What should be the size of the order? Ideally, the computer would place an order for 7 units in period 3 to cover the 7-unit deficit expected in period 5. However, the minimum order quantity for this item has been specified as 25, and that is what shows up in the planned order release row of period 3.

If the MRP planner accepts the computer software's recommendation, he or she will convert the computer planned order into a scheduled receipt when period 3 becomes the current period (period 1), and a surplus of 18 units will be available in period 5, as reflected in the bottom half of the cell (13 + 25 − 20).

An important point is now being made. In order for a computer planned order to be recognized as a scheduled receipt, the scheduler or planner must take affirmative action. Remember, only orders placed by a scheduler or planner appear in the scheduled receipt row. It follows that once the computer planned order is converted to a scheduled receipt, the CPO will be deleted when MRP is next run. Lower-level requirements are maintained when the system creates an allocation for each lower-level part or item required to support the scheduled receipt. These allocations are maintained automatically by the system's software and stored in a requirements file.

Looking ahead to future periods, no activity takes place in period 6, so the projected available balance remains at 18 units. In period 7 a demand for 20 units creates a projected negative balance of 2 units (18 + 0 scheduled receipts − 20). The origin of this demand is the computer planned order for 20 flashlights in period 8 of the master schedule. Using the planned lead time of one period for the flashlight has resulted in this CPO's generating a projected gross requirement in period 7 in the MRP matrix. The computer cannot abide a negative balance for the light subassembly, so another planned order must be released, this time in period 5 (taking into account the light subassembly's two-period lead time) to ensure sufficient supply of the light subassembly in period 7. If the computer's recommendation is followed and the computer planned order is converted into a scheduled receipt to be received in period 7, a projected surplus balance of 23 units will be available at the end of period 7 (18 + 25 − 20).

In period 8, the projected available balance will either remain at −27 units if no action is taken, or at 23 units if the CPO releases are converted to scheduled receipts when appropriate. The CPO scheduled for release in period 3 should be converted to a scheduled receipt two periods prior to the CPO scheduled for receipt in period 5.

The projected gross requirements (demand), projected available balance, and planned order release (supply) rows are automatically calculated by the MRP software system. Only the scheduled receipt row is maintained by MRP schedulers and planners.

Analysis

Using the on-hand balance, projected gross requirements, and scheduled receipts, the MRP system will project the available balance over each planning period, making it possible for the system to determine the true material need dates. If the projected available balance goes negative and then returns to positive, the system recognizes that a timing problem exists—i.e., there is enough on order, but some of the orders are scheduled too late. If the projected available balance goes negative and stays negative, the system recognizes a volume problem and calls for additional orders.

Reviewing the MRP matrix for the light subassembly we observed in periods 5 through 8, the projected available balance went negative and remained negative (top set of numbers)—evidence of a volume problem. Some type of order action has to take place, and the computer has suggested that two releases be made to put the supply and demand for light subassemblies back into balance. The scheduled receipts of 25 units in periods 1 and 3 are both necessary and scheduled properly to prevent the close-in projected available balance from becoming negative, which would have otherwise signified a timing problem.

Each time that MRP is run, this kind of analysis takes place within the computer and action messages are generated as appropriate. Based on the analysis just completed, the MRP system would not recommend that any action be taken until period 3 becomes the current period.

The flashlight example just given has explained the basics of both the MPS and the MRP logic, how internal calculations are made, and how the system—with the input of the scheduler or planner—maintains a balance of demand and supply. Just as important, the example showed the connection between the master schedule for the flashlight and how it is supported by the MRP system for each of the flashlight's components, examining one of those components—the light subassembly—in detail.

Experienced manufacturing people will be quick to recognize this as a very simplified case. Few manufactured products are as simple as the one just shown, and even a flashlight is more complex in its component makeup than this illustration has revealed. In fact, each of the flashlight components used in the example (head subassembly, light subassembly, and body subassembly) can be exploded into its components and their subcomponents. This complexity of detail, even for a simple flashlight, is more typical of the multilevel product structure that most schedulers experience.

This added detail is brought in here to make the point that MRP will continue to explode requirements through the defined bills-of-material in order to generate an MRP plan for every one of the items identified as part of the final flashlight.

Safety Stock

Master schedulers and planners must understand safety stocks, why they are used, and their impacts on master scheduling and material requirements planning. In developing illustrations of a fairly simple master schedule and showing how it explodes down through the MRP system we have, thus far, made some convenient assumptions. We have assumed that our inventory records are accurate—i.e., if the on-hand balance said 12 units, we assumed it reflected reality. We also assumed the demand at the MPS level, bills-of-material, and the projected gross requirements at the MRP level were realistic and accurate. Based upon these assumptions, we constructed a master schedule, supported by lower-level schedules, and assumed that production as well as our suppliers would perform to a high standard of timely completion relative to those schedules.

However, forecasted demand is not always accurate, and non–

Class A companies' inventory records[4] are notoriously inaccurate—meaning that items we assumed to be on hand were not. Even if the inventory records are accurate, other problems could occur. The production floor may run the number of items scheduled, but some of these may be found to be defective. Suppliers sometimes fill a purchase order for 100 parts, but 97 are found to be in the box; and sometimes these parts arrive late.

A system in which one set of assumptions is layered upon others is bound to contain surprises. Often surprises do not work in our favor.

Safety Stocks as a Hedge

Safety stocks can be used as a hedge against unanticipated variations in both demand and supply. If the supplier delivers fewer parts than requisitioned, if the production floor builds items that fail to meet quality specifications, or if the demand forecast is for 10 and orders come in for 12, safety stocks, used with caution, can be strategically planned to fill out the difference.

What to Safety Stock

In a world where inventory had no carrying costs for the company, virtually every finished item, every parent part, and every component could be safety stocked—as long as there was room to store it. But why stop there? Why not have extra personnel on hand, just in case someone has to go home early? In the imperfect world, however, this is impractical and expensive, so management teams have to determine what is important to safety stock from a strategic standpoint. The immediate choices that come to mind are finished goods, subassemblies, intermediates, components, and raw materials. However, there are several other candidates for safety stocking, some of which are discussed in greater detail later in this book. Here, our concern is the mechanics of how MPS and MRP software accommodate safety stocks.

[4] Class A companies have inventory record accuracy that exceeds 95 percent.

In the flashlight example, the company could decide to always maintain an inventory of 10, 20, or 40 finished flashlights. Additionally, it could also consider safety stocking certain components—like flashlight bulbs or even the raw materials used to make the components. Whichever level it chooses to safety stock, there should be a strategic purpose to offset the extra cost of inventory. Here are a few strategic purposes:

• Items with long lead times can add to the cumulative time needed to build the product. By strategic or safety stocking those items with the longest lead times, the cumulative lead time to build the product may be reduced.

• If a family of finished product is available in many options (colors, trim pieces, etc.), the forecast for the entire family is likely to be more accurate than the forecast for the specific configured product. Thus, the surprises in demand are likely to be most pronounced among the options; therefore, these semifinished options would be candidates for strategic stocking.

• For many businesses, customers expect that the producer will have certain items on hand *all of the time*, other items *some of the time*, and other items *occasionally*. Consider the analogy of the automotive service station. Its customers expect that gasoline and certain selected auto parts (fan belts, oil, oil filters, etc.) will *always* be available. It would be unacceptable for an auto service station to be out of these for any length of time. Customers would expect replacement batteries and spark plugs to be available, but they would not be shocked or disappointed if the station was temporarily out of stock. They might be willing to wait a day or two for their replacement batteries or spark plugs (many companies have a one- or two-day restocking policy for items like these). These same customers, however, would *not* expect the service station to have a replacement transmission for a 1975 Ford, and would be prepared to wait for a special order on this part to come in. In this example, gasolinelike items are candidates for safety stock if there is a reasonable chance for unexpected demand or a shortfall. This analogy applies to manufacturers who place a high premium on customer service for their basic, core products or service parts business.

The Mechanics of Using Safety Stocks

With modern MPS software, the desired stocking level for a master scheduled item is entered into the system, and the system flags any situation in which the projected on-hand balance falls below the safety stock level. Consider the example in Figure 3.7. This company desires, as a matter of policy, a safety stock of 50 units. Here, forecasted demand is also for 50 units per period. Seventy units are shown to be on hand—all but 20 representing safety stock (70−50). In the MPS line, the master scheduler has laid in four separate orders of supply to meet the anticipated demand. A quick glance at the projected available balance line reveals that in periods 1, 3, and 4, the

Figure 3.7 Safety Stock Example

Safety stock: 50 Units
On hand: 70 Units
Lot size: 125 Units

	Past Due	1	2	3	4	5	6	7	8
Item Forecast		50	50	50	50	50	50	50	50
Option Forecast									
Actual Demand									
Total Demand		50	50	50	50	50	50	50	50
Projected Available Balance	70	20	95	45	−5	70	145	95	170
Available-to-Promise									
Master Schedule		←	125	←	←	125	125		125

projected number of units on hand is expected to fall below the safety stock level or turn negative. For example, with 70 as a starting on-hand balance, less the 50 needed in period 1, only 20 will remain—less than the safety stock policy requirement. Here the master scheduler would receive an action message to shift the period 2 supply order in the MPS line to period 1, as indicated by the arrow. Following the same logic, the master scheduler would receive an action message to shift the 125 scheduled in period 5 to period 3 because the projected available balance falls below the safety stock policy of 50. If period 5's supply order is moved to period 3 or 4, the projected shortage in period 4 will not occur. These shifts would keep the projected available balances above 50 in all periods.[5] After these shifts in the timing of supply, the matrix for this master scheduled item would appear as shown in Figure 3.8.

Figure 3.8 Same Example After Shifting Supply Orders

Total Demand		50	50	50	50	50	50	50	50
Projected Available Balance	70	145	95	170	120	70	145	95	170
Available-to-Promise									
Master Schedule		125		125			125		125

In this instance, none of the periods have a projected available balance less than the safety stock level.

Alternative Safety Stock Display Format

Many people today have checking accounts that require a minimum balance of $300. By agreeing to maintain this minimum balance, they are not charged the normal account service fees. While most of these

[5] The computer would recommend these changes by means of action messages, which are detailed later in chapter 4.

people keep track of their checkbook balances in the normal way and avoid slipping below the $300 minimum, some people simply reduce their actual balance by $300. This way, when the checkbook register says $0, they know they cannot write any more checks—even though there is $300 in the account. Some MPS and MRP computer software handles safety stocks the same way. The MPS matrix for these systems does not reflect the safety stock in the projected available balance line. It is there, but the computer software does not show it. This means that the master scheduler can take those balances down to zero without violating safety stock policy.

Planning Time Fences

As previously discussed, projected gross requirements, scheduled receipts, on-hand balances, lot sizes, and safety stocks affect the placement of computer planned orders. Also, each part's lead time is used to offset the placement (release date) of computer planned orders from the need date. In the flashlight example, we saw lead times of 1 period for flashlights and 2 periods for the light subassembly. But what would happen if the lead time for flashlights or light subassemblies was 5 or more periods? By definition, the planned order release for light subassemblies would be past due. Another way to say this is that there would be inadequate lead time for the proper placement of the light subassembly order. Of course, this is not a desired condition.

Fortunately, there is a way in master scheduling to control lead time issues. Modern software links master scheduling requirements to the MRP systems, which schedules descending levels of parts and materials. It efficiently performs calculations and recommends actions, freeing the scheduler from the drudge work and allowing him or her to focus on critical decision making.

One of the truly valuable features of MPS software is the "planning time fence." A planning time fence (PTF) restricts the computer software system from automatically adding to the master schedule within a specified zone. If, for example, the master scheduler wants to maintain complete control of all flashlight supply orders within periods 1 through 6, a planning time fence can be placed at the end of period 6 (see Figure 3.9), forming a boundary within which only the master scheduler can place supply orders (by definition these orders then must be released orders or firm planned orders—no computer planned orders, which are created by the computer, being permitted inside the planning time fence). Outside the planning time fence, the computer can continue to place CPOs.

The planning time fence can be used to implement management policies and guidelines. For example, managers may determine that changes to the master schedule can be accomplished easily beyond the cumulative lead time—i.e., the total time needed to build the product from its lowest MRP level up—whereas making supply changes at points inside the cumulative lead time become progres-

Figure 3.9 Planning Time Fence Example

← PTF (between periods 6 and 7)

	Past Due	1	2	3	4	5	6	7	8
Item Forecast		70	70	70	70	70	70	70	70
Option Forecast									
Actual Demand									
Total Demand		70	70	70	70	70	70	70	70
Projected Available Balance	135	65	125	55	115	45	–25	–95 35	–165 95
Available-to-Promise									
Master Schedule			130		130			130	130

sively more difficult as they take on the characteristics of last-minute changes. The planning time fence can create a boundary between these areas.

The planning time fence also satisfies the master scheduler's need to restrict the master scheduling software so that only released orders and firm planned orders can be created within close-in time periods. These are time periods within which the master scheduler's attention must be focused and within which the scheduler—not the computer—must make the decisions.

Areas of Control

To better understand how the planning time fence functions, look at Figure 3.9. Let's assume the cumulative lead time of this MPS item is six periods. The master scheduler has decided to place a planning time fence[6] at the end of period 6. The PTF indicates that the master scheduler controls all the supply orders up through period 6, while the computer can add or make changes in periods 7 and 8. With a cumulative lead time of six periods, the master scheduler may want these periods "locked up" and not subject to any mindless changes made by the computer software to balance out a deficiency in some period without careful analysis.

To understand the utilization of the planning time fence, consider again the problem represented in Figure 3.9. In this case, forecasted demand for the master scheduled item is 70 per period. The starting on-hand balance is 135 units. The on-hand balance plus the scheduled receipt of 130 units in period 2 is sufficient to cover the demand through that period and leaves a projected available balance of 125. That surplus supply is enough to meet the next period's demand, but not enough to meet that of period 4. However, a firm planned order of 130 is scheduled in period 4, and this should leave a projected balance of 115. Taking this order into account, the projected inventory is sufficient to meet demand through period 5, but as we observe, a

[6] Where to place the time fence for various master schedule items is discussed in chapter 4.

potential shortage appears in period 6. Here the available balance at the end of period 6 is 25 units short of meeting the demand of 70 in the period. In the absence of a released order or firm planned order in the MPS row of period 6, the MPS display shows a −25 projected available balance. That deficit would increase by 70 per period through the horizon if no additional orders were placed, which is indicated by the negative available balances in periods 7 and 8 (−95 and −165 respectively).

Maintaining Supply/Demand Balance Inside the Planning Time Fence

Since master scheduling software cannot tolerate a supply shortage (its circuits get upset when a negative available balance appears), it would normally place a CPO in the MPS row of period 6 to cover the −25 projected available balance. However, the planning time fence restricts the computer software from any CPO activity through period 6. If it could speak (and it probably will some day), the computer software would shout to the master scheduler, "Wake up and fix that deficit in period 6!" Since it cannot do that, the computer software settles for piling enough CPOs into period 7 (the first period outside the planning time fence) to create a positive projected available balance, and informs the master scheduler by means of an action (or exception) message that a negative availability condition exists inside the planning time fence. With this action or exception message, the decision of what to do is dropped directly into the master scheduler's lap.

Converting a CPO to an FPO

The master scheduler must take some sort of action in period 6 if the potential supply deficit in that period is to be avoided. It would appear that the computer planned order of 130 in period 7 must be converted into a firm planned order with a due date in period 6. First, though, the master scheduler should be sure that this action is in the best interest of the company. Several questions must be answered:

- Can we get the material to produce these items in time?
- Does the capacity to produce these items exist?
- Will the forecast of 70 units really turn into customer orders?
- What will it cost to make this change?
- Does authorization exist to make this change?

Determining the answers to these questions takes master scheduling beyond the straightforward job of juggling numbers to keep supply and demand in balance. This is an area in which the computer can provide assistance but not a final judgment—at least not yet. What we are now talking about is the real job of the master scheduler. This chapter has described what the master scheduling system mechanics do to support the master scheduler. The next chapter begins the discussion of how the master scheduler uses this data in order to manage the production plant. But before this discussion begins, we must conclude this chapter with a discussion on some of the design criteria of the master scheduling process.

Master Schedule Design Criteria

In order to make MRP II function properly, the master scheduling and material requirements planning system must be carefully linked. This linkage is done via bills-of-material. Besides tying the two systems together, the MPS system should adhere to a set of design criteria.

While there is some flexibility in the design of any MPS process, certain guidelines should be observed. These guidelines reflect the cumulative experience of many companies in many different industries. The following design areas need to be addressed:

Time Criteria

Most MPS software now on the market manages all supply and demand by dates. If the real dates are known, master schedule data can be displayed in any variety of ways. It is recommended that the maximum length of a scheduling display period be no greater than one week. In many cases, a daily time period will be preferred. Monthly increments are simply unsatisfactory; attempting to manage time blocks of this size increases the chances that the master scheduler will miss the details necessary to convert production rates into specific part numbers, quantities, and due dates. The result: completion dates not met and missed deliveries.

Planning Horizon

At the master schedule level, it is necessary to deal with two different types of lead times. One is the lead time required to produce the master scheduled item itself when all items one level down in the item's bill-of-material are available. The second is the cumulative lead time—the longest planned length of time required to produce the master scheduled item from scratch. This takes into account *all* the lead times of *all* the items that go into the master scheduled item. In short, it is the critical path that recognizes all processes that can be done in parallel.

Many companies find it necessary to extend the planning horizon beyond the cumulative lead time if they need additional visibility for procurement planning or establishing supplier agreements. Extension of the planning horizon may also be required to properly assess capacity requirements. Thus, while some companies have a short material lead time, they may need to extend the overall horizon because of heavy equipment or other capacity needs.

Frequency of Review

Ideally, the master schedule will be reviewed continuously or daily using an on-line computer system. At a minimum, it should be reviewed weekly. With today's technology it is possible to keep the master schedule constantly on-line, where changes can be seen on the MPS screen as they are made. As chapter 14 on demand management and available-to-promise (ATP) will make clear, the ATP row of the master schedule screen needs to be analyzed in a real-time environment if customer orders are received on a regular basis.

This chapter covered the basic MPS matrix and the calculations used in the master scheduling process. Some basic guidelines on the design of MPS process have also been addressed. The fact is, however, that we have only described how to get information into a format that the master scheduler can use. The next step is to understand how to manage with the MPS system. This is discussed in the following chapters.

4

Managing with the Master Schedule

If you don't have time to do it right the first time, when are you going to find time to do it again?

On Wednesday morning, just as she was preparing to go off to lunch, Judy Wilson, master scheduler for Criterion Electric Controls Company, received a call from the vice president of sales.

"Judy. I just got a call from our sales representative in Philadelphia. He has a chance of making an important sale of an A3 control system to a big company out there if we can beat Drumlin Electronics in making delivery."

"Well, that's good news," Wilson replied. "An A3 is a $120,000 unit."

"Right," said the sales vice president, "and this would be a new and important account for us—one that Drumlin has always controlled. Once we get our foot in the door, other business should follow."

Wilson knew that the sales vice president had not called just to announce some good news. The phrase "if we can beat Drumlin

Electronics in making delivery" was to be the real reason for this conversation. The master scheduler braced herself for what was surely coming next.

"Here's the deal, Judy. Delivery is the big issue in the sale. Drumlin has promised to expedite the order and deliver in just four weeks—not their usual five." The sales vice president paused for just a moment, preparing to drop his bomb on Wilson. "We have to do better to get the business. Could we have an A3 unit for this customer in three weeks?"

Wilson had just looked at the master schedule for A3s that morning and knew that the production line was totally committed through the period in question. She also knew that the cumulative lead time for a finished A3 was six weeks. "Is that three weeks to ship?" she asked.

"I'm afraid not," the vice president responded. "That's three weeks to the customer's loading dock."

Both knew that the product was too heavy to air freight, and that express trucking would take a full two days.

"Let me work on it," Wilson said. "I'll call you back in a couple of hours. I need to check the schedule and talk with some other people."

While the sales vice president was off to a business lunch, the master scheduler went to work on the problem. She would spend the next hour or more reexamining the master schedule for A3s, several of which were on order and in various stages of production for other customers. She would consider current capacity and materials. And she would do whatever she could to make it possible for Criterion to deliver its A3 for the sales representative to open this important new account, and to ensure that all other customer commitments are satisfied. It was her job to make these things happen when she could.

By 1:30 that afternoon, Wilson was on the phone to the sales vice president. "Tell your sales representative in Philadelphia that he'll get his A3 three weeks from today . . . on the customer's loading dock."

"Great, Judy! How did you manage it?"

"Well, we had an A2 already in production. I had your assistant call the account representative for the A2's customer to determine if he could live with a two-week delay. We worked out a deal with that customer to offer a free extension on his warrantee if he would take it two weeks later. The customer had no problem with it, and finance has approved the deal. I can upgrade that A2 to an A3 with available materials and capacity and deliver as promised. Tell your sales representative that he has a green light on this one, if we can solve one problem."

"What's that?" the vice president asked apprehensively.

"Your Michigan representative has an A3 on order that will be delayed by three to four days if we make these changes. Is that all right with you?"

The ball was back in the sales vice president's court. But he was used to this give and take with Wilson, who had educated everyone to the fact that when the production system was carefully scheduled, even the most creative rescheduling to satisfy customers usually carried some sort of penalty.

"Yes, I can deal with the customer on that delay," the vice president ended. "We'll fax you the order in an hour."

As this story makes clear, there is much more to master scheduling than knowing how to move numbers around on the MPS matrix. Proficiency with the mechanics of scheduling is essential, but other skills are equally important: a sense of the company's overall business and its customers, knowledge of its products and production processes, and understanding of the reliability of its suppliers, to name just a few. These are areas in which judgment combined with a good business sense are critical, and they relate closely with the ability to use the mechanics of the MPS system to manage production operations.

In this story, the master scheduler used her MPS software tool to get a picture of current A3 production, capacity, and materials. But she went beyond this, thinking creatively about how the picture could be tactically rearranged to meet the interests of her company and its customers. Her knowledge of the company's products and how they are manufactured allowed her to see how an A2 could be converted into an A3 on short order. And she had the organizational skills to work through other parts of the company—sales, marketing, engineering, finance, manufacturing, and management—to create a solution in a way that would be supported by all affected parties.

The mechanics of master scheduling (described in chapter 3) provide an important management tool, but the master scheduler must know how to use that tool, which is the focus of this chapter.

The Master Scheduler's Job

One way to understand how to manage with the master scheduling system is to consider the job requirements of the scheduler. (A detailed sample job description is supplied in chapter 15.) Basically, the master scheduler is responsible for creating and maintaining a master schedule that satisfies all demands. This is not a task restricted to the factory or plant floor, but one that coordinates with other important functions of the company and its constituency of suppliers and customers:

- *Sales.* Sales personnel live to secure orders on which, hopefully, a profit can be made and commissions earned. Their task is made easier when the product can be delivered when the customer wants it and in the correct quantities. In a competitive world, stockouts, missed delivery dates, and the inability of the manufacturing facility to fill rush orders makes the lives of sales personnel more difficult. Conversely, the ability to avoid stockouts, meet promised delivery dates, and accommodate special customers with rapid delivery helps secure both sales success and the overall success of the company.

- *Marketing.* Marketing personnel are skilled in bringing product into the marketplace and communicating its features and benefits to potential customers. They work on forecasting issues, pricing strategies, distribution systems, product promotions, and so forth. Untimely production delays, stockouts, and unreliable service to distributors and dealers are issues that require regular interaction with the master scheduler. The better they can work together, the more effective their marketing and manufacturing programs will be.

• *Engineering.* Design engineers live for the day when development projects, which for months and years had been merely ideas or drawings, emerge from the plant as finished new products. Anything that reduces manufacturing and material complications or failures ranks high on their list of important issues.

• *Finance.* Financial managers measure the world in monetary terms. Inventory requires costly capital. Surpluses of materials and finished goods are nonproductive assets that create expense and no income. On the other hand, shortages of deliverable products and the materials from which they are made can result in expensive unplanned air freight, overtime pay, performance penalties, and lost sales. Finance wants the factory to walk a fine line between too much inventory and stockout situations.

• *Manufacturing.* Plant managers like to maintain an orderly flow of production—one that levels the load on the factory over extended periods. An orderly flow facilitates optimal plant usage, steers a course between layoffs and overtime, and eliminates the stresses that create the end-of-the-month nightmares described at the beginning of chapter 1.

• *Top management.* The role of top management is to harness the capital and human resources of the company to a strategy that will result in economic prosperity for the organization and its owners. Top management has to steer the company into the future, and that is possible only when all the machinery of the organization is working together. The ability of management to control and lead is compromised with shipping delays, confusion on the manufacturing floor, excessive expenses in production, poor quality, and other internal emergencies.

The activities of the master scheduler are important to each of these functions of the company. Sales and marketing must be accommodated to the greatest extent possible to win orders, but undisciplined demands for large inventories and expedited production need to be balanced against other concerns. The desire of finance to reduce inventory expenses must be balanced against the requirements of the competitive marketplace and the needs of production to keep the plant running in a sensible way. The desire of manufacturing to produce steady runs and level the load on the plant must be judged in the context of foreseeable customer demand for the plant's output.

In some respects, the master scheduler attempts to do from the middle management level of the organization what senior management attempts to do from the top, namely, optimize the cooperation of the company's many functions in serving the needs of the customer. This is a job for which master scheduling software is clearly just one tool; a job for which an acute sense of factory dynamics as well as negotiating and communication skills are critical. The following case illustrates how master scheduling is more than a mindless numbers tool, but one that requires finesse on the part of the scheduler.

MOVING A CUSTOMER ORDER TO AN EARLIER DATE

"We'd like to reschedule our order."

This is not the worst kind of message to get from a customer. It's certainly preferable to "We'd like to *cancel* our order." Still, it can present problems for manufacturing and challenge the ability of management to run the business in a way that delivers a profit to shareholders and satisfies customers—which are the two bases for being, and *staying*, in business.

Consider the case of Acme Glassworks, a producer of plate glass. One of its major customers, a manufacturer of commercial windows and glass sheathing for buildings, has called to request a change in its scheduled orders, from 10 pallets in each of the next three months (30 pallets in all), to 10 this month, 14 next month, and 6 the following month (again, 30 in all).

The master scheduler at Acme Glassworks recognizes this as a straightforward timing change, one that will require some shifting from month to month. If capacity and materials were no issue, this could be accomplished as follows:

PERIODS	MO1	MO2	MO3	QTR.
Customer Orders (pallets)	10	14 ~~10~~	6 ~~10~~	30
Master Schedule	10	10	10	30

On the surface, a request to move up an order would seem like a clear-cut opportunity for the manufacturer to please and satisfy the customer. But is it, really? This move-up request may actually have some source other than the customer. The order might have been triggered by one of the company's own sales representatives. With the sales contest for the trip to Hawaii coming into the final stretch, the representative in Omaha might have pleaded with a customer to place the order early, thereby pushing his sales numbers up in the contest period.

In another situation, the order might originate on a clerk's computer screen. The "customer" in this case might be a clerk in the company's inventory control group whose computer software flagged the item, indicating a demand change due to arbitrary safety stock requirement.

If a great fuss is to be made in moving an order in, then we need to be sure that all the pain and suffering will have a positive result: that of profitably serving a paying customer.

Issues of Management

Even the simple Acme Glassworks situation raises a host of important issues for managers and supervisors.

• *Can we get the capacity?* Sure, you want to satisfy the customer's request to move up an order! But it's often easier said than done. Will this gesture of customer service overload the schedule and throw a monkey wrench into the production facility?

• *Can we get the materials?* Even if the capacity problem is solved, a manufacturer might not be able to move up his own order for materials. With so many companies operating on razor-thin parts and materials inventories, the materials might not be obtainable.

• *How much will it cost?* If overtime is part of the capacity solution, and if expedited purchases and air freight of materials are part of the materials problem, then this order change may squeeze any profit out of the order that so many people will be scrambling to accommodate.

• *What will this change do to morale and teamwork on the floor?* Personnel close to the action may be working diligently to create a stable and smooth-running operation for management. Will this order change and disrupt the efficient routines and undercut the progress personnel has made in creating an orderly workplace?

These are important issues for management. Others in the organization will have their own issues of concern. Marketing may see the order change as important for market penetration. In the absence of any explanation, manufacturing may see the order change as just another headache. Finance may see a revenue opportunity. Of course, they may also recognize a cash-flow problem—namely, how will the company pay for the material and manufacturing costs that are now being moved up and out of its budget?

Typically, requests to move up an order in the schedule come from someone in sales, and they usually want an answer right away—while they are still on the telephone. "Well, can you do it or not?" We all like to please, but moving an order usually requires some checking: with the current schedule, the stockroom, and sometimes with suppliers. There is nothing wrong with saying, "I'll need to do some checking and call you back. It may take a day or two to get you an answer, depending on which suppliers we need to check with to see if we can get the materials." To imply otherwise is to send the signal that schedules are of no great importance and can be changed at will.

Sometimes, we simply have to say no to change requests. But instead of an absolute no, we should say something like this: "I can't move that order up because the production schedule is currently booked. If you would be willing to move one of your other orders to a later date, however, I might be able to use that capacity. Do you want me to look into that?" This response helps the salesperson understand the limits of schedule flexibility, and the important idea that tradeoffs are often the answer.

For companies whose traditions have been to reflexively accept order changes, the greater care and study suggested above may not be agreeable to everyone—especially at first. Sales representatives who routinely telephone in order changes and get an instant answer will not like being told "we'll get back to you after we do some checking." One of management's challenges is to help these people see that a more thoughtful way of handling order changes is in the company's best interests.

Action Messages

The MPS computer system proposes; the master scheduler disposes. Chapter 3 explained that the computer looks for imbalances in supply and demand, and places computer planned orders where necessary, given product lead times, lot sizes, and safety stock requirements. We also observed how a planning time fence can be used to create a boundary between time periods in which the computer "proposes" and the master scheduler "disposes."

One way in which computer and scheduler communicate is through "action messages" (also known as "exception messages"). Action messages are the MPS software's way of getting the master scheduler's attention, and directing it to areas of potential problems. They identify the need for intervention to correct a current problem or to avoid a potential one. Examples of action messages are: release an order, reschedule-in, reschedule-out, cancel, convert a computer planned order to a firm planned order, and so forth.

Figure 4.1 provides an example in which several of these action messages appear. Here, the planning time fence is somewhere beyond period 8, thus, all the numbers in the MPS row represent firm planned orders.

Demand for the product is stated as 50 units per period. With 70 units on hand, the MPS logic projects the available balance for each period. An FPO for 115 is scheduled to be received in period 2. (The lot size was 115 when the firm planned order was created, or the

Figure 4.1 Action Message Example

On hand: 70 units
Lead time (one level): 1 period
Cumulative lead time: > 8 periods
Lot size: 125 units
Safety stock: None

PTF →

MPS Matrix	Past Due	1	2	3	4	5	6	7	8
Item Forecast		50	50	50	50	50	50	50	50
Option Forecast									
Actual Demand									
Total Demand		50	50	50	50	50	50	50	50
Projected Available Balance	70	20	85	35	–15	60	135	85	160
Available-to-Promise									
Master Schedule			115		←	125	125	→	125
			Release			R/I	R/O		Cancel

ACTION MESSAGES:

1. Release FPO in period 2; start building in period 1.
2. Reschedule-in FPO in period 5 to period 4.
3. Reschedule-out FPO in period 6 to period 7.
4. Cancel FPO in period 8.

master scheduler had decided to override the lot size specification of 125 when the order was placed, or 10 have been received or scrapped, etc. This could be true if the company manufactures to a rate and expresses this rate using firm planned orders.) It is the master scheduler's job to keep the MPS line valid in quantity and due date. Remember, inside the planning time fence only the master scheduler can create orders and alter released and firm planned order data. Additional FPOs for 125 have previously been placed in periods 5, 6, and 8.

A potential shortage of 15 units is projected for period 4, but a positive available balance reappears in the next period (60 in period 5). Subsequent periods project additional positive balances (135, 85, and 160). Because the projected available balance goes negative and then returns to positive, the master scheduling system recognizes that a timing, and not a volume, problem exists. The MPS system notes this and looks into future periods for orders that could be moved up. Since an FPO for 125 units is scheduled to be received in period 5 and really is needed in period 4, the system generates an action message recommending that the FPO be "rescheduled-in" to period 4, thus solving the deficit problem.[1] The computer would also scan future periods and spot the larger than needed available balance of 135 in period 6. If the scheduled FPO for this period were not received, the 60 remaining from the previous projected balance would be more than enough to cover period 6's demand of 50 units; 10 units would, in fact, be left over. This being the case, the software would send an action message to "reschedule-out" the 125 units from period 6 to period 7.

Scanning still further, it would be clear that the FPO of 125 units in period 8 is not needed if the projected demand beyond period 8 is less than 35 units and a "cancel" message would be sent to the master scheduler for his or her consideration.

In addition to the action messages discussed above, the master scheduling system would notify the scheduler that the firm planned

[1] Only 15 units are needed here, but most MPS and MRP systems recommend bringing in the entire lot. The master scheduler has several options: Split the lot of 125 into 15 and 110; increase the planned order in period 2 to 130; do nothing; etc.

order due in period 2 should be released (converted to a released order, such as a work order) since the item under evolution has a one-period lead time.

To review, a master scheduling system generally has the capability to analyze the supply/demand balance and to generate the following action messages:

- Convert firm planned orders into released orders.
- Convert computer planned orders into firm planned orders.
- Reschedule released or FPOs into a closer time frame.
- Reschedule released or FPOs into a future time frame.
- Cancel a released or firm planned order.
- A negative available balance exists within the planning time fence.
- Demand requirements are past due.
- Scheduled receipts or FPOs are past due.
- A planned order release has inadequate lead time to properly order material or secure the necessary capacity.

Five Key Questions

Action messages contain the recommendations of the software system. These systems range in price from several thousand to a few million dollars and are terrific for making calculations and linking those calculations horizontally across time periods, and vertically through the bills-of-material and MRP systems. They are practically infallible in the black-and-white area of numeric logic, but even the best systems are not capable of dealing with the many gray areas that permeate the complex manufacturing environment. It is the gray areas in which the human master scheduler is superior to the machine, and in which his or her natural skepticism about demand forecasts, intuitions about risk, and so forth are essential. These gray areas may be defined in terms of five key questions that no computer can completely answer but which must be addressed before computer-directed reschedules and order launches are executed.

Question 1: Has Demand Really Changed?

The computer can look up the demand number, compare it to the supply, and recommend action. However, it would never challenge the validity of that demand number. If the demand number is seriously in error, the reschedule or order message may be invalid. Maybe a customer has just shifted an order out of one period; the period demand has changed, but the aggregate demand remains the same. Before making changes on the shop floor, a human operator must ask: "How realistic is this demand?" or "What caused the change?" or "Should we react to this demand?"

Consider a product that normally has demand for 50 units per period. A period with 80 units appears in the total demand row on the planning horizon. The master scheduler must make a decision with respect to creating supply to match this demand. Certain subtle clues may suggest that the high demand is not genuine. For example, if this high demand comes in just prior to the end of the annual sales bonus period, could the sales force be "stuffing" their regular customers with sales, robbing the next period just to enhance this period and reach their bonus requirements? Meeting this abnormally high demand might likely mean paying high overtime rates, costly special freight charges, and general stress on the factory. A telephone call or two might determine how genuine the demand really is. Changes can then be made accordingly.

Question 2: What Is the Impact on the Production Plan?

A computer-generated action recommendation may put the master scheduler at odds with one or more top-management plans. In a Class A MRP II environment, aggregate monthly production rates by product family are reviewed and authorized by senior management; these constitute a production plan that the master scheduler must support in aggregate. This means that individual line item master schedules can be altered only in a way that preserves the validity of the overall monthly production plan totals. One master schedule change may have to be counterbalanced by an equal but opposite change for another item in the same product family. If this is not possible, higher-level approval may be needed for a change that would disrupt the production plan volume.

Question 3: Is Capacity Available?

The desire to make a change to the master schedule may be constrained by available resources. A manufacturing facility is like a piece of rubber: You can stretch it in a number of different directions to accommodate production level changes (extra shifts, outsourcing, etc.). However, when action recommendations appear, capacity must be ensured before taking the recommended steps.

Question 4: Is Material Available?

Capacity alone does not manufacture products; the right materials in the right quantities are also essential to making schedule changes. If the recommendation is for supply increases, there must be materials. Conversely, if demand is being reduced, it may be necessary to consider added space requirements for materials inventory.

Question 5: What Are the Costs and the Associated Risks?

In most cases, extra capacity can be found and more materials can be obtained to accommodate changes made within the lead time. Almost everything is possible—but at a cost. Express delivery companies have multibillions of dollars in annual revenues, much of it earned from companies and individuals rushing documents and materials around to met deadlines and schedules. But revenues to express delivery companies are expenses to companies that use their services.

In manufacturing, freeing up capacity, shifting work, and expediting materials delivery and product shipments all raise the cost of production. They also increase the risk of producing poor-quality products and damaging important customer relationships due to failure to keep delivery promises.

From a management viewpoint, the costs and risks of MPS changes have to be measured and compared to the benefits of these changes. Does management understand the impact on financial performances due to these changes? Will the changes impact support for other customers and products? In the end, management needs to ask the question: "Is it a smart business decision to make this change?"

Answering the Five Questions

Each of the five questions must be answered before any master schedule change is made. Obviously, in complex environments involving many materials and many products, answering each question in complete detail would be enormously time consuming. In these cases, time-saving tools like rough cut capacity planning (explained in chapter 13)—which focuses attention on only key resources and materials—are invaluable. Also, operating on a computer platform that can generate simulations in minutes or even seconds is desirable. However, no matter how difficult the task, answers to these questions need to be determined if sound business decisions are to be made.

Equally invaluable is the master scheduler's experience and judgment. That experience and judgment will make answers to some of the questions intuitively obvious. In other cases, hours and days of investigation by the master scheduler and other personnel may be required to gather the data on which analysis and an informed decision can be made.

A good master scheduler satisfies demands from forecasts, contracts, customer orders, and other sources, along with the demand variations that inevitably occur, through the use of effective schedules, safety stock, safety capacity, and selective overplanning. Building a good master schedule, however, is just half of the challenge; operating a master schedule within 95 percent of plan is the other half. This is as much art as science, because the master scheduler must balance time and resources against the goals and needs of other parts of the business.

Time Zones as Aids to Decision Making

The example given in Figure 4.1 on page 88 allowed the master scheduler to use judgment in rebalancing the MPS through change orders. For a number of reasons to be discussed soon, it is beneficial to have a set of guidelines, or "rescheduling time zone rules," to aid master schedulers and management in making decisions. These rules are linked to management policies that determine what kinds of changes can be made to the master schedule at certain points in time. Figure 4.2 is an abridgment of the MPS matrix, and shows how the time horizon of periods can be grouped into zones for managing schedule changes.

The meaning of these time zones for management is fairly intuitive. Zone A includes the current period and close in periods, and is one in

Figure 4.2 Rescheduling Time Zones

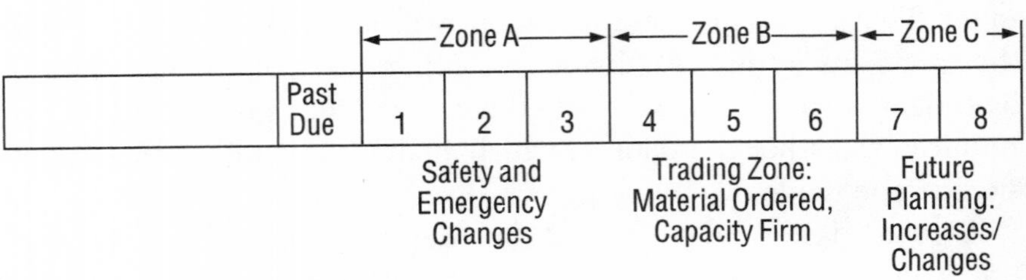

		←Zone A→			←Zone B→			←Zone C→	
	Past Due	1	2	3	4	5	6	7	8
			Safety and Emergency Changes			Trading Zone: Material Ordered, Capacity Firm		Future Planning: Increases/ Changes	

which management must carefully investigate all suggested changes. Because these periods are almost always within the cumulative and possibly the finishing or final assembly lead time of the master scheduled item, any changes will be disruptive and probably costly. Generally, safety and emergency changes are honored here. All others need high-level approval.

Zone B is one within which caution should be exercised with respect to changes. Capacity and material availability for changes need scrutiny here, and prioritizing of different orders may be required. Generally, this zone is known as the "Trading Zone"—material has been ordered, capacity is firm. Changes that cannot be traded with other demand need some level of approval.

In Zone C the master scheduler, and often computer, are free to make changes. This period is by definition far enough into the future that the master scheduler can modify the MPS without affecting the procurement of material or the process of getting the product to market. Generally, this zone is known as the "Future Planning Zone." Changes in this zone can generally be approved by the master scheduler without further management analysis or discussion.

Guidelines for Establishing Zones

There are no hard and fast rules for establishing where each zone starts and stops. These are totally dependent upon the nature of the product and the market and manufacturing strategy of the company. As a general rule, it is useful to think about the boundary separating Zones A and B as a point at which the production process is highly locked in—where changes will be quite costly and disruptive (Zone A) and in which a certain amount of careful trading can take place (Zone B). The boundary between these two zones often coincides with the final assembly or finishing process.

The next step is to determine the boundary between Zones B and C. When in doubt, the product's cumulative lead time is a logical candidate for this boundary. The logic here is that beyond the cumulative lead time, the master scheduler has the time necessary to obtain the required lower-level materials and move capacity around. In some cases, however, Zone B could extend beyond the cumulative lead time. This happens when management wants more control over the schedule and schedule changes. The down side of this, however, is the human effort required to approve changes within this zone.

The opposite is also possible—management might make Zone B smaller, thereby extending the area of Zone C. If a scheduled item had, for example, a cumulative lead time of two months, and fewer approvals and less control were wanted near the end of that period, the boundary could be brought *inside* the cumulative lead time. This provides greater people empowerment in making changes. However, the risk of not making the time, capacity, materials, and financial resources come together as necessary is certainly there due to changes occurring inside of lead time.

Before leaving this subject, let's consider the following case of an order change.

MOVING A MANUFACTURING ORDER TO AN EARLIER DATE

The new production facility of Bordertown Salsa Company had not only been able to meet its scheduled production load but had actually gotten ahead of the game. It now felt capable of taking on more work. For a new production facility this was an encouraging development. The general manager, however, was cautious and reluctant to push the new plant to the limits. "No sense in giving them so much that they choke themselves," he thought.

Bordertown's production manager told the general manager that he would like to move in 2 units of scheduled output from period 3 to period 2. This would provide a test of the plant's productive capacity

PERIOD	1	2	3
Demand	10	10	10
Schedule	10	12 ~~10~~	8 ~~10~~

in period 2 and, if that went well, would open up some slack time in period 3 to do some line adjustments. The general manager agreed.

Pulling work forward is not always a bad idea. In this case, it is done for a rational purpose: to test the limits of a new production facility and to create future slack time for line adjustments. Another instance might involve the opportunity to fill unused production capacity. Likewise, a company may find that its parts or materials inventories are too large, and moving orders in can help reduce these inventories and associated carrying costs if the product built can be sold, shipped, and invoiced. The reasons to move a manufacturing order to an earlier date are numerous. However, moving up an order involves more than just a change in the due date.

Management Issues

Some orders are moved in because they *must* be moved: a batch of finished product was damaged and must be quickly replaced, preshipment product testing found many defective units, a cycle count found an inventory error placing the company out-of-stock on a popular product, a new safety stock level has been approved, etc. Other move requests may have less merit, and part of management's job is to create a working environment in which necessary and frivolous change requests can be sorted out on a rational basis.

It takes very little effort to request an order change, but implementing the change is often difficult, disruptive, and costly. Management needs to determine if a change request is frivolous or essential to the goals of the business, and whether it can be justified from a cost standpoint. If the move-up request is simply to satisfy some internal convenience—such as an arbitrary safety stock requirement—that might not represent a genuine business need. If the move is to satisfy an important customer, we should measure the benefit of greater customer satisfaction against the cost of making the change. We need to ask: "What would happen if we didn't make the change?"

Here are some other issues that management must think through:

- *The order movement may be inside the lead time.* One or more components needed for this stage of production may not be available at the newly scheduled date. This could create a materials problem as well as a credibility problem for the scheduler (i.e., by asking manufacturing to make product without materials).

• *Is there sufficient capacity?* Whoever approved the move-in order may not have checked (or had the experience to determine) that the capacity was available. If the factory cannot respond, what purpose would be served by moving the order?

If an order *must* be moved forward, yet the plant cannot respond, then management must make hard choices. Being between a rock and a hard place is a dilemma that is common in the business world. Management's job is to exercise judgment and creativity in dealing with these dilemmas.

Naturally, management is not the only party concerned when the idea of moving in a manufacturing order is considered. If manufacturing resists, marketing may respond: "You've done it before. Why not now?" Manufacturing may counter with: "We are flexible—to a point—and can handle this one moved-up order. But we cannot handle three, five, or ten such orders." Manufacturing rightfully wonders why they are seldom notified of opportunities to move *out* orders to make room for the orders in question. Finance, as always, is concerned with the costs of the change and how it will enhance or reduce profits. The master scheduler, whose job it is to satisfy customers within the capabilities and capacities of production, may rightfully muse that "nothing seems impossible to the person who doesn't have to do it."

Planning and Policy

Chapter 3 described the use of planning time fences, which is a system technique in which the master scheduler interacts with the computer. It is not unusual to see the planning time fence (PTF) established at a product's cumulative lead time. In fact, if you do not know where to put the PTF, this is where to start. The master scheduler may, however, want to take more control of the horizon. This can be done by putting the PTF further out onto the horizon. This gives the master scheduler more control but also requires more effort since there are more FPOs to control. The master scheduler could also decide to take less control. This can be done by putting the PTF *inside* the cumulative lead time. While this requires *less* effort, the master scheduler is turning over more control of the product to the computer. Care is needed here since any time the PTF is placed inside the cumulative lead time, some strategic stocking of long lead time items should also be taking place in order to ensure material availability. In addition to the PTF and computer logic, we must also consider the relationship between the managerial decision zones just described and the position of the rescheduling timing zones.

The Hierarchy of Change Approvals

The establishment of zones within which a descending hierarchy of cautions prevails suggests a corresponding hierarchy of authorities for approving master schedule changes. Thus, changes in Zone C, which involve little risk and cost, can be made by individuals lower in the hierarchy of authority, while changes in Zone A should be scrutinized and approved at a higher level. This is the sort of policy that prevails in Class A MRP II companies and is analogous to other corporate policies that involve commitments of resources.

A caution in the development of a change-approval policy is that the list of people needed to approve a change should not be so formidable as to make needed changes overly difficult to implement. If a master scheduler has to run around to seventeen people to get approval for necessary changes, one of two things will happen: 1) the changes will never be made, or 2) the master scheduler will ignore the policy and make changes arbitrarily. There is a fine line between overburdening the approval process and giving out too much authority to lower-level functions.

Figure 4.3 illustrates this hierarchy of authority to approve changes against the background of the schedule time horizon and Zones A, B, and C previously mentioned. The exact location of the zones in the figure is hypothetical and strictly for illustration purposes. In any Class A organization, however, these demarcations are thoroughly thought out and communicated through written policies.

Figure 4.3 Time Zones and Approval Policy Example

		←Zone A→			←Zone B→			←Zone C→	
MPS Matrix	Past Due	1	2	3	4	5	6	7	8
		----- Cumulative Lead Time ---------							

Zone A	Zone B	Zone C
Approvals by:	Approvals by:	Approvals by:
Pres., VP Manufacturing, VP Sales, and/or VP Finance	Manufacturing Dir., Plant Mgr., and/or Sales Dir.	Master Scheduler and/or Materials Mgr., Demand Mgr.

The Placement of Approval Zones

While approval policies that govern the domain of humans are divided into three or more time zones, the domain of the computer software is generally broken in two by means of the planning time fence: one in which the computer software has no control and another in which it operates freely. The point has already been made that in the absence of any other guidelines, a good place to put the PTF is at the end of the cumulative lead time.

In the development of a formal policy with respect to the re-schedule approval zones, a good place to put the break between Zones C and B is also at the end of the cumulative lead time. A logical place for the break between Zones A and B is at the finishing or final assembly process. These are not hard-and-fast rules by any means, but they are good rules of thumb when the company has insufficient information to place the decision points elsewhere.

Managing with Planning Time Fences

It is now useful to return to planning time fences to discuss how the master scheduler can use them to more effectively manage production schedules. Consider again the MPS matrix used to introduce the concept of planning time fences, reintroduced here as Figure 4.4. Let us consider this to be the master schedule for an A3 unit manufactured by Criterion Electric Controls Company, introduced earlier in the chapter.

Figure 4.4 Managing with Planning Time Fences

← PTF (between periods 6 and 7)

	Past Due	1	2	3	4	5	6	7	8
Item Forecast		70	70	70	70	70	70	70	70
Option Forecast									
Actual Demand									
Total Demand		70	70	70	70	70	70	70	70
Projected Available Balance	135	65	125	55	115	45	–25	–95 35	–165 95
Available-to-Promise									
Master Schedule			130		130			130	130

Criterion has forecasted level demand at 70 units per period. The master scheduler, Judy Wilson, has placed a PTF at the end of period 6, and as before, the computer has spotted the potential deficiencies beginning in period 6 and generated two CPOs of 130 each to counteract the deficiencies. However, since a PTF has been established between periods 6 and 7, the first of these CPOs has been placed in period 7 with an action message (negative availability inside the PTF) being sent to the master scheduler. Moving the first of those CPOs into period 6 as a firm planned order is necessary from the vantage point of the computer. However, additional analysis must be done before taking action. To learn something new from this situation, consider the following scenario.

The sales group has just returned from a major trade show where customer response to the A3 unit has been extraordinary. Each of the regional sales managers has told the national sales vice president that its sales representatives will be submitting new and higher forecasts for A3 units within the near term. This is truly good news for the company, and the sales vice president is anxious to ensure an adequate supply of A3 units to meet the tremendous demand he expects to materialize soon. Normally, he would have consulted with the vice president of finance on any major change in the sales forecast, but today he was so excited by future sales prospects and so uneasy about the company's ability to satisfy orders, that he picked up the telephone and called Judy Wilson first.

"Judy, this is Phil. Good news on the sales front. We have big orders ready to come in on A3s, so we are increasing the forecast in period 4."

"I'm glad to hear about the big sales, Phil, but could you give me a figure for how much higher your forecast will go?"

"Sure," said Phil, proudly. "Right now it is 70 units in period 4. We plan to knock that up to 270. Wait, on second thought, let's go to 370. No sense in getting caught short, is there?"

Wilson knew immediately that she would earn her paycheck this day. Several things would happen if she entered this order as requested. The obedient computer software would place a series of CPOs for 130 units in the MPS row of period 7, along with an action message to convert three CPOs for 130 units to FPOs and move them into period 4. Figure 4.5 demonstrates just what Wilson's computer screen would show her.

Figure 4.5 MPS for A3 Units, with Increased Demand in Period 4

Lot size: 130 units
Multiples: 130 units
Lead time: 2 periods
Cumulative lead time: 6 periods

PTF

	Past Due	1	2	3	4	5	6	7	8
Item Forecast		70	70	70	370	70	70	70	70
Option Forecast									
Actual Demand									
Total Demand		70	70	70	370	70	70	70	70
Projected Available Balance	135	65	125	55	–185	–255	–325	–395 125	–465 55
Available-to-Promise									
Master Schedule			130		130			520	

ACTION MESSAGES:

1. Convert CPO to FPO.
2. Negative availability inside PTF.

The large new demand forecasted for period 4 would create a projected deficit in periods 4, 5, and 6. The computer software would never dial the sales vice president to ask how realistic this demand forecast was; the computer would respond in the only way available to it: it would place a very large computer-generated supply order—520 units, four complete lot sizes—in period 7, just outside the planning time fence. These large CPOs would solve the volume problem for

Wilson, but certainly not the timing problem in periods 4 through 6. An action message would recommend firming the CPO of 520 units into a FPO and moving the FPO into period 4, or moving two FPOs of 130 each into period 4, one of 130 to period 6, and creating one for 130 in period 7 (dependent upon the software logic).

Keeping the CPOs outside the planning time fence has the benefit of avoiding unexamined new demand forecasts from automatically exploding downward through the MRP system, where materials would be ordered and expected as well as capacity called for on short order. The planning time fence permits the master scheduler to keep this change in suspension while she considers its consequences on the entire production and materials system.

As an experienced master scheduler, Judy Wilson knew that she would not be changing the master schedule on the sales vice president's request alone. A few things were out of order:

1. This change would take place within Time Zone B, and company policy required the approval of *both* the sales vice president and the plant manager. The reason for this policy was to avoid the chaos that normally resulted from unauthorized changes made within the cumulative lead time. Wilson would first check to see if the plant manager had signed off on this proposed schedule change.

2. Wilson's natural suspicion was aroused by both the timing of this request and the sales vice president's initial tentativeness with respect to the number of orders he expected to receive. Saying "on second thought, let's go [from 270] to 370" was not reassuring to Wilson. Also, forecasted demand increases typically followed the annual trade show attended by the company and, historically, many of these sales failed to materialize in the forecasted period—if at all.

Aside from these two concerns, Wilson knew intuitively that if she brought the CPOs into period 4 that the magnitude of the increased supply would create material and capacity problems below the level of the master schedule. Completing this volume of A3 units would require evening shifts at double-time wages, rushed materials purchased at premium prices, and expedited shipments to customers—all very costly to the company. "Had anyone even spoken with the vice president of finance?" Wilson wondered aloud.

In the case described above, the master scheduler earned her pay by being both open- and tough-minded. She had to be open-minded to the possibility of increasing shipments by considering possible alternatives to the computer action messages, like bringing some of the 520 units into periods 4 and 6—capacity, materials, and costs permitting. She also had to be tough-minded in observing change policies that support smooth operations and collaboration of different functions of the company. Finally, she needed to answer the five questions with respect to demand, the impact of demand changes on production, materials and capacity availability, costs, risks, and opportunities.

Planning time zones help master schedulers manage this difficult process. Planning time fences hold automatic MPS changes outside of Zones A and B, where unexamined changes invariably cause problems; and they prompt the master scheduler with action messages to either implement its suggestions or think of better alternatives.

Load-Leveling the Manufacturing Floor

Every plant manager's dream is to run the factory at a steady pace—i.e., at a level load. Ideally, this level load is very close to peak operating capacity yet provides enough slack for periodic repairs and maintenance. In a perfect world, overtime and expediting costs are eliminated, and workers are spared the scourge of forced layoffs. The top half of Figure 4.6 represents this idyllic condition. The bottom half, however, represents every plant manager's nightmare and a condition all too common among traditional production plants. In the bottom half, the factory load varies widely: underutilizing capacity in some periods and demanding more than the factory can deliver—except with costly overtime—in others. These variations may be attributed to fluctuating demand, equipment downtime, or just poor scheduling. The master scheduler cannot always make the plant manager's dream come true, but he or she can even out some of the peaks and valleys of production.

Figure 4.6 Load-Leveling

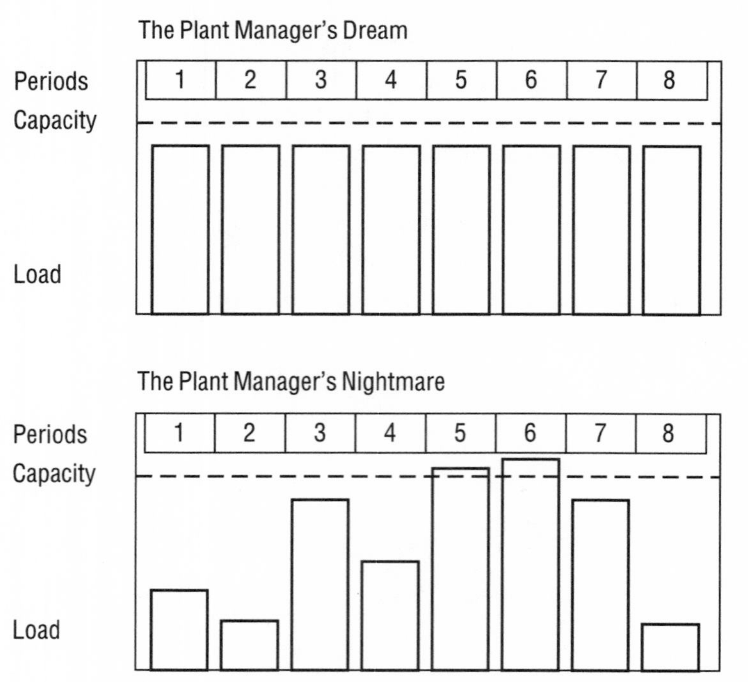

Since a major cause of load-level problems is demand fluctuation, consider the following situation. The company forecasts total demand for 400 units at a very uneven rate over the next eight weeks. One approach to leveling production is to plan orders for 400 units at a level rate of 50 per week (400/8 = 50). Figure 4.7 demonstrates the result of this naive approach. Assume that the company starts with a zero on-hand balance and that the scheduler has effectively leveled production at 50 units per week. The resulting projected available balance line indicates that promises to customers will be broken in five of the eight weeks. The first-cut level load will not work.

Figure 4.7 A Naive Approach to Level-Loading

	Past Due	1	2	3	4	5	6	7	8	Total
Total Demand		30	80	60	70	20	20	80	40	400
Projected Available Balance	0	+20	−10	−20	−40	−10	+20	−10	0	0
Master Schedule		50	50	50	50	50	50	50	50	400

Several possible solutions present themselves:

1. Anticipating this situation, the master scheduler might build up inventory to a point where the company would start week 1 with an on-hand balance of 40 units. This would render PAB positive in all subsequent weeks. The negative side of this approach is inventory costs for certain periods.

2. Work with the sales department to shift demand so that it takes on a more level profile. Discounts or other inducements could be effective in this effort.

3. Break the eight-week time span into blocks that can be level-loaded. A quick review of the demand figures indicates that the first four weeks is a block of fairly high demand (30 + 80 + 60 + 70 = 240); weeks 5 through 8 have less demand (20 + 20 + 80 + 40 = 160). By simply scheduling orders for 60 units in each of the first four weeks (240/4 = 60), and 40 units in each succeeding week (160/4 = 40), as

demonstrated in Figure 4.8, two level-loaded blocks of production are created that satisfy all customer orders with a minimum of excess inventory. This might not be the perfect solution of 50 units per week, but it is very close.

Figure 4.8 Level-Loading by Blocks

	Past Due	1	2	3	4	5	6	7	8	Total
Total Demand		30	80	60	70	20	20	80	40	400
Projected Available Balance	0	30	10	10	0	20	40	0	0	0
Master Schedule		60	60	60	60	40	40	40	40	400

The company can come closer to the perfect solution if it implements a continuous improvement program with just-in-time characteristics that makes use of mixed-model scheduling.

Just-in-Time and Continuous Improvement

Over the past decade much attention has been paid to improving the manufacturing process, and largely as a result of the continuous improvement (CI) and Just-in-Time (JIT) movements. As manufacturers learned more about CI/JIT, they came to realize that improving their processes involved more than simply getting material to arrive at the factory every two hours. They began to see CI/JIT in a broader sense—as a continuous improvement program that has as its objective the elimination of waste—where waste is defined as any activity that does not add value to the product.

Consider a three-step process that produces a plastic part (see

Figure 4.9). In Step 1, the part is formed in a mold; this step adds cost (machine, material, labor, electricity, etc.). This step also adds value. Step 2 moves the molded part some one hundred feet to the packaging line. Again, this step adds cost (material handling equipment, labor, etc.). But does Step 2 add value to the final part? Absolutely not! The customer is no better off for the fact that the part moved one hundred feet across the manufacturing floor. Step 3, part packaging, adds both cost and value.

Figure 4.9 Value-Adding and Nonvalue-Adding Operations

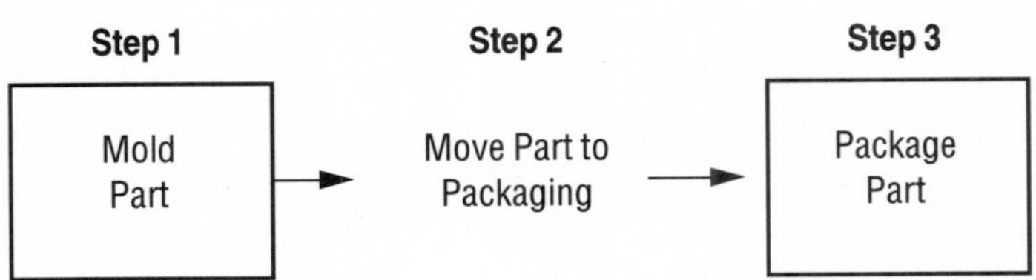

The principles of continuous improvement suggest that the nonvalue-adding activity of Step 2—physically moving the molded part around the facility—should be eliminated. One way to do this would be to place the packaging line next to the molding machine. Besides this obvious candidate for elimination, there may be other, less obvious nonvalue-adding activities associated with this molded part: the preparation of schedules, dispatch lists, hot lists, shortage reports, work orders, etc. The use of these traditional control mechanisms is today being challenged by many manufacturers. Those activities that cannot be shown to add value are being eliminated.

The same scrutiny is being applied to traditional lot sizes and safety stocks, two factors that produce inventory. Inventory does not directly add value for the customer, even though the company may have reason to maintain it. However, any increments of inventory that can be reduced without impairing customer service and satisfaction may legitimately be viewed as waste. Lot sizes are generally the result of long setups and complex changeovers. Continuous improvement programs suggest that the way to reduce lot sizes is to reduce setup times.

Safety stocks are used as protection against demand/supply variation. As this book intends to demonstrate, careful management of demand and supply is effective in reducing the need for wasteful safety stocks.

Mixed-Model Scheduling

Traditionally, manufacturers have attempted to build products in large lots to take advantage of cost savings associated with volume. Today, the cost savings associated with volume production are being challenged. As companies move closer to the Just-in-Time environment, they are discarding the ideas of large production runs in favor of smaller ones that match incoming customer orders. Since demand for many different products or models may require shipment of many products on the same day, a growing number of companies are implementing a technique called "mixed-model scheduling," which allows them to reduce order quantities, build less of a product at one time, build the product more often, and provide better customer satisfaction and service. Paradoxically, they can do this without increasing costs.

Mixed-model scheduling means building a small volume of each product every day or every week. Consider, for example, a company that produces a five-member family of golf carts—Types 151 through 155—with a mixed-model sequence. For this producer, 50 percent of its unit business is represented by Type 151; the other types normally account for sales as follows: Type 152, 10 percent; Type 153, 10 percent; Type 154, 20 percent; and Type 155, 10 percent. Under traditional methods, the firm would produce each type of golf cart in a batch to minimize production costs. The mixed-model method, however, schedules each type of cart as needed. Figure 4.10 represents the schedule of a company that builds 10 units per week. The top part of the figure is the traditional approach, and the bottom is the mixed-model approach.

Figure 4.10 Weekly Production Schedule for Golf Carts

Traditional Approach

	1	2	3	4	5	6	7	8	9	10
Item	151	151	151	151	151	152	153	154	154	155

Mixed-Model Approach

	1	2	3	4	5	6	7	8	9	10
Item	151	154	151	152	151	153	151	154	151	155

In the traditional approach, the customer who orders a Type 154 cart at the beginning of the week must wait until Thursday for shipment. In the mixed-model approach, that cart can be shipped on Monday. This method reduces the chance of a stockout and the overbuilding of inventory. As a scheduling method it is not perfect, but manufacturers that use it have reported good results.

One such manufacturer is Tennant Company, which makes industrial floor sweepers. Tennant implemented mixed-model scheduling to improve delivery times and reduce the need to carry large finished goods inventory. To accomplish this, Tennant needed to reduce setups, lead times, and cycle times (from four weeks to one week).

The three parts of Figure 4.11 (see page 112) show the company's transition from a traditional economic order quantity (EOQ) producer—one that optimizes order size relative to carrying costs—to a mixed-model producer. Section A of the figure identifies Tennant as an EOQ producer. Looking at the assembly line starts and the "part kitting" activities supporting those starts, we see an unbalanced load on the people doing the kitting—21 kits to be pulled in week 1; 17 kits in week 2; 49 kits in week 3; no kits at all in week 4; and so forth. Section B of the figure shows Tennant still as an EOQ-based product producer, but level-loading the kitting area at 17 pulls per week. Section C of the figure indicates that Tennant has completed the

Figure 4.11 Tennant Company Transition from Traditional Economic Order Quantity Producer to Mixed-Model Producer

A. Economic Order Quantity Producer

Week #

Model	1	2	3	4	5	6	7	8	9	10	11	12	13	14	Total
A	21→							21→							42
B		17→							18→						35
C			49 →							49 →					98
D						21→							21→		42
E							11							10	21
Total # of Units Kitted per Week	21	17	49	—	—	21	11	21	18	49	—	—	21	10	238

B. Level-Load Producer

Week #

Model	1	2	3	4	5	6	7	8	9	10	11	12	13	14	Total
A	17	4						17	4						42
B		13	4						13	5					35
C			13	17	17	2				12	17	17	3		98
D						15	6						14	7	42
E							11							10	21
Total	17	17	17	17	17	17	17	17	17	17	17	17	17	17	238

C. Mixed-Model Producer

Week #

Model	1	2	3	4	5	6	7	8	9	10	11	12	13	14	Total
A	3	3	3	3	3	3	3	3	3	3	3	3	3	3	42
B	2	3	2	3	2	3	2	3	2	3	2	3	2	3	35
C	7	7	7	7	7	7	7	7	7	7	7	7	7	7	98
D	3	3	3	3	3	3	3	3	3	3	3	3	3	3	42
E	2	1	2	1	2	1	2	1	2	1	2	1	2	1	21
Total	17	17	17	17	17	17	17	17	17	17	17	17	17	17	238

transition to a mixed-model producer, building a small amount of everything every week, *and* level-loading the kitting area. The secret to the company's transition was regular, incremental process improvement.

Mixed-model scheduling is an important part of being a Class A company. It requires good communication among sales, marketing, engineering, finance, and manufacturing. There is just no substitute for people working as a focused team. Companies that have not adopted mixed-model scheduling are advised to consider it as a method for improving the customer service process.

Planned Plant Shutdowns

In many industries, customer demand is fairly continuous, yet production facilities are shutdown periodically for vacations, scheduled maintenance, refitting, and other purposes. Accommodating demand when the plant is idle is a regular and important responsibility of the master scheduler and is usually accomplished by a steady buildup of inventories in the periods prior to the shutdown. To demonstrate this process, consider Minuteman Electronics Company (MEC). MEC has planned a shutdown of its Boston production facility during the weeks beginning 7/12 and 7/19 to accommodate annual maintenance and cleaning. Many of its regular production workers will take those weeks as vacation; those who do not will assist the maintenance and cleaning crews.

Demand from customers and from its two regional distribution centers is forecasted at 3,000 units per week during the period before and during the shutdown, meaning that MEC must go into the shutdown period with a reserve quantity of 6,000 units if it hopes to satisfy all forecasted orders. Thus, MEC's master scheduler must plan to build enough product to cover the regular forecasted demand *and* build up the reserve quantity during the weeks prior to shutdown.

Figure 4.12 shows the situation at MEC, where the master scheduler has created three firm planned orders of 7,500 each in periods 6/8, 6/22, and 7/5 to complete the reserve quantity. By the end of period 7/5, the projected inventory balance is 9,700, enough to cover the shutdown as well as any demand in 7/26, while the plant is coming back up. However, as the master scheduling software analyzes the projected available balance line, it will notice that the firm planned orders in 6/22 and 7/5 can be rescheduled-out (the projected available balance will remain positive if this is done), and will signal the master scheduler with action messages.

Figure 4.12 Plant Shutdown Planning

Reserve quantity: 0
Cumulative to date: 0
On-hand balance: 5,200 units
Start build: 6/8
Stop build: 7/5
Release date: 7/12

Shutdown

	Past Due	6/1	6/8	6/15	6/22	6/29	7/5	7/12	7/19
Forecast		3000	3000	3000	3000	3000	3000	3000	3000
Projected Available Balance	5200	2200	6700	3700	8200	5200	9700	6700	3700
Master Schedule			7500		7500		7500		

The master scheduler may want to get rid of these correct, though unwanted, action messages. There are three approaches to do this:

1. Use a nonmovable firm planned order if the MPS software offers this capability
2. Create artificial demand by placing a reserve requirement in the system over the course of the buildup period

3. Modify the software so that it will create artificial demand equal to the amount needed during the shutdown period

Figure 4.13 indicates how the artificial demand suggested in the last two alternatives may be implemented.

Figure 4.13 Plant Shutdown Planning with Artificial Demand

Reserve quantity: 6,000 units
Cumulative to date: 0
On-hand balance: 5,200 units
Start build: 6/8
Stop build: 7/5
Release date: 7/12

	Past Due	6/1	6/8	6/15	6/22	6/29	7/5	Shutdown 7/12	7/19
Forecast		3000	3000	3000	3000	3000	3000	3000	3000
Reserve Quantity			1200	1200	1200	1200	1200	–6000	
Projected Available Balance	5200	2200	5500	1300	4600	400	3700	6700	3700
Master Schedule			7500		7500		7500		

As the figure indicates, an artificial demand equal to the forecasted demand for the shutdown period has been created and placed in the master scheduling matrix under the Reserve Quantity line. As each period's projected available balance is calculated, the shutdown demand is taken into account. This process continues until period 7/5, when the entire buildup quantity is released (7/12) and recorded in the inventory balance. The projected inventory balance in 7/12 is determined by summing the 3,700 projected to be available in 7/5 and the reserve quantity of 6,000 (3,700 + 6,000 = 9,700). From this the forecast of 3,000 units is subtracted, leaving a projected available balance of 6,700, which will be used to satisfy demand in periods 7/19 and 7/26.

Of course, plant shutdowns can also result from the termination of a particular product or from a corporation's need to reduce overall manufacturing capacity. Witness, for example, the continuing efforts of General Motors Corporation to slash its auto- and part-making capacities. The following case situation speaks to a similar situation, and one that points out the important implications for both senior management and the master scheduler.

THE PRODUCTION SHUTDOWN

In 1976 a leading medical group announced its conclusion that women below the age of fifty-five should *not* have regular mammograms. The danger of repeated radiation exposures, in its view, outweighed the benefits of regular mammograms in the detection of breast cancer among younger women.

For Xerox Corporation's Xeroradiography Operations Unit, this announcement struck like a torpedo amidships. Almost overnight, a large chunk of the market for its expensive mammography machines was blown out of the water. Though some of its backlogged orders held firm in the wake of the announcement, many were canceled, and few new customers appeared. With its demand forecast sinking quickly, managers and production schedulers in the Xerox unit had to make new estimates of future demand and reflect these in dramatic revisions of the production plan.

In the fast-paced business environment, when products are quickly undercut by new technology and new competitors, the situation faced by Xerox in 1976 is not uncommon, and just about everyone in the affected business unit—including the master scheduler—is forced to make dramatic course corrections. Consider the following set of numbers for a hypothetical operation. The original forecast had been for 100 units per period, but new developments have cut deeply into that figure. With future demand slowed to a trickle, and the future of the product clearly in doubt, management sees a shutdown of the production line as its best option. But how should that shutdown be scheduled?

Original Forecast	100	100	100	100
New Forecast	30	10	10	10
Master Schedule	60	0	0	0

In this simple example, management decides to keep the production line open during the next period, building for *all* demand anticipated over the next four periods. This plan will result in heavy initial inventory, but financial managers determine that the inventory costs will be less than the costs associated with maintaining a low-volume production line over time. Once its inventory of built products is exhausted, the product will be terminated due to insufficient demand.

In the case of Xerox, the Xeroradiography Operations Unit determined that the combination of existing finished goods, current production scheduled through the next several months, and machines sent back for refurbishing would be sufficient to satisfy reduced market demand for a period of two years—an estimate that proved to be remarkably accurate. Current work was completed and the line was shut down. Two other developments occurred within two years: medical opinion on the risk/benefits of mammograms for women under fifty-five took an about-face and engineering changes at Xerox were successful in reducing the radiation levels of the next generation of mammogram machines.

Management Issues

Production shutdowns can result from several causes: a dramatic reduction in market demand (as described above), recall of the product because of safety or sabotage problems (e.g., Johnson & Johnson's recall of Tylenol), among others. Whatever the cause, a number of important issues confront management:

- Should we continue production and simply build inventory until the horizon is clearer, or should we shut down the line?
- If we reduce or halt production, what will we do with materials in inventory and on order, with production personnel, and with the production facility itself?
- Should we fight the issue and rebuild demand by pumping resources into public relations and advertising?

If managers are paid to make decisions, they *really* earn their pay during episodes like these, when the stakes are high and the future is uncertain. Worse still, the best solutions may only *reduce* the financial damage to the company. For business managers, all the choices may be undesirable, but choices nevertheless must be made.

Abrupt production shutdowns affect everyone, not just senior management. Financial managers analyze the costs of the alternative solutions and project their effects onto the bottom line. Sales and marketing personnel must deal with affected customers and wonder what other products they should be selling. Manufacturing personnel contemplate line changeovers to other products as they await the decision of senior management. Engineers and quality people scramble for solutions that will put the product back into the market.

The two preceding chapters should have imparted a general understanding of master scheduling and materials requirements planning mechanics, time zones, action messages, and what the master scheduler needs to do in order to successfully guide the company. The next two chapters deal with how to use the master scheduling system output in the make-to-stock environment and *what* to master schedule. The mechanics discussed so far are important, but not nearly as important as how the master scheduler makes decisions using the generated information.

5

Using the MPS Output in a Make-to-Stock Environment

It requires a very unusual mind to make an analysis of the obvious.

This chapter examines the software output—or screens—used by the master scheduler in managing supply, demand, and the timing of production. Understanding its many elements and how they interact is essential in that important management task. Once the MPS screen is introduced, we will see how it can be used in scheduling an actual product—an industrial winch.

The manufacturer of the winch in our example follows a "make-to-stock" manufacturing strategy. This is a fairly common strategy followed by companies that make everything from felt-tipped pens to books like the one you are holding in your hand. Make-to-stock companies build products to put directly on the shelf—either in their own stockrooms or in those of their distribution centers. The relative simplicity of the make-to-stock strategy versus the make-to-order strategy makes the chore of explaining the MPS output straightforward. Subsequent chapters will show you how to work the MPS output in other manufacturing environments.

The MPS Screen

Previous chapters have presented matrices for the master schedule. Hopefully, these have been useful to the reader in learning the mechanics of the scheduling process. Here we encounter a computer-generated master schedule screen typical of those used in modern manufacturing facilities and whose elements should now be familiar to the reader (see Figure 5.1).

This screen is divided into three major sections:

1. Item information
2. Planning horizons
3. Detail data

Item Information Section

This section occupies the top portion of the screen and contains information about the product, planning data, and production policy guidelines. Here is a brief description of each field of this section.

Part Number: The unique identification assigned to the master scheduled item.

Primary Description: Provides a brief description of the scheduled item and can include name, model number, or other data.

Item Status: Describes the item by stocking status (e.g., indicates whether the part is a stocked, pseudo, or phantom).

Product Family: The product family to which the item belongs. For example, an AM radio might be part of a family that includes AM/FM radios, AM/FM radios with cassettes, AM/FM radios with CD, etc.

Figure 5.1 Sample Master Schedule Screen

Item Information Section

Part Number	Primary Description			Item Status	Product Family			Master Scheduler		Forecast Source
Balance On Hand	Lot Size		Safety Stock		Time Fence			Lead Time	Cuml. Lead Time	Stnd. Cost
	1	2	Policy	Factor	1	2	3			

Forecast Consumption	Resource Profile	Critical Resources							
		RES.	QTY.	RES.	QTY.	RES.	QTY.	RES.	QTY.
Selling Price	Special Instructions		Date Run		Actions Recommended				

Planning Horizons Section

Period Item Forecast Option Forecast Actual Demand Proj. Available Balance Available-to-Promise Master Schedule	Past Due						

						Period Item Forecast Option Forecast Actual Demand Proj. Available Balance Available-to-Promise Master Schedule

Detail Data Section

Master Schedule Detail

Req'd Date	Order Number	Lot No.	Order			Recom. Action
			Qty.	Type	Status	

Actual Demand Detail

Req'd Date	Order Qty.	Refer. Number	Order Number	T	S	C	Req'd Date	Order Qty.	Refer. Number	Order Number	T	S	C

Master Scheduler: Contains the initials or name of the individual scheduler responsible for this master schedule item. The data also allows the master scheduling system to sort reports for distribution of hard copies.

Forecast Source: Indicates the source of forecasted demand (i.e., demand from a statistical forecasting system, developed through an explosion using planning bills, or a manually input judgmental number).

Forecast Consumption: Shows the master scheduler how the forecast is consumed when orders are booked.

Resource Profile: Indicates the resource profile to which the item is tied (to its own profile, to the product family profile, or to a similar item). This resource profile is used in rough cut capacity planning, which is discussed in detail in chapter 13.

Critical Resources: Four critical resources could be displayed for this item. These include the name of the resource and the required quantity/time, depending on how the profile was designed.

Balance On Hand: The quantity of the master scheduled item on the shelf as of the date the MPS data was run.

Lot Size: Indicates the preferred ordering practice for the item. This category contains two fields. The first field includes the lot sizing rule used (discrete or lot for lot; a fixed quantity; a period order quantity; etc.). The second field contains the modifier attached to whatever lot size rule is used. For example, if period order quantity is used, a modifier of 2 specifies that enough material to cover two periods of demand should be ordered. If a fixed quantity is used, the modifier might be, say 100, indicating that 100 is the minimum order amount.

Safety Stock: This displays two types of information: 1) the policy, which refers to a quantity or time; and 2) a factor, which describes the lower limit (e.g., "never less than 100 units") or how many periods early the recommended order release and receipt will be specified (e.g., "two periods earlier than required").

Time Fences: This field shows where the planning time fence is set (e.g., between periods 6 and 7). If a demand, material, capacity, or release time fence is used, this, too, is indicated.

Lead Time and Cumulative Lead Time: The first field is planning lead time for one level of the product. It shows how long it should take to get the product on the shelf once all the subassemblies or intermediates one level down are available. The second field, cumulative lead time, indicates how long it takes to build the product from scratch (i.e., the longest leg or critical path of this item).

Standard Cost: The target cost of the item (material content, labor content, direct overhead, outside processing, etc.). The information in this field is helpful in determining the impact on cost resulting from changes in the master schedule.

Selling Price: Indicates the list price of the item in the marketplace. Selling price is useful in determining operating margins and in quantifying the impact of master schedule changes on total revenues.

Special Instructions: These include reminders such as, "see note 11." Note 11 in turn might instruct the master scheduler to check with engineering before releasing another FPO because of a planned change.

Date Run: The date on which the computer system prepared the screen or report.

Actions Recommended: A summary of recommendations, such as reschedule-in or -out, release the order, convert a computer planned order to a firm planned order, etc. (Refer to chapter 4 for a discussion of the various action messages.)

Planning Horizons Section

The planning horizons section describes supply and demand data for a specific time period, typically one week. The format in the screen is almost identical to the format used in previous chapters. The first period is generally the past-due period, the second is the current period, and each subsequent period extends the time line into the future (Note: The number of periods shown varies from company to company. Also, the master scheduler can often define how many days are in each period; the scheduler may, for example, define the first five periods in individual days, the next eleven in weeks, and the six following these in bi-weeks.) Each period includes the following information:

Item Forecast: Generally independent demand. This line is used to display spares or service forecast for the master scheduled item.

Option Forecast: Generally dependent demand. The option forecast is the quantity directly forecasted for the item or the result of forecasted requirements from a top-level model or family planning bill exploding dependent forecasted requirements for this item.

Actual Demand: Indicates customer orders already held by the company. In a make-to-stock environment, the interval between the receipt of customer orders and ship date is often so short that little unshipped actual demand is reflected on the master schedule screen.

Projected Available Balance: The quantity expected to be available at the end of each planning period. This is the balance between supply and demand. A positive number shows potential surplus stock, negative numbers show a potential shortage, and zero reflects potential perfect balance. (Note: A positive value can also reflect potential perfect balance if safety stock is being used and the positive value equals the desired safety stock level.)

Available-to-Promise: Shows the amount of product that can be committed to customers (not used extensively in make-to-stock environments). It is equal to the master scheduled quantity less the actual demand for all periods, except period 1, where the quantity on hand is added to the MPS lot since it is available-to-promise.

Master Schedule: Shows the anticipated build quantity per period and consists of released orders and firm planned orders within the planning time fence. Beyond the planning time fence, the computer can place its own orders. All MPS quantities are shown in the period in which they are due.

Detail Data Section

This section of the master schedule screen shows actual data by date and is subdivided into "Master Schedule Detail" on the left side and "Actual Demand Detail" on the right. All data appearing here is linked to the planning horizons data above it and constitutes the supporting detail for the master schedule.

MASTER SCHEDULE DETAIL. This portion of the detail section is found in the lower left corner of the screen. It supplies detail information on each expected master schedule receipt that appears in the master schedule row. Action messages are printed for any expected receipt that requires scheduling, rescheduling, cancellation, etc.

Required Date: Shows the actual date the scheduled receipt is expected to be completed or received. This date is the one used to place the quantity on the master schedule row of the planning horizon.

Order Number: Shows the manufacturing, firm planned, or purchase order number assigned by the master scheduler.

Lot Number: Is a suffix applied to manufacturing, firm planned, or purchase orders that further defines the expected receipt by lot, run, campaign, or other unique characteristic.

Order Quantity: Indicates the quantity remaining open on the scheduled receipt.

Order Type: Distinguishes between manufacturing and purchase receipts or orders.

Order Status: Indicates whether the expected receipt is released, firm planned, or computer planned.

Recommended Action: Displays the computer's recommendation for each receipt (e.g., reschedule-in or -out, release, etc.).

ACTUAL DEMAND DETAIL. This portion of the detail section occupies the lower middle and lower right area of the MPS screen. Like the master schedule detail, it provides important details on the demand figures that appear in the planning horizons section. This information is provided in terms of the following categories:

Required Date: Displays the ship date or final assembly start date (depending on which date is being used to synchronize the planning) for the customer order.

Order Quantity: Shows the amount of product remaining open for the customer order.

Reference Number: Is the particular customer name (which, in a make-to-stock environment, may just be "finished goods").

Order Number: Indicates the actual customer order number for the make-to-order environment and the manufacturing order for the make-to-stock environment.

Demand Type (T): Indicates the type of demand, such as assemble-to-order (A), finished goods (F), etc.

Demand Status (S): Notes whether the demand is a released requirement (R), a customer order in the quotation state (Q), an on-hold customer order (H), a shippable item (S), or demand that has been generated from an upper-level item (F), etc.

Demand Code (C): Indicates whether the demand is abnormal (A) or normal (blank). If abnormal, it is added to the forecast amount in the period in which it occurs.

Working a Make-to-Stock Master Schedule

Now that the basic components of the master scheduling screen are understood, it can be used in master scheduling an actual manufactured product, in this case an industrial winch.[1] But first we need to understand this product in terms of its product family, product structure, and cumulative lead time. These are best understood by examining the bill-of-material (see Figure 5.2 on page 128).

The top portion of the figure is a hierarchy representation of the WA01 winch and its underlying components and subassemblies. The winch has four levels: a finished part level (LO) and three lower levels (L1, L2, and L3).

The bottom half of the figure is called an "indented" or "multilevel" bill-of-material (BOM). This bill reveals all the items necessary to produce the WA01 winch from scratch. The various column headings in this indented BOM, however, require some explanation:

LVL: Refers to the level in the BOM. Level 3 items are components of level 2 items, level 2 items are components of level 1 items, and level 1 items are all components of the finished part—the level 0 item.

[1] The winch product structure example used in this chapter and chapter 9 was created and published in the initial APICS *Bill-of-Material Training Aid* (Falls Church, VA: American Production and Inventory Control Society). The master schedule and material requirements planning examples were originally developed at Arista Manufacturing Systems by a number of people. The intention of these two chapters is not to perform mechanics on the numbers; but to discuss what a master scheduler does with data once it is available. For this purpose these examples work well.

Figure 5.2 WA01 Winch Multilevel Bill-of-Material

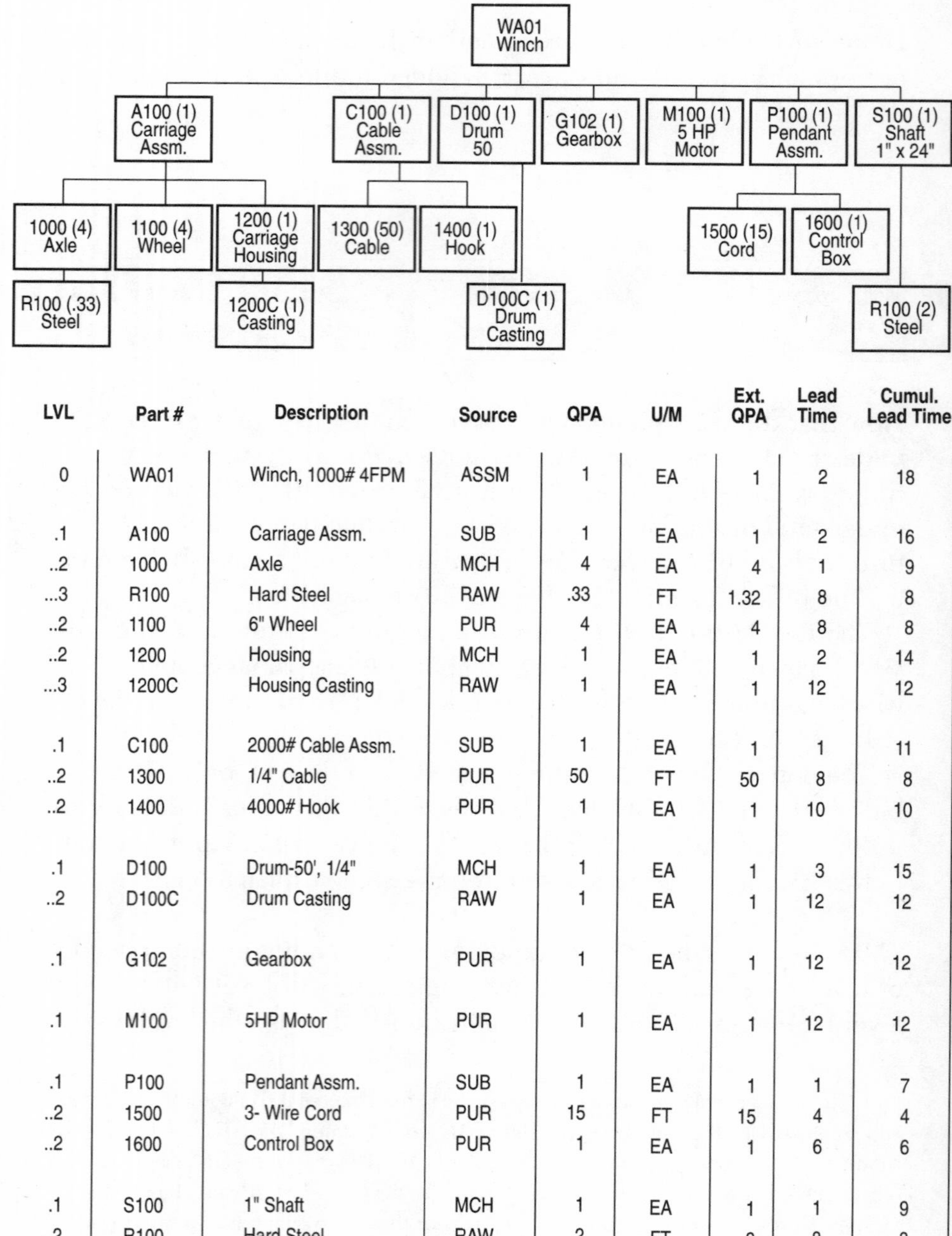

LVL	Part #	Description	Source	QPA	U/M	Ext. QPA	Lead Time	Cumul. Lead Time
0	WA01	Winch, 1000# 4FPM	ASSM	1	EA	1	2	18
.1	A100	Carriage Assm.	SUB	1	EA	1	2	16
..2	1000	Axle	MCH	4	EA	4	1	9
...3	R100	Hard Steel	RAW	.33	FT	1.32	8	8
..2	1100	6" Wheel	PUR	4	EA	4	8	8
..2	1200	Housing	MCH	1	EA	1	2	14
...3	1200C	Housing Casting	RAW	1	EA	1	12	12
.1	C100	2000# Cable Assm.	SUB	1	EA	1	1	11
..2	1300	1/4" Cable	PUR	50	FT	50	8	8
..2	1400	4000# Hook	PUR	1	EA	1	10	10
.1	D100	Drum-50', 1/4"	MCH	1	EA	1	3	15
..2	D100C	Drum Casting	RAW	1	EA	1	12	12
.1	G102	Gearbox	PUR	1	EA	1	12	12
.1	M100	5HP Motor	PUR	1	EA	1	12	12
.1	P100	Pendant Assm.	SUB	1	EA	1	1	7
..2	1500	3- Wire Cord	PUR	15	FT	15	4	4
..2	1600	Control Box	PUR	1	EA	1	6	6
.1	S100	1" Shaft	MCH	1	EA	1	1	9
..2	R100	Hard Steel	RAW	2	FT	2	8	8

PART #: Refers to the specific identification number of the raw material, component, machined part, or subassembly, etc.

DESCRIPTION: Provides a brief description of the raw material, component, intermediate, subassembly, parent assembly, or finished item.

SOURCE: Describes where the item comes from. These sources may be any of the following:

RAW: Raw materials or components, which are used to create machined parts or subassemblies.

PUR: Purchased parts.

MCH: Machined or fabricated parts, in which raw materials are converted into other intermediates (in some cases, the machined or fabricated parts may be end items in themselves).

SUB: Subassemblies, which consist of a configuration of parts, components, machined parts, or raw materials.

QPA: Stands for "quantities per assembly" and defines the quantity needed at the next higher level. Thus, the carriage assembly consists of 4 axles, which in turn require .33 feet of hard steel (see next column for units), 4 purchased wheels, 1 machined housing, and 1 housing that is machined from a housing casting.

U/M: Indicates the "unit of measure" for each quantity in the preceding column. The units in this example are feet (FT) and each (EA).

EXT. QPA: Is the "extended quantities per assembly." For example, as we saw in the QPA column, 4 axles are needed for each carriage assembly. Each axle in return requires .33 feet of hard steel, so 4 axles will require 1.32 feet of hard steel (4 × .33).

LEAD TIME: Refers to the amount of time it takes to procure or make the individual part (hours, days, weeks).

Cumulative LT: Indicates how long it takes to build the item from scratch. Note that it is *not* the sum of the individual lead times below it; rather, it is based on the critical path—the longest path in time that it takes to produce the referenced item from scratch. The difference is that many of the processes will be carried on in parallel.

In Figure 5.2 it can be seen that each intermediate has its own cumulative lead time. In the case of the pendant assembly, that time is seven periods. For the carriage assembly, the lead time is sixteen periods. The carriage assembly in fact, has the longest lead time of any of the intermediates. Since the final winch assembly requires two periods to build once all the intermediates are in place, the cumulative lead time for the WA01 winch is eighteen periods.[2]

Time-Phasing the BOM

With the information contained in the BOM, the master scheduler knows the items, levels, quantities, and lead times. Using this information, a time-phased bill-of-material is developed that shows the relationship of each item in the winch to each other in terms of level and in terms of when work on it must be started if the final winch is to be built within the planning lead time—eighteen periods (see Figure 5.3).

The time-phased BOM in this example makes it visually clear that to produce the WA01 winch, the carriage assembly (A100), cable assembly (C100), drum (D100), pendant assembly (P100), and shaft (S100) must be completed and available two periods before the WA01 winch is scheduled for completion. In addition, the gear box (G102)

[2] If a winch is to be completed eighteen periods from today, a parts planner must order the housing casting today, because it requires twelve periods to procure the raw material, two periods to machine the housing, another two periods to include the housing casting in the carriage assembly; a total of sixteen periods. Add the two periods for putting the finished winch together and the total time is eighteen periods.

Figure 5.3 Time-Phased Bill-of-Material

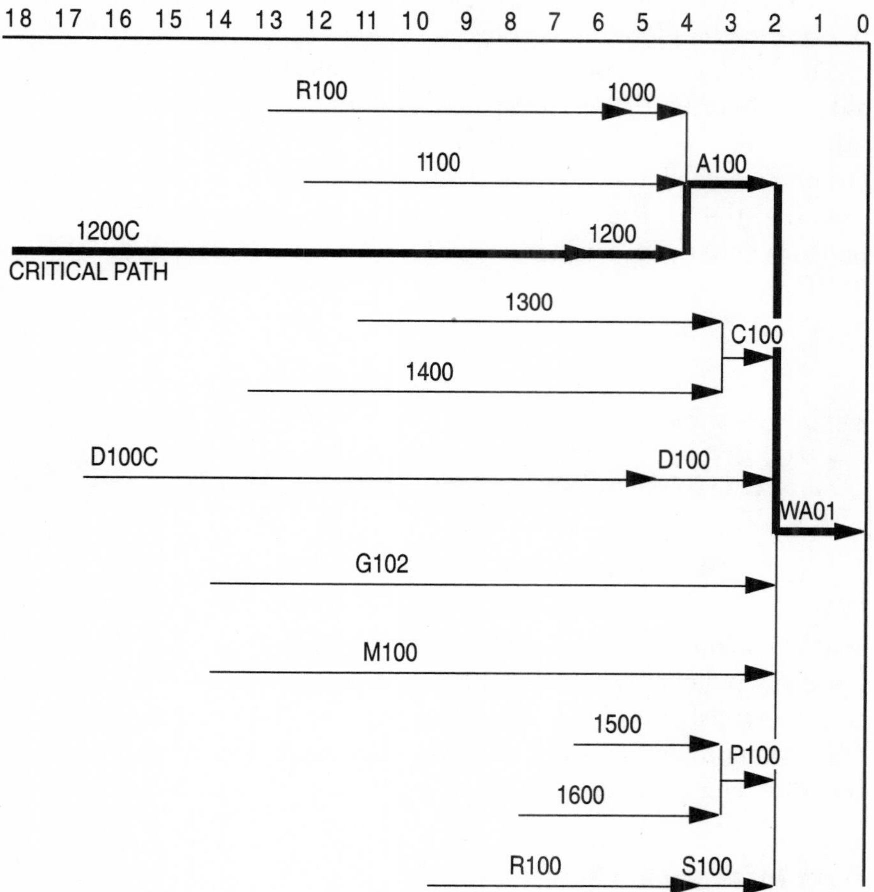

and motor (M100) must be received from the supplier. This is true because of the two periods of lead time associated with the WA01 winch. Looking at just one of the subassemblies for the winch, the A100 carriage assembly, it is easy to see that work on its component parts must be initiated still earlier if the carriage assembly is to be ready in time for work on the final WA01 winch to begin. To pick just one of A100's component parts as an example, work on part 1100 (the 6-inch wheel) must begin ten periods before the A100 carriage assembly is due to be finished (eight periods to secure the wheel and two periods to complete the carriage assembly).

The term "critical path" is used by schedulers and project managers alike to describe the longest path in the entire operation. As long as other work can be done in parallel to this critical path, it defines the cumulative lead time to build the entire item. In this particular example, the critical path travels from housing casting (1200C), to housing (1200), to carriage assembly (A100), and to winch (WA01) itself.

Understanding the Action Messages

Figure 5.4 (see pages 134–135) is the master schedule screen for the WA01 winch. This screen will be our tool in learning how the master scheduler integrates the information available about the winch with company policies, demand, supply, and the master scheduler's strong desire to satisfy the customer with competent, businesslike judgments concerning manufacturing stability, inventories, capacity constraints, schedule change costs, etc.

Item Information Section

In the WA01 example, 138 units are on hand, and the lot size method chosen is period order quantity (POQ) for two periods of demands. The safety stock policy is by quantity, and the factor is 100 (the company desires not to drop below 100 winches in stock at any time). The planning time fence is set at 20 periods.

"Since the cumulative lead time is 18 periods," one might ask, "why set a planning time fence at 20 periods?" In this case, the answer may simply be that the master scheduler has elected to gain an extra two periods of control. Remember, inside the planning time fence, the master scheduler has control of the planning horizon and creates or places released or firm planned orders. Outside the planning time fence, the computer software generates computer planned orders.

Finally, the actions recommended in the WA01 example include a reschedule-in, a computer planned order that needs to be converted to a firm planned order, and a firm planned order that needs to be released. Those actions are reflected in the master schedule detail section of the screen, as explained below.

Planning Horizons Section

In the past-due column of the planning horizons section, there is an unconsumed forecast of 22 items. This means that the item probably started with a forecast of 100 for the period, 78 of which were sold and consumed, leaving 22 units unconsumed.[3]

The second number in this column is the projected available balance (PAB) of 116 units. The system calculated this as follows: 138 units are on hand and 22 are still forecasted to be sold (the unconsumed forecast). Here the system assumes that the forecasted 22 will in fact be sold, leaving 116 (138 − 22) as the PAB to start the first period.

Now consider that first period (the current period) during which 200 units (on the master schedule line) are scheduled to be received. Combining those 200 units with the 116 available balance creates a total supply of 316 units. The demand for this period is 100 units, as shown in the forecast line. Assuming that those will be sold, the system subtracts 100 units from the 316 units available, leaving a projected available balance at the end of the first period of 216 units. This same logic is used to calculate the projected available balance throughout the entire planning horizon.[4]

[3] Different master scheduling systems would display that 22 in several ways—either as shown here or added to the first period's demand of 100, making it 122 (refer to chapter 9 for a discussion of forecast consumption).

[4] Note: If you have trouble understanding the basic calculations and mechanics, refer to chapter 3 for a review.

Figure 5.4 Master Schedule Screen, Winch WA01

Part Number	Primary Description	Item Status	Product Family	Master Scheduler	Forecast Source
WA01	WINCH	STK	WAXX	PROUD	JUDMNT

Balance on Hand	Lot Size		Safety Stock		Time Fence			Lead Time	Cuml. Lead Time	Stnd. Cost
	1	2	Policy	Factor	1	2	3			
138	POQ	2	QTY	100	P-20			2	18	2170

Period	Past Due	1	2	3	4	5	6
Item Forecast							
Option Forecast	22	100	100	100	100	105	105
Actual Demand							
Proj. Available Balance	116	216	116	216	116	211	106
Available-to-Promise							
Master Schedule		200		200		200	

Period	13	14	15	16	17	18	19
Item Forecast							
Option Forecast	115	115	115	115	120	120	120
Actual Demand							
Proj. Available Balance	216	101	211	96	226	106	236
Available-to-Promise							
Master Schedule	225		225		250		250

Period	26						
Item Forecast							
Option Forecast	125						
Actual Demand							
Proj. Available Balance	–634						
Available-to-Promise							
Master Schedule							

Master Schedule Detail

Req'd Date	Order Number	Lot No.	Order Qty.	Order Type	Order Status	Recom. Action	Req'd Date	Order Quantity
1	WA01	012	200	MFG	RLSD			
3	WA01	013	200	MFG	FIRM	RELEASE		
5	WA01	014	200	MFG	FIRM			
7	WA01	015	200	MFG	FIRM			
9	WA01	016	225	MFG	FIRM	R/I-01		
11	WA01	017	225	MFG	FIRM			
13	WA01	018	225	MFG	FIRM			
15	WA01	019	225	MFG	FIRM			
17	WA01	020	250	MFG	FIRM	R/I-01		
19	WA01	021	250	MFG	FIRM			
21			234			PLAN		

Forecast Consumption	Resource Profile	Critical Resources							
		Res.	Qty.	Res.	Qty.	Res.	Qty.	Res.	Qty.
ADJUST	WAXX	MCH	5.0	SUB	3.0	ASSM	14.0	PKG	2.0

Selling Price	Special Instructions	Date Run	Action Recommended		
3100		XX-XX-XX	R/I	PLAN	REL

7	8	9	10	11	12	Period
105	105	110	110	110	110	Item Forecast
						Option Forecast
						Actual Demand
201	96	211	101	216	106	Proj. Available Balance
						Available-to-Promise
200		225		225		Master Schedule

20 P	21	22	23	24	25	Period
120 P	125	125	125	125	125	Item Forecast
P						Option Forecast
P						Actual Demand
116 P	–9	–134	–259	–384	–509	Proj. Available Balance
P						Available-to-Promise
P	234		250		250	Master Schedule

						Period
						Item Forecast
						Option Forecast
						Actual Demand
						Proj. Available Balance
						Available-to-Promise
						Master Schedule

– – – – – – – —Actual Demand Detail— – – – – – – – – – – – – – – – –

Refer. Number	Order Number	T	S	C		Req'd Date	Order Quantity	Refer. Number	Order Number	T	S	C

The Reflection of Supply and Demand in the Details Section

Supply and demand activities throughout the planning horizon are illuminated in the details section. For example, the 200 units in the master schedule line of period 1 are reflected as the first entry under master schedule detail. Here, the master scheduler can see that this is more than just a supply of 200 scheduled WA01 units, which is all the planning horizon data reveals. In the master schedule detail section, it is defined as lot number 012. Its required date is period 1; it is a manufacturing work order (MFG); and it has been released to the manufacturing floor. And if it's on the floor, the assumption is that the material required to make it is likewise on the floor, unless an allocation or shortage shows up on the WA01 components' MRP screens.

In period 3, 200 units are also shown on the MPS line. In the master schedule detail for period 3, an action message to release indicates that it's time to convert the firm planned order into a released order. The reason for this action is that the winch has a lead time of two periods, and period 3 is within one period of that lead time. That means it is time to cut a work authorization and send it out to the floor.

Further down in the master schedule detail is lot 016, a firm planned order of 225, with a required date of period 9. Here, the system is recommending a reschedule-in of the order by one period, back to period 8. To the master scheduler, this message is a cue to examine the supply/demand situation in the planning horizon for periods 8 and 9. In period 8, the projected available balance is 96 units, 4 short of the company's desired safety stock requirement of 100. Therefore, the firm planned order of 225 in the MPS line of period 9 needs to be moved back into period 8. The same logic applies to the order in period 17, where another reschedule-in recommendation appears in the master schedule detail (the same situation: the projected available balance has fallen below the desired safety stock level of 100 units).

To ignore the computer's recommendation on the basis that "we need only 4, not 225 units" would be a legitimate response to the potential safety stock shortfall in period 8. The experienced master scheduler would understand that the forecasted demand in each period between 1 and 8 is only a prediction or request for product, and that actual demand may easily fall short by 4 or more units over that period, entirely eliminating the need for an early resupply of WA01 winches. And even if the demand does materialize, the company would still have an inventory of 96 units.

Besides the alternatives of slavishly following the computer software's recommendation to reschedule-in 225 units from period 9 to period 8, or simply ignoring the recommendation for action altogether, the master scheduler has at least two other alternatives to choose from:

1. Split the lot of 225 scheduled for period 9 into two orders: one for 4 units in period 8, and another for 221 in period 9; or
2. Simply change the order of 200 in period 7 to 204.

Either of these options would eliminate the action message. The first, however, might be somewhat costly in that an extra order involves extra paperwork, reporting, material issuing, and possibly changeover costs. In fact, the changeover cost to build just 4 units may, in itself, be sufficiently high as to disqualify this as a viable solution. The second solution might cause less paperwork, reporting, and changeover but could still disrupt manufacturing.

Both cases contain other issues that need to be addressed before changing the schedule. Chapter 4 went over five important reschedule change questions that should be answered before any rescheduling is done. It is worth reviewing them here:

1. *Has demand changed?* The screen merely represents a snapshot of the master schedule and does not provide the data necessary to answer this question. However, a working master scheduler in the plant would be able to secure the information necessary. We want to know if we *should* change.

2. *What is the impact of the change on the production plan volumes?* The production plan is created and approved during the sales and operations planning process. The master scheduler has a respon-

sibility to work within the constraints of approved production plan volumes. If a change is made, will the master schedule still summarize up to the approved rates? Here we want to know if we are *authorized* to make the change.

3. *Can the capacity be obtained?* In both cases we need to know if there is enough capacity in period 7 or period 8 (depending upon our choice) to do the work. If the capacity is not available or cannot be available, then it will do no good to reschedule. We want to know if we are *able* to change.

4. *Can we obtain the material?* In both cases we must know if the required material can be procured in time. To determine what material, we would refer back to the time-phased BOM (Figure 5.3 on page 131). Drawing a line on the WA01 winch BOM, at period 7 through 9, we see the material that is affected: hard steel (R100), wheel (1100), housing casting (1200C), cable (1300), hook (1400), drum casting (D100C), gear box (G102), motor (M100), and control box (1600). It may not be easy to cut one or two periods of lead time from these items. Again we want to know if we are *able* to change.

5. *What is the cost of changing?* Changing schedules generally costs money, in fact, the closer the change comes to the completion date, the greater the cost in overtime, subcontracting, extra shifts, premium payments to suppliers, air freight, expediting, etc. We want to know the *cost* of changing.

Only after the master scheduler has the data to answer these reschedule change questions can an informed decision be made. No one ever said master scheduling was easy. This is why Class A companies have very creative, organized, and knowledgeable people doing the job.

Finally, period 21 details a system recommendation to convert a CPO to a firm planned order (PLAN). Here's why: The system shows a projected available balance of −9 in period 21. The lot sizing rule tells the master scheduling system that any time a computer planned order is placed, it must cover the next two periods of demand. So, in period 21, nine units are needed, and in period 22 the demand is 125, leaving a projected deficit of 134 (9+125). A total of 134 units will thus cover demand in periods 21 and 22, but the safety stock rules specify that 100 units must always be in stock, so the MPS system recommends releasing an order for 100 additional units, for a total of 234.

Bridging Data and Judgment

This computer-driven reporting system projects what the plant or factory will look like in the future. It provides supply and demand information, summaries of company policies about lot sizes and safety stocks, and asks the master scheduler to intervene in situations where imbalances and policy violations occur. This is the mechanical or scientific part of master scheduling; the remainder is art—or, more accurately, judgment formed with experience. Armed with the information and recommendations provided by the system, the master scheduler uses judgment in making decisions on a multitude of quantitative *and* qualitative factors.

Seeing the Big Picture

The computer software's posting of demand data over long periods allows the master scheduler to see patterns in the ebb and flow of demand. In the case of the WA01 winch, for example, demand grows steadily in step-wise fashion (100, 105, 110, 115, etc.) every four periods. As a percentage of total demand, however, each step is smaller than the one before. From the MPS line of the screen, we observe that the master scheduler has not responded to the steady growth in demand with an equal increase in supply—at least not at first. Instead—perhaps to better manage growth in output, perhaps owing to production constraints not revealed here—the master scheduler builds supply gradually, but deliberately. Over the periods shown in the screen, demand exceeds supply in periods 5 through 8 and in periods 13 through 16, but supply exceeds demand in periods 9 through 12 and periods 17 through 20. If we were to represent this situation conceptually, ignoring the step-wise changes, it would appear something like Figure 5.5. Here, a small supply deficit develops in the early periods, but that deficit turns into a surplus in the intermediate periods, which then turns back into a supply deficit in later periods.

Figure 5.5 Supply Deficit Turns to Supply Surplus

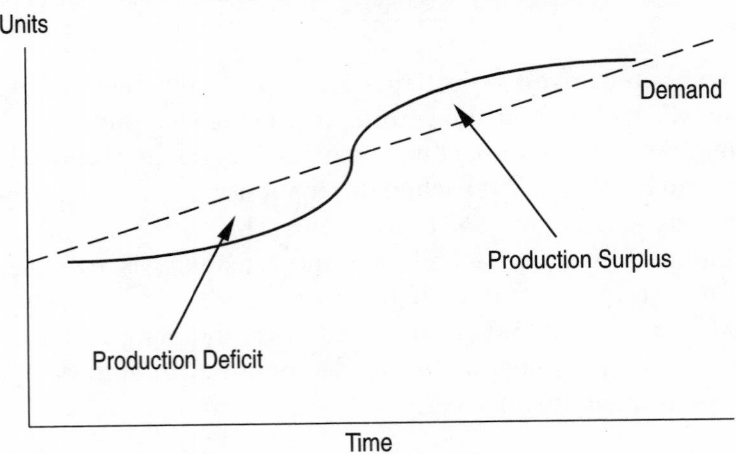

So how can this be possible? And why would the master scheduler, whose first responsibility is to balance supply and demand, do this?

As to *how*, the answer is safety stock. Safety stock is not there to be worshipped or admired, but to provide some utility to the company. Sometimes this utility takes the form of a supply bank from which the master scheduler can do a little judicious borrowing. In the example, the master scheduler has borrowed a little supply in the early periods, but like any savvy borrower, he or she pays back what he or she owes. Thus, in later periods, any reduction in safety stock is redressed with a supply surplus.

Conceptually, this is how farmers finance their seasonal businesses and how manufacturers maintain manageable loads on their factories in the face of seasonal demand cycles. While on this topic, let's look at a seasonal business and address some of the management issues involved.

SEASONALITY AND INVENTORY BUILDUP

Bernard Baruch once said that the way to get rich was to "buy straw hats in January"—the presumption being that you could buy them cheaply and resell them at a premium in July and August. Mr. Baruch was a wizard at the investment game of buying low and selling high, but he probably didn't know much about the cost of holding inventory.

For businesses with strong seasonal demand, planning production to meet anticipated demand while minimizing current inventory and possibly unsold units is a tremendous challenge. Consider the case of Datebook Publishing Company, whose main products are calendars and appointment books. It experiences strong demand during the late fall months and virtually no demand for the rest of the year, as shown below. Any calendars not sold during the period between October and December most likely end up at the paper shredder.

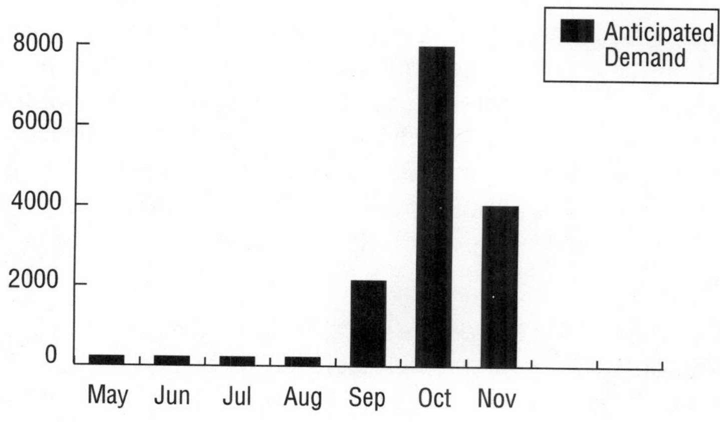

Fortunately, this company has other contract printing and publishing work during other seasons. Still, to meet anticipated demand, it must begin production and start building inventory as early as May.

Forecasted Demand	0	0	0	0	2000	8000	4000
Master Schedule	2000	2000	2000	2000	2000	2000	2000

Management Issues

For companies like Datebook Publishing, seasonality of demand creates a number of management issues to which ingenuity and judgment must be applied.

• *Demand forecasting takes on greater importance.* In most businesses, if you are caught short on product availability, the customer might be induced to delay the order while more products are built. In seasonal businesses, you either have product or miss the sale entirely. Conversely, building too many products generally leads to obsolete inventory, particularly if a shelf-life or model-year issue is involved. This means that everyone in the organization must understand the importance of accurate forecasting and must have an incentive to provide good numbers and continuous monitoring of anticipated demand.

• *Inventory and fixed capacity are major concerns.* Management faces an important trade-off between building large manufacturing capacity or building large inventories. Large amounts of capacity make it possible to meet the seasonal demand spike without reliance on inventory. It is the difference between being a make-to-order and a make-to-stock business. The problem is using that expensive capacity during the rest of the year. By contrast, keeping fixed capacity low forces the company to build and hold expensive inventory. Finding the optimal condition demands the collective attention of managers in all functions.

• *Can the either/or dilemma of capacity versus inventory be altered through design?* For years, managers subscribed to the idea that you either produced in high volume at low cost or in low volume at high cost. The notion that high quality costs more to build was also universally accepted. The experience of the past ten years has shown that both of these "iron laws" of manufacturing were wrong. Quality *can* cost less to produce, and short production runs are *not* absolutely synonymous with high costs.[5] The either/or dilemma of high capacity or high inventory for the seasonal business may be equally antiquated. Managers need to step outside of these constraints and think creatively about alternative ways of producing. They may be able to break out of this dilemma through redesigning products or processes: by creating unique products from a combination of common and unique parts that are configured *after* receiving the customer order; and, by implementing manufacturing processes with the flexibility to respond to seasonal spikes in demand as they occur.

Senior managers are not the only ones who should be concerned with these issues. Marketers have to think deeply about the validity of their demand forecasts. Errors are expensive when you have just one shot at the customer. Salespeople are naturally concerned about their booked orders being filled in the event that the company builds too few products. Financial managers are justly concerned with the cost of building and carrying inventory, some of which might never be sold. They need to communicate those concerns to others in the organization and to work with top management in creating incentives for all concerned to forecast, build, and inventory only what can be sold.

The Five Important Questions Revisited

Computer-generated data and the ability of MPS software to create action recommendations give the master scheduler every opportunity to bring judgment to bear in managing the supply and timing of

[5] See James P. Womack, Daniel T. Jones, and Daniel Roos, *The Machine That Changed the World: The Story of Lean Production* (New York: Rawson Associates, 1990) and Joseph Pine, *Mass Customization: The New Frontier in Business Competition* (Boston: Harvard Business School Press, 1992).

production. Managing change is, in fact, the master scheduler's highest responsibility. Like other managers, the master scheduler must make decisions on the basis of factual information that is often incomplete, ambiguous, or reflective of conflicting goals within the company. The choice of accepting or rejecting a computer-software generated reschedule-in recommendation to cover a potential supply or safety stock problem is typical of the hard decisions the master scheduler must make. To the computer software, the answer is clear: A safety stock violation exists, therefore reschedule-in; to the master scheduler, violation of this simple decision rule merely provokes a number of questions for which there may be no simple answers. A good start is to secure the answers to the five questions previously discussed. Thinking through each of those questions is the first step in reaching an informed scheduling decision.

Scheduling in a World of Many Schedules

The detailed example of winch WA01 should not lull the prospective master scheduler into the illusion that the real world of manufacturing is this simple. WA01, it should be remembered, is just one of many members of the WAXX winch family, each of which has its own time-phased bill-of-materials, its own ordering policy, its own scheduling requirements, etc. Like the game of chess, there are many different types of players on the board at the same time. And like a chess game, we cannot play each item in turn—i.e., we cannot deal first exclusively with the pawns, then the bishops, then the knights, etc.—but we must know how to move them about as part of a single game. This makes master scheduling a *dynamic* as opposed to a *linear* process. Thus, in scheduling the WA01, we must realize that other product family members share the same manufacturing floor, the same materials stockroom, and probably the same product line.

Figures 5.6 and 5.7 (see pages 146–147 and 150–151 respectively) are master schedule screens for WA01's cousins: WA04 and WA06 winches respectively. A quick glance at these screens indicates that they have much in common with WA01: the same family, the same lot size and safety stock policies (but not the same factors), the same lead times and planning time fences. Because WA01 is forecasted to account for two thirds of all winch sales, all demand and supply figures for WA04 and WA06 are proportionally less.

An experienced master scheduler who knew nothing about these winches—who had in fact just walked in off the street—would nevertheless spot an important relationship among these three different winches. He or she would notice that all MPS quantities for WA01 are due in odd-numbered periods, and MPS quantities for WA04 and WA06 are due in even-numbered periods. To the veteran scheduler, this would suggest that all three winches share an important critical resource: the same production line. This can also be seen by evaluating the critical resources noted on the top of each master schedule under critical resources. Therefore, a schedule change for any one winch may affect a resource required by the other two. Rough cut capacity planning is one of the useful tools in testing the viability of schedule changes that impinge upon other schedules.

Working the WA04 Reschedule-in Action Message

Referring to period 10 master schedule detail in Figure 5.6, notice a reschedule-in message for lot 306. Reviewing period 9 of the planning horizons data section, the MPS system is recommending that the master scheduler pull in the lot of 75 by one period to stop the projected inventory balance from falling below the safety stock level (19 units as opposed to the required 30). That is what the system says to do. However, pulling in the entire lot might overload the production line or critical resources in period 9, the period the WA01 winch is planned to run. So, here are the master scheduler's alternatives:

- Ignore the action message. By doing this, the master scheduler will use safety stock inventory to satisfy expected demand.

Figure 5.6 Master Schedule Screen, Winch WA04

Part Number	Primary Description	Item Status	Product Family	Master Scheduler	Forecast Source
WA04	WINCH	STK	WAXX	PROUD	JUDMNT

Balance On Hand	Lot Size		Safety Stock		Time Fence			Lead Time	Cuml. Lead Time	Stnd. Cost
	1	2	Policy	Factor	1	2	3			
82	POQ	2	QTY	30	P-20			2	18	2310

Period	Past Due	1	2	3	4	5	6
Item Forecast							
Option Forecast	4	30	30	30	30	30	30
Actual Demand							
Proj. Available Balance	78	48	68	38	73	43	63
Available-to-Promise							
Master Schedule			50		65		50

Period	13	14	15	16	17	18	19
Item Forecast							
Option Forecast	34	32	32	32	35	35	35
Actual Demand							
Proj. Available Balance	39	82	50	93	58	98	63
Available-to-Promise							
Master Schedule		75		75		75	

Period	26						
Item Forecast							
Option Forecast	35						
Actual Demand							
Proj. Available Balance	–109						
Available-to-Promise							
Master Schedule							

Master Schedule Detail

Req'd Date	Order Number	Lot No.	Order Qty.	Order Type	Order Status	Recom. Action	Req'd Date	Order Quantity
2	WA04	302	50	MFG	RLSD			
4	WA04	303	65	MFG	FIRM			
6	WA04	304	50	MFG	FIRM			
8	WA04	305	50	MFG	FIRM			
10	WA04	306	75	MFG	FIRM	R/I - 01		
12	WA04	307	75	MFG	FIRM			
14	WA04	308	75	MFG	FIRM			
16	WA04	309	75	MFG	FIRM			
18	WA04	310	75	MFG	FIRM			
20	WA04	311	75	MFG	FIRM			

Forecast Consumption	Resource Profile	Critical Resources							
		Res.	Qty.	Res.	Qty.	Res.	Qty.	Res.	Qty.
ADJUST	WAXX	MCH	6.0	SUB	3.5	ASSM	15.0	PKG	2.0

Selling Price	Special Instructions	Date Run	Action Recommended		
3300		XX-XX-XX	R/I		

7	8	9	10	11	12	Period
						Item Forecast
30	30	34	32	32	32	Option Forecast
						Actual Demand
33	53	19	62	30	73	Proj. Available Balance
						Available-to-Promise
	50		75		75	Master Schedule
20 P	21	22	23	24	25	Period
P						Item Forecast
35 P	35	35	35	35	35	Option Forecast
P						Actual Demand
103 P	68	33	–2	–37	–72	Proj. Available Balance
P						Available-to-Promise
75 P			67		70	Master Schedule
						Period
						Item Forecast
						Option Forecast
						Actual Demand
						Proj. Available Balance
						Available-to-Promise
						Master Schedule

— — — — — — —Actual Demand Detail— — — — — — — — — — — — — — —

Refer. Number	Order Number	T	S	C		Req'd Date	Order Quantity	Refer. Number	Order Number	T	S	C

• Split the lot and pull in only the required 11 units. Of course, there is nothing sacred about the 11 units except that 11 are needed to bring the projected available balance up to the desired safety stock.

• Increase the firm planned order in period 8 to 61 units (the master scheduler is planning to increase the schedule by 25 units in period 10 anyway). Again, the only reason for choosing 61 is that this is the quantity required to satisfy the safety stock policy.

• Some combination of the above. The master scheduler could choose to pull a few items forward, increase the quantity in period 8, and still be projected to drop below safety stock policy.

• Follow the computer software's recommendation.

In order to determine the best course of action, the master scheduler must first decide whether he or she is comfortable cutting into safety stock by approximately 35 percent. If the answer is yes, then the best action would probably be to take *no action*. However, if this cut into safety stock disturbs the master scheduler's comfort level, a different course of action should be taken.

One of the challenges of master scheduling is to balance supply and demand while maintaining as much stability as possible. Therefore, looking at the example, the master scheduler may not wish to disrupt the production flow of running the WA04 and WA06 in the even periods. If this is the case, a change in the quantity for period 8 seems like the best alternative. However, the five important reschedule change questions must be asked—and answered—before making a change.

Since the recommended schedule adjustment is for periods 9 and 10, several items in the WA04's bill-of-materials are affected (refer to Figure 5.3 on page 131) and assume the WA04 product required materials are similar to WA01's). So, if any change is to be made, a lot of homework must be done to ensure that the change is not only made in the master scheduling system, but also is successfully made on the plant floor and in purchasing.

One last point on this example: Period 11 projects an inventory balance of 30 units, exactly the desired safety stock quantity. This is only two periods away from the projected problem. This might be another reason for the master scheduler to use some safety stock if necessary and leave the schedule as currently written.

Working the WA06 Reschedule-in Action Messages

Two back-to-back reschedule-in messages appear in periods 8 and 10 (Figure 5.7 on pages 150–151). Using the same logic as with WA04, there seems no point in pulling up the 50 units in period 8 to period 7 because of a projected 8 percent dip into safety stock. Why disrupt the production line for 2 units of safety stock? Besides, we are halfway through the lead time and any change to the master schedule will affect many material items as well as capacity. And then there is the cost associated with every change at the MPS level within the product's lead time. The best choice seems to be to leave the schedule stand.

Consider the next message. The suggestion of pulling up the 75 units in period 10 to period 9 requires more analysis. If we let the schedule stand, we anticipate going into planned safety stock by approximately 40 percent. If this is no problem, then the best choice again is to opt for stability by leaving the schedule alone. However, if depletion of safety stock threatens our ability to satisfy variable future demand, then raising the quantity in period 8 to, say, 64 units would take care of the action message and meet management's objective of holding one period's worth of safety stock (demand is increasing from 25 to 30 through period 9). If the master scheduler plans to make this change, the five reschedule change questions must again be asked. Again, the only magic about 64 is that an increase of 14 is required to bring the company's projected available balance position back in line with safety stock policy.

Given the expected deep cut into safety stock, it would be worth the master scheduler's time to consider the history of the product. A new product might call for greater caution, since demand patterns are unknown. An established product whose demand patterns are stable

Figure 5.7 Master Schedule Screen, Winch WA06

Part Number	Primary Description	Item Status	Product Family	Master Scheduler	Forecast Source
WA06	WINCH	STK	WAXX	PROUD	JUDMNT

Balance On Hand	Lot Size 1	Lot Size 2	Safety Stock Policy	Safety Stock Factor	Time Fence 1	Time Fence 2	Time Fence 3	Lead Time	Cuml. Lead Time	Stnd. Cost
74	POQ	2	QTY	25	P-20			2	18	2450

Period	Past Due	1	2	3	4	5	6
Item Forecast							
Option Forecast	3	25	25	25	25	29	27
Actual Demand							
Proj. Available Balance	71	46	71	46	56	27	50
Available-to-Promise							
Master Schedule			50		35		50

Period	13	14	15	16	17	18	19
Item Forecast							
Option Forecast	34	32	32	32	35	35	35
Actual Demand							
Proj. Available Balance	42	85	53	96	61	101	66
Available-to-Promise							
Master Schedule		75		75		75	

Period	26						
Item Forecast							
Option Forecast	40						
Actual Demand							
Proj. Available Balance	–124						
Available-to-Promise							
Master Schedule							

Master Schedule Detail

Req'd Date	Order Number	Lot No.	Order Qty.	Order Type	Order Status	Recom. Action	Req'd Date	Order Quantity
2	WA06	404	50	MFG	RLSD			
4	WA06	405	35	MFG	FIRM			
6	WA06	406	50	MFG	FIRM			
8	WA06	407	50	MFG	FIRM	R/I-01		
10	WA06	408	75	MFG	FIRM	R/I-01		
12	WA06	409	75	MFG	FIRM			
14	WA06	410	75	MFG	FIRM			
16	WA06	411	75	MFG	FIRM			
18	WA06	412	75	MFG	FIRM	R/I-01		
20	WA06	413	75	MFG	FIRM	R/I-01		

Forecast Consumption	Resource Profile	Critical Resources							
		Res.	Qty.	Res.	Qty.	Res.	Qty.	Res.	Qty.
ADJUST	WAXX	MCH	6.5	SUB	4.0	ASSM	16.5	PKG	2.0

Selling Price	Special Instructions	Date Run	Action Recommended		
3500		XX-XX-XX	R/I	R/O	

7	8	9	10	11	12	Period
						Item Forecast
27	27	30	30	30	30	Option Forecast
						Actual Demand
23	46	16	61	31	76	Proj. Available Balance
						Available-to-Promise
	50		75		75	Master Schedule
20 P	21	22	23	24	25	Period
P						Item Forecast
35 P	39	37	37	37	40	Option Forecast
P						Actual Demand
106 P	67	30	–7	–44	–84	Proj. Available Balance
P						Available-to-Promise
75 P			69		80	Master Schedule
						Period
						Item Forecast
						Option Forecast
						Actual Demand
						Proj. Available Balance
						Available-to-Promise
						Master Schedule

— — — — — — —Actual Demand Detail— — — — — — — — — — — — — — — —

Refer. Number	Order Number	T	S	C	Req'd Date	Order Quantity	Refer. Number	Order Number	T	S	C

or more predictable, however, may suggest using safety stock in lieu of schedule changes.

These simple examples again demonstrate the need for a knowledgeable master scheduler; left to its own devices, the computer software would initiate the reschedule actions, disrupting the production line and possibly frustrating many. Worse still, the computer software cannot be held accountable for its reschedule decisions. Of course, this is not true when it comes to the master scheduler and his or her decisions. The master scheduler is accountable for maintaining a realistic, valid, and achievable master schedule.

Working the WA06 Reschedule-out Action Messages

For WA06, the system recommends moving lot 412, a firm planned order of 75 units, out one period, from period 18 to 19. It also recommends moving lot 413 from period 20 to 21. The reason for this message in period 18 is the projected ending balance of 101 units in that period. If the 75 units do not arrive as scheduled, we would still have a projected inventory balance of 26 units, one more than the current desired safety stock level of 25. Thus, it is not necessary to have the lot for 75 arrive in period 18. The same logic applies to period 20; if the 75 units do not come in as scheduled, we will still end period 20 with a balance higher than the current desired safety stock.

The cumulative lead time for WA06 is eighteen periods. This means that any action taken by the master scheduler on the FPO in period 18 will affect purchasing, which will be starting to acquire the long lead time items. If the lot is pushed out to period 19, the potential overstocking problem will be solved. Of course, another problem may be created by doing this; period 19 may become capacity constrained.

Another possibility is not to run as many as planned—perhaps 65 units instead of 75 (the right lot size is, in fact, 67 or 68) starting in period 10. Therefore, knowing the product, the best approach might be to reduce the FPOs in periods 10, 12, 14, 16, 18, and 20 to some lower amount. This action would stop the projected inventory buildup, thereby eliminating the two action messages.

From Master Scheduling to Material Requirements Planning

Now that it is understood how the MPS system recommends actions for individual items, and how the master scheduler must analyze these recommendations, the next step is to test changes to the master schedule using rough cut capacity planning. This technique is described in chapter 13. Only when the RCCP step has been completed and the master scheduler is satisfied that changes to the schedule are reasonable are those changes passed down to the MRP system, where materials are ordered and capacity and components are earmarked for availability.

Figure 5.8 on pages 154–155 shows the MRP computer-generated screen for the A100 carriage assembly, a common part in the WAXX winch family. Like the MPS screen, it has three main sections. The top section contains information about the part itself. The middle section contains planning horizons data. The bottom section contains details: "scheduled receipts detail" on the left; "requirements detail" on the right. While many features of the MRP screen are shared with the MPS screen already explained, others are unique and in need of explanation here.

Item Information Section

Item Type: Here SUB is "subassembly."

Commodity Code: A code indicating the basic characteristics of a purchase order.

Value Class: Refers to a hierarchy of dollar cost among parts in which "A" is high cost and "C" is low cost. This hierarchy can connote either high unit cost or high total cost (as in the case of a low-priced but high-usage item).

Figure 5.8 Material Requirements Planning Screen, Carriage Assembly (A100)

Part Number	Item Status	U/M	Primary Description	Item Type	Comm. Code	MRP Planner	Value Class
A100	STK	EA	CARRIAGE ASSM	SUB		SMITH	A

Balance On Hand	Safety Stock		Scrap Factor	Annual Gross Requirement	Total Released Requirements
	Policy	Factor			
0	NO			10400	0

Period	Past Due	1	2	3	4	5	6
Service Requirements							
Production Requirements		200	100	200	100	200	100
Scheduled Receipts		300					
Proj. Available Balance	0	100	0	–200	–300	–500	–600
Planned Order Release		300		300		375	

Period	13	14	15	16	17	18	19
Service Requirements							
Production Requirements	225	150	250	150	250	150	234
Scheduled Receipts							
Proj. Available Balance	–1950	–2100	–2350	–2500	–2750	–2900	–3134
Planned Order Release	400		400		234		386

Period	26						
Service Requirements							
Production Requirements	0						
Scheduled Receipts							
Proj. Available Balance	–3920						
Planned Order Release							

– – – – – – – – Scheduled Receipts Detail – – – – – – – – – – – – – – – – –

Req'd Date	Promised Date	Order Number	Lot No.	Rem. Qty.	Received	Type	Status	Recom. Action	Req'd Date	Req'd Qty.
1		A100	26	300		MFG	RLSD		1	200
3		A100	27	300				ORDER	2	65
									2	35
									3	200
									4	50
									4	50
									5	200
									6	50
									6	50
									7	225
									8	75
									8	75
									9	225
									10	75
									10	75
									11	225

Lead Time	Cuml. LeadTime	Order Policy	Order Qty./Time	Minimum Order Qty.	Maximum Order Qty.	Multiple Order Qty.
2	16	POQ	2	100		

Total Sched. Receipts	Special Instructions	Date Run	Action Recommended
300		XX-XX-XX	ORDER

7	8	9	10	11	12	Period
						Service Requirements
225	150	225	150	225	150	Production Requirements
						Scheduled Receipts
–825	–975	–1200	–1350	–1575	–1725	Proj. Available Balance
375		375		375		Planned Order Release

20	21	22	23	24	25	Period
						Service Requirements
0	386	0	400	0	0	Production Requirements
						Scheduled Receipts
–3134	–3520	–3520	–3920	–3920	–3920	Proj. Available Balance
	400					Planned Order Release

						Period
						Service Requirements
						Production Requirements
						Scheduled Receipts
						Proj. Available Balance
						Planned Order Release

Requirements Detail

Refer. Number	Order Number	Lot	T	S	Req'd Date	Req'd Qty.	Refer. Number	Order Number	Lot	T	S
WA01	A100	013	M	F	12	75	WA04	A100	308	M	F
WA04	A100	303	M	F	12	75	WA06	A100	410	M	F
WA06	A100	405	M	F	13	225	WA01	A100	019	M	F
WA01	A100	014	M	F	14	75	WA04	A100	309	M	F
WA04	A100	304	M	F	14	75	WA06	A100	411	M	F
WA06	A100	406	M	F	15	250	WA01	A100	020	M	F
WA01	A100	015	M	F	16	75	WA04	A100	310	M	F
WA04	A100	305	M	F	16	75	WA06	A100	412	M	F
WA06	A100	407	M	F	17	250	WA01	A100	021	M	F
WA01	A100	016	M	F	18	75	WA04	A100	311	M	F
WA04	A100	306	M	F	18	75	WA06	A100	413	M	F
WA06	A100	408	M	F	19	234	WA01	A100		P	P
WA01	A100	017	M	F	21	250	WA01	A100		P	P
WA04	A100	307	M	F	21	67	WA04	A100		P	P
WA06	A100	409	M	F	21	69	WA06	A100		P	P
WA01	A100	018	M	F							

Cumulative LT: Cumulative lead time is calculated as in the master schedule system. In the case of the carriage assembly, this is sixteen periods—the time needed to build A100 from scratch. This lead time number is determined from the time-phased BOM. Here cumulative lead time is two periods less than the finished winch, which makes sense in that the final assembly of the winch from A100 and the other required parts requires two periods.

Scrap Factor: A bit of information that allows the scheduler to figure gross production needed to yield an after-scrappage net production equal to product demand (sometimes referred to as shrinkage).

Annual Gross Requirements: Strictly memo information.

Total Released Requirements: Summary information computed by aggregating data from the requirements detail section.

Total Scheduled Receipts: Summary information computed by aggregating data from the scheduled receipts detail section.

Planning Horizons Section

This section contains five lines of data for each period. The first two lines reflect requirements; the third, scheduled receipts; the fourth, the projected available balance; and the fifth, the planned order releases. Each is worth examining in some detail.

Service Requirements: If an item is sold as an independent item, and orders are taken directly against the item, then these orders show up here. If marketing and sales forecasted that some of the carriage assemblies would be needed as spares, that forecast would also appear here.

Production Requirements: Indicates dependent demand for the part caused by the master schedule or a higher-level MRP part. All dependent requirements for the carriage assembly are summarized and appear on this line.

Scheduled Receipts: Identifies actions taken by the planner or scheduler for the carriage assembly. When the planner or scheduler creates a work order, manufacturing order, purchase order, or run rate, the order quantity appears on this line.

Projected Available Balance: Displays the projected inventory balance for each period in the part's MRP horizon. The PAB line is used to critique the balance between supply and demand.

Planned Order Release: All computer planned orders are shown on this line. When MRP recognizes an imbalance between supply and demand, and the supply is projected to be short, the computer places its own orders in the form of CPOs to restore the balance. These orders are placed by the MRP system logic in the time period in which they are scheduled to be released or started. Some MPS systems put CPOs in the period in which they are due and some may reflect both.

Detail Data Section

The detail data section of the MRP screen, like that of the MPS screen, is divided into two major parts, here called "Scheduled Receipts Detail" and "Requirements Detail."

Scheduled Receipts Detail: In the lower left corner of Figure 5.8 (see page 154), the first line indicates that in period 1, 300 units remain to be received (remaining quantity) for lot 26. Lot 26 is a manufactured item (MFG) that has already been released (RLSD). The next line indicates that a computer planned order (lot 27) for 300 has been created by the computer; an action message, prompted by the two-period lead time, recommends that the planner/scheduler convert this CPO into a scheduled receipt.

Looking briefly at the requirements detail, the first date with a requirement is period 1, which has a demand of 200 carriage assemblies, which we know originates in the WA01 winch. Two quantities totaling 100 units are required for period 2 (the 65 necessary to start building WA04s and 35 to start building WA06s). Back in the first line of the scheduled receipts detail is an entry for 300 units, which is scheduled for receipt in period 1. Since there is no on-hand balance for carriage assemblies, the scheduled receipt of 300 is expected to be used to satisfy the demand in period 1 of 200 units, leaving a projected available balance of 100 units. This quantity is expected to be used in period 2 to satisfy the demand for 100 carriage assemblies needed to support the build plan for the WA04 and WA06 winches. In period 3 there is a PAB of −200. Recognizing a two-period lead time, MRP logic recommends in period 1 the releasing of an order for 300 units to be due in period 3. This amount is 100 over the requirement for that period, but since the order policy is to order enough to cover two periods of demand, the 300 are just enough to satisfy the 200 required in period 3 and the 100 required in period 4.

REQUIREMENTS DETAIL: As the requirements detail shows, a quantity of 200 is needed in period 1 to satisfy a demand from the WA01 winch. A quick look back at the MPS schedule for WA01 (Figure 5.4 on page 134) shows a FPO for 200 in period 3, lot 013 (remember, the lead time to build the WA01 when all parts one level down are available is two periods). This FPO is both the trigger for this 200-unit requirement at the carriage assembly MRP level and the ultimate destination of the completed A100 parts. This linking of parts requirements to the source of demand is an example of "pegging" and is a very essential part of any MRP system.

The next two lines in the requirements details indicate quantities of 65 (from WA04), and 35 (from WA06). The MPS screens for those two different winches indicate that those quantities are needed at the completed winch level in period 4, which means that they are required to be started in period 2—two periods earlier. This is when the carriage assemblies are needed.

* * *

As this chapter's discussion should make clear, it is important that the master scheduler and material planner understand the relationship between what appears on the MPS screen and the underlying MRP system. Less obvious, but just as important, are the productive working relationships among master schedulers, planners, and shop schedulers. However, there is another level of understanding that the master scheduler must possess. We have discussed in some detail how the master schedule itself drives requirements down to lower levels. But where does the master schedule get its data? We have mentioned the likes of a production plan, which is a volume plan by product family. To be effective, a master scheduler must understand the ins and outs of the sales and operations planning process (discussed in chapter 12), which is the source of the production plan.

However, there is another issue to address, that of *what* to master schedule. This chapter has reviewed the process of master scheduling in a make-to-stock environment where finished goods are often the items master scheduled. But what about the make-to-order, assemble-to-order, design-to-order, engineer-to-order, and make-to-contract products? What items do we master schedule in these environments. This question is the subject of our next chapter.

6

What to Master Schedule

When you think you have all the answers, it may be time to reask the question.

Like any tool, master scheduling software is useful only if it is applied in the right way. Here, the right way begins with knowing *what* to master schedule. In the case of a simple product, like the flashlight in chapter 3, it may be the final assembly of the flashlight that needs master scheduling. In a more complex product, like an automobile, master scheduling may be done at a number of intermediate steps—engines, transmissions, radios, etc.

Knowing what to master schedule presupposes a clear understanding of the process by which the product is transformed from either raw materials or purchased components into a shippable configuration. Generally, that process begins with the ordering of the raw materials to be available when the product is to be built. In traditional manufacturing, these materials are inspected by the receiving department as they arrive to ensure their conformance to order specification and quality standards. Items that "pass muster" are then stored and issued to the manufacturing floor as needed. At the point of issue, the conversion of raw materials through the processes of assembly, fabrication, mixing, forming, machining, etc., to final product begins to take place. The item may move into a subassembly or filling area, and then into a final assembly, finishing, or packaging area. The last step typically involves crating and shipping the finished product either to a warehouse or directly to the customer.[1]

Manufacturing Strategies

The master scheduler's company adheres to one or more manufacturing strategies deemed most appropriate for its business. Each of these strategies is defined in terms of *the point in the manufacturing process at which the customer enters the picture*.

Make-to-Stock (MTS)

Company A makes a very simple family of products—plastic wall plates to cover electrical outlet boxes. With just a few exceptions, its products are manufactured by continuous processes of plastic molding, with no assembly except packaging. This company has determined that it must follow a make-to-stock strategy—i.e., a strategy in which raw materials are ordered and the final product made in advance of any orders by the final consumer. From the customer's perspective, these are "off the shelf" products. Fasteners, note pads, photographic film, and countless other commoditylike items are typically made on this basis.

Companies follow this strategy when the market dictates that their products be finished and available for immediate purchase and use.

Engineer-to-Order (ETO)

Company B designs and builds process equipment for the chemicals industry. Its products are large, complex, and very expensive; most are

[1] "Finished" is a relative term. In many cases the finished product of manufacturer A is a component in the finished product of manufacturer B.

built on a base of standardized liquid and dry materials, mixing and moving equipment, with computerized monitoring systems. Because each piece of its equipment is expensive and specially tailored to the requirements of the individual customer, work can begin only when a customer order is received and detailed specifications are developed.

Company B follows an engineer-to-order strategy, which is at the opposite end of the spectrum from the make-to-stock company. While make-to-stock products tend to be generic and easily substituted within a product class, engineer-to-order products are, by definition, either unique (as in custom-made) or very complex and produced only in small quantities. Aircraft, special-purpose machine tools and other process equipment, and space shuttles are all engineer-to-order products. In ETO companies, no product is engineered and/or manufactured until the company has at least a letter of intent, a contract, or a customer order. At that point the design process can begin, after which material is ordered and the product is produced and delivered to the customer.

Make-to-Order (MTO)

Between the extremes just cited is the make-to-order company, in which *some* material may be ordered and *some* parts of the product may be produced before receipt of a customer order. With a pure MTO strategy, product is designed, but the company does not start manufacturing until a customer order is received. Highly customized products are generally made in this fashion.

Two variations on the make-to-order theme are "finish-to-order" (FTO) and "assemble-to-order" (ATO). In the case of the former, the company may build product through all but the finishing stage and may proceed only when a customer order has been received. The basic product, a conference room table, for example, may be completed, but the customer's logo etched in the middle of the table is not done until the order is received. Furniture makers often use an FTO strategy, building product up to the point of applying the customer's choice of finishing stain or fabrics as the last step. Assemble-to-order is an analogous manufacturing strategy. Automobiles, with their many options, are good examples of ATO products.

Company C follows an assemble-to-order strategy. It is a leading producer of elevators for commercial buildings. It offers an array of elevator products, featuring dozens of capacities and hundreds of possible car interior decors. Because its customers—architects and building contractors—have long planning schedules, Company C does not need any off-the-shelf items (except for replacement parts), but the economics of its business encourages it to produce most of the components from which its product variety can be fabricated within three weeks.

Make-to-Contract (MTC)

Whereas all of the above strategies generally apply to commercial businesses, another variant of the make-to-order strategy applies to government contractors. Like make-to-order, "make-to-contract" (MTC) companies wait until a contract is issued before ordering material (many government contracts specify when the company can procure materials). The MTC strategy can thus be thought of as a make-to-order or engineer-to-order approach in which the contract takes the place of the customer order.

Choosing the Right Strategy

The right strategy for a particular company depends on where it intends to "meet the customer," which is largely dictated by the demands of the marketplace and the company's competitive position within its own marketplace. The strategy chosen determines where, in the product structure, master scheduling will take place. In addition, where a company chooses to meet the customer influences the actual structuring of the bills-of-material.

The choice of where to meet the customer really depends on a company's competitive position, which is determined by a balance of delivery, service, price, quality, and technology. If a company's service, price, technology, and quality are competitive, its delivery performance may be the deciding factor. The tremendous impact of master scheduling on meeting schedules is therefore an important competitive weapon.

Before examining the master scheduling component, though, we need to reexamine the options for meeting the customer, which are represented in Figure 6.1. The "stair step" diagram indicates the many points in the manufacturing process at which the actual order may be received—i.e., where the company meets the customer. Each step up the stairway represents a higher degree of product completion or "value added." In selecting "ship finished goods," a company has, by definition, chosen a make-to-stock strategy. The company that meets its customer at the engineering level has chosen an ETO strategy. At the purchasing, fabrication, or intermediate assembly step, it has chosen one of the make-to-order approaches.

Figure 6.1 Strategies to Meet the Customer

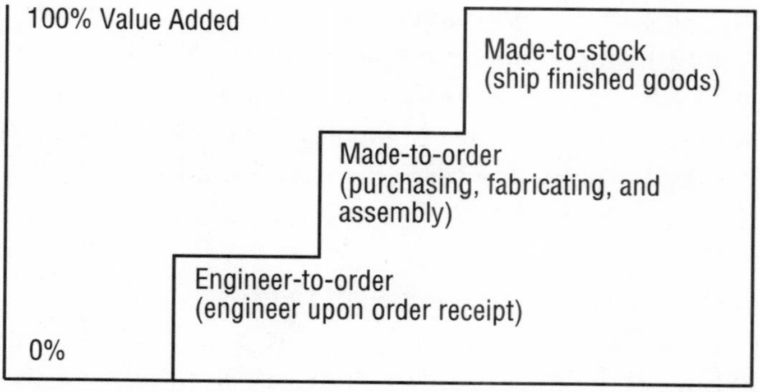

Inventory and Capacity Requirements

In selecting a strategy, two other factors should be considered: inventory investment and the capacity to complete the product. Any company that chooses to meet the customer at the finished goods (make-to-stock) level, must be willing to make a substantial investment in inventory. This company must be prepared to ship finished goods as customer orders appear. In contrast, the engineer-to-order company has minimal or zero inventory requirements, since no product building takes place in the absence of an order. But it must have the engineering, manufacturing, and finishing capacity necessary to complete the order within a quoted lead time and by a specified date.

In the make-to-order strategy, particularly finish- and assemble-to-order situations, companies must be willing to invest in inventory up to the point where they plan to meet the customer (stocking level), such as subassemblies, and must secure the capacity necessary to complete and ship the defined products.

It is important to understand that wherever a company chooses to meet the customer, its objective must be to provide timely delivery, first-class service, competitive pricing, high quality, and leading-edge technology. The next section demonstrates how master scheduling can greatly enhance at least two of those critical components of success: timely delivery and competitive pricing.

Manufacturing Strategy and Product Life Cycles

Like living organisms, products experience life cycles of growth, maturity, and decline. Business scholars have described this process as shown in Figure 6.2. Here, the introductory stage (measured in sales revenues or units) is fairly flat until such time as the product catches on. At this point it enters a period of rapid growth, followed by a maturity period of large but flat sales, followed by a period of decline.

Obviously, not every product experiences each of these cycles. Many new products never get beyond the introductory stage, and a fortunate few products forestall decline for extended periods through the introduction of product enhancements ("new and improved") and long-term growth of their markets.

A company may treat the same product with different manufacturing strategies at various stages of its life cycle. Thus, in the introductory stage, when demand is largely unknown, an engineer-to-order strategy may be most appropriate (more on this aspect of ETO in chapter 11). As the product enters its rapid growth period, a make- or assemble- or finish-to-order strategy may be ideal. Once the period of rapid growth gives way to a long stretch of flat, but predictable

Figure 6.2 Product Life Cycles

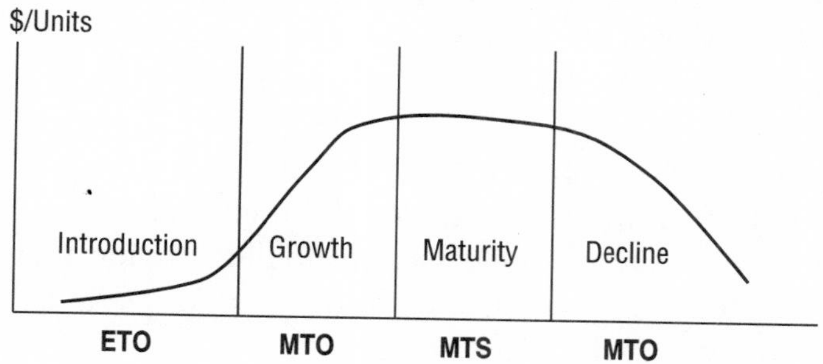

demand from established customers, make-to-stock may be most suitable. As the product goes into decline and customer orders become less reliable, going back to finish- or assemble- or make-to-order may be sensible.

MPS and Product Structures

In making the determination of *what* to master schedule, it is necessary to consider the different possible types of product structures (see Figure 6.3). In each of the product structures, the top portion represents finished goods, and the bottom represents raw materials.

Figure 6.3 Product Structure

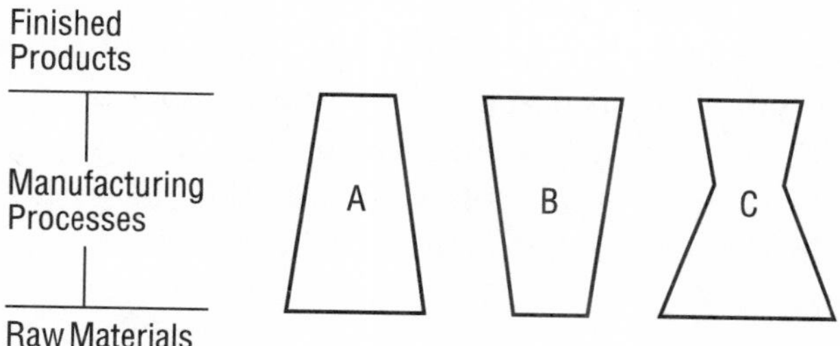

Pyramid structure. Figure 6.3A represents a business that makes a limited number of standard items from many semifinished items or components. Small appliances, staplers, ballpoint pens, watches, lamps, and telephones fit this type of product structure.

Inverted pyramid structure. Many items are made from a limited number of raw materials. Steel, for example, is used to make everything from shopping carts to scaffolding. Nylon thread is the main ingredient in thousands of fabric products. Figure 6.3B describes this product structure.

Hourglass structure. Many items are made from common, semifinished items or part sets. The automobile is a classic example (see Figure 6.3C). At the top level is the car; at the "pinch point" is the semifinished product (the engine, the chassis); at the bottom level are the thousands of components used to make the semifinished parts.

The Optimal Point to Master Schedule

In each of the preceding product profiles, the idea is to master schedule at the *narrowest* part of the diagram; doing so provides the greatest flexibility and control. The reason for this is that at this narrow point there are the fewest number of items to forecast, and desired customer requirements can be configured from this point using the fewest number of master scheduled items (a point expanded upon during the discussion of MTO environments in chapters 7 through 9). With fewer items to deal with, the narrowest point is also the *easiest* place to master schedule. Besides, master scheduling at the top level will require an investment in inventory at all subsequent levels.

If a product has the pyramid structure, the top of the pyramid—where the product is finished into a limited number of end items—is probably the place a company would like to master schedule. If, for instance, a company was in the business of selling electric coffee pots off the shelf, it may decide to master schedule the various standard colored pots.

The inverted pyramid presents the opposite situation, and the master scheduler may want to focus at the bottom, the pinch point. Of course, master scheduling at this level would mean that material requirements planning would be of little assistance in the planning process. This fact is probably obvious since the master schedule would be for the lowest level in the structure, leaving little for MRP to do. To get more help from MRP, the master scheduler may decide to move up into the structure and master schedule at some higher level, even though control may be more difficult. In moving to a higher level, common product groupings that use like resources and common base stocks should be considered. By doing so, the master scheduler can plan the common materials, schedule focused resources, and get some help from the material requirements planning logic.

The pinch point in the hourglass structure provides a useful master scheduling point. Consider how difficult it would be to master schedule automobiles at the top level: millions of option permutations are possible at the top (e.g., two-doors, V6, air-conditioning, and special interior features to name just a few). Two issues immediately surface when discussing this environment. The first relates to the possible number of bills-of-material for a company that offers several configurations; it would be impossible to structure and maintain all the possible bills-of-material. Without a bills-of-material data base, MRP is also impossible to implement. The second issue is that of securing a reasonable forecast (statement of demand) for each and every possible detailed configuration.

These are general guidelines, and the optimal place to master schedule within a product structure ultimately depends upon the needs of the company and where it intends to meet the customer.

Depending on specific needs, each of the following is a candidate for the status of a master scheduled item:

- end items
- subassemblies
- options or features

- add-ons or attachments
- purchased components
- raw materials
- service or spare parts
- capacity or key resources
- activities or events

The point is: One can master schedule *anything that makes sense to the business*. All of the factors and issues discussed above must be taken into consideration when a company is identifying what it plans to master schedule. And we're not done. To make this an even more complex decision, a company can elect to master schedule at multiple levels in its product structure.

Multilevel Master Scheduling

We have seen above that there are times when it may make sense to master schedule at levels other than the top, or final, product. A part that is expensive, difficult to obtain, or difficult to manufacture may need the kind of attention that a master scheduled item deserves. Thus, since there are no hard-and-fast rules for deciding *what* to master schedule, the management team and the master scheduler may elect to master schedule not only end items, but other items one, two, or three levels deep in the product structure. This approach is known as "master scheduling at multiple levels," or sometimes referred to as "master scheduling at two levels."

There are also times when two-level master scheduling, which is technically different from multilevel master scheduling, is necessary.

For example, the first level in two-level master scheduling logic would be at the product family level, as stipulated in the sales and operations planning process. At some point, the discrete demand and due dates for lower-level members that make up that product family need to be determined; one could drive the product family demand through a planning bill in order to forecast demand for the product family members. When a company uses a planning bill to predict demand at a lower level, it is using a two-level master scheduling approach.

We will get into two-level master scheduling and planning bills later, but for now, think about the issue raised in the following situation.

TYING THE MPS AND THE PRODUCTION PLAN

No business can operate for long without coordination between its functional parts. All must coordinate their efforts if a company is to survive and prosper. For the manufacturing company, sales and operations planning serves as an important coordinating function, bringing together customer demand, financial capabilities, and the goals of management in a quantitative form, describing—in aggregate—what needs to be built in future periods.

Consider the case of Deskmasters Corporation, a manufacturer of office furniture. As its managers emerge from their monthly sales and operations planning meeting, the manufacturing vice president hands the master scheduler a copy of the new production plan, which, for simplicity's sake, we will describe as covering only the month of April. The plan calls for the production of 1,200 desks.

The master scheduler takes this *aggregate* plan and uses it to create a more specific plan—breaking it into different types of desks to be produced in varying quantities in each week of the month. In this simple example, the desk product family has just two members: oak and pine.

	April Production Plan = 1,200 desks				
	Week 1	Week 2	Week 3	Week 4	Total
MPS oak	200	200	200	200	800
MPS pine	100	100	100	100	400
Total	300	300	300	300	1200

You will notice that the various quantities *total* 1,200 desks, pointing up an important principle: *The sum of the master schedule must equal the production plan.*

Management Issues

For management, the production plan serves as an important control mechanism over manufacturing resources, indicating the level of overall production. For those who do the work, and who may have more intimate knowledge of current inventories, work-in-process, plant capacities, and material availabilities at any given moment, the master schedule provides specificity and direction, namely, how many of *which* products will be built, and *when*. The requirement that master scheduled quantities equal those of the production plan provides an important check against unauthorized and ill-directed activities on the factory floor. Without this check, the master scheduler would, in effect, be in sole control of the factory and its various costs. When product families contain dozens of different members, the damage done by uncontrolled master scheduling can very quickly get out of hand.

For practical purposes, there may be times when it makes sense to *exceed* production plan limits in a particular period. Perhaps production wants to build up inventory in advance of a previously unscheduled maintenance shutdown or pending strike? Perhaps the master scheduler wants to overplan unique options and features in some product family because of product mix uncertainty? Management needs to have a clear policy concerning these situations and the link between the master schedule and the production plan.

Master Scheduling Capacities, Activities, and Events

Thus far, our discussion has concentrated on master scheduling only one of the productive resources of the company—materials. Equally important to the production process is another resource—capacity.[2] Master scheduling techniques can be applied to capacity as well as to parts or items. Understanding this point is especially important for those companies whose business is that of selling capacity. For example, job or machine shops that make buildings, irrigation, and other large-scale products fall into this category. For such businesses, it is critical to know what machinery will be required so that customer orders can be booked against the uncommitted—or unconsumed—capacity of that machine. When the next customer places an order, the shop needs to know how much capacity is left so that product completion can be properly quoted and delivered on the promised date.

Other situations may require a company to master schedule not items or capacity, but activities and events. A testing lab, for example, sells a service that can be broken down into a series of activities. The product that the testing lab sells is capacity, and that capacity is spread among several events that must occur. Chapter 11 will detail how activities and events can be harnessed within a structure analogous to that of a bill-of-material and shows how points within this structure can be scheduled, and capacity can be planned.

This chapter has explained the importance of knowing *what* to master schedule. It has shown that this "what" is not preordained as

[2] Here we should not think so narrowly as to construe capacity as applying solely to labor, machine time, and production space on the factory floor. As master scheduling becomes more broadly applied within companies, capacity can also be construed (and scheduled) in the context of services.

the last step in the value-adding process, but may focus elsewhere, depending upon the manufacturing strategy selected by the company.

Manufacturing strategies are largely geared to where a company intends to meet its customers, and this is determined by customer needs, competition, market requirements, willingness to invest in inventory, and the company's position on employing resources and capacity. Besides these elements, where the company's product is on its life cycle and what the product structures look like have a good deal of impact when choosing what to master schedule.

The important point to carry forward from this discussion to succeeding chapters is that the master scheduler must be fully versed in the nature of his or her company's products, how they are built, and the competitive constraints under which the company operates. A simple-minded default to end item master scheduling may work in some competitive environments, but in most will be inappropriate, resulting in loss of control of the schedule and its underlying levels of materials management. In addition, succeeding chapters will help the reader determine what to master schedule in any given manufacturing environment. In fact, not until the reader completes reading this entire book will all the decision points and master scheduling techniques be on the table. At that point, answers to "what to master schedule" can be obtained.

So far, we have discussed why manufacturing companies need to master schedule, the mechanics of master scheduling, managing with the master schedule, and using the master schedule in a make-to-stock environment. In the next four chapters we will turn our attention to master scheduling in other environments, starting with the assemble-to-order, finish-to-order, and make-to-order worlds. In these environments planning bills are usually necessary to aid the master scheduling process. Planning bills and their use are the subjects of our next discussions.

7

Planning Bills

An assumption is the first step toward a screwup.

Imagine a company that sells conference center chairs "off the shelf." To remain competitive, the company determines that it must expand its product line—customers want a variety of colors beyond the current black-only model. To accomplish this product expansion, the company must evaluate both its marketing and manufacturing strategies. Under its current make-to-stock strategy, the customer simply asks for a chair, and that item is shipped from finished goods. This system works fine for a product family with a limited number of members. But if a company is going to offer greater product variety without a change in its manufacturing strategy, it will be very expensive to maintain a finished-goods inventory for off-the-shelf shipment. Its forecasting job will be much more difficult, too; if it guesses wrong on demand for its variety of products, it risks having obsolete inventory. As the company continues to offer more options to the customer in order to remain competitive, the problem becomes more significant. Therefore, it may be necessary to choose a new manufacturing strategy.

Make-to-stock manufacturing strategy has already been discussed. This chapter describes an alternative strategy—make-to-order (MTO). First, though, we review the potential strategies at our disposal, using the familiar fast-food industry as a model. At one extreme, a fast-food restaurant can make-to-stock ready-to-eat hamburgers and keep them hot under heat lamps. Some would have ketchup, some mustard, some pickles, others lettuce, and some combinations of the various condiments. The advantage is that the customer gets instant gratification; the disadvantages, of course, are the high cost of finished inventory and the difficulty in forecasting the mix. Some items would move quickly, but others would grow stale and have to be discarded.

At the other extreme, the restaurant could wait for the customer's order and then do the following: bake the buns, run to the grocery store for some ground beef, prepare sliced pickles and other condiments from scratch, and cook and prepare the order as given. Such a "design-to-" or "engineer-to-order" approach would, of course, be impractical for a fast-food restaurant. The customer would grow tired of waiting.

In between these two extremes, the restaurant could maintain certain items in a finished state—the burgers and the buns. Condiment options could be added on request. This is a form of a make-to-order, or "finish-to-order" or "assemble-to-order" situation. The customer walks in and says, "I'll have a hamburger with lettuce, pickles, and tomatoes." The hamburgers are sitting on the grill and the buns are in the warmer; the restaurant simply adds the requested options.

Whether a company makes burgers or bolts, the production issues and master scheduling techniques needed are basically the same for the make-to-order business. However, these product configurations must be planned prior to receipt of the order to avoid high inventory investments and to reduce delivery time to the customer.

While make-to-order approaches to manufacturing offer significant advantages in terms of reducing finished-goods inventory costs, they have the potential disadvantage of creating unwieldy and complex bills-of-material as the number of product options grows. They also create potential forecasting problems in terms of estimating the right mix of options. This chapter is concerned primarily with the BOM aspects of make-to-order strategies, demonstrating how to set up the product structures in a database so that master scheduling in a make-to-order, assemble-to-order, and finish-to-order environment is feasible.

The Overly Complex Bill-of-Material

Earlier in the book it was explained that to gain a strategic edge, a company must match or surpass its competitors in terms of delivery time, price, quality, service, and technology. If product quality, technology, service, and price are equal among competitors, then the battle for customer allegiance must be won on the grounds of delivery performance, a factor of competitiveness that falls squarely in the domain of the master scheduler.

With proper scheduling techniques, it may be possible to meet the customer at a prefinished stage yet still provide product within a competitive time frame. If so, a competitive advantage will have been gained by offering the same or better delivery times but with substantially lower costs. Since the producer will have the opportunity to carry less inventory, its operating costs will be lower, making it possible either to reduce product price or increase margins or both.

From the master scheduler's perspective, a change to a make-to-order strategy means, first, deciding where to meet the customer. ("Come in and we will hand you a burger. . . . Give us two minutes and we will put it together for you. . . . Give us two hours and we'll run to the store for the ingredients and prepare it from scratch.") The decision about where to meet the customer impacts the decision of *what* will be master scheduled. Recalling the previous chapter, any of three types of product structures are possible within a company's framework (see Figure 7.1). In the case of the finish-to- or assemble-to-order environment, the hourglass structure (C) is the relevant shape.

Figure 7.1 Standard Manufacturing Configurations

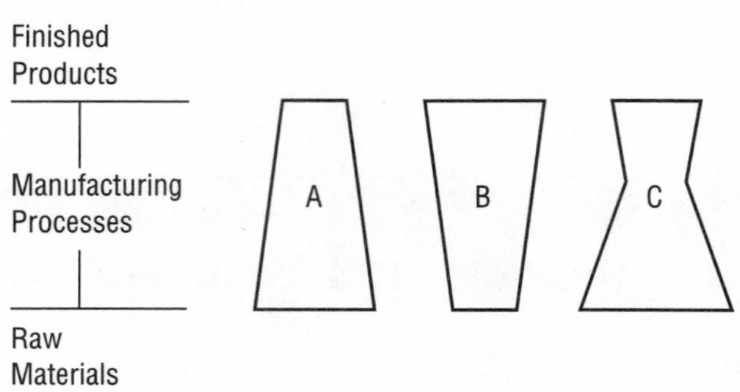

The hourglass structure represents a situation in which the customer buys a certain item from a product family, then selects additional options; like a hamburger, which can be configured in any number of ways. But whether the customer buys a plain hamburger or a cheeseburger with the works, he still must buy a burger (which, here, is one item represented in the pinch point of the hour glass). The buns, lettuce, tomatoes, pickles are "options" added later. The automobile offers a similar example: No matter which radio is ordered (AM, FM, CD player, or audio cassette), or which type of seat covers, the customer is still buying a car with bumpers, wheels, chassis, etc.

The hourglass is the structure most relevant to the assemble-to- or finish-to-order environment, and it addresses a key question for the master scheduler: How many bills-of-material must be created to accommodate all the possible options? Consider the BOM for a hypothetical product shown in Figure 7.2.

As Figure 7.2 makes clear, the purchaser of one of the products has a choice of ten different A Options. Assuming that all options are mutually compatible, the buyer then needs to select from among eight B Options. This equates to 80 possible configurations just among the A and B options. But there are more! Option C lists two

Figure 7.2 Options Availability for Hypothetical Product

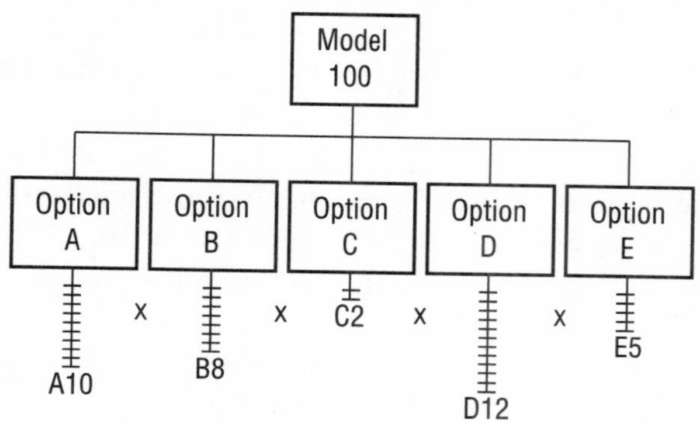

choices. A quick calculation of all possible options A through E reveals a staggering 9,600 possible configurations (10 × 8 × 2 × 12 × 5). The job of creating and maintaining separate bills-of-material for each configuration would be staggering. Now, what if a single new Option E were added to the list of choices. How many *new* BOMs would need to be created? Answer: 1,920 new bills-of-material (10 × 8 × 2 × 12 × 6 = 11,520 minus the earlier 9,600) each time a change is made to Option E.

This situation requires the master scheduler to work with sales and marketing to create the best forecast of demand for the various options—no easy task. Imagine the novice master scheduler approaching the marketing manager and saying, "I need to know how many Model 100s you're going to sell with the A1, B1, C1, D1, and E1 options next August." The marketing manager, a savvy veteran of the manufacturing world, rubs his chin, looks the new master scheduler straight in the eye, and says with great deliberation: "Seventeen."

Of course, the marketing manager has absolutely no idea of how many Model 100s will be sold with those options some months from now, and perhaps the master scheduler will catch on to his little joke. The point is, there has to be a better method for getting a handle on products that have potentially enormous BOMs. One solution is to figure out a way to master schedule one level below the finished product level—at the A1 and A2 and B1 levels, etc. How many BOMs would be needed if this approach was followed? Answer: a total of 10 BOMs for A, 8 for B, 2 for C, 12 for D, and 5 for Es. In other words, 37 BOMs would be needed (see Figure 7.3). This represents quite an improvement over the 9,600 BOMs for the full product!

Dropping down a level also benefits the design engineers. If an engineer wants to add a sixth E option, he or she needs to create *one* new BOM instead of having to gin up 1,920 new ones.

Of course, it is still necessary to determine how many Model 100s will be sold in a given month.

Once the aggregate number is determined, another key question must be answered: For every Model 100 sold, what is the probability that it will be shipped with the A1 option? With the A2 option? And so forth. Sales and marketing can answer these questions by saying something like this: "Whenever we sell a Model 100, we anticipate that 20 percent of the time we'll sell it with Option A1." This is essentially a forecast for the requirement of the option, and being a forecast, it is bound to be inaccurate to some extent. But for the time being, it may be the best number available to the master scheduler and will be used to estimate demand for the product mix.

Figure 7.3 Effect of Master Scheduling One Level Down in the Product Structure

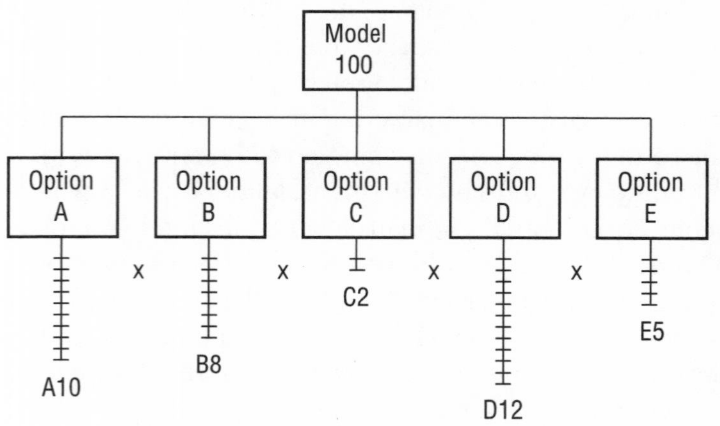

After the mix percentage has been determined, the next step is to forecast demand at the lower levels. The following discussion covers a tool for doing just that—"the planning bill." A planning bill is an artificial grouping of items or events in a bill-of-material format (see Figure 7.4).

Figure 7.4 Sample Planning Bill

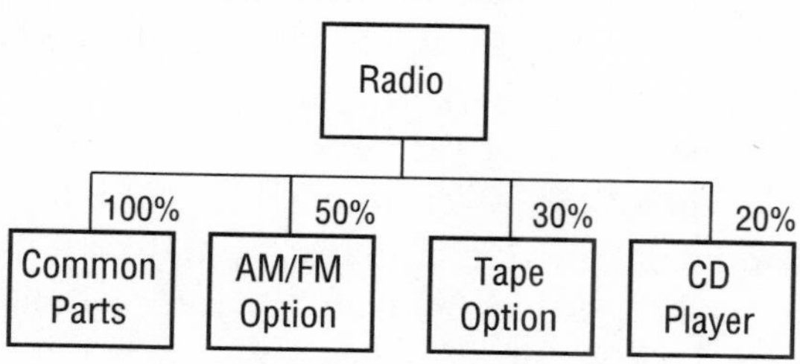

Planning bills are referred to as "pseudo bills"—false or artificial bills. They cannot be used to actually build any configuration of the product. The reason is two-fold. First, a product cannot be built with less than 100 percent of a given part. In other words, you cannot take 50 percent of an AM/FM radio, add it to 30 percent of a radio with a tape cassette, and then add this to 20 percent of a radio with a CD player. Second, it takes more than just unique parts to build the product—common parts are also needed. However, an item with a pseudo bill attached to it can be master scheduled. The planning bill can then be used to predict what items may be needed to produce the product the customer may request.

An Example

Consider this simple example. If we know that we will sell 1,000 Model 100s, we also know that 1,000 sets of the common parts (those used in *all* Model 100s, no matter which options are selected by the customer) will be needed. Nothing could be more simple. The difficulty comes in determining the mix of the *unique* items. Suppose that 20 percent of the Model 100s sold in any given month are expected to contain option A1. In this case we would convert the 20 percent to a decimal (.20) and enter that value into the BOM quantity field (some MPS software has a probability field as well as the quantity field—in this case the value is entered in the probability field) for the A1 option, as shown in Figure 7.5. The same would be done for each of the other options—say, .15 for the B1 option, indicating that 15 percent of the Model 100s are expected to contain the B1 option.

These numbers are best obtained through a mixture of science and art. The process begins by asking the right people, who in this case happen to be individuals in marketing and sales—who, after all, has a more complete knowledge of the product, the market appeal of its options, and the intentions of customers? Their information comes through sales and delivery (demand) history and what might be called "future history"—i.e., orders booked for future delivery. At some point, what is booked for future delivery becomes sales history. Sales and marketing personnel also keep close tabs on their list of current and prospective accounts, often compiling lists of expected orders months in advance of when those orders are actually received. These lists are used by marketing to focus sales attention on near-term orders that need to be closed, but they can also be used in forecasting. The bottom line in planning bill accuracy is that sales and marketing

Figure 7.5 Planning Bill with Percentages of Options

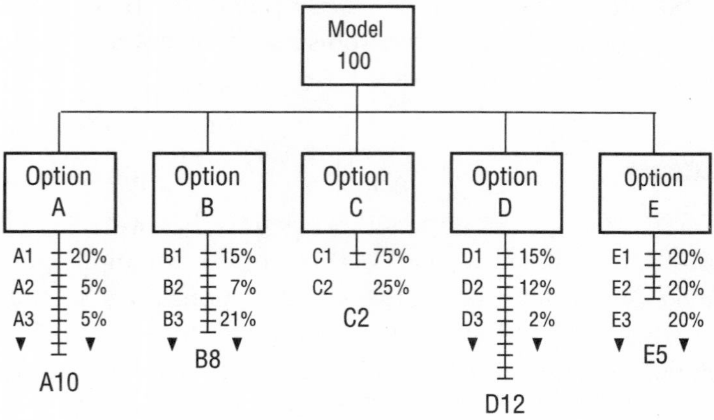

must be accountable for creating and maintaining the planning bill percentages.

Once the percentages are obtained, they are entered into the option planning bill. But should they add up to 100 percent? If the options are required, the answer would be yes. But if the options are "add ons," then the percentages or probabilities of sales may be less than or greater than 100 percent. For example, consider a bicycle with numerous configurations—different frame sizes, a rear derailleur (gear assembly), pedals, etc. No matter what size frame, what gear ratios, or what style of pedals are selected, every bicycle *must* have a frame, a gear assembly, and a pedal set. On the other hand, it is not necessary to have a front derailleur (which doubles or triples the number of available gears). The front derailleur is therefore an add-on option, and the total forecast for units with this option could be equal to, less than, or greater than the number of bicycles to be sold.

As more options are added, the complexity of the bicycle increases, creating a more difficult situation for manufacturing and the master scheduler. One technique for managing this complexity is to group common parts (those that are always needed, such as wheels, brakes, seat stems, wire cables, etc.). Every bicycle in a given family will have common parts, though these may be unique to the product family. One family, for example, might always have an eight-inch seat stem and a standard front axle, regardless of frame size, wheel size, etc. Those items would be listed together on a common parts bill. The common parts bill is also a pseudo, since nothing can be built with just a seat stem and front axle. But the common parts bill can be married with an option bill-of-material to build the bicycle. Why do this? Because of the existence of common parts, certain probabilities remain constant; the probability that common parts will be needed is 100 percent. That fact is very important. If a set of common parts for every bicycle is needed, the job of forecasting the mix is certainly reduced. All that is needed then is to get enough sets of common parts to match the demand forecast generated in the S&OP process.

Now consider handlebars. Perhaps option C1 represents dropped bars, and C2 represents upright bars. According to marketing, 75 percent of the bicycles sold will have dropped bars, and the remaining

25 percent will have straight bars. In the planning bill C1 would be indicated as .75, and C2 would be listed as .25. Manufacturing cannot produce a handlebar using .75 of a dropped bar and .25 of a straight bar. Again, for this reason, the planning bill is called a "pseudo bill-of-material" and is used for planning purposes only. To build the product, manufacturing must use an actual bill-of-material and process instructions created by engineering.

How does the pseudo bill work? Suppose that marketing predicts 1,000 bicycles will be sold in the next month. By exploding 1,000 through the planning bill, and multiplying the aggregate quantity by the projected percentages, one can forecast how many unique and common items will be needed. In this case, if the dropped bars are forecasted at a 75 percent probability, and upright bars at 25 percent, then 750 bikes with dropped handlebars and 250 with upright bars will be needed. Naturally, the number of common parts needed will equal the number of bicycles required—1,000.

With this understanding, consider a familiar product and how the planning bill assists the company and its master scheduler in getting the job done in the assemble-to- or finish-to-order environment.

Soft Seat Listens to Customers, Expands Product Offerings

The Soft Seat Corporation designs and manufactures a successful line of conference center chairs that it sells "off the shelf" throughout North America and parts of Europe. During a monthly sales and operations planning meeting, the CEO announced that market research indicated that to remain competitive the company must expand its product line to provide models in colors other than its traditional black. "Customers are telling us that they want a variety of colors to coordinate with modern office decors. The increasing success of the one competitor that does provide color choices confirms the research."

Soft Seat had built a successful business on just one product in one color. This simple product situation made planning fairly straightforward. Since the company's market forecast was generally reliable, it could satisfy customer orders by keying production to the market forecast. There was no need to guess how many orders there would be for various model options.

The announcement by the CEO would make life more difficult for just about everyone. Marketing would find forecasting more challenging; they would have to estimate demand not just for chairs, but for black chairs, red chairs, and so forth. If estimating demand for plain black chairs was difficult from month to month, breaking that total forecast into segments represented by different colors would prove more difficult—and surely less reliable.

The chief financial officer would surely find the new strategy troubling. This was a "get the order and ship it" business. Soft Seat had to have a sizable finished goods inventory to meet the competitive requirement for fast delivery. Now he feared he would be required to finance not one inventory, but several, one for each color plus the various mixed colors—red back with a black seat is quite fashionable.

The manufacturing manager was even less thrilled by the announcement because it would greatly complicate what had been a fairly simple and routine manufacturing operation. Nevertheless, he knew that he and his staff were up to the challenge.

The sales force was entirely behind the color idea. Since the other competitive parameters of their business—price, delivery, quality, service, and technology—were closely followed by everyone in the business, this color-option strategy gave them one more piece of selling ammunition. The manufacturing and finance issues were not their concern.

Until now, Soft Seat merely had to secure the customer order and ship from its finished-goods inventory. It followed a classic make-to-stock manufacturing strategy, typical of businesses in which either 1) the competitive environment requires rapid order fulfillment, or 2) simple, low-priced products prevail. Manufacturers of office supplies, tire companies, and small appliances fit this description. When a customer wants a box of ten 3.5-inch computer diskettes, she wants them now, not two weeks from now. She will not submit an order to the manufacturer to begin production.

The make-to-stock manufacturing strategy works well in the environment just cited, but if a company adopts a new product strategy—as Soft Seat has—then a new manufacturing strategy logically follows.[1] Here we describe a make-to-order strategy. Recall from chapter 6 that a make-to-order strategy occupies a middle position between the extremes of make-to-stock and engineer-to-order. According to APICS, a make-to-order product is one that is finished after receipt of a customer order. In make-to-order, *some* material may be ordered and *some* parts of the product may be produced before receipt of a customer order. With a pure MTO strategy, the product is designed, but no manufacturing occurs until a customer order is received. Highly customized products are generally made in this fashion. Finish-to-order (FTO) and assemble-to-order (ATO) are variants of this strategy. Here, the company may build product through all but the finishing stage, which is triggered by a customer order.

Anatomy of a Planning Bill

Figure 7.6 shows a planning bill for the new Soft Seat chair product family. Here, four different color options are available. (Note: Colors are coded using a significant part number scheme in the form of a suffix. For example, the basic conference center chair is model 260;

[1] Over the past ten years, the business strategy of competing on the basis of rapid introduction of new and varied products has gained many adherents. Japanese companies have led the way in this: Honda with literally dozens of new motorcycle model introductions in just a few years; Casio with over 100 different watch models (on less than a dozen internal cores); Sony with multiple varieties of its popular Walkman cassette player. Business scholars have written extensively on the competitive advantages to be gained by this strategy; almost none, however, have focused on the manufacturing issues that underlie the strategy and, in fact, make it possible.

Figure 7.6 Soft Seat Planning Bills for Options and Common Parts

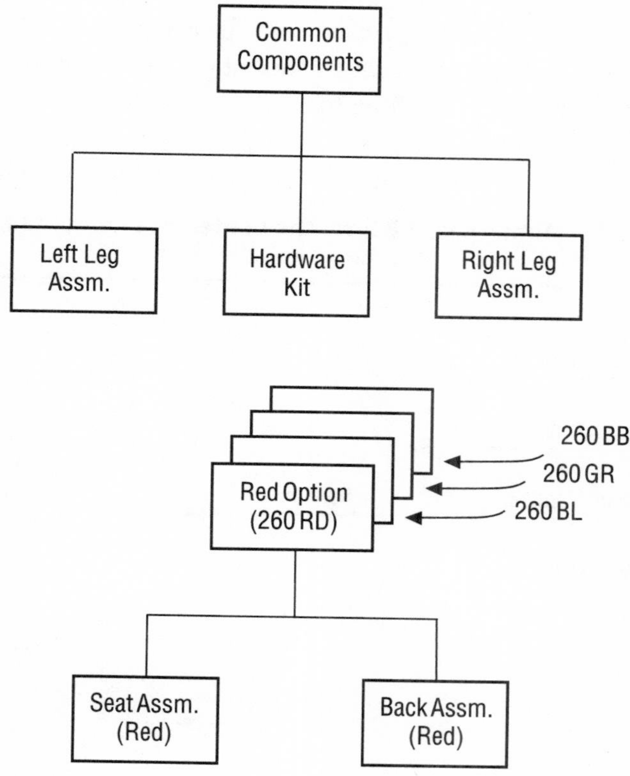

the suffix, BL, indicates black; RD indicates red; GR indicates green; and BB indicates blue.)

In a make-to-stock environment, all four colored conference center chairs would be built and held as finished goods pending the receipt of customer orders. Looking at the chair one level down (see Figure 7.7 on the following page), we see that the following items are needed: a seat assembly, a back splat assembly, a left leg assembly, a hardware kit, and a right leg assembly. Notice that neither the hardware kit nor the leg assemblies have a color designation. This means that these are common to all chairs, regardless of color, and *not* unique.

Time Phasing

At this point we need to *time phase* the bill-of-material, as shown in Figure 7.7. In a make-to-stock environment, chairs would be stocked at the *zero* time line. In switching to a make-to-order or assemble-to-order strategy, however, time phasing would become critical, since completed chairs would no longer be stocked. Instead, we may stock

Figure 7.7 Time-Phased Bill for the Conference Center Chair Product Family

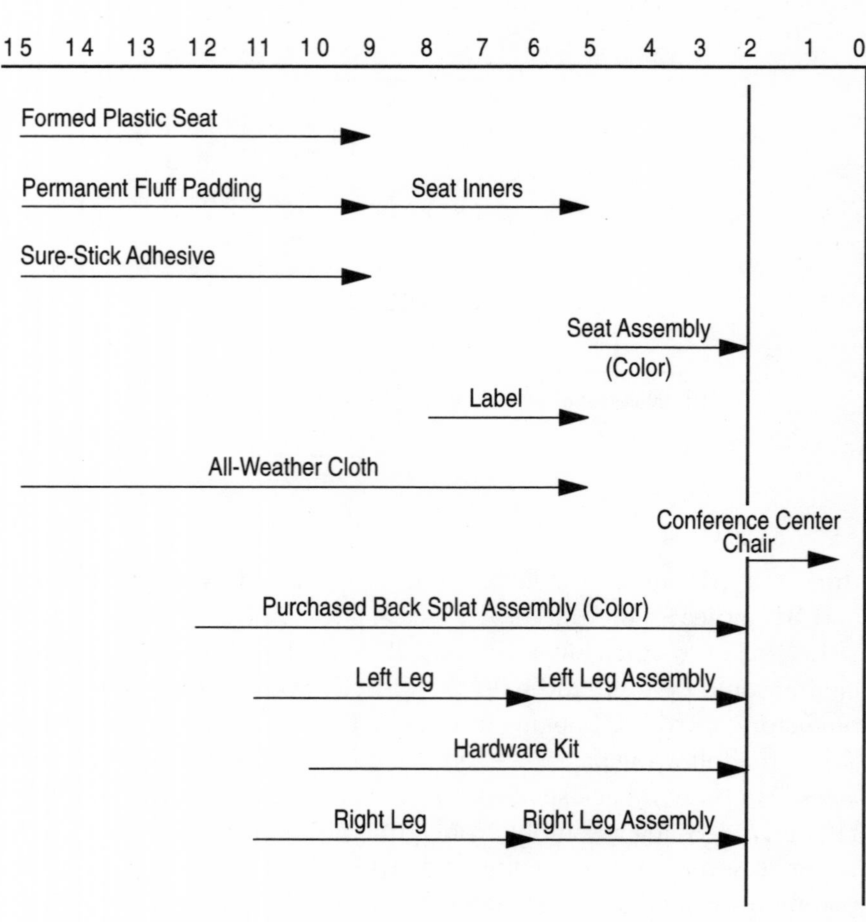

seat assemblies (color-sensitive), back splat assemblies (color-sensitive), hardware kits (common), right leg assemblies (common), and left leg assemblies (common). The ability and decision to do this depend on where the company intends to meet its customers. The capacity to configure these stocked items into customer-defined requirements would also be required within the defined time period. For illustration purposes, let's assume we plan to meet the customer with the defined modules, which means that we would need two periods to complete the product once the customer order is placed.

To deploy to an assemble-to- or finish-to-order strategy, bills-of-material need to be structured for the common components as well as for each offered option. This means that the red option bill will contain a red seat assembly and a red back assembly. The black option will likewise contain a black seat assembly and a black back assembly.

Figures 7.6 (see page 187) and 7.8 show the planning bills for the entire conference center chair family. The common parts planning bill is shown at the top of Figure 7.6, while the lower portion of the figure contains the unique items: red option, black option, etc. This bill restructuring makes it possible to greatly reduce the number of bills in the data file. With this done, another pseudo bill is created for the conference center chair family itself (Figure 7.8). In this planning bill we structure the common parts plus all the options that can be requested. By so doing, we have made it possible to tie the output of the sales forecasting process to the lowest component in the chair

Figure 7.8 Planning Bill for the Conference Center Chair Product Family

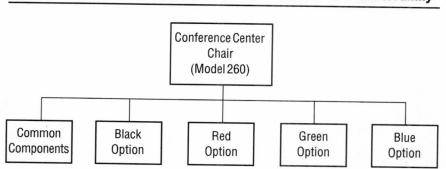

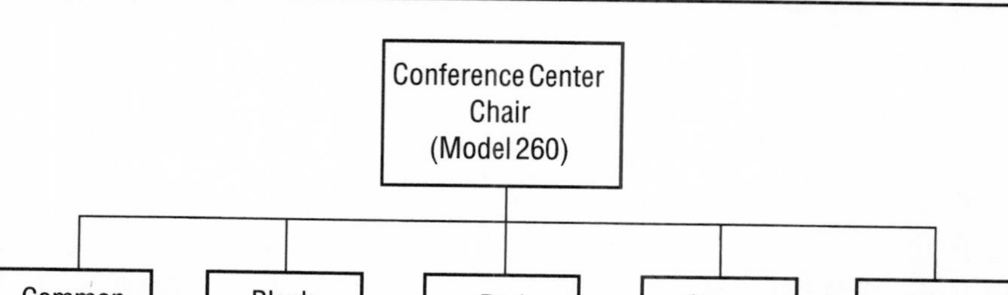

family. To see how, follow it all the way to the bottom. The conference center chair calls out the red option, which calls out the red seat assembly, which calls out the seat inners (see Figure 7.7 on page 188), which call out the formed plastic seat, permanent fluff padding, and sure-stick adhesive. The chair also calls out the common parts, which call out the hardware kit, which would call out the hardware.

The key concept here is that the forecasting done at the sales and operations planning meeting is done at the product family level (conference center chairs) and the top-level planning bill is also structured at the generic chair level. This provides the vital link needed to tie the aggregate planning to the detail planning.

During the master scheduling process, the numbers created during the S&OP plan are exploded through the planning bill. Since every conference center chair requires one set of common parts, the percentage attached to the common parts kit is 100 (or 1.0). Now, according to sales and marketing, every time a chair is demanded, there is a 40 percent chance that it will be black. If you planned to sell 1,000 conference center chairs, you would anticipate needing 1,000 sets of common parts (1,000 × 1.0), 400 black seat assemblies (1,000 × .40), and 400 black back splat assemblies (1,000 × .40). The other 600 conference center chairs would require red, blue, and green options. In this way the MPS software using the planning bills can calculate the expected mix demand at the next lower level, which is where master scheduling would take place.

What we have done in this example is create pseudo bills-of-material: one for the common items and one for each of the color options. When a customer orders a chair, that customer will indicate a color preference. If the order is for three red chairs, then the company needs to configure a customer order comprised from three sets of red options and three sets of common items.

Knowing that, the company will structure the five pseudo bills into a conference center chair family (Figure 7.8 on preceding page). The purpose is to tie all the option bills to the sales and operations planning process output—i.e., to the level where top management creates the product family plans that includes the conference center chair family.

The chair family pseudo bill is also known as a "super bill" or the top-level planning bill. The master scheduler can take the S&OP output and explode it through the planning bill by time period to determine the expected demand at the MPS mix level (the demand for different color options). Demand for the common parts is determined at the same time. With that demand determined, a master schedule can be created at the common parts and option levels, and that master schedule data can be passed down to lower levels via material requirements planning logic.

Creating Demand at the Master Schedule Level

The next step is to calculate demand for the various options. Here our novice master scheduler (who has since been educated on make-to-order scheduling techniques and is now a journeyman), must go back to marketing and sales with some questions. But the questions will now be quite different. Instead of asking how many of a particular configuration (such as red, green, blue, or black chairs) will be sold in future periods, the first question is: How many chairs are anticipated to be sold in August, *regardless* of color? The answer has been determined in the S&OP meeting. The second question is: What are the probabilities that chair sales will be red, green, blue, or black?

To determine the expected option mix demand, the master scheduler takes the estimate for August chair sales (of all color options) and explodes it through the planning bill using the probability percentages to determine the expected demand for each option. Thus, if 1,000 conference center chairs are expected to be sold in August, and if the red option has a 25 percent probability, then 250 sets of red option parts will be required to satisfy the product family's sales plan of 1,000 units. With this information the master scheduler is in a position to put together the master schedule for the common items and the various color options, which is a topic covered in the next chapter.

RESTRUCTURING COMPANY BILLS INTO PLANNING BILLS: A CASE STUDY

Dynoline is a major manufacturer of turbine engines used to drive electrical generators in industry and in smaller public utility plants. The company manufactures a variety of engines, each of which can be ordered with one of three different fuel systems: natural gas, liquid, and dual fuel. Because customer preferences for fuel systems are largely dictated by prevailing market prices for different fuels, Dynoline's marketing department has never been successful in forecasting the fuel options ordered by customers. The result is that the company operates on a strictly make-to-order basis, starting the build process once it has the order with the specifications, including the fuel system specification.

The company maintains three different bills-of-material for the fuel system on each engine. It also has a cumulative lead time (CLT) of eight months to complete each engine—from start to ship date. In 1993, faced with a tougher competitive environment, Dynoline sought a competitive edge in time-to-delivery. If it could deliver a complete turbine engine with the specific product features required by the customer in less time than competing producers, Dynoline would win more business. Thus, reducing lead time was a mandated improvement. Further, Dynoline's chief executive officer announced that the goal would be to reduce lead time to the point that the customer could have any of the company's turbine engines within three months of placing an order. The CEO also made it clear that solutions to this time compression challenge would have to be made within four weeks.

Walt Webber was vice president of manufacturing for Dynoline. Over lunch, he and the master scheduler, Virginia Hall, discussed the problem of slicing five months from their lead times. "Marketing and sales would say that the way to handle this would be to build an inventory of engines with each fuel system," Virginia joked.

"Sure," said Walt, "the finance department would love to keep an inventory of a dozen or so $250,000 engines. They could take the carrying costs out of the soft drink machine fund!"

"Or out of your salary, Walt," she quipped. "I suggest that we take a look at our time-phased bills-of-material as a first step," Virginia offered. "This is probably the best place to start looking for ways to cut lead times. The time-phased bills will show us at a glance the time line for each engine and the cumulative lead times for each component."

Walt agreed, and they went to his office to examine the BOMs. For simplicity, they started with the turbine engine with gas-fuel system, which appears in Figure 7.9.

It was clear from this time-phased bill-of-material that the cumulative lead time—the total elapsed time required to acquire or build the entire gas-fuel engine from start to finish—was eight months. Walt

Figure 7.9 Dynoline Gas-Fuel Turbine Engine Time-Phased Bill-of-Material

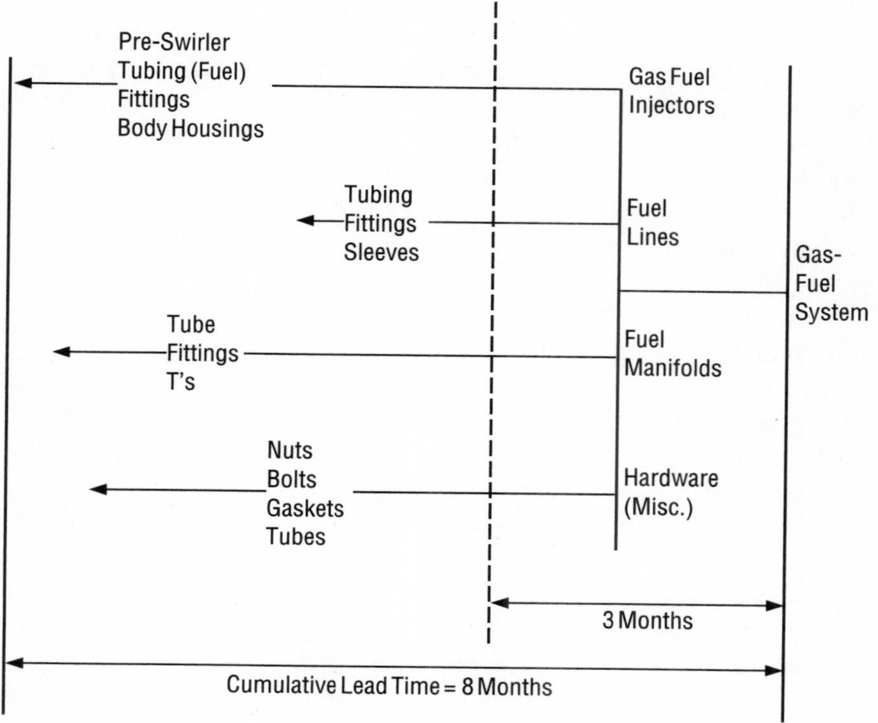

took a pencil and drew a dashed line vertically through the time-phased bill-of-material at month 3. "This is it," he said. "We have to be able to ship product in three months from this point. This shows us what we need in stock in order to compress the lead time by five months. So, how can we restructure our engineering bills into planning bills that will allow us to effectively plan these stocked options?"

Both Virginia and Walt knew that they had various options for reducing the cumulative lead time. The most drastic of these was to redesign Dynoline turbine engines to have fewer parts, simpler assembly procedures, etc., so that they could be built from start to finish in just three months. This was "design for manufacturability," a process used by many companies to improve their products and their lead times. In the long run, this was probably the best solution, but not one that could be accomplished within the four weeks mandated by the CEO.

Another option would be to systematically work on process improvements to reduce the build or order times for a variety of operations. By squeezing these into shorter lead times, the overall lead time for the completed product could be reduced. But there was another way.

"The most obvious way to reduce our lead time," Walt remarked, "without stocking completely built engines, is to work back through the time-phased bills-of-material from expected ship date to three months before expected ship date. Assuming that we cannot compress the lead times for all activities in these three months, we must have everything else in stock and ready to go just as soon as the customer order arrives."

"But will three months give us enough time to handle the fuel-system option?" Virginia asked.

They examined the gas engine BOM carefully and determined that all of the requirements specific to this being an engine with a gas-fuel system were addressed within the final three months of the CLT. "Yes, Virginia, it can be done," Walt responded. "For the gas engine, at least, everything up to three months could be based upon one set of common parts and various stocked options. We could build-to-stock up to that level of uniqueness and commonality, then finish the engine off after the order is received." But would this work for the other engines? The only way to know was to check the BOM for each.

Later that day, Walt assigned the job of examining the BOMs for the liquid-fuel and dual-fuel systems to a staff assistant, who later reported that the requirements for these other systems, like the natural gas–fuel system, could all be handled within the three-month lead time. The assistant also reported that fully 90 percent of all the fuel-related parts were common.

Sensing that he was near a solution to the CEO's three-month delivery challenge, Walt changed the agenda of that week's upcoming master scheduling meeting from routine items to an initial attempt at restructuring the planning bills for Dynoline's turbine engines. In addition to Virginia and the other production people, Walt invited the sales manager, who understood the typical order patterns for the different fuel-system options.

As the meeting came to order, Walt's assistant rolled in a chalkboard on which a graphic representation of a fuel system, showing its common and unique parts, had already been sketched out (Figure 7.9 on page 193). Walt explained to the assembled group that their job that morning would be to attempt to cut the time to delivery by sorting out what was common to each of the three engine fuel systems, what was unique to each, and what had to be stocked if the company had only three months to build the product after receipt of an order.

"Today we are going to examine the bills-of-material for each of our turbine-engine fuel systems," he explained, "and sort out what is common and what is unique up to a point three months prior to the completion time for a turbine engine. We will go through the BOMs for each of the different fuel systems in turn, and Virginia will lead the discussion of the first one."

Virginia Hall walked up to the front of the room and taped five cards to the wall, as shown in Figure 7.10. The words *Fuel System, Common*

Figure 7.10 Product Family Fuel System

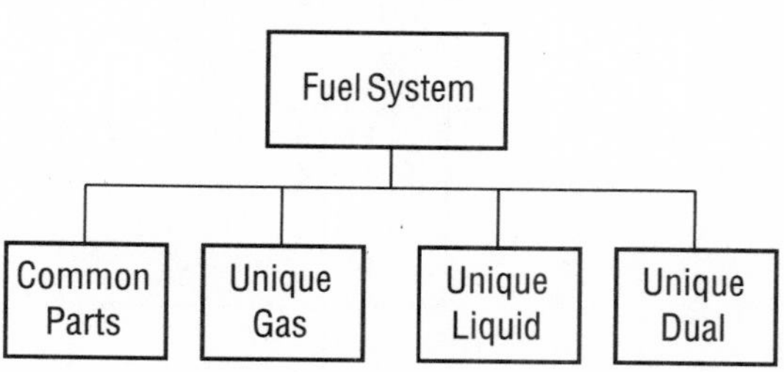

Parts, Unique Gas, Unique Liquid, and *Unique Dual* were boldly lettered on the cards.

"To get things started, I thought we could *deconstruct* our engine by identifying which of its many parts are common and which are unique. You have the BOMs for the natural gas–, liquid-, and dual-fuel systems in front of you." (Figure 7.11 is a cut down version of the product.)

"Let me begin by saying that Level 0 is our finished gas-fuel turbine engine. Level 1 represents all of those items that are required to make one Level 0 product, and Level 2 represents all of those items required to make one Level 1 item. Is everyone with me?" All nodded in agreement.

Over the course of the next thirty minutes, Virginia and other attendees of the meeting went through the entire bills-of-material for the fuel systems; each part was identified on a Post-it Note by item number, description, unit of measure, whether it was a make or buy item, and by lead time, and stuck under one of the five cards taped to the wall (Figure 7.10 on preceding page). At the end of the exercise all the required stocked items were identified as common to the fuel system or unique to the gas-, liquid-, or dual-fuel system. As the group sat back to admire their work, the group knew that it had restructured the engineering bills into a planning bill. By using this planning bill to plan materials and resources, a customer requirement could be met in the three-month time frame.

Figure 7.11 Indented Bill for Gas Turbine Engine

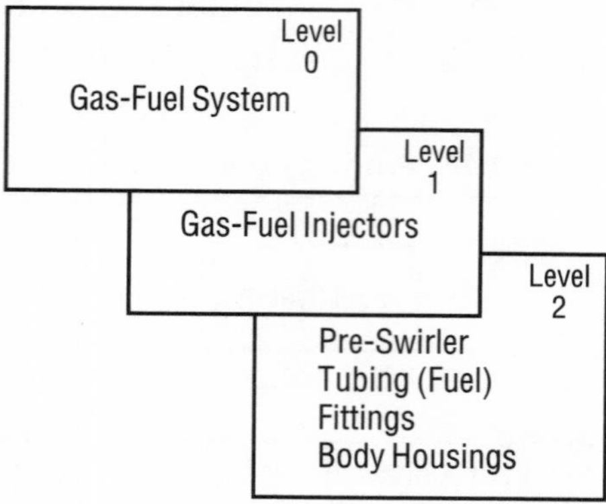

"Okay," Walt said, "is this it? Do we have our new planning bill?" The group nodded its approval. "Virginia, you will be responsible for putting the planning bill into the computer system. In order to do this, you need to know the quantities for each component."

Walt looked over at the sales manager. "Here's where you come in, Al. We need to know the probabilities of the gas, liquid, and dual systems to be ordered. We will take your probabilities, convert them to decimals [50 percent = .5], and enter the results into the quantity field on the planning bill. By doing this we will be able to take the output of the sales and operations planning meeting and determine the expected option requirements. Of course, the common parts are always required and will carry a 100 percent probability [or a quantity of 1.0]. Can you get us those numbers?"

The sales manager indicated that he had done his homework and knew the probabilities. He told the group that he used a combination of order history and future-order forecasts. The numbers were given to Virginia so that she could create the planning bills as directed.

The last thing the group did was to identify who in the organization was going to be responsible for the planning bill database. It was decided that the master scheduler would be responsible and accountable for the planning bill structure (ensuring compatibility with engineering design and proper maintenance of the planning bill), and sales and marketing would be responsible and accountable for the quantities that contained the probability numbers. At this time, the members of the group patted one another on the back and gave compliments for a job well done.

With the planning bills in place, the master scheduling system could now use the structures and probabilities to generate option forecasts for each master scheduled component called out. This logic, plus the actual creation of the master schedule, is the topic covered in the next chapter.

8

Two-Level MPS and Other Advanced Techniques

Without data, you are just another person with an opinion.

The previous chapter introduced the conference center chair product family of the Soft Seat Company, posing a key question: For every chair sold, how many are anticipated to be sold with the black option? Red option? Black-and-red option? The answers to these questions are necessary to complete the forecasting process, which in turn is essential to creating a master schedule. Before continuing our discussion of master scheduling and the forecasting process, another component of the master scheduling process must be examined—the "backlog" or "order book curve."

The Backlog Curve

"Backlog" is defined as orders booked but not shipped. This definition does not say that the orders are past due, which are referred to as "backorders"; many, and sometimes all orders in the backlog curve—

or "order book"—are *expected* to ship in the future. The backlog curve is a profile of those booked but not shipped orders in the framework of the company's planning forecast. Virtually all make-to-order (MTO) and engineer-to-order (ETO) companies have backlogs, and each must understand the nature and shape of that backlog in scheduling current and future production.

Figure 8.1 is a conceptualized view of the backlog profile. In the earliest periods of the planning horizon (the leftmost extreme) the demand pipeline is filled with booked but unshipped orders. These may be orders where production has yet to begin work, others in some stage of work-in-process, and still others ready to be crated for shipment. The opposite extreme (the rightmost portion of the planning horizon) contains no backlog; the only demand here is "forecasted" orders. Between these two extremes are a number of planning periods containing both backlog and forecasted orders.

Master schedulers segment the backlog curve into zones that de-

Figure 8.1 The Backlog Curve

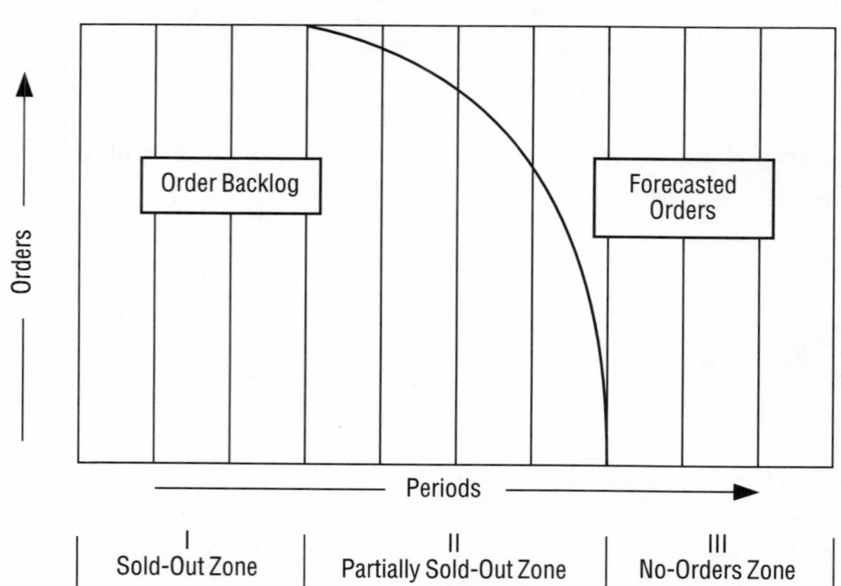

fine the status of orders in each. These are the "Sold-Out Zone" in which all expected demand is backed by an actual order; a "Partially Sold-Out Zone" in which some of the demand is supported by actual orders and the remainder is supported strictly by a forecast; and a "No-Orders Zone" that extends beyond the backlog in which all production, material planning, and resource planning is geared to forecasted sales (whereas in the first two zones, some or all production, material planning, and resource planning is geared to satisfy real customer orders).

To understand how the master scheduler deals with the backlog curve, we return to the Soft Seat Company where, following the S&OP monthly meeting, top management has determined product demand or a production rate of 40 (could be 4,000 or 40,000) conference center chairs per month. (Remember that this is a make-to-order example where deliveries are quoted into the future after the order is booked.) Figure 8.2 shows a two-month demand or production rate of 40 units per month (assumes four periods in each month), and these are broken down into 20 units in every other period.

Thus, product demand and the production rate are set at 20 in periods 2, 4, 6, and 8, for a total of 80 for the two-month horizon. The demand rate is the same as the production rate, because Soft Seat operates in a make-to-order environment—i.e., the production rate equals the expected shipment rate, which is keyed to the customers' expected product receipt minus transportation time.

It is easy to see from Figure 8.2 that Soft Seat's backlog curve has

Figure 8.2 Backlog for the Conference Center Chair Product Family

	Past Due	1	2	3	4	5	6	7	8
Production Rate			20		20		20		20
Actual Demand			20		16		8		0
Available-to-Promise (ATP)		0	0 0	0	4 4	4	12 16	16	20 36

the three zones just mentioned. In period 2 it has customer orders equaling its current capacity level of 20 chairs every two periods. This, then, is a sold-out zone in which there are 0 chairs available-to-sell or available-to-promise (ATP). However, period 4 contains only 16 customer orders that have consumed the 20 units scheduled for production, leaving 4 available-to-promise to any customer who happens to call. ATP increases to 12 in period 6 and to 20 in period 8 as fewer orders are booked relative to the planned production rate. Notice that in the ATP line the top set of numbers is the number available-to-promise for that particular period (as in period 6 where 20 are expected to be produced less 8 units of actual demand leaving 12 ATP). The bottom set of numbers is *cumulative* ATP—i.e., the total number of units available-to-promise, which is the ATP in that period *plus* all the previous ATP quantities, which are units still unsold.

Figure 8.3 shows the current backlog curve for Soft Seat and the position of its various zones. Periods 1 through 3 are sold out; periods 4 through 7 are partially sold out; and period 8 is in the zone contain-

Figure 8.3 Soft Seat Backlog Curve

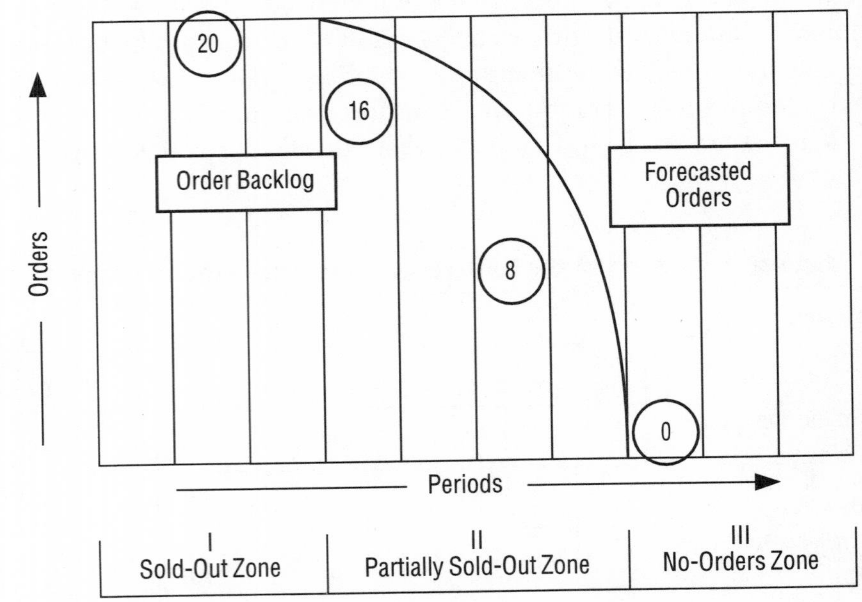

ing no customer orders. The shape of the curve and duration of the zones will differ for each company and industry. In an engineer-to-order company, we would expect the sold-out zone to be very lengthy, stretching far out into the future. For a company that is strictly make-to-stock, the sold-out zone may be very short.

Scheduling and the Backlog Curve Zones

From the perspective of master scheduling in the assemble-to-order, finish-to-order, and buy-to-order environments, the sold-out zone is the easiest to deal with—the customer requirements and the specifications for each in the form of customer orders are already in hand. In Zone I the master schedule (supply) for all pseudo items (see chapter 7) should be made to equal the customer orders (demand). No forecasting is required. The no-orders zone is likewise easy for the master scheduler to plan out. With no customer orders in hand, sales and marketing plans provide the guidance. And barring products with short lead times, time is on the side of the master scheduler.

It is generally the middle area—the partially sold-out zone—that can give master schedulers fits. Here, time is slipping away and there is still forecasted order demand for which neither quantities nor configuration specifications have been established. As discussion of the configure-to-order environment continues, keep this thought in mind.

Identifying Demand

Since the demand and production rates for product families over the planning horizon have been determined during the S&OP process, the next step is to determine the demand for each master scheduled item—for example, the demand for every item that goes into the conference center chair family. This is done by taking the S&OP output and converting it into discrete part numbers, quantities, and due dates.

In the previous chapter we created a series of planning bills that identified common parts along with the red, blue, green, and black options. In order to simplify the example, this chapter will deal with only two options, red and black, each of which has a 50 percent probability. For the sake of discussion, sales and marketing have pulled the green, blue, and mixed options from the company's offerings. The focus in this section will be on the red option, which contains a red seat assembly and a red back splat assembly. The red option bill has already been described as a pseudo in that manufacturing cannot create a finished chair from a red seat assembly and back splat assembly; only when these are united with a set of common parts does a red chair became a real, shippable product. But even though true pseudos cannot be built, they can be master scheduled.

Figure 8.4 presents the MPS matrix for the red option components. Note the forecast line. If the red option was a real part (remember, it's a pseudo or artificial item) and if there was any independent demand, it would show up on this line. But since this part has been identified as a pseudo, there is no service demand in our example. If, for some reason, the seat and back are sold as a kit, independent demand would then appear.

The Actual Demand Line

When the planning bill for the conference center chair family in this chapter was set up, the red option was given a probability of 50 percent—i.e., if 20 units were sold and committed, Soft Seat expects 10 to be sold as red chairs. So when the 20 units were sold for delivery in period 2, the company would have expected 10 to be red. However, in the case of period 2, 12 of the 20 units of *actual* demand for the chair family (see Figure 8.4) turn out to be red chairs requiring the red option (example displays when option items are required to be delivered to the finishing line). In period 4, a total of 16 chairs

Figure 8.4 MPS Matrix, Red Option Components (50 percent probability)

MPS Matrix	Past Due	1	2	3	4	5	6	7	8
Item Forecast		0	0	0	0	0	0	0	0
Option Forecast			0		2		6		10
Actual Demand			12		7		5		0
Total Demand			12		9		11		10
Projected Available Balance	0	0	0	0	2	2	2	2	2
Available-to-Promise		0	0 0	0	4 4	4	6 10	10	10 20
Master Schedule			12		11		11		10

were sold. Here, Soft Seat would have expected 8 to be red, but out of the 16 sold, only 7 were red units. While the predicted sales were wrong, they were nevertheless close; many companies, in fact, would be glad to come this close to the product mix forecast. In period 6, 8 conference center chairs were sold, of which 5 were red, as shown in the actual demand line in period 6 of Figure 8.4. Again, the actual demand did not match the expected demand, but the forecaster was not far from the mark.

The Option Forecast Line

Now that the master scheduler knows the expected service demand (zero has been forecasted in this example) and the actual demand supported by real customer orders, the piece of the total demand picture that remains unknown is the option forecast—how many red chair orders are still anticipated to be received over the eight-period horizon in the example. To answer this question we need to revisit the backlog curve and the conference center chair product family data contained in Figure 8.2 (see page 201).

The Sold-Out Zone

The data in the matrix tells the master scheduler a good deal. Period 2 is in the sold-out zone. The master scheduler knows that 12 red options are required in this period (see actual demand line, period 2, Figure 8.4 on page 205). The master scheduler also knows that no red options are required in period 2 to support expected service demand (see forecast line, period 2, Figure 8.4). So the only open question is: How many additional red options will be required in period 2 to support any additional expected sales? The answer is straightforward: Zero! Since period 2 is in the sold-out zone, the master scheduler should not expect sales to book any more orders requiring a period 2 delivery. Now, can you imagine telling sales that they cannot commit any deliveries until period 4 (the first period in which product is available-to-promise)? But that's exactly what must be done—to a point.

This is a very key point in our discussion of two-level master scheduling. When top management determines a demand rate in the make-to-order environment, it is in a sense communicating to the master scheduler how many sets of common parts will be required, since there is a one-for-one relationship between a product family and common parts. If the demand rate for the conference center chair family is 20 in period 2 and all 20 have customer orders attached, there are no more common parts available in period 2 to satisfy additional orders. Therefore, any booked order that promises a period 2 delivery may be a bad promise unless something can be done to reschedule the booked demand.

Upon hearing that the company cannot take any more orders for delivery in period 2, sales may suggest that the master scheduler get 22 or 24 sets of common parts—a few extra just in case. If sales wants more than 20, however, it must get the participants in the sales and operations planning process to agree upon a demand rate that translates into a higher production rate. The master scheduler will then make preparations to have those extra sets of common parts ready to satisfy customer demand as booked by sales. However, there is no reason for the master scheduler to hedge any bets or second-guess the need for common parts. Common parts are not the planning problem in this environment; the planning problem is the unique parts (red and black option parts).

A company need not put an absolute freeze on orders. It may be good business sense to take and commit to a delivery inside the sold-out zone. However, there are no "free lunches" here, and sales must be asked, and must answer to, which currently booked order or orders scheduled for period 2 delivery are to be shipped later. The answer to this question establishes order priorities and tells the master scheduler how to reschedule delivery dates.

At this point the master scheduler knows that the expected demand for the option in question is the sum of the top three lines in the MPS matrix—the item forecast (independent demand), the option forecast (dependent demand), and actual demand (customer orders). Thus, in period 2, the total demand is 12 red options, since there is no service demand, no option forecast, and 12 committed to customers.

The Partially Sold-Out Zone

In the partially sold-out zone, total expected demand is not so easily identified. Here, some orders are in hand and others are anticipated by the forecast. The item forecast line states that no service demand is expected while the actual demand is for 7 red options in period 4 and 5 red options in period 6 (obtained through an order-entry process). The remaining question is: How many additional red options should be forecasted to satisfy anticipated demand in period 4 and period 6?

Here the master scheduler is faced with a range of alternatives. Period 4 is analyzed first:

1. *No chairs requiring the red option.* Even though red is a 50 percent option, the four chairs remaining to be sold in period 4 may not be red. Perhaps red has simply gone out of fashion. Or a sales

representative has just landed an order for 4 black conference center chairs and committed them to a period 4 delivery. The right answer in this case is 0.

2. *One chair requiring the red option.* Sales of 40 conference center chairs are anticipated for each month (periods 1 through 4 and periods 5 through 8), with a probability of 50 percent (20) being red. Actual demand for red chairs during the first month (periods 1 through 4) indicates that 19 red chairs have been sold to date and scheduled for delivery (12 in period 2 and 7 in period 4). Therefore, current sales information combined with historical knowledge make it plausible that only one more red chair will be sold and scheduled for delivery during the month. This logic assumes that the events that have already occurred in the month will have impact on events yet to occur.

3. *Two chairs requiring the red option.* A case can also be made that 2 of the 4 chairs (50 percent probability) still left to promise in period 4 will be red. The ATP in period 4 at the conference center chair level is 4 units. The important point here is that the master scheduler has 4 sets of common parts available-to-promise in that period. To build a chair, the company needs a set of common parts as well as the black or red option parts. Therefore, we expect a demand for only 4 more chairs in period 4.

If the red option has a 50 percent probability, the option forecast for that red option in period 4 is 2. This case proceeds from the notion that the probabilities for chair sales in periods 1, 2, and 3 are *independent* of the probabilities for chair sales in subsequent periods—just as the probability of a coin's turning up as heads is 50 percent, even though previous coin flips may have all been heads or all tails.

4. *Three chairs requiring the red option.* According to the established demand and production rate for the conference center chair family, 20 chairs are anticipated to be promised for delivery in period 4. Since the red option is a 50 percent option, we might have expected that 10 promised chairs for the period (50 percent of the aggregate 20) would require the red option. A review of the actual demand in period

4 for the red option shows that 7 chairs have already been committed, leaving 3 out of the next 4 to require this option. This logic assumes that the previous events in the order placing cycle affect future events.

5. *Four chairs requiring the red option.* Even though red is a 50 percent option, the 4 chairs remaining to be sold in period 4 may be all red. Perhaps red is a new “hot” color. Or a sales representative just landed an order for 4 red conference center chairs and committed them to a period 4 delivery. The right answer in this case is 4.

Master scheduling systems generally support three of the types of logic represented above—specifically, option forecasts in examples 2, 3, and 4. In example 2, the master scheduling system takes the aggregate production rate for a group of periods and explodes it through the planning bill; it then subtracts the actual demand for those periods to determine the option forecast. In example 3, the master scheduling system takes the available-to-promise value and explodes it through the planning bill, multiplying ATP by the probability associated with the option in question. In example 4, the master scheduling system takes the planned demand rate for the period and explodes it through the planning bill; it then subtracts the actual demand for that period to determine the option forecast.

The ATP approach is probably the most commonly used, and for that reason is the basis for the examples used in this book. Applying this logic, the forecast in period 4 for the red option is identified as 2. With this information, the master scheduler knows that 9 is the total expected demand for the red option in period 4—2 to support the option forecast, and 7 to support actual demand.

Continuing use of the ATP explosion logic, look at period 6, where 12 more conference center chairs are available-to-promise. If that ATP is exploded through the planning bill, a demand for 6 red options are identified in period 6. The same logic can be applied in period 8, where 20 conference center chairs are available-to-promise. Exploding that quantity through the planning bill results in a red option forecast of 10.

Regardless of the method chosen, the total demand for each of the master scheduled options must be determined before a master schedule that satisfies demand and stays within production plan constraints can be created.

Creating the Master Schedule in a Make-to-Order Environment

A make-to-order product is one finished *after* receipt of a customer order. Frequently, long lead-time components are planned prior to receipt of an order as a means of reducing delivery time to the customer. In cases in which options or other intermediates are stocked prior to order receipt, the terms "assemble-to-order" or "finish-to-order" are commonly used.

The master scheduler working in this environment needs to understand the shape of the company's backlog curve and which periods are sold out, partially sold out, or void of booked orders. The following sections analyze each of these zones in terms of the conference center chair used in this chapter.

The Sold-Out Zone

The first demand appears in period 2—when 12 red options are expected to be delivered to the finishing process (refer to Figure 8.4 on page 205). Here the question becomes, How many red options should be currently scheduled to be available in period 2? This question suggests three others:

1. What is the very *least* that should be scheduled?
2. What is the very *most* that should be scheduled?
3. What number will *most likely* satisfy demand?

The answer to the first question (the least) for period 2 is 12 because 12 customer orders are already booked and promised. If less than 12 are scheduled, a risk of missing a customer promise in period 2 is not only possible, but probable.

The answer to the next question—the *most* that should be scheduled—is, again, 12. This is the sold-out zone, and there are no more red options and common items to promise. The reason the ATP at the conference center chair product family level is 0 is that all 20 sets of common parts are committed—12 to red chairs and the other 8 to black chairs. "Theoretically that's fine," a master scheduler might argue, "but if sales has an opportunity to sell an additional conference center chair and commit it for delivery in period 2, can I really tell them not to take the order? After all, we're not in the business of turning away orders." No one wants to lose orders but consider the risk of committing it for delivery in period 2. Based on the S&OP process, top management has agreed that 20 conference center chairs should be promised for delivery in period 2. This decision has been made in consideration of capacities, materials, capital, marketplace presence, quality, and competition. Therefore, the master scheduler has planned to have 20 sets of common parts. Since every chair needs a set of common parts, selling more chairs than there are common parts is to make a bad promise. The sales force could, however, book and commit an additional order in the sold-out zone and shift a set of common parts from, say, a customer who ordered a black chair to a customer who ordered a red chair. Or sales could request the shifting of the common parts from one order to another, both for the same colored option. In either case, the parts in the options must be available before the shift can take place. But the fact that such a manipulation is possible is no basis for scheduling more than the anticipated volume of conference center chairs.

Now consider the converse situation—sales books only 18 orders, 2 *less* than the expected demand. Since a complete chair cannot be made from the 2 sets of uncommitted common parts, the master scheduler must either reschedule them out into the future, move something up earlier, produce something to stock, or place the individual completed common parts to inventory.

Finally, the third question—the number *most likely* to satisfy demand. Answer: The aggregate of the three demands. Figure 8.4 indicates an item forecast of 0, an option forecast of 0, and an actual demand of 12; the most likely demand is 12, and we should expect that 12 would be scheduled for receipt in period 2. Thus, an important rule in the make-to-order environment: **For a *pseudo*, the master schedule should equal the actual demand for all periods in the sold-out zone.** This rule makes master scheduling in the sold-out zone relatively easy compared to the partially sold-out zone, the next subject for discussion.

The Partially Sold-Out Zone

In the conference center chair example, the partially sold-out zone lies somewhere between periods 3 and 7 (refer to Figure 8.4 on page 205). Here, 4 chairs remain in period 4's available-to-promise, the first period in the partially sold-out zone. As a first step in determining how many to master schedule, again ask the three questions: What is the *least* that should be scheduled? What is the *most*? What number will *most likely* satisfy demand in the period?

The actual demand line for period 4 indicates that 7 red options are committed to customer orders, so the *very least* that should be scheduled is 7—enough to satisfy real customer demand. That covers the red chairs already sold, but how many more chairs requiring the red option could possibly be promised in this period? The answer is 4 because even though half of the remaining 4 required conference center chairs are predicted to be red, it is possible that *all* could be sold as red chairs. Therefore, the *most* that should be master scheduled in period 4 is 11 (the 7 already promised to customer orders and the 4 that *could* be so promised).

Finally, what is the *most likely* number of red options that could be scheduled to satisfy expected demand in period 4? Answer: 9. This is determined as follows:

1. There is 0 service demand.
2. Four more sets of common parts are available-to-promise; half of these are expected to go with the red option. Therefore 2 of the 4 expected demand should be red.

3. Seven orders for red chairs are already in hand and require the red option.

4. The most likely total demand is 9 (0 + 2 + 7).

Moving on to period 6, ask the three questions again. The answers are: the least that should be scheduled would be 5—the actual demand; the most that should be scheduled is the 5 that are committed plus the conference center chair ATP of 12, or 17; and the most likely number to satisfy demand is the sum of the three demand lines, or 11 (0 + 6 + 5). So the range for period 6 is between 5 and 17, with 11 the most likely (refer to Figure 8.4 on page 205).

The No-Orders Zone

The no-orders, or forecast, zone is by definition one in which (theoretically) no product configurations have been ordered and committed. With no orders in hand, and with the forecast as a sole guide, the master scheduler must nevertheless plan and schedule materials and capacities; and again, the three questions offer guidance. The period in question is period 8.

The *least* that could be scheduled is 0, since no actual demand exists. The *most* that should be scheduled is 20 (0 actual demand plus the 20 ATP from the product family). Here, the assumption is that every one of the conference center chair sales forecasted for delivery in period 8 would require the red option.

What about the *most likely* scenario for the red option. Here again, the answer is the sum of the three demand streams: the service demand of 0, the actual demand of 0, and the option forecast of 10. Thus, 10 is the *most likely* value. This scenario assumes 50 percent of the chairs sold requiring a period 8 delivery will have the red option.

So what should the master schedule for the red option be for periods 2, 4, 6, and 8?

- Period 2. It should have 12 red options scheduled for receipt—no more, no less. For a pseudo item like the red option, the master schedule should equal the actual demand in the sold-out zone.

• Period 4. We have already determined that in period 4 the *least* was 7, the *most* was 11, and the *most likely* was 9. Hold that thought for now, as the next section on overplanning will shed more light on what should be scheduled in this period.

• Period 6. This is similar to period 4 in that it is in the partially sold-out zone. For now, let's say the master schedule should have 11 in period 6—the most likely expected demand.

• Period 8. The master scheduler should adopt the *most likely* expected demand and schedule 10 units in this period.

Option Overplanning

As has been stressed so far, the more difficult issue is not coming up with a forecast for common parts, but with the forecast for the right mix of unique option-related parts. The question always remains, What are the chances that the actual sales will come in right on the forecast? Since the answer is invariably not very high, it may be necessary to protect the company and its ability to satisfy customer demand from possible forecast error.

One way to protect against forecast error is to provide safety stock for the items required to build a conference center chair. This could be expensive, and if the safety stock carried is forecasted wrong the company may pay for the error at least four times:

- In stocking parts not required by actual booked customer orders
- In lost sales because the wrong items were stocked and the company lacked the complete sets of parts to build entire products for shipment
- In stocked parts being broken, lost, stolen, or otherwise unavailable when needed

- In over stocking parts that are common to each product sold and thereby not needing forecast error protection

Alternately, a company could safety stock finished products to cover their bases. But that would be both impractical and expensive in terms of inventory, space, production, obsolescence risk, etc.[1]

A much better approach to protecting the plan from forecast error is "option overplanning," a technique that entails increasing the master schedule for unique options in the partially sold-out zone to provide protection against demand variation. To understand option overplanning, ask this question: When a customer places an order, when does he or she usually want delivery? In most cases, the answer is "yesterday," "as soon as possible," or "right now!"

Look again at the backlog curve for Soft Seat shown in Figure 8.3 on page 202. If a new customer order appears now, the earliest that delivery can be promised (if other orders and the master schedule are not manipulated) is the first period of the partially sold-out zone. This makes sense, since all production capacity and materials in the sold-out zone are already committed to customer orders.

In the Soft Seat example, the first unsold period is period 4, and that is where protection should be applied (refer to Figure 8.4 on page 205). But what should be protected? Earlier discussion suggests that no protection for common parts is needed since a one-for-one relationship exists within the product family. If 4 conference center chairs remain available-to-promise, then 4 sets of common parts should be available since the master schedule for common parts is set up to match expected demand. Again, the problem surfaces with respect to the *unique* items, the color options in our example.

From earlier discussion we know that the least number of red chairs that should be scheduled for period 4 is 7, the most is 11, and the most likely is 9. To provide 100 percent forecast-error protection to the first unsold period (period 4 in the example) we would schedule to match the *most* demand that could be received. In the case of the

[1] One wonders how often manufacturers have disassembled finished stock to retrieve common parts needed for the product configurations the customers actually wanted.

red option, that is 11. Thus, there would be adequate supply of red options to cover demand even if the forecast were 100 percent wrong.

Just exactly what does option overplanning buy a company?

- Option overplanning provides protection against demand variation in the first unsold period. It is in this period that the customer usually wants delivery.
- Option overplanning drives the material requirements planning system. MRP in turn tells planners and schedulers what must be done to satisfy the master schedule in *matched* sets of parts, ensuring that master scheduled items can be produced as promised.
- Option overplanning creates inventory *only* for components with a lead time greater than the backlog horizon. The benefit, of course, is the reduction of unneeded inventory (a company does not need safety inventory across the sold-out zone—the customer has told the company what they want).

Although overplanning is a powerful technique, it potentially creates inventory and must be used with caution; it must be managed in terms of quantities and dates. Overplanning also tends to move around, as we will observe later in this chapter. It must be managed and scheduled properly, usually in the first unsold period of the partially sold-out zone.

Calculating Projected Available Balance

Once the master schedule is created, the system will calculate the projected available balance (PAB). As shown in Figure 8.4 on page 205, there is a starting PAB of 0—not surprising, since the red option is a pseudo and, thus, cannot be built. Nor should it be surprising to see that PAB remains 0 through period 3 since this is a pseudo item. In creating the master schedule for these periods we said that the master schedule line must balance with the actual demand line. This done, the PAB will be 0.

In period 1 there is no activity, and in period 2 there are 12 units master scheduled against an equal total demand. Period 3 is 0 because there is no additional activity. Calculating period 4, 0 units are projected to be available at the end of period 3; these are added to the 11 master scheduled (expected receipts) resulting in a total supply of 11 against a total demand of 9. The difference of 2 represents the overplanned quantity.

As stated earlier, a pseudo cannot be built, but it can be master scheduled. And if a pseudo can be scheduled, it is possible that the projected available balance could be calculated to be a positive number. If this is so, as Figure 8.4 period 4 indicates, the system is telling us how much overplanning the master scheduler is doing. In this instance there are 2 extra sets of the items that make up the red option pseudo.

The projected available balance remains 2 in period 5, since there is no activity. In period 6, there are the 2 from period 5's PAB plus the 11 from the MPS line, minus total demand of 11, which again leaves 2. The same logic applies to periods 7 and 8.[2]

[2] Note: Overplanning is generally done in the first unsold period, although for various reasons (e.g., budget) the master scheduler may wish to spread the overplanning over the first few periods in the partially sold-out zone for forecast-inaccuracy protection. For example, since period 6 is still in the partially sold-out zone, the master scheduler could overplan and schedule up to a total of 17 units, the most red options that could be required to service customer needs in that period.

Calculating Available-to-Promise

In calculating the available-to-promise (ATP) quantity for the red option, we work backward from period 8. The first step is to take what is master scheduled and subtract the commitments (orders booked but not yet shipped).

The idea of ATP is to protect the company's promises to customers. A forecast is not a commitment, but rather a prediction or request for product; thus, forecasts are generally ignored in the ATP calculation. Working right to left starting in period 8, 10 red options are master scheduled, and 0 are committed (see actual demand line period 8), so the ATP is 10—a noncumulative value.

For period 6, 11 red options are master scheduled, and the actual demand is 5, leaving 6 available-to-promise in that period (noncumulative) to any incoming new orders. In period 4, the 11 master scheduled units have commitments against them of 7, resulting in 4 available-to-promise. For period 2, 12 units are master scheduled and 12 are committed, leaving an ATP of 0.

These ATP values are noncumulative. To calculate a cumulative value or carry over the values, simply add the ATP from each period working left to right. Why is this important? What if a customer calls and asks, How many red chairs can you give us by period 8? The answer is 20 (see ATP, period 8, cumulative value, Figure 8.4).

At this point, you would have a complete master schedule, not only for the red option but for the common parts and the other colors as well (see Figure 8.5 on pages 220–221); for simplicity the only other option color in the discussion is black. The next step in understanding the process is to actually commit an order using ATP.

Using ATP to Commit Customer Orders

In the next example, the customer has requested 10 conference center chairs to be delivered in period 6: of these, 9 are to be red and 1 black. Can this order be accepted? Use Figure 8.5 on the following pages to answer this question. Period 6 in the ATP line for the common parts indicates that 12 sets of common items are available-to-promise. In fact, a total of 16 sets of common parts are available-to-promise as shown on the cumulative ATP line. The cumulative ATP in period 6 of the red option schedule indicates that 10 sets of red option parts are available-to-sell. And 10 sets of black option parts are available through period 6, as the master schedule for that option makes clear. Thus, customer order entry, demand management, and the master scheduler know that the order *can* be taken.

Committing to customer orders always requires that two questions be asked. The first is: Can the order be taken? ATP provides the answer. The second question is: Do we want to take the order and commit to its delivery requirements? In other words, in this example is the company willing to sell 10 conference center chairs here and have only 6 left to sell for the next six periods of which only 1 can be red? This second question requires a management decision. If both questions are answered in the affirmative, the next step is to book the order.

First, look at period 6, the actual demand line, in the conference center chair family schedule (top of Figure 8.5). Currently it is 8, but with the new order of 10 it will become 18 (see Figure 8.6 on pages 222–223). The ATP of 12 will be reduced by 10, leaving an ATP of 2 for the same period and 6 cumulative. The same process is true for the common parts. Now, dropping down to the red option schedule for this same period, the actual demand of 5 in period 6 will increase by 9, to 14. The black option's actual demand in period 6 will increase by 1, to 4. The master scheduling system then recalculates

Figure 8.5 Complete Master Schedule for Chair Family, Common Parts, and Options

Conference Center Chair Product Family

MPS Matrix	Past Due	1	2	3	4	5	6	7	8	Total
Item Forecast			0		4		12		20	36
Option Forecast			0		0		0		0	0
Actual Demand			20		16		8		0	44
Total Demand			20		20		20		20	80
Projected Available Balance	0	0	0	0	0	0	0	0	0	0
Available-to-Promise		0	0 0	0	4 4	4	12 16	16	20 36	36
Master Schedule			20		20		20		20	80

Common Parts (100 percent probability)

MPS Matrix	Past Due	1	2	3	4	5	6	7	8	Total
Item Forecast			0		0		0		0	0
Option Forecast			0		4		12		20	36
Actual Demand			20		16		8		0	44
Total Demand			20		20		20		20	80
Projected Available Balance	0	0	0	0	0	0	0	0	0	0
Available-to-Promise		0	0 0	0	4 4	4	12 16	16	20 36	36
Master Schedule			20		20		20		20	80

Figure 8.5 (Continued)

Red Option (50 percent probability)

MPS Matrix	Past Due	1	2	3	4	5	6	7	8	Total
Item Forecast			0		0		0		0	0
Option Forecast			0		2		6		10	18
Actual Demand			12		7		5		0	24
Total Demand			12		9		11		10	42
Projected Available Balance	0	0	0	0	2	2	2	2	2	2
Available-to-Promise		0	0 0	0	4 4	4	6 10	10	10 20	20
Master Schedule			12		11		11		10	44

Black Option (50 percent probability)

MPS Matrix	Past Due	1	2	3	4	5	6	7	8	Total
Item Forecast			0		0		0		0	0
Option Forecast			0		2		6		10	18
Actual Demand			8		9		3		0	20
Total Demand			8		11		9		10	38
Projected Available Balance	0	0	0	0	1	1	2	2	2	2
Available-to-Promise		0	0 0	0	3 3	3	7 10	10	10 20	20
Master Schedule			8		12		10		10	40

Figure 8.6 Complete Master Schedule for Chair Family, Common Parts, and Options After Booking Order for 10 Chairs—9 Red and 1 Black

Conference Center Chair Product Family

MPS Matrix	Past Due	1	2	3	4	5	6	7	8	Total
Item Forecast			0		4		2		20	26
Option Forecast			0		0		0		0	0
Actual Demand			20		16		18		0	54
Total Demand			20		20		20		20	80
Projected Available Balance	0	0	0	0	0	0	0	0	0	0
Available-to-Promise		0	0 0	0	4 4	4	2 6	6	20 26	26
Master Schedule			20		20		20		20	80

Common Parts (100 percent probability)

MPS Matrix	Past Due	1	2	3	4	5	6	7	8	Total
Item Forecast			0		0		0		0	0
Option Forecast			0		4		2		20	26
Actual Demand			20		16		18		0	54
Total Demand			20		20		20		20	80
Projected Available Balance	0	0	0	0	0	0	0	0	0	0
Available-to-Promise		0	0 0	0	4 4	4	2 6	6	20 26	26
Master Schedule			20		20		20		20	80

Figure 8.6 (Continued)

Red Option (50 percent probability)

MPS Matrix	Past Due	1	2	3	4	5	6	7	8	Total
Item Forecast			0		0		0		0	0
Option Forecast			0		2		1		10	13
Actual Demand			12		7		14		0	33
Total Demand			12		9		15		10	46
Projected Available Balance	0	0	0	0	2	2	–2	–2	–2	–2
Available-to-Promise		0	0 0	0	1 1	1	0 1	1	10 11	11
Master Schedule			12		11		11		10	44

Black Option (50 percent probability)

MPS Matrix	Past Due	1	2	3	4	5	6	7	8	Total
Item Forecast			0		0		0		0	0
Option Forecast			0		2		1		10	13
Actual Demand			8		9		4		0	21
Total Demand			8		11		5		10	34
Projected Available Balance	0	0	0	0	1	1	6	6	6	6
Available-to-Promise		0	0 0	0	3 3	3	6 9	9	10 19	19
Master Schedule			8		12		10		10	40

the option forecast; it takes the ATP for the chair family, 2 in this case, and explodes it through the planning bill, applying the probability of 50 percent, leaving an option forecast of 1 for both red and black options. What we have just seen is the system automatically consuming the forecast at the option level.

Total demand for the red option increases to 15 in period 6, which is the total of 0 service forecast, an option forecast of 1, and 14 actual demand. The black option's total demand in period 6 is 5. To recalculate the red option ATP, we note that 9 additional red options have been booked, resulting in a total committed demand of 14 for that period (5 + 9). Since 11 units are master scheduled in period 6 and 14 have been committed, the resulting ATP is −3. Since an ATP of −3 does not make much sense for the red option, the ATP in period 6 will become 0 (the total master schedule in period 6 is consumed). To protect the entire commitment of the 9 additional units, the master scheduler must cover 3 more units of demand (the negative 3). The MPS line shows an MPS lot of 10 in period 8, but these units will be too late to commit to period 6. Working back in time, the master scheduler finds 4 available-to-promise in period 4. By using 3 of these units for period 6 coverage and taking them out of ATP, 1 red option set would remain available-to-promise in period 4. By working back into time, from period 6 to period 4, a master scheduler can use ATP to protect customer promises without committing current inventory any earlier than necessary. To complete the example for the red option, the cumulative ATP would then drop to 1 up through period 7, while period 8 would drop to 11. (Remember, we started with a total ATP of 20 red options and sold 9, leaving 11.) The same process would be done to complete the black option. The good news is that most master scheduling software does these mechanics for us, allowing the master scheduler to manage the data and the business situation.

Changes in Projected Available Balance

The projected available balance is also affected by the booking process. Periods 1 through 5 remain the same, since no activity occurred to change the total demand; the booking took place in period 6. Two red options were originally projected to be available at the end of period 5, due in part to overplanning. If these 2 are added to the master schedule of 11 in period 6, the result would be a projected available balance of 13 (11 + 2). The new red option total demand is 15 (1 option forecast, 14 actual demand), leaving a potential deficit of 2. Periods 7 and 8 also have a cumulative potential deficit of 2, since the master schedule in period 8 equals the total demand.

Returning to periods 4 and 6, 2 additional units over the current actual demand are expected to be required in period 4 and 1 in period 6 (option forecast line), yielding a total red option forecast of 3 through period 6. Look at the master schedule line in period 4. Remember that we overplanned the red option by 2. If that had not been done, then the ATP would have been 2 instead of 4, which means that we would not have been able to satisfy the customer's request for all the conference center chairs—only 8 red could have been committed. But because of the overplanning, we could commit to fulfilling the entire request, 9 red and 1 black.

Period 4 was overplanned by 2 units. At this point, 1 of the overplanned red options has been given up. In period 6, you have a projected deficit of 2. Remember the option forecast above of 3. If that 3 does not come in, then the projected available balance will be plus one. That plus one is the remaining overplanned red option. So you can take only 1 more red chair order through period 6, but not 3, unless an adjustment is made to the master schedule.

Option Overplanning in the Make-to-Stock Environment

Working in a make-to-stock environment forces the manufacturing company to build to a forecast so that product is available when the customer requests it. We have spent enough time discussing the fact that forecasts usually contain some degree of error. So, look at this situation. The sales and operations planning output calls for the company to build and deliver 100 products to the marketplace during a particular month. For discussion purposes, this product family has two items in it. Therefore, marketing must forecast the expected demand—let's say they forecast that 60 will be A units and 40 will be B units. Since this is a forecast, what are the chances of the sales force's bringing in orders that will perfectly match this expected demand? We should not be surprised if the answer is not very good!

If this fact is true, then the chance of the company's meeting the overall volume target is nil. If the company sells 61 units of A and 39 units of B, the total product that can be delivered on time is 99, assuming manufacturing built 60 A and 40 B. To protect itself from this condition, many manufacturing companies carry safety stock on A and B units (say they hold 10 extra A and 8 extra B). While this approach may work, it can be expensive. Is there another way? Sometimes a company may be able to provide forecast-error protection in the MTS environment by overplanning some of the unique items that make up the finished product.

Figure 8.7 is an example of a make-to-stock strategy being employed on products A and B. As the figure illustrates, product A is made from parts W and X and the 25 common components. Product B is made from parts Y and Z and 25 common components. In this example we will assume that a short finishing cycle exists, there is a

Figure 8.7 Make-to-Stock Product Structures for Stocked Parts A and B

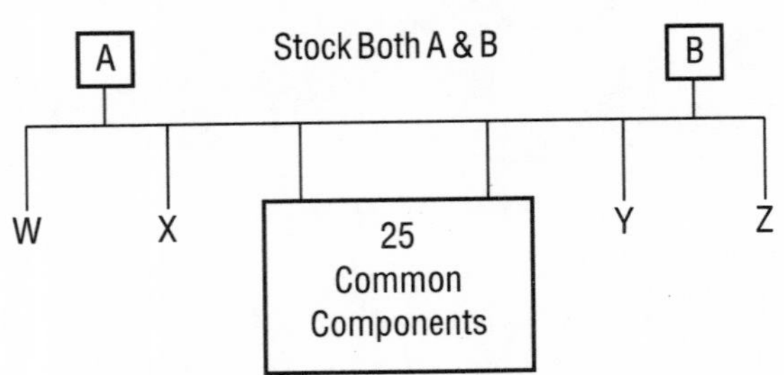

variable demand pattern, and unique items W, X, Y, and Z are used in other places. The master scheduler has decided to do some dependent overplanning and use the MRP system to overplan in matched sets of parts.

To do this, two planning bills are created—one for A's unique items and one for B's unique items. Figure 8.8 shows these simple planning bills with their option bills, identified as A-op and B-op. Both items are pseudos.

The next step is to create a master schedule for A option and B option equal to the overplanning desired. Since period 1 may be inside the finishing lead time, the overplanning in the example has been done in periods 2 and 3. The master scheduler has placed firm planned orders for A option in period 2 for 20 and in period 3 for 10. The B option has been scheduled for 15 receipts in period 2 and 5 receipts in period 3. The total overplanning is 50 sets for both periods. (Remember: We are overplanning only the unique items, W, X, Y, and Z.)

By creating the unique parts planning bills and master scheduling the A option and B option pseudos, the master scheduler has provided protection for expected forecast error in matched sets of parts. This is done by driving the material requirements planning system with the

Figure 8.8 Planning Bills for Unique Items in Product Structures A and B (A-op is A Option Bill and B-op is B Option Bill)

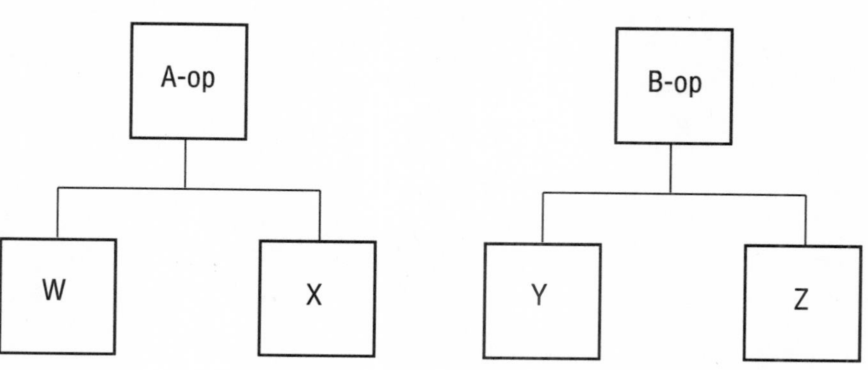

master schedule for A option and B option. Refer to Figure 8.9 to see how it actually works.

Products A and B are forecasted at the 60/40 split. Using these probabilities, 60 A are produced in periods 1, 2, and 3. At the same time, 40 B are produced in each period. Using the A-op schedule, 20 sets of items W and X are planned to be available in period 2, while 10 are scheduled to be available in period 3. Using B-op's master schedule, we expect 15 Y and Z to be available in period 2, and 5 more sets to be available in period 3. So, what has this bought the master scheduler? To answer this, let's ask the following questions: What is the maximum number of A that could be committed in period 2? What is the maximum number of B that could be committed in period 2? What is the maximum number of A that could be committed in period 3? What is the maximum number of B that could be committed in period 3?

Using Figure 8.9 to answer each question shows us the benefit of this overplanning technique. The maximum number of A that can be

Figure 8.9 Master Schedule for Products A, B, A-op, and B-op

A & B Family		100 Units/Period			
	1		2		3
A	60		60		60
B	40		40		40
Total	100		100		100
A-op	0		20		10
B-op	0		15		5
Total	0		35		15
A	60	(45)	(80)	(55)	(70)
B	40	(20)	(55)	(30)	(45)
Total	100		135		115

committed in period 2 is 80 (60 A and using the 20 A-op overplanning). However, if 80 A are committed in period 2 then only 20 B can be committed (a total of 100). The maximum number of B that can be committed in period 2 is 55 (40 B and using the 15 B-op overplanning). However, if 55 B are committed in period 2, only 45 A can be committed (a total of 100). This is true because we have only 100 sets of common parts—no overplanning has been done for those 25 items.

What does this really mean? Imagine going to sales and telling them that they had to create the perfect forecast or the company would not be able to achieve its overall plan. Or telling finance that a safety stock for all stocked items must be carried or the company would not be able to achieve its delivery plans. Finance might ask if inventory goals and targets are more important to the business than making money and a profit.

By employing the technique in the example, the master scheduler can respond in a different way. If sales brings in orders for A in period 2 somewhere between 45 and 80, and for B somewhere between 20 and 55, the company will be able to reach their goals. But remember, only 100 units (A and B together) can be sold because of the common parts constraint. Looking at period 3, if A orders are somewhere between 55 and 70, and B orders are between 30 and 45, the plan can be achieved. By using this overplanning technique, a wide range of possibilities will now satisfy management's plan. And it didn't cost the master scheduler or the company a great amount of time or money.

Master Scheduling in Make-to-Order and Make-to-Stock Environments: A Comparison

Make-to-stock companies generally master schedule at the end item level. By contrast, the make-to-order environment calls for master scheduling below the end item level, often working with pseudo bills-of-material to manage hundreds of options.

Another difference is that make-to-stock transactions are often simpler—the customer wants a standard electric switch box, and the manufacturer simply pulls one out of finished-goods inventory. Transactions in the make-to-order environment, though, are more complex in that several actions must take place. First, the customer must indicate product specifications and a desired delivery date. Second, the manufacturer must match the desired specifications and delivery date with the requisite common and unique parts. Third, the order must be booked identifying the demand date for all the unique items plus the common parts. Finally, the timing of production and meeting promised deliveries must be coordinated through the master scheduling and finishing functions.

To ensure customer satisfaction in the MTS environment (where immediate or near immediate delivery is required), conventional statistical techniques are used to analyze desired customer service levels and compute how much safety stock should be carried for each end item being master scheduled. But in a make-to-order environment, it doesn't make sense to stock completed items, since the final configurations required by customers will be unknown until the order appears. Trying to safety stock individual parts is also impractical. How do you decide which items need safety stock, in what quantities, etc., when literally thousands of unique products are made by a single company? Therefore, techniques such as option overplanning in the first unsold period should be used.

Yet another difference concerns finishing schedules (to be discussed in depth in chapter 11). In the MTS world, finished products are usually built to a forecast using available capacity. In an MTO environment the customer order must precede the finishing or final assembly process. Moreover, information in the customer order must be communicated to the manufacturing floor; all the required items listed on the pseudo bills-of-material must be sent to the right operation on the finishing line at the right time. In addition, process instructions detailing the configured customer order must be developed. In short, planning and scheduling in the MTO environment is a lot tougher than simply building a red conference center chair and placing it on the shelf.

In regards to the bills-of-material being used, make-to-stock companies use standard engineering BOMs for the entire planning, scheduling, and building phases. In a make-to-order environment, though, standard BOMs are not universally used, at least at the upper levels. Instead, planning and pseudo bills are common. Many times in an MTO environment, a conventional bill is restructured into a planning bill, possibly several levels down, based on the competition's lead time, the company's cumulative lead time, the company's willingness to invest in inventory, and the capacity needed to finish the order to a customer specification. This restructuring is done for three reasons: first, to allow a company to master schedule the fewest number of items; second, to give marketing and sales a better chance at creating an accurate forecast (the accuracy of the forecast will always be better at the aggregate level than at the detail level); third, by separating the common items from the unique items, option overplanning can be applied to just the unique items, thus reducing the inventory carried as protection against demand variability.

Most of the discussion in this chapter concerns itself with the mechanics of two-level master scheduling and how the planning bill is used to assist the master scheduler in forecasting demand at the MPS second level. It also has dealt with the logic used to create the master schedule, and how and when and where to use option overplanning. With the knowledge of two-level master scheduling, we are now ready to return to the job of the master scheduler and scheduling in make-to-order environments.

The next chapter follows the same format as chapter 5, which presented situations for the master scheduler to analyze along with information screens to use in drawing conclusions. The goal of the chapter is not to provide a set of "right" answers, but rather an understanding of the job of master scheduling in the make-to-order and option-planning environments.

9

Using MPS Output in a Make-to-Order Environment

In the absence of facts, arguments will persist.

This chapter considers how the master scheduler working in a make-to-order (MTO) environment uses the information presented by the MPS system. Special attention is given to the following:

- Differences in the information used in make-to-stock (MTS) and make-to-order environments
- Using the planning bill to generate forecasts for master scheduled items
- Balancing the master schedule to the actual demand for pseudo items
- How available-to-promise (ATP) information and forecast consumption are handled
- Overplanning at the option level in the partially sold-out zone
- Action messages supplied by the system and how the master scheduler may respond to them

To maintain continuity, this chapter uses the winch example introduced in chapter 5. Figure 9.1 describes the three winch models WA01, WA04, and WA06, listing all major components. The matrix used here is a helpful way of identifying what is common and what is

Figure 9.1 Winch Product Comparison

		WAO1	WAO4	WAO6	Characteristic
A100	Carriage Assm.	1	1	1	Common
C100	2000# Cable Assm.	1			
C101	4000# Cable Assm.		1		
C102	6000# Cable Assm.			1	Unique
D100	Drum - 50', 1/4" Cable, 1"	1			
D102	Drum - 50', 3/8" Cable, 1.5"		1		
D103	Drum - 50', 1/2" Cable, 1.5"			1	Unique
G102	Gearbox 4 FPM, 1" Shaft	1	1	1	
M100	5 HP Motor	1			
M103	8 HP Motor		1		
M105	10 HP Motor			1	Unique
P100	Pendant Assm.	1	1	1	Common
S100	Shaft, 1" x 24"	1			
S101	Shaft, 1.5" x 24"		1	1	Unique
	Lift Speed (feet per minute)	4	4	4	
	Capacity (in thousand pounds)	1	4	6	

unique in the product family. Notice the A100 carriage assembly and the P100 pendant assembly are common to all three winches. These winches have the same lift speed—4 feet per minute (fpm)—but vary as to lift capacity (1,000, 4,000, and 6,000 pounds). The G102 gearbox is a common part as long as the lift speeds remain at 4 fpm. However, this has changed as described in the next paragraph.

Using Planning Bills to Simplify Option Scheduling

Assume for a moment that management of the company producing the winch wants to expand its offerings. Instead of offering just 3 winches with the same lift speed, the company will offer winches that operate at 4, 6, and 10 feet per minute. In addition, winches with 2,000, 3,000, and 5,000 pound (#) capacities will be added to the product line. Thus, the company will make available winches with three different lift speeds and six different capacities—18 different configurations instead of the previous 3.[1]

The company's decision to expand its winch product family means that master scheduling at the end item will be significantly expanded and made more complex. To simplify matters, the company has decided to create a planning bill-of-material for the winch family (WXYY) that contains both a common parts bill (A100 and P100) and various option bills for the different capacities and lift speeds (1,000#, 2,000#, 3,000#, 4,000#, 5,000#, 6,000#, 4 fpm, 6 fpm, and 10 fpm). With the planning bill structure in place, marketing and sales provided the probability of sales for each of the various options.

[1] Here we make the assumption that all of the gear boxes work with any of the capacity options.

This winch family planning BOM with the best estimate for each of the various options is shown in Figure 9.2.

The planning bill thus reflects all options as well as common parts.

Figure 9.2 Winch Product Family Planning Bill-of-Materials

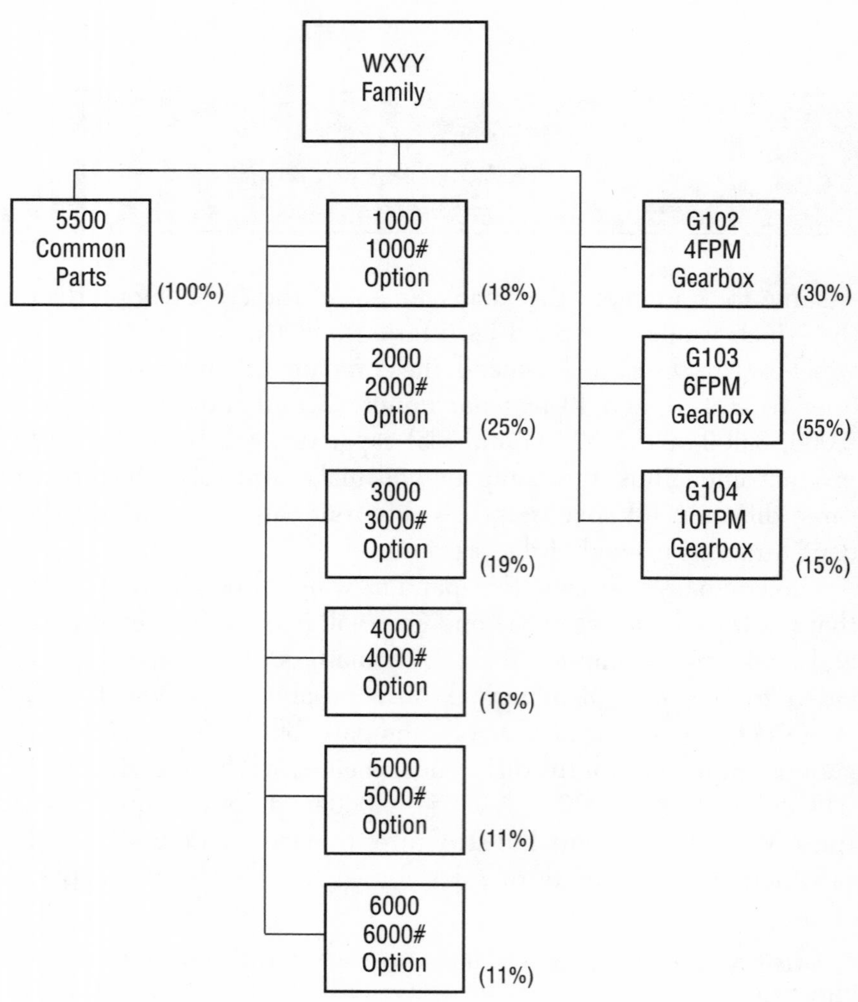

This bill makes it possible to cut out 45 percent of the otherwise master scheduled items, reducing their numbers from 18 to 10. The 10 items are the common parts (1), capacity options (6), and lift speed gearboxes (3).

The chapters on planning bills and master scheduling in the make-to-order environment show that master scheduling is done at the option or feature level, and not at the level of the end item. Applying this logic, the master scheduler for the winch product family does the same, dropping down one level to get better control, ease the job of forecasting, add flexibility in manufacturing, and better serve the customer.

The Scheduling Process

In the example, the winch family's common parts and various capacity option bills are all pseudos—i.e., artificial groupings of parts that can be scheduled, but not built. The gearboxes are purchased subassemblies and therefore *not* pseudos. Since the gearboxes are purchased complete, the common parts bill contains only common parts from the capacity options (no common parts between the various gearboxes are included). If the gearboxes were manufactured, an opportunity to add the common parts in the gearboxes to the common parts bill would exist, and the company should seize the opportunity.

Time-Phased BOMs

Once structured, the planning bill for the common parts as well as each of the capacity options can be time-phased. Time-phasing the master scheduled items simply means that each item is exploded into its underlying raw materials, components, subassemblies, and assemblies, and the length of time required for material procurement, manufacturing, and assembly is noted. Time-phased bills-of-material for the common parts and for one of the capacity options (3,000#) are shown in Figures 9.3 and 9.4 respectively. (Refer to chapter 5 for details on creating time-phased bills.)

The figures indicate a cumulative lead time for the common parts and options as sixteen weeks, with the greatest lead time component being the housing casting (1200C) in the common parts and the drum casting (D101C) in the 3000# option bill. Figure 9.3 indicates that two major assemblies make up the common parts: the A100 carriage assembly and the P100 pendant assembly. The A100 is itself made from part 1000 (an axle), part 1100 (a 6-inch wheel), and part 1200 (a housing). Figure 9.4 shows that the capacity option is also made up of two major assemblies, a 7 horsepower motor (M102) and a winding assembly (3001).

For purposes of illustration, assume that manufacturing has added the winding assembly (3001) to increase efficiency in production. This winding assembly includes a ⅜–1″ drum, a shaft, and a cable assembly. Grouping and assembling parts into subassemblies is often done for purposes of efficiency, control, and manufacturing flexibility. These subassemblies can either be built and placed in stock or remain on the shop floor for immediate consumption by a parent assembly. In the later case, the subassembly is commonly referred to as a "phantom" assembly—i.e., an assembly that is real, but not planned to be stocked.

In the example, the 3001 winding assembly is actually a produced item. This not only creates greater efficiencies but allows for the creation of a modular subassembly. The same logic can be used in the other capacity option bills. Such time-phased bills can help the master scheduler determine which parts will be affected by a process change. For example, if a change were to be made nine weeks prior to shipment, the time-phased planning bill would make it possible for the master scheduler to quickly identify the several affected parts. Thus, among the common parts in Figure 9.3, the hard steel and housing casting would be affected. In the 3,000# option in Figure 9.4 the motor, drum casting, hard steel, ⅜″ cable, and hook are affected.

Figure 9.3 Time-Phased Common Parts Planning Bill-of-Material

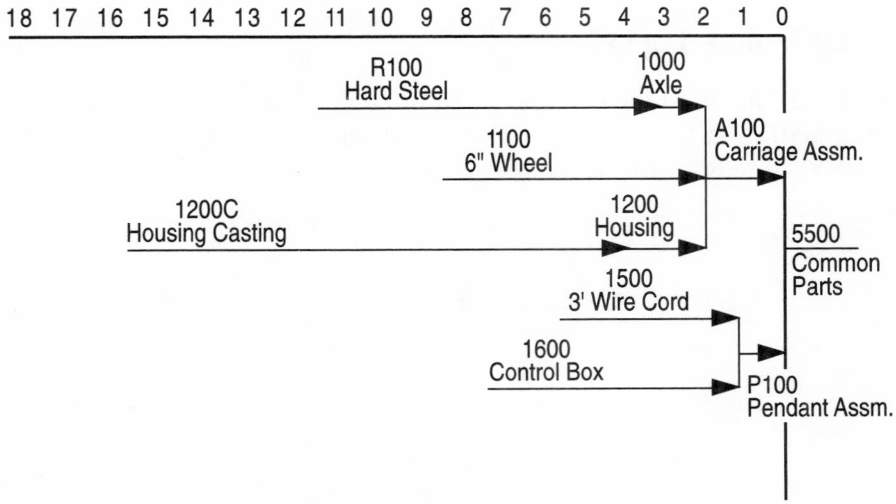

Figure 9.4 Time-Phased 3000# Option Planning Bill-of-Material

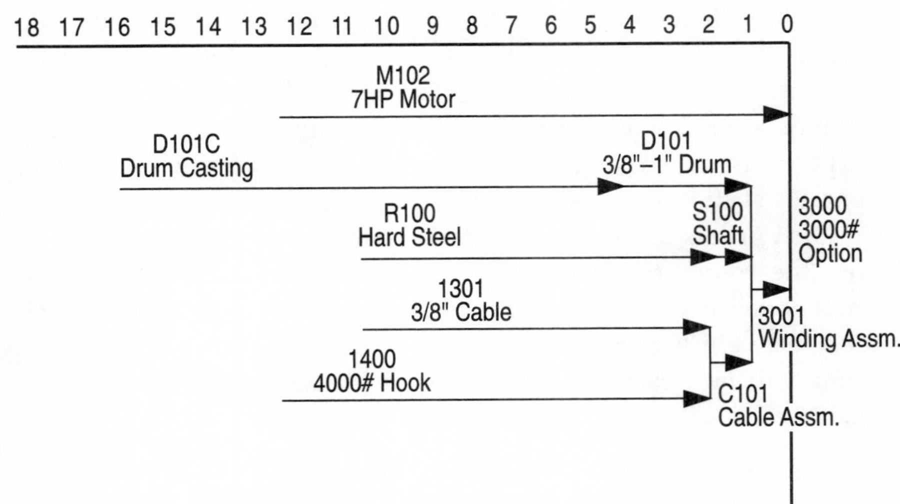

Part Numbering System

To continue with the example, assume that a significant part numbering system is being used at the end-item level.[2] Now consider the WXYY family in terms of its significant part number system, as described in Figure 9.5.

Figure 9.5 Significant Part Numbering System (WXYY)

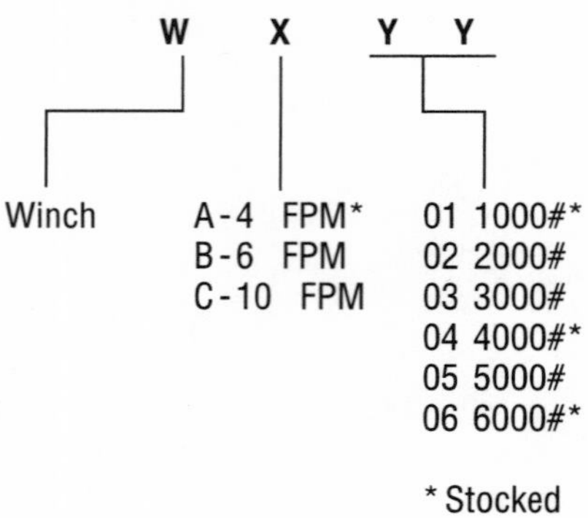

The first character defines the product family (W = winches); the second character defines the lift speed; and the last two define capacity. With 18 possible configurations to deal with, this significant part number approach is useful in sales planning and for order-entry purposes. In such a case, the sale of a WC05 would mean a winch that operates at 10 fpm and lifts up to 5,000 pounds.

When orders are received in this environment, the customer defines the configuration required, the number of units needed, and product delivery date. For example, the customer order–entry screen reproduced in Figure 9.6 indicates that the customer has ordered 2 6-fpm winches, each with 3,000-pound lift capacity, for delivery on October 14.

[2] This is not a recommendation, but is simply used here for illustration purposes. Some companies use product configurations driven by a significant part numbering scheme for entering customer order requirements.

Figure 9.6 Customer Order-Entry Screen

Order#	Customer Name	Credit
C3456	Liftum-High Machine Tool	S

Line	Item	Descripticon	Qty. Req'd	Date Req'd
1	WB03	3000#, 6 FPM Winch	2	10/14
2	5500	Common Parts	2	10/14
3	3000	3000# Option	2	10/14
4	G103	6 FPM Gearbox	2	10/7

To satisfy this particular customer order, the master scheduler needs the following:

- Two sets of common parts
- Two sets of 3,000# option parts
- Two 6-fpm gearboxes

With this background for the winch example, attention can be turned to using the MPS data to make decisions in the make-to-, assemble-to-, and finish-to-order environments, starting with the common parts.

The Common Parts Master Schedule

Figure 9.7 on pages 242–243 is the master schedule for the common parts (5500) used in the winch. This is typical of the MPS screen formats produced by contemporary software programs.

Figure 9.7 Master Schedule Screen, Common Parts

Part Number	Primary Description	Item Status	Product Family	Master Scheduler	Forecast Source
5500	COMMON PARTS	PSDO	WXYY	PROUD	PLANBL

Balance On Hand	Lot Size		Safety Stock		Time Fence			Lead Time	Cuml. Lead Time	Stnd. Cost
	1	2	Policy	Factor	1	2	3			
0	LFL		NO		P-13	C-12		1	16	

Period	Past Due	10/13	10/20	10/27	11/03	11/10	11/17
Item Forecast							
Option Forecast		10	0	265	370	400	400
Actual Demand		385	405	135	30		
Proj. Available Balance	0	5	0	0	0	0	0
Available-to-Promise		10	0	265	370	400	400
Master Schedule		400	400	400	400	400	400

Period	1/12	1/19	1/26	2/02	2/09	2/16	2/23
Item Forecast	P						
Option Forecast	440 P	440	440	440	440	440	440
Actual Demand	P						
Proj. Available Balance	0 P	0	0	0	0	0	0
Available-to-Promise	430 P	440	440	440	440	440	440
Master Schedule	430 P	440	440	440	440	440	440

Period	4/13						
Item Forecast							
Option Forecast	440						
Actual Demand							
Proj. Available Balance	0						
Available-to-Promise	440						
Master Schedule	440						

Master Schedule Detail

Req'd Date	Order Number	Lot No.	Order Qty.	Order Type	Order Status	Recom. Action	Req'd Date	Order Quantity
10/13	5500	413	400	MPS	FIRM		10/13	35
10/20	5500	414	400	MPS	FIRM		10/13	60
10/27	5500	415	400	MPS	FIRM		10/13	45
11/03	5500	416	400	MPS	FIRM		10/13	25
11/10	5500	417	400	MPS	FIRM		10/13	15
11/17	5500	418	400	MPS	FIRM		10/13	40
11/24	5500	419	400	MPS	FIRM		10/13	14
12/01	5500	420	400	MPS	FIRM		10/13	70
12/08	5500	421	420	MPS	FIRM		10/13	20
12/15	5500	422	420	MPS	FIRM		10/13	36
12/22	5500	423	420	MPS	FIRM		10/13	25
1/05	5500	424	430	MPS	FIRM		10/20	40
1/12	5500	425	430	MPS	FIRM		10/20	50
1/19	5500		440			PLAN	10/20	10
							10/20	60

Forecast Consumption	Resource Profile	Critical Resources							
		Res.	Qty.	Res.	Qty.	Res.	Qty.	Res.	Qty.
PLANBL	WXYY	MCH	6.0	SUB	3.5	ASSM	10.0	KIT	1.0

Selling Price	Special Instructions	Date Run	Action Recommended		
	SAFETY-HSING CAST	XX-XX-XX	PLAN		

11/24	12/01	12/08	12/15	12/22	1/05	Period
					C	Item Forecast
400	400	400	400	400	400 C	Option Forecast
					80 C	Actual Demand
0	0	20	40	60	10 C	Proj. Available Balance
400	400	420	420	420	350 C	Available-to-Promise
400	400	420	420	420	430 C	Master Schedule

3/02	3/09	3/16	3/23	3/30	4/06	Period
						Item Forecast
440	440	440	440	440	440	Option Forecast
						Actual Demand
0	0	0	0	0	0	Proj. Available Balance
440	440	440	440	440	440	Available-to-Promise
440	440	440	440	440	440	Master Schedule

						Period
						Item Forecast
						Option Forecast
						Actual Demand
						Proj. Available Balance
						Available-to-Promise
						Master Schedule

Actual Demand Detail

Refer. Number	Order Number	T	S	C	Req'd Date	Order Quantity	Refer. Number	Order Number	T	S	C
MAIN MFG	C1759	A	R		10/20	30	TORO MFG	C1819	A	F	
WA01	M0814	F	R		10/20	15	GEN ELEC	C1825	A	F	
WA04	M0815	F	R		10/20	5	ALLIS CHAM	C1831	A	F	
WA06	M0816	F	R		10/20	10	TRW	C1832	A	F	
ALLEN MFG	C1802	A	R		10/20	50	XEROX	C1829	A	F	
WC02	M0817	F	R		10/20	35	GEN DYN	C1830	A	F	
SALEM CO	C1746	A	R		10/20	100	FORD MR	C1849	A	F	
WHITE MFG	C1811	A	R		10/27	60	WA01	M0820	F	F	
GEN MTRS	C1814	A	R		10/27	40	AMER MTR	C1835	A	F	
AMF	C1815	A	R		10/27	10	DUKE PWR	C1837	A	F	
SHELL OIL	C1821	A	R		10/27	25	NORTH TEL	C1841	A	F	
DUPONT	C1823	A	R		11/03	30	CUTL HAM	C1856	A	F	
WC04	M0818	F	R		1/05	80	AT&T	C1801	A	F	A
PULLMAN	C1824	A	F								
WA06	M0819	F	F								

The screen format is divided into several major sections: item information; planning horizon summaries of supply and demand; and detail data sections containing information on requirements and replenishment order status, action messages, and various reference data. The MPS screen summarizes critical details used by the master scheduler in managing and timing supply and demand. These screen formats are the same as those used in chapter 5. Here it would be useful to highlight some of data that makes this particular screen unique to a make-to-order scenario.

Item Information Section

This section of the MPS screen contains background information about the item being scheduled: part number, part description, product family, etc. It also contains information specific to the item that helps the master scheduler to properly manage the item's progress through production: lot size, lead time, the position of planning time fences, and so forth.

In chapter 5, the *item status* on the winches was "STK" (stock). In this case the common parts bill is a pseudo; thus its item status is "PSDO." Under *forecast source* and *forecast consumption*, the screen notes "PLANBL" for planning bill. This means that the forecast source (identified as "judgment" in chapter 5) is the planning bill, and the items in the planning bill are forecasted automatically. Also, the forecast is automatically consumed using the planning bill. The technique used to consume the forecast is to explode the available-to-promise quantities through the percentages that reside in the planning bill, as explained in the previous chapter.

On the next information line, the *balance on hand* is 0, which is not surprising since a pseudo cannot be built or stocked. As for *lot size*, discrete lot sizing rules are applied to pseudos; therefore, lot-for-lot ("LFL") is used in the example. Also, since a pseudo cannot be stocked, it should have no *safety stock* indicated.

The *lead time* one level down is set to 1 (week in the example), while the *cumulative lead time* is 16 (the time required to pull together all the common parts from scratch). To shorten that lead time the master scheduler has chosen to safety stock the housing casting, which in the time-phased BOM was shown to be the long lead-time item. He or she is reminded of this decision by the text under *special instructions*. By safety stocking the housing, its contribution to cumulative lead time is effectively reduced and the manufacturer is able to deliver the common parts 4 periods sooner. This explains why the planning *time fence* may be set at 13 periods, which is inside the cumulative lead time of 16 periods. Of course, there is no reason why the master scheduler could not set the planning time fence at 12 periods. It also could be set at 14 periods. The setting of the planning time fence does not need to line up exactly with the cumulative lead time or any other lead time.

Planning Horizons Section

This section of the screen contains the supply-and-demand information needed to manage the master schedule. In contrast to the screens in chapter 5, booked orders are summarized on the actual demand line by period. In addition to showing actual demand, the screen provides the available-to-promise quantity described in chapter 8. Thus, for period 10/13, there are booked orders needing 385 sets of common parts.

The master scheduler has placed two time fences in this example, a capacity fence set at the end of week 1/05, and a planning time fence at the end of the following period. The capacity time fence is a memo-type time fence indicating that it is difficult to make capacity adjustments within the fence. The planning time fence is used to control computer behavior; all master scheduled orders within the planning time fence are controlled by the master scheduler, while those outside the fence are generally controlled by the computer.

Detail Data Section

The bottom portion of this screen contains two separate categories of information—both generated by the MPS software system using data from various order files—i.e., manufacturing and purchase orders on the supply side, and customer and stocked orders on the demand side.

The first category of information is the *master schedule detail*, which identifies the released as well as the firm planned orders already placed, along with their respective identification numbers (lot) and required dates. The MPS detail section also includes a column for *recommended action*. In the case of the last supply order (required date 1/19), the recommended action is "PLAN," or "it is time to convert the computer planned order in question into a firm planned order."

The section labeled *actual demand detail* indicates the source of demand on the line of that name in the planning horizon summaries. This section calls out required date, quantity ordered, order reference number, and order number.

Analyzing the Detail Data

With the general sections of the MPS screen understood, we consider the finer details. Begin with the planning horizon in the 10/13 column. In the MPS line of that period, the master schedule shows a firm planned order for 400 sets of common parts ready to be applied to customer orders. That was the plan, but a review of the plan for this period indicates actual demand is for only 385 sets of common parts.

Eleven separate customer orders, each listed individually in the actual demand detail section of the screen, are the source of this demand. For example, on 10/13 there is an order for 35 units for "Main Mfg" (customer order C1759). The "A" in the *T* column indicates that the unit is assemble-to-order. The order beneath this indicates a quantity of 60 units required on 10/13. This requirement has a reference number—WA01—which is not the name of a customer, but one of the company's own product numbers. In this case the master scheduler has committed 60 sets of common parts to a finished-goods order. (In addition to building and configuring to customer orders, the master scheduler may at times choose to build popular configurations to stock.)

"M0814" indicates that the order is a manufacturing order rather than a customer order. The "F" next to it indicates that the product is being built for finished goods. Thus, the master scheduler is building to order as well as to stock.

Determining ATP. Since the 11 lines of detail demand summarize to the 385 shown in period 10/13's actual demand, the available-to-promise quantity for this period can be calculated by subtracting actual demand for the period from the 400 sets of common parts scheduled to be due in 10/13, yielding an ATP of 15 units.

Oddly, the screen shows an ATP in period 10/13 of only 10, which is explained as follows. Looking ahead to period 10/20, we can see that the master scheduler has planned for another 400 sets of common parts to be available. Since actual demand for that period is 405 (5 over the amount master scheduled), the need for common parts in that period is overbooked by 5 units. To ensure the company's ability to satisfy each customer promise, the master scheduler plans to use 5 sets of the 10/13 period common parts' surplus to cover the 10/20 overbooking. As a result, the ATP in 10/13 is reduced by 5, resulting in the indicated ATP of 10.

ATP and the Sold-Out Zone. Periods 10/13 and 10/20 are in the sold-out zone, meaning that no more customer orders are expected. This zone is sold out even though 10 units are still available-to-promise. To understand this, ask the question: Will sales be bringing in a last-minute order? If the answer is yes, it's time for sales to define the configuration needed. Remember, we're talking about the current period. If sales does not have an order, the master scheduler must take other action.

What is to be done with the 10 sets of common parts available-to-promise in period 10/13? If no action is taken by the master scheduler, and if no customer orders appear at the beginning of the period, then there will be 10 sets of common parts for which there is no home.

Balancing the Sold-Out Zone for Common Parts

As period 10/13 begins, the master scheduler must ask, What are the chances of an order coming in the door with a delivery time of one period or less? To make good on such an order, the order must appear right away, and the winch configuration must be known. If an order for 10 winches magically appeared, the excess common parts problem would go away, as the order would consume the option forecast and planned production (ATP would become zero). More likely than not, an order will not appear just in time to solve the master scheduler's common parts problem, and the company will face two undesirable realities, that of 1) having the capacity to assemble 10 winches that will remain idle, and 2) carrying inventory of all items in the common parts bill. Neither of these is satisfactory from the company's point of view, but what alternatives are available?

The master scheduler has four alternatives for meeting the challenge presented in the example's sold-out zone. The first alternative is to look into the future and see if any customer order can be moved up. For instance, the actual demand detail section in Figure 9.7 (see page 243) indicates a customer order of exactly 10 units (TRW, order number C1832) required for delivery in period 10/20. Perhaps this customer would be agreeable to taking early delivery, making it possible to pull that 10-unit order into period 10/13. But first the master scheduler must determine which capacity options and gearboxes that customer has requested, and examine the various option screens to make sure that those options are also available in 10/13.

This alternative would solve only the current period issue—not the sold-out zone problem. Available capacity would be shifted out to period 10/20. So, the master scheduler should look beyond the sold-out zone for other possible orders to move up. In this case, the entry for Duke Power in period 10/27 is a possible candidate. The Duke Power order of 10 units is scheduled for the first period of the partially sold-out zone. If this order can be pulled into either the 10/13 or 10/20 period (the sold-out zone), the problem of losing the capacity in that zone can be solved. But first, the master scheduler must look up Duke Power's customer order (C1837) and find out which capacity options and gearboxes go with it, then check the master schedule for those options to be sure that the needed materials are or will be available.

The second alternative is to split a customer order into multiple deliveries. There are some large orders in period 10/27 and further out that might be split up—some to be produced with the capacity available in the sold-out zone and the remainder to be produced in the originally scheduled period. The order of 40 units for American Meter, for example, might be broken into 10 and 30, with 10 units moved into period 10/13 and the remaining 30 staying where they are. It might be better from a business sense to produce the 10 early and hold them as inventory than to lose the capacity. Of course, the customer should be given the opportunity to accept an earlier delivery; the earlier delivery would be the best of both worlds for the company, allowing it to build earlier yet not carry the inventory.

Instead of getting the demand to match the master schedule, a third alternative is to decrease the master schedule so that it equals the actual demand. In this example, the total of the master schedule for the sold-out zone must be 790 (385 for the demand in period 10/13 and 405 for the demand in period 10/20). The perfectly balanced schedule would require reducing the lot of 400 in period 10/13 to 385, and increasing the master schedule in period 10/20 to 405. This would mean that 5 sets of common parts would be rescheduled into 10/20 and 10 sets would be rescheduled into some period beyond 10/20.

The fourth alternative is to build some popular configuration to stock. As already discussed, the winch company seems to do this. Look at the actual demand detail: You see WA01, WA04, WA06 winches being built on manufacturing orders for finished goods. The master scheduler should analyze the options to determine what material is available. That information and consultation with sales, marketing, demand management, manufacturing, and finance should lead to a decision and possibly production authorization with respect to the inventoried configuration.

Handling Abnormal Demand

With the immediate problem of cleaning up the sold-out zone (reducing the ATP to 0) taken care of, the master scheduler must look further into the future to determine what else needs to be done. For the company represented in the Figure 9.7 screen, the future planning zone for common parts 5500 begins 11/10 and continues to the end of the horizon. Normally, this zone contains no orders. But in this case, an order for 80 sets of common parts exist in period 1/05 of the planning horizon. This order is from a customer with whom the company normally does no business, which means that it represents "abnormal demand." Abnormal demands are comprised of orders not anticipated by the regular sales forecast. In this case, sales/customer service has indicated that the order for 80 units represents abnormal demand (code "A") in the detail section.

Period 1/05 contains an option forecast of 400 units and actual demand (known to be abnormal) of 80. Since we know that abnormal demand is not part of the forecast, some adjustment to the master schedule must be made to ensure that an extra 80 sets of common parts are available to satisfy that abnormal demand. The master scheduler has, in this example, already made that adjustment. The Figure 9.7 screen indicates that by period 1/05, 90 more units are scheduled than are forecasted. This was done by increasing the master schedule by 20 units in periods 12/08, 12/15, and 12/22 and again by 30 in period 1/05. The master scheduler has decided to get the common parts ready early, thus ensuring that sufficient common parts are available to handle the abnormal demand.

But the abnormal demand is only 80; why the 10 extra units? The answer is that the forecast for period 1/12 jumps abruptly from the typical 400 to 440. By increasing the MPS schedule in period 1/05 to 430 and holding it through 1/12 (stabilizing the MPS and using small, incremental adjustments), the expected demand orders can be satisfied.

The buildup thus helps solve the abnormal demand issue and in addition helps to solve the expected increased demand in the forecast. In planning the buildup over the six periods in question, the master scheduler would have returned to the time-phased BOM for the common parts (Figure 9.3, page 239) to make sure of the availability of materials. So, starting with period 12/08, when the MPS amount increases to 420, the master scheduler would have to check the R100 hard steel and the 1200C housing casting. The beauty of the time-phased BOM is that the master scheduler can instantly determine the parts that are impacted by the change in the schedule.

To review how the master scheduling system handles abnormal demand, look at period 12/22, where there is a projected available balance of 60. The master scheduler has arranged for an additional 430 sets of common parts to be available in period 1/05, making a total of 490 sets of common parts available (60 + 430 master scheduled = 490). With a forecast demand of 400, 90 will be left over. Since the 80 is abnormal demand—and not considered part of the forecast—it is also subtracted from the remaining 90, leaving a projected available balance of 10.

Action Messages

As the master scheduler looks further into the horizon, he or she observes in period 1/19 a computer planned order of 440 and in the master schedule detail section a recommendation to convert that computer planned order to a firm planned order. The reason for the recommendation stems from the fact that 1/19 is the first period outside the planning time fence. Therefore, the master scheduler should convert this CPO to a FPO, so that the 440 shows up inside the planning time fence the next time the master scheduling system is run.

At the end of the current period, 10/13, we would expect the 385 units to be shipped and all subsequent periods to shift to the left. But at this point, the 440 is still a computer planned order, and the master scheduler needs to convert it to a firm planned order. If no action is taken, the planning time fence would móve to the end of period 1/19, and the 440 in that period would be moved with it to the right—outside the time fence, since computer planned orders cannot exist inside the planning time fence. In that case, the master scheduled lot of 440 in period 1/26 (the *new* first period outside the planning time fence after the system shifts all periods to the left) would be double, from 440 to 880. An accompanying message would also inform the master scheduler of a negative available balance inside the planning time fence. The ATP would drop to 0 in period 1/19 because the master scheduled lot is moved out of the period.

Working the Pseudo Options

With the current situation for the common parts in the continuing example now understood, and some actions in future periods taken, the next step is to analyze the remainder of the options to determine what further actions might be necessary to ensure a complete and valid master schedule. Here, the option issues are illustrated through analysis of the 1,000# and 3,000# lift capacity options, and by the G102 gearbox assembly.

The 1,000# Option

ITEM INFORMATION SECTION. The data contained in this section of the screen (Figure 9.8 on pages 254–255) for the 1,000# option is basically the same as the item information in the common parts screen; however, there are a few differences. Under *special instructions*, for example, the option is listed as being part of the winch product family, 18 percent of whose sales are expected to require this option configuration (note that the 18 percent is taken directly from the planning bill).

Master Schedule Detail Section. This section shows a series of action messages for the master scheduled item. Here, the software logic recommends a number of reschedule-ins and the conversion of a computer planned order to a firm planned order. The master scheduler would quickly see that 12 of the 13 MPS lots are currently scheduled incorrectly, as evidenced by the R/I-01 ("reschedule-in") messages. At first blush there appears to be a serious timing problem. But a complete analysis should take place before any knee-jerk action is taken.

Planning Horizons-Section. The first step toward determining the source of the problem is to examine the sold-out zone, periods 10/13 and 10/20. Period 10/13 has 72 sets of the 1,000# option scheduled to be received. In-house customer orders, however, total 74 units for this period and there are still 2 more units forecasted. Therefore, the total demand shown is 76 (74 + 2). Since only 72 units are scheduled to be available, the projected demand exceeds supply by 4 option sets.

Now review the next period, 10/20. Again, 72 sets of the 1,000# option are scheduled against a total projected demand (all in-hand orders) of 75, resulting in demand exceeding supply by 3 option sets. The projected available balance in that period has gone from −4 to −7, because of the 3 overbooked options. The difference between the −7 projected available balance, which is a cumulative figure, and the cumulative ATP for the two periods (−5) is the option forecast for period 10/13 (remember, ATP does not take forecast into account, whereas projected available balance accounts for *all* demand).

At this point, the master scheduler must ask: Is current scheduling in the sold-out zone a problem? Here it must be remembered that in the current period of the sold-out zone, the chance of bringing in an order to use the common parts was slim. So when analyzing the common parts earlier in this chapter, the master scheduler decided to

Figure 9.8 Master Schedule Screen, 1000# Option

Part Number	Primary Description	Item Status	Product Family	Master Scheduler	Forecast Source
1000	1000# OPTIONS	PSDO	WXYY	PROUD	PLANBL

Balance On Hand	Lot Size 1	Lot Size 2	Safety Stock Policy	Safety Stock Factor	Time Fence 1	Time Fence 2	Time Fence 3	Lead Time	Cuml. Lead Time	Stnd. Cost
0	LFL		NO		P-13	M12		1	16	

Period	Past Due	10/13	10/20	10/27	11/30	10/10	11/17
Item Forecast							
Option Forecast		2	0	48	67	72	72
Actual Demand		74	75	60			
Proj. Available Balance	0	–4	–7	–30	–25	–25	–25
Available-to-Promise		–2	–3	20	72	72	72
Master Schedule		72	72	85	72	72	72
Period	**1/12**	**1/19**	**1/26**	**2/02**	**2/09**	**2/16**	**2/23**
Item Forecast	P						
Option Forecast	80 P	79	79	79	79	80	79
Actual Demand	P						
Proj. Available Balance	–26 P	0	0	0	0	0	0
Available-to-Promise	80 P	105	79	79	79	80	79
Master Schedule	80 P	105	79	79	79	80	79
Period	**4/13**						
Item Forecast							
Option Forecast	79						
Actual Demand							
Proj. Available Balance	0						
Available-to-Promise	79						
Master Schedule	79						

— — — — — — — — — — — Master Schedule Detail — — — — — — — — — — — —

Req'd Date	Order Number	Lot No.	Order Qty.	Order Type	Order Status	Recom. Action	Req'd Date	Order Quantity
10/13	1000	226	72	MPS	FIRM		10/13	60
10/20	1000	227	72	MPS	FIRM	R/I - 01	10/13	14
10/27	1000	228	85	MPS	FIRM	R/I - 01	10/20	40
11/03	1000	229	72	MPS	FIRM	R/I - 01	10/20	35
11/10	1000	230	72	MPS	FIRM	R/I - 01	10/27	60
11/17	1000	231	72	MPS	FIRM	R/I - 01		
11/24	1000	232	72	MPS	FIRM	R/I - 01		
12/01	1000	233	72	MPS	FIRM	R/I - 01		
12/08	1000	234	72	MPS	FIRM	R/I - 01		
12/15	1000	235	72	MPS	FIRM	R/I - 01		
12/22	1000	236	72	MPS	FIRM	R/I - 01		
1/05	1000	237	72	MPS	FIRM	R/I - 01		
1/12	1000	238	80	MPS	FIRM	R/I - 01		
1/19	1000		105			PLAN		

Forecast Consumption	Resource Profile	Critical Resources							
		Res.	Qty.	Res.	Qty.	Res.	Qty.	Res.	Qty.
PLANBL	WXYY	MCH	7.0	SUB	3.5	ASSM	10.0	KIT	1.0

Selling Price	Special Instructions	Date Run	Action Recommended		
	WXYY-18% OPTION	XX-XX-XX	NEGATP	R/I	PLAN

11/24	12/01	12/08	12/15	12/22	1/05	Period
					M	Item Forecast
72	72	75	76	75	63 M	Option Forecast
					M	Actual Demand
–25	–25	–28	–32	–35	–26 M	Proj. Available Balance
72	72	72	72	72	72 M	Available-to-Promise
72	72	72	72	72	72 M	Master Schedule

3/02	3/09	3/16	3/23	3/30	4/06	Period
						Item Forecast
79	79	79	80	79	79	Option Forecast
						Actual Demand
0	0	0	0	0	0	Proj. Available Balance
79	79	79	80	79	79	Available-to-Promise
79	79	79	80	79	79	Master Schedule

						Period
						Item Forecast
						Option Forecast
						Actual Demand
						Proj. Available Balance
						Available-to-Promise
						Master Schedule

— — — — — — —Actual Demand Detail— — — — — — — — — — — — — — —

Refer. Number	Order Number	T	S	C	Req'd Date	Order Quantity	Refer. Number	Order Number	T	S	C
WA01	M0814	F	R								
SALEM CO	C1746	A	R								
DUPONT	C1823	A	R								
GEN DYN	C1830	A	F								
WA01	M0820	F	F								

either pull in an order that had been scheduled already and possibly ship it early, split a customer order and move some forward, decrease the master schedule to equal the actual demand, or build a popular configuration to stock. In each case, the ATP at the common parts and product family levels would go to 0. Remember, that is a responsibility of the master scheduler to make the master schedule line equal to the actual demand line in the sold-out zone for all *pseudo* items. If the ATP of 10 goes to 0 at the product family level, that 0 will be exploded through the planning bill (which obviously yields 0) to generate a forecast for all options and common parts. When this is done, the option forecast for the 1,000# option will become 0 in period 10/13. The additional forecast of two 1,000# options then vanishes. If the option forecast of 2 in period 10/13 disappears, the projected available balance increases from −4 to −2. In period 10/20, it increases from −7 to −5.

Solving the Problem. The solution to bringing the MPS into balance begins by examining the actual demand detail section of Figure 9.8 on the preceding page. Seventy-four and 75 units of actual demand appear in periods 10/13 and 10/20 respectively. The actual demand detail section indicates the sources of those numbers.

With respect to the 74 units of demand, the detail section indicates two sources. The first is an order for 60 for WA01, under manufacturing order M0814. The second is for 14 units for the Salem Company, customer order C1746. The customer order for Salem Company is a regular assemble-to-order; we know this because of the code "A" in order type. But the order for 60 is being built for stock on a manufacturing order; again, the code "F" (for finished goods) makes this clear. In other words, 60 of those 74 are for the company's own stockroom! In attempting to bring actual demand and the master scheduled quantities into equality, which of these two demand sources might be easier to manipulate? The Salem Company order may be untouchable for customer service purposes, but perhaps the order to add to the company's stockroom could be reduced from 60 to 58 or even something less? If that were possible, the problem in 10/13 would be solved.

Period 10/20 is also oversold, as evidenced by the negative ATP, this time by 3 units. Again, the solution begins with determining the source(s) of actual demand. Here, there are two orders, one of 40 units for du Pont, and one for 35 units for General Dynamics. These are real customer orders for which promises have been made. The question must be asked, Can we reduce the finished goods order in the first period from 60 down to 55 or less? If we can, the problem is solved. This would, in fact, result in 3 units being on hand as period 10/13 ends, enough to cover the deficit in period 10/20, and provide a perfect balance through the sold-out zone.

Thus, what appears to be a complicated and messy situation can be resolved simply by the demand side of the house reducing one stock order. The moral of this example? Know the customers, including the needs of internal customers; don't panic and jump to first conclusions; analyze the horizon as a whole; and use people's product and process knowledge to do what's best for the company.

When examining MPS screens it is easy to believe that the numbers represented in them are scientifically derived and absolutely valid. This is rarely the case. In searching for ways to rebalance the schedule, it is legitimate to continually challenge these numbers.

- Are items being made for inventory really critical?
- Is the lot size optimal, or has it been arbitrarily set?
- Is there a bias in the forecast to ensure abundant supply?
- Is the ship date for a big order being dictated by the customer's needs, or by a salesperson's commission calendar?

These are all legitimate questions for the master scheduler to ask as he or she attempts to balance supply and demand within a time frame that meets market needs.

Returning to period 10/13 for the 1,000# option (Figure 9.8 on pages 254–255), we see that by dropping the WA01 demand order to 55, the first two reschedule-in messages would vanish—there would be no need to reschedule the MPS lot in 10/20 into 10/13, or the 85 in

10/27 into 10/20 as the projected available balance at the end of 10/20 would be 0, not negative.

In 10/27, another demand order for 60 is on tap. Above that is demand for 48 additional sets of the 1,000# option, which was generated by the WXYY family above, exploding its ATP through the planning bill (18 percent probability). To see how that happens, return to the common parts (Figure 9.7 on page 242). There, the ATP in 10/27 is 265 units for the common parts set (same as the product family). By exploding that 265 through the planning bill at the designated 18 percent probability for the 1,000# option, the result is 48 units, which appear in the option forecast line of that option's master schedule screen. Adding the 48 forecasted to the 60 already booked yields a total demand of 108 units against a master schedule of 85. Therefore, since the 60 units booked are for inventory (as indicated in the actual demand detail), the source of the problem is once again internal demand.

Demand is managed by marketing; the MPS is managed by manufacturing. The problem revealed in our example is that the company has overbooked the master schedule—in this case with demand from a finished-goods stockroom.

Another of the master scheduler's challenges is to understand what constitutes *real* demand, and how to satisfy it. As the example implies, not all demand is real and necessary. The master scheduler works closely with the demand manager and with sales and marketing when determining who gets what and which orders receive priority.

The last item for discussion on the 1,000# option is the ATP in period 10/27. Eight-five options sets are scheduled for receipt.[3] Actual demand is 60, which is subtracted from the MPS receipt of 85, leaving 25, not 20. The ATP of 20 is a result of the system's using 5 available options to cover the oversold 5 units in periods 10/13 and 10/20. In other words, the master scheduler should not commit more than twenty 1,000# options through 10/27.

[3] This is a good example of overplanning since the other master schedule receipts are for 72; this 85 is also scheduled in the first unsold period.

Handling the Action Messages. Getting the 60-unit inventory orders reduced makes all the reschedule action messages in this example disappear. The last task of the 1,000# option master scheduler is to convert the CPO for 105 units in 1/19 (just beyond the planning fence) to a FPO. As time passes and period 10/13 disappears, all remaining periods shift to the left, but no computer planned orders in the MPS line can shift inside the planning time fence without their conversion to FPOs by the master scheduler. Failure to do so would result in the CPO being moved out into period 1/26. The master scheduler should follow the system's recommendation and convert the CPO into an FPO.

The 3,000# Option

The 3,000# option is another pseudo option, just like the 1,000# option. The difference is simply the lift capacity. The item information indicates nothing unusual (refer to Figure 9.9 on pages 260–261). The planning time fence is the same for the for both options, as are the lot sizes. One difference is that the 3,000# option is planned as a 19 percent option, instead of 18 percent.

Next, the master scheduler should look at the planning horizons data. In period 10/13, notice the option forecast of 2 units. This will automatically vanish when the common parts and winch product family's sold-out zone is cleaned up. Also in period 10/13, there is an actual demand of 71, and a MPS lot of 76. The projected available balance in that period will now be 5 (adding 2 to the PAB of 3 to take into account the option forecast dropping to 0), indicating that 5 more sets of the 3,000# option are scheduled than exist as in-house orders. Since the chances of bringing in an order of 5 for this period are slim, the master scheduler needs to "clean up" the sold-out zone for the 3,000# option.

"Clean up" first requires a look ahead to period 10/20, where the actual demand is 75 and the option forecast is 0—the company is not expecting to sell any more winches during the first two periods. In the example the master scheduler needs to cover the actual demand of

Figure 9.9 Master Schedule Screen, 3000# Option

Part Number	Primary Description	Item Status	Product Family	Master Scheduler	Forecast Source
3000	3000# OPTION	PSDO	WXYY	PROUD	PLANBL

Balance On Hand	Lot Size		Safety Stock		Time Fence			Lead Time	Cuml. Lead Time	Stnd. Cost
	1	2	Policy	Factor	1	2	3			
0	LFL		NO		P-13	M12		1	16	

Period	Past Due	10/13	10/20	10/27	11/03	11/10	11/17
Item Forecast							
Option Forecast		2	0	50	70	76	76
Actual Demand		71	75	25			
Proj. Available Balance	0	3	18	19	25	25	25
Available-to-Promise		5	15	51	76	76	76
Master Schedule		76	90	76	76	76	76

Period	1/12	1/19	1/26	2/02	2/09	2/16	2/23
Item Forecast	P						
Option Forecast	84 P	83	84	84	83	84	83
Actual Demand	P						
Proj. Available Balance	23 P	0	0	0	0	0	0
Available-to-Promise	84 P	60	84	84	83	84	83
Master Schedule	84 P	60	84	84	83	84	83

Period	4/13						
Item Forecast							
Option Forecast	83						
Actual Demand							
Proj. Available Balance	0						
Available-to-Promise	83						
Master Schedule	83						

— — — — — — — — — — — Master Schedule Detail — — — — — — — — — — — — — —

Req'd Date	Order Number	Lot No.	Order Qty.	Order Type	Order Status	Recom. Action	Req'd Date	Order Quantity
10/13	3000	216	76	MPS	FIRM		10/13	35
10/20	3000	217	90	MPS	FIRM		10/13	36
10/27	3000	218	76	MPS	FIRM		10/20	15
11/03	3000	219	76	MPS	FIRM		10/20	10
11/10	3000	220	76	MPS	FIRM		10/20	50
11/17	3000	221	76	MPS	FIRM		10/27	25
11/24	3000	222	76	MPS	FIRM			
12/01	3000	223	76	MPS	FIRM			
12/08	3000	224	76	MPS	FIRM			
12/15	3000	225	76	MPS	FIRM			
12/22	3000	226	76	MPS	FIRM			
1/05	3000	227	76	MPS	FIRM			
1/12	3000	228	84	MPS	FIRM			
1/19	3000		60			PLAN		

Forecast Consumption	Resource Profile	Critical Resources							
		Res.	Qty.	Res.	Qty.	Res.	Qty.	Res.	Qty.
PLANBL	WXYY	MCH	7.0	SUB	3.5	ASSM	10.0	KIT	1.0

Selling Price	Special Instructions	Date Run	Action Recommended
	WXYY-19% OPTION	XX-XX-XX	PLAN

11/24	12/01	12/08	12/15	12/22	1/05		Period
						P	Item Forecast
76	76	80	80	79	67	P	Option Forecast
						P	Actual Demand
25	25	21	17	14	23	P	Proj. Available Balance
76	76	76	76	76	76	P	Available-to-Promise
76	76	76	76	76	76	P	Master Schedule

3/02	3/09	3/16	3/23	3/30	4/06	Period
						Item Forecast
84	84	83	84	83	84	Option Forecast
						Actual Demand
0	0	0	0	0	0	Proj. Available Balance
84	84	83	84	83	84	Available-to-Promise
84	84	83	84	83	84	Master Schedule

						Period
						Item Forecast
						Option Forecast
						Actual Demand
						Proj. Available Balance
						Available-to-Promise
						Master Schedule

Actual Demand Detail

Refer. Number	Order Number	T	S	C	Req'd Date	Order Quantity	Refer. Number	Order Number	T	S	C
MAIN MFG	C1759	A	R								
AMF	C1815	A	R								
GEN ELEC	C1825	A	F								
TRW	C1832	A	F								
XEROX	C1829	A	F								
NORTH TEL	C1841	A	F								

146 (71 + 75) for the sold-out zone, for which one hundred sixty-six (166) 3,000# option sets are scheduled, leaving a surplus of twenty (20) 3,000# options.

Also notice in period 10/20, the projected available balance is 18, and the ATP is 15. This PAB will increase to 20 once the option forecast in period 10/13 is reduced to 0. A majority of this surplus is caused by the master schedule receipt of 90. A significant portion (14) of this MPS lot probably represents option overplanning done to compensate for expected forecast error. Here, the overplanning has moved into the sold-out zone. Since no additional winch orders are planned to be received for immediate delivery in the sold-out zone, it makes no sense to schedule more 3,000# options than are required by customer orders. Therefore, the master scheduler should reschedule the overplanning (at least the 14 option sets) to the first unsold period in the partially sold-out zone—which is period 10/27. Most master scheduling software systems will not make this suggestion; thus, the master scheduler may have to personally and carefully manage the overplanning dates and quantities.

Here the same alternatives confront the master scheduler as those presented earlier with respect to common parts. The availability of the 3,000# option suggests the pulling up of a customer order. Looking at the actual demand detail we see that the company has an order for Northern Telecom (C1841) requiring 25 of the 3,000# option winches in 10/27. This being the case, the master scheduler could elect to build some of these configurations ahead of time and either ship early (with customer approval) or store the completed products for a period or two.

The master scheduler could also choose to build a *popular* configuration early, using the common parts available and overplanned gearboxes, whatever they may be. (An examination of the gearbox master schedule's ATP would determine the feasibility of this alternative.) The point here is that demand, as well as supply, can be managed in an effort to balance the master schedule in the sold-out zone.

If demand cannot be altered, then the supply must be changed. If the master scheduler decides to reduce supply, the purist approach would entail moving the 14 overplanned options to period 10/27 from

10/20. The purist would again lower the 76 in period 10/13 to 71, and in 10/20, the MPS would read 75. The master scheduler should also pay attention to the fact that the projected available balances in the future are too high, indicating an inventory buildup. The overplanning quantity appears to be 14. Is this too much? Since the projected available balance continues to be positive, overplanning may need to be reduced.

Consider the master schedule detail in Figure 9.9 for period 1/19. The system is recommending the conversion of the CPO for 60 to a FPO. The planning horizons data for this same period indicates that it is time to make this conversion. But why the quantity of 60? The lot size for a pseudo is generally lot-for-lot (LFL). Using this logic, the computer software asks, What should be released to put supply and demand in balance? In period 1/12, the projected available balance is 23, indicating that there is expected to be 23 option sets available at the end of this period. Since demand for the 3,000# option in 1/19 is 83, and 23 are projected to be available at the end of the previous period, a computer planned order for 60 is created. As the example highlights, the computer software adjusts the supply to equal the demand in the first period outside the planning time fence, the first period where CPOs can be placed.

Master Scheduling a Purchased Item in the Planning Bill

Now we turn to the MPS screen for the 4-fpm gearbox, a purchased assembly (Figure 9.10 on pages 264–265). Master scheduling a purchased item in the MTO environment is a combination of the logic discussed in chapter 5 (using the MPS in an MTS environment) and this chapter's logic on using MPS in an MTO environment supported by planning bills.

Figure 9.10 Master Schedule Screen, 4FPM Gearbox

Part Number	Primary Description	Item Status	Product Family	Master Scheduler	Forecast Source
G102	4FPM GEARBOX	STK	WXYY	PROUD	PLANBL

Balance On Hand	Lot Size		Safety Stock		Time Fence			Lead Time	Cuml. Lead Time	Stnd. Cost
	1	2	Policy	Factor	1	2	3			
320	FIXED	500	QTY.	100	P-12			12	13	

Period	Past Due	10/13	10/20	10/27	11/03	11/10	11/17
Item Forecast		8			20		
Option Forecast		3	0	80	111	120	120
Actual Demand		120	110	77			
Proj. Available Balance	320	189	79	422	291	171	51
Available-to-Promise		90		423			
Master Schedule				500			
Period	**1/12**	**1/19**	**1/26**	**2/02**	**2/09**	**2/16**	**2/23**
Item Forecast				20			
Option Forecast	129	132	132	132	132	132	132
Actual Demand							
Proj. Available Balance	159	527	395	243	111	479	347
Available-to-Promise		500				500	
Master Schedule		500				500	
Period	**4/13**						
Item Forecast							
Option Forecast	132						
Actual Demand							
Proj. Available Balance	383						
Available-to-Promise							
Master Schedule							

Master Schedule Detail

Req'd Date	Order Number	Lot No.	Order Qty.	Order Type	Order Status	Recom. Action	Req'd Date	Order Quantity
10/27	G102	005	500	PUR	RLSD	R/I - 01	10/13	60
11/24	G102	006	500	PUR	RLSD	R/I - 01	10/13	45
12/15	G102	007	600	PUR	RLSD		10/13	15
							10/20	60
							10/20	30
							10/20	15
							10/20	5
							10/27	60
							10/27	10
							10/31	7
							11/28	20
							1/05	80

Forecast Consumption	Resource Profile	Critical Resources							
		Res.	Qty.	Res.	Qty.	Res.	Qty.	Res.	Qty.
PLANBL									

Selling Price	Special Instructions	Date Run	Action Recommended		
	WXYY-30% OPTION	XX-XX-XX	R/I		

11/24	12/01	12/08	12/15	12/22	1/05	Period
	20				20 P	Item Forecast
120	120	126	126	126	105 P	Option Forecast
20					80 P	Actual Demand
411	271	145	619	493	288 P	Proj. Available Balance
480			520		P	Available-to-Promise
500			600		P	Master Schedule
3/02	3/09	3/16	3/23	3/30	4/06	Period
20					20	Item Forecast
132	132	132	132	132	132	Option Forecast
						Actual Demand
195	563	431	299	167	515	Proj. Available Balance
	500				500	Available-to-Promise
	500				500	Master Schedule
						Period
						Item Forecast
						Option Forecast
						Actual Demand
						Proj. Available Balance
						Available-to-Promise
						Master Schedule

— — — — — — — Actual Demand Detail— — — — — — — — — — — — — — — — — —

Refer. Number	Order Number	T	S	C		Req'd Date	Order Quantity	Refer. Number	Order Number	T	S	C
WA01	M0814	F	R									
WA04	M0815	F	R									
ALLEN MFG	C1802	A	R									
WA06	M0819	F	F									
TORO MFG	C1819	A	F									
GEN ELEC	C1825	A	F									
ALLIS CHAM	C1831	A	F									
WA01	M0820	F	F									
DUKE PWR	C1837	A	F									
LIFTUM-HI	C1834	S	S									
GSA	C1813	S	F	A								
AT&T	C1801	A	F	A								

Item Information Section. The item information section contains the part number (G102) and other key information used by the master scheduler:

- On-hand balance equals 320 (this is a *real* part).
- Lot sizes are fixed at 500 units per order (minimum order quantity).
- The company intends to maintain a safety stock of 100 units.
- The gearbox is a stocked ("STK") item, not a pseudo.
- The lead time is 12 periods—it takes 12 weeks to receive a gearbox from the supplier after an order is placed. The planning time fence is set at 12.
- Thirty percent of winch family sales are forecasted to include this 4-fpm gearbox feature.
- Reschedule-in action is recommended.

Planning Horizons Section. Beginning in period 10/13, there is a service forecast demand of 8 units, indicating that not only is the gearbox part of the winch's final assembly but it is sold as a "spare" or "service" part. This means that the gearbox option has a dual demand stream. A forecast of 20 units for expected service demand is found in the first period of each month, rather than spread evenly at five per period.

Returning to period 10/13, where the remaining service forecast is 8, one might speculate that the original quantity for the month of October was 20. In this case the 8 tells us that orders have been taken for 12, leaving the 8 of the original 20 unconsumed. How have those 12 been consumed? The actual demand detail section for 10/31 provides part of the answer: A customer order for seven 4-fpm gearboxes has been promised to customer Liftum-High (C1834), with a promised delivery of 10/31. This order has consumed the forecast that precedes it by date. In period 10/27, there is actual demand of 77—and 7 of those are the service order ("S") from Liftum-High. Since no more service orders are listed in the demand detail section, we would have to assume that the missing 5 service orders have already been shipped or the original forecast for October was 15, not 20.

The option forecast line for the 4-fpm gearbox is simply derived by exploding the ATP of the product family through the 30 percent in the planning bill. Thus, if 400 winches (of all descriptions) were forecasted for period 11/10, then 120 of the 4-fpm gearboxes would be forecasted (400 × 30 percent = 120). This gearbox option forecast is automatically consumed every time an order for a winch is booked (this is so because the gearbox is part of the winch's planning bill). In this gearbox's MPS screen (Figure 9.10), forecast consumption is taking place two different ways: one by the planning bill (affects the option forecast), and one by the forecasting logic in the system (service forecast).

Troubleshooting the Planning Horizon. The fact that the example company has a safety stock policy of maintaining a 100-unit inventory of gearbox G102 should send a signal to the master scheduler to scan the planning horizon for any violation of that requirement. The projected available balance line tells the tale. There are two violations—in period 10/20 (79 projected to be available) and in period 11/17 (51 projected to be available).

These safety stock policy violations are the source of the action messages in the master schedule detail section and the reason for the recommendations to move 500 gearboxes into the 10/20 and 11/17 periods. If left to its own devices, the master scheduling software system would follow these recommendations. However, before the master scheduler does any rescheduling, some thought should be given to the company's unwritten policy of stable master schedules, avoiding mountains of stock, and having enough inventory to satisfy customer demand. Before moving in an order of 500 gearboxes to satisfy a 21-unit safety stock problem (100 − 79 = 21), the master scheduler should make an attempt to finesse the situation.

The search for a solution to this problem begins at the sources of demand for the 4-fpm gearboxes: the various finished-goods winch configurations for which this gearbox is a BOM item, service or spares demand, and safety stock.

We have already seen how the master scheduler got demand reduced for the 1,000# option. One part of that reduction was the product family's ATP of 10 being reduced to 0. That reduction would also explode down to the 4-fpm gearbox in question, reducing demand for it by 3. Suppose, as discussed earlier in this chapter, that the master scheduler got the finished-goods order for the WA01 (1,000# options, 4-fpm gearboxes) reduced from 60 to 55 in 10/13, and from 60 to 30 in 10/27. These reductions of 35 units would flow down to the 4-fpm gearbox level, reducing demand for it—more than enough to eliminate the first reschedule-in recommendation. Of course, the reason for this reduction is that the stocking orders in question use the 4-fpm gearbox.

Another point to consider before blindly following the computer software's rescheduling recommendations is the safety stock policy itself. Safety stock is not sacred; it is there to be used when it suits the best interests of the company and its customers: when unexpected orders need to be satisfied, when production shortfalls occur, and to save the company from ordering 500 gearboxes (may be the supplier's required order quantity) when only a handful are needed!

Period 11/17 shows a projected available balance of 51—49 units fewer than the 100 required by the safety stock policy. The demand reductions for WA01 winches just mentioned would reduce that shortfall, leaving what many experienced master schedulers would view as a somewhat comfortable level of safety stock. A novice might jump in and act on the second reschedule-in message (which is why so many are nicknamed "Pogo"), while the veteran master scheduler would likely ignore it and move on.

Abnormal Demand. Finally, looking out period 1/05, the 80 units in the actual demand line of Figure 9.10 represents abnormal demand (the order for AT&T we saw listed on the common parts screen).

On 11/28 there is another abnormal demand—20 for GSA (see actual demand detail). Since this GSA order is a service requirement (indicated with an "S") and is abnormal, the booking of these 20 units did not consume the spares forecast. Remember, abnormal demand is incremental demand and a system with an automated forecast consumption mechanism should not consume the forecast with any demand indicated as "abnormal." The handling of the 80 units of abnormal demand in period 1/05 has already been discussed under common parts. The difference between master scheduling this gearbox and the pseudo common parts above basically centers around the fact that gearboxes can be inventoried, while pseudo items cannot.

Linking MPS and MRP

To understand the connection between the master schedule and material requirements planning for pseudo items, refer back to the 3,000# option (see Figure 9.9 on pages 260–261). Recall that a winding assembly (part 3001) had been structured in as part of this option, and therefore demand for the 3,000# option triggers a one-for-one demand for the winding assembly through the MRP system. The MRP screen for the 3001 winding assembly is seen in Figure 9.11 on pages 270–271.

The MRP screen format is the same as the one introduced in chapter 5 and similar to the MRP screens worked through earlier in this book. However, there are a few differences. Generally, the MRP system is driven by the MPS line of the master schedule. Thus, if the MPS for the 3,000# option calls for 90 units in period 10/20, that triggers a projected gross requirement of 90 winding assemblies in period 10/13—one lead-time period earlier. However, the 3,000# option is a pseudo and requires a slight modification to that logic.

Figure 9.11 Material Requirements Planning Screen, 3001 Winding Assembly

Part Number	Item Status	U/M	Primary Description	Item Type	Comm. Code	MRP Planner	Value Class
3001	STK	EA	WINDING ASSM	SUB		SMITH	A

Balance On Hand	Safety Stock		Scrap Factor	Annual Gross Requirements	Total Released Requirements
	Policy	Factor			
249	NO			4180	136

Period	Past Due	10/13	10/20	10/27	11/03	11/10	11/17
Service Requirements							
Production Requirements	41	90	76	76	76	76	76
Scheduled Receipts	8						
Proj. Available Balance	216	126	50	–26	–102	–178	–254
Planned Order Release			178			228	

Period	1/12	1/19	1/26	2/02	2/09	2/16	2/23
Service Requirements							
Production Requirements	69	84	84	83	84	83	84
Scheduled Receipts							
Proj. Available Balance	787	–871	–955	–1038	–1122	–1205	–1289
Planned Order Release		251			251		

Period	4/13						
Service Requirements							
Production Requirements	84						
Scheduled Receipts							
Proj. Available Balance	–1874						
Planned Order Release							

— — — — — — — — — Scheduled Receipts Detail — — — — — — — — —

Req'd Date	Promised Date	Order Number	Lot No.	Rem. Qty.	Received	Type	Status	Recom. Action
10/06	10/06	3001	86	8	220	MFG	RLSD	R/0 - 3
10/27	10/27	3001	87	178				Order

Req'd Date	Req. Qty.
10/07	36
10/07	5
10/13	15
10/13	15
10/13	10
10/13	50
10/20	25
10/20	51
10/27	76
11/03	76
11/10	76
11/17	76
11/24	76
12/01	76
12/08	76

Lead Time	Cuml. Lead Time	Order Policy	Order Qty./Time	Minimum Order Qty.	Maximum Order Qty.	Multiple Release Requirements
1	16	POQ	3	100		

Total Sched. Receipts	Special Instructions	Date Run	Action Recommended	
8		XX-XX-XX	R/O	ORDER

11/24	12/01	12/08	12/15	12/22	1/05	Period
						Service Requirements
76	76	76	76	76	84	Production Requirements
						Scheduled Receipts
–330	–406	–482	–558	–634	–718	Proj. Available Balance
	228			237		Planned Order Release

3/02	3/09	3/16	3/23	3/30	4/06	Period
						Service Requirements
84	83	84	83	84	83	Production Requirements
						Scheduled Receipts
–1373	–1456	–1540	–1623	–1707	–1790	Proj. Available Balance
250			84			Planned Order Release

						Period
						Service Requirements
						Production Requirements
						Scheduled Receipts
						Proj. Available Balance
						Planned Order Release

Requirements Detail

Refer.	Order Number	Lot	T	S	Req'd Date	Req. Qty.	Refer.	Order Number	Lot	T	S
AMF	C1815		A	R	12/15	76	3000		226	P	F
3000		216	P	F	12/22	76	3000		227	P	F
3000		217	P	F	1/05	84	3000		228	P	F
GEN ELEC	C1825		A	F	1/12	69	3000			P	P
TRW	C1832		A	F	1/19	84	3000			P	P
XEROX	C1829		A	F	1/26	84	3000			P	P
NORTH TEL	C1841		A	F	2/02	83	3000			P	P
3000		218	P	F	2/09	84	3000			P	P
3000		219	P	F	2/16	83	3000			P	P
3000		220	P	F	2/23	84	3000			P	P
3000		221	P	F	3/02	84	3000			P	P
3000		222	P	F	3/09	83	3000			P	P
3000		223	P	F	3/16	84	3000			P	P
3000		224	P	F	3/23	83	3000			P	P
3000		225	P	F	3/30	84	3000			P	P

The MRP System

The *past due* period in Figure 9.11 indicates projected gross requirements of 41 units of part 3001 and a scheduled receipt of 8 units. Therefore, the starting projected available balance can be calculated as follows:

	249	On hand
−	41	The number needed to satisfy the past-due requirement (The master scheduler should challenge why these items have not been issued if they are on hand.)
+	8	Past due, but expected to be received instantly since they have not been rescheduled
	216	Starting Projected Available Balance

Requirements Detail Section. The requirements detail in Figure 9.11 is analogous to the actual demand detail of the MPS screen and explains the origins of demand for the item being analyzed. In this case, notice the first two lines of the requirements detail. The first line is for 36 units for customer AMF, the second is for 5 units for the 3,000# option. The 36 units for AMF is a customer requirement. The second is to fill an expected requirement for the 3,000# option. Looking back to the actual demand detail in the MPS screen for the 3,000# option (Figure 9.9 on pages 260–261), that requirement—36 units for customer AMF—is for 10/13. That is the required date to the finishing line. But to meet this date, the one-period lead time for option 3,000# requires work to start on the item in period 10/07. This can be observed both in the planning horizon for that date and in the requirements detail section.

The 5 units from the second line of the requirements detail (Figure 9.11) represent the winding assemblies expected to be required by the 3,000# option in period 10/13 and are a direct result of the available-to-promise quantity at the MPS option level, the quantity still not committed. Therefore, what is passed to material requirements

ments planning from the master schedule for a pseudo item is a combination of the actual demand and the available-to-promise.

Now look at the 3,000# option in period 10/13 of Figure 9.9, where the actual demand is 71 units. Two orders are found in the details section of that screen: one for 35 and one for 36 (refer to Figure 9.11). Since only the order for 36 appears in the MRP screen, the master scheduler knows that the requirements for 35 units of the 3001 winding assembly have already been satisfied. The remainder of this MRP screen example is provided as reference material for the reader who wants to dig a little deeper into the MPS and MRP integration program.

In working through the several make-to-order examples in this chapter, the reader should get a sense of the difficulty of master scheduling in the MTO environment—the use of pseudo planning bills having contributed an added level of complexity. Difficult though it may be, it is a job that must be done if companies hope to be successful in satisfying customer orders within the lead time demanded by the marketplace.

The next chapter considers another environment: custom products and engineer-to-order (ETO). Here the master scheduler must make decisions in an environment in which bills-of-material, routings, lead times, and completion dates are not predetermined. In addition to addressing the ETO world, we shall take a look at the make-to-contract environment, which has some similarities to the make-to-order as well as the engineer-to-order environments.

10

Master Scheduling in Custom-Product Environments

Failure to plan on your part does not constitute an emergency on my part.

Back in chapter 6, several manufacturing strategies—make-to-stock, finish-to-order, assemble-to-order, make-to-order, engineer-to-order, and design-to-order—were introduced and discussed. Each strategy was partially dictated by the competitive environment faced by the company, and the need to meet the customer at some point in time earlier or later in the production process. In this chapter our focus will be on the design-to- or the engineer-to-order (ETO) strategy, and on the particulars of scheduling in these environments. The process of developing and introducing a new product for which no actual demand yet exists, whether it be in a make-to-stock or make-to-order company, is a unique application of the engineer-to-order strategy.

As a brief review, recall that ETO companies generally do not begin the design and/or production process until an order or letter of intent is actually in hand. Producers of specialized industrial equipment, large passenger aircraft, high-tech military equipment, and commuter subway cars are typical of ETO companies. Because these products are expensive and suited for a limited number of customers and applications, their manufacturers cannot afford to design, build, and hold them in inventory in the expectation of future orders. Unlike make-to-stock companies that meet their customers at or near the time of delivery, ETO companies and their customers may meet months and even years before completion and delivery of the final product.

This is not to say that ETO companies do not, or need not, forecast future business activity or practice the disciplines of sales and operations planning and demand management. The mere fact that these companies have engineers, designers, and manufacturing personnel on the payroll is clear evidence that future manufacturing activities are anticipated and that some forecasting is, in fact, taking place. Only the time horizons are different.

The Unique Challenges of the ETO Environment

To appreciate the challenges facing master schedulers within the ETO company, consider Figure 10.1, which roughly describes the value-adding activities that must go on within the company between its contract with the customer and actual delivery of the finished product. For perspective, MTS and MTO companies are added to the figure. The bottom axis of the figure is a time line along which these activities are listed. As the figure makes clear, the ETO company faces the demand management and resource/capacity planning chores of other companies, but these are just the tip of the iceberg, so to speak—other major planning and scheduling tasks lie beneath the surface:

- Product specifications must be worked out, usually in collaboration with the customer;

Figure 10.1 Tasks of Manufacturing Strategies Compared

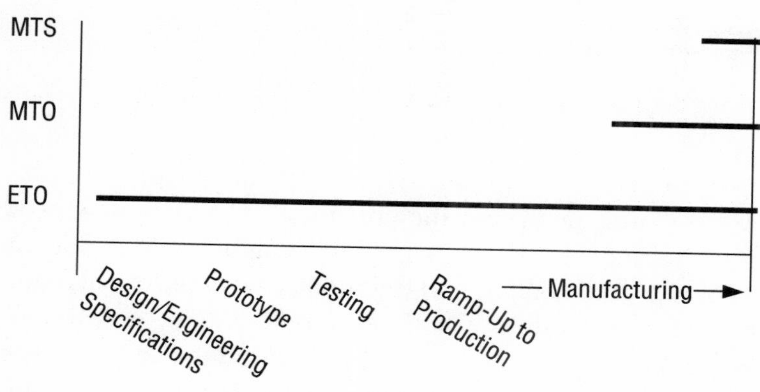

- A prototype or sample must be produced and tested;
- Feedback from prototype testing must be reflected in engineering and design changes;
- Bills-of-material and process routings must be created; and
- Ramp-up to final manufacturing level must begin.

Many of these activities precede the traditional master scheduling and material requirements planning activities so far discussed. This does not mean, however, that the master scheduler and the tools for balancing supply and demand cannot be useful in these earlier activities. Quite the contrary; the master scheduler, being one of the persons responsible for getting the final product to the customer, is the logical coordinator of ETO activities, and MPS techniques are eminently suited to ETO activities from design/engineering through final manufacturing. The main difference between master scheduling manufacturing activities and engineering activities is that instead of bringing materials and manufacturing capabilities together within certain "build times," the ETO master scheduler must provide for human resources and elapsed times for "products" thought of in a much broader sense: engineering drawings, tooling configurations, testing activities, and so forth.

The Case of New-Production Introductions

Engineer-to-order scheduling issues are equally relevant to MTS and MTO companies when they plan and introduce new products. In these instances, a product is being engineered-to-order at the behest of top management and the marketing department, who have determined the feasibility and sales potential of the item. New products for these companies must pass through the same development activities—design, engineering, prototype, testing, ramp-up, and full manufacturing phases—as do ETO products. The same challenges apply. Demand must be forecasted; product specifications must be developed; design changes based on prototype testing must be made; and processes for manufacturing the final new product must be arranged. In fact, new products create two extra levels of scheduling difficulties regardless of the manufacturing strategy chosen: 1) timing the introduction, and 2) planning for the impact of the new product on current lines of business. These two difficulties are not unrelated.

Timing New-Product Introductions

New-product introductions are always risky. Product development requires high expenses for research and development, design, engineering, and the tooling to bring the product to market. These costs are incurred before even one dollar of revenue is generated and must be paid, even if the product is a failure. And there is no assurance that the new product will succeed. No matter how much thought goes into market research, no matter how much money is spent on promotion designed to introduce the new product to the market, high failure rates for new products are the rule.

Minimizing the risks associated with new-product introductions requires careful forecasting and coordination of production with sales and marketing. From the master scheduler's perspective, this means working closely with marketing and design engineering to hit roll-out dates planned in the company's promotional strategy. The confusion and damage caused by poor coordination between production and promotion can be great and are well illustrated in these two recent cases:

- In the late 1980s, Lotus Development Corporation spent months and millions preparing its large base of Lotus 1-2-3 users to switch over to a forthcoming upgrade of its popular spreadsheet program. The customers were ready, but the product was not. Month after month of production delays caused confusion and frustration for both the company and the market.

- In late 1991, Apple Computer Company introduced its low-priced Classic model of the Macintosh. The product rolled off Apple's new, state-of-the-art plant built especially for this machine; they were right on time for the Christmas buying season. The Classic was an immediate success in all but one respect: Demand was more than twice what had been forecast. The result: angry dealers who were "allocated" a few machines at a time, demoralized salespeople, and many customers who simply gave up waiting for their promised Classics and bought competing machines to put under the Christmas tree.

Planning for the Impact on Existing Products

The introduction of a new product generally has some impact on a company's existing products. In some cases the new product is an intended *replacement* and, except for spare parts, production of the existing product is discontinued; the annual model changes of automobiles are a good example. In other cases, it is assumed that the new product will cannibalize some sales from the company's existing products; one might assume Apple's introduction of the Powerbook surely had that effect on its other basic, monochrome screen models. How about the over-the-counter drug manufacturers who promote a new, improved aspirin on television, causing significant impact on demand. In some cases, as with the introduction of new products in separate product markets, no impact on existing products would be expected; Sony's introduction of a new video camera, for example, would have no measurable impact on sales of its popular Walkman.

Consider a company preparing for the introduction of a new product that it hopes to eventually replace demand for an existing product. In planning its initial periods of production, the company needs to do several things: It must continue satisfying demand for the old product until the new product catches on in the marketplace; it must plan on the elimination of inventory for the old product; and it must phase in production of the new product as demand and production for the old one taper off (see Figure 10.2).

Figure 10.2 Introduction of a New Product (in Period 3)

	1	2	3	4	5	6
Old Product	20	20	15	10	5	0
New Product	0	0	5	10	15	20
Total Production	20	20	20	20	20	20

In this case, the company planned the new-product introduction for period 3, and planned for the gradual displacement of the old product by the new product over periods 3 through 6. This is a simple case without lead time or inventory complications. Nor does it recognize the possibility that the production line may have to be shut down for product changeover. But this case should make the point about the issues the master scheduler must consider in planning new-product introductions. Let's take a look at the process for getting a new product to the marketplace.

Launching a New Product

The job of putting a new product into the marketplace in a respectable time frame has proven to be a frustrating experience for many organizations. To improve the process, a number of companies have adopted a four-step approach to new-product introductions.[1]

1. Use a task force to plan and create data structures, and maintain control of these structures. The task force usually consists of four to seven people representing design engineering, marketing, manufacturing engineering, master scheduling, planning, operations, and purchasing.

2. Make all new products and their market introductions part of the sales and operations planning process. Each new product is added to the monthly agenda, with discussions revolving around engineering, manufacturing, sales promotion, pricing, and strategy issues.

3. Create a bill-of-events that includes all activities and events that must take place between product idea approval and actual product launch. Couple this bill-of-events with resource templates to generate priorities and resource requirements. Eventually, these will be replaced with actual bills-of-material and process routings.

4. Use planning and control concepts of master scheduling and MRP II to execute materials and activities requirements. This makes it possible for the company to plan, schedule, and report progress, and to know at all times what needs to be done, the nature of resource requirements, and when each activity is to be completed.

[1] For a complete discussion of new-product launches, see Jerry Clement, Andy Coldrick, and John Sari, *Manufacturing Data Structures* (Essex Junction, VT: Oliver Wight Publications, Inc., 1992).

Master Scheduling Events and Activities

Virtually any set of items, events, or activities can be master scheduled. In the traditional sense, master scheduling typically means scheduling production of tangible materials: putting together the parts to produce a ballpoint pen, a chair, an automobile, etc. In the ETO and new-product environment as seen in Figure 10.3, many of those events and activities take place at CAD-CAM screens, in testing

Figure 10.3 Bill-of-Events for Hoist

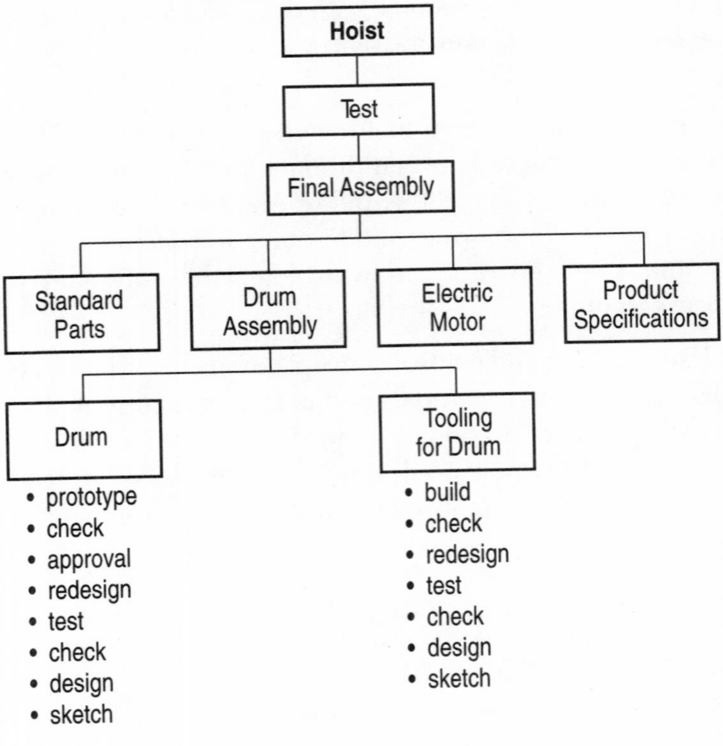

laboratories, in sales brochures, and around conference tables. *These can, nevertheless, be scheduled.* This goes back to the earlier discussion of *what* do we master schedule? End items? Options? Here we schedule events and activities, and instead of scheduling from bills-of-materials, "bills-of-events" or "bills-of-activities" are among the tools of the master scheduler's trade.

Consider Levitation Lift Corporation (LLC), which is in the heavy-duty hoist and crane business. Working with top management and the marketing department, LLC's research and development center has proven a new hoist technology that it is ready to give to manufacturing. A small-scale model based on off-the-shelf materials has been tested in the lab and in the field, and it is time to bring it up to full scale through design and engineering and ready it for production.

No design specifications and no bills-of-material currently exist for this new product, but the master scheduler can still apply his art and tools to this project following these steps:

1. *Classify the scope of the change.* Is the hoist a major or minor product change, or does it represent a new-product concept? Does it fit into any existing product family? This information imparts a feel for the complexity and difficulty associated with the upcoming change.

2. *Create a "dummy" item number for the finished hoist.* Ask engineering to release a number that will be used for planning purposes. At some future point the new product will either carry this number or be assigned a new one.

3. *Identify significant activities.* Here the scheduler or task force would list the set of important tasks necessary for designing and producing the hoist—ideally, in the sequence in which they must take place. In this case, design/engineering, detail engineering, perhaps a customer approval of the detailed design, drafting, checking the drawings, creating of a prototype, and so forth, all the way through the assembly and shipping activities. Even significant marketing activities should be identified.

Naturally, the master scheduler cannot know in detail all significant events and activities associated with the creation of this hoist: they do not yet exist. But knowledge of the products of his or her business, and close consultation with relevant parties within the company, make a close approximation possible. And at this stage, a close approximation is all that is required.

4. *Create a bill-of-events.* At this point a bill-of-events like the one in Figure 10.3 can be constructed. The product will be built from the bottom up, but anyone looking at the bill will know that to get the special hoist onto the shipping dock, a test will have to be made. Four significant events must take place before that test can be made: Product specifications must be developed and produced; an off-the-shelf motor must be obtained; a drum assembly must be designed and built; some standard parts must be procured as their significance to the hoist is spelled out. Each of these four significant events has its own subbill-of-events, or defined bill-of-materials. As unknown events are entered into the bills-of-events, use dummy numbers.

5. *Estimate total resources and lead time for each event or activity.* In the example, we would consider the resources required to complete each of the four significant activities (and their subactivities) and the test involved in making the special hoist (see Figure 10.4). The lead times for performing each of these activities can be estimated from past projects and conversations with the relevant departments, and these can be used to create the planning lead times and a cumulative time frame for the entire ETO project.

Taking just one activity as an example, LLC might schedule the "tooling for the drums" as follows:

The schedule for the drum tooling is combined with similar schedules for each of the other significant activities to construct an overall project lead-time schedule. This is then available for the next step.

6. *Rough cutting the project lead-time schedule.* The methodology for rough cut capacity planning (chapter 13) is here brought to bear on the hoist's schedule of the project to determine if the plan is feasible, given the company's resources and other commitments.

7. *Replace "dummy" item numbers with real numbers.* As the bill-of-events becomes more fully articulated with design specifications

Figure 10.4 Loading and Scheduling the Events

Activity	Elapsed Time (weeks)	Hours Required	Competition/ end of week #:
Sketch	3	120	3
Design	4	165	7
Check	1	15	8
Test	1	10	9
Redesign	2	80	11
Check	1	15	12
Build	3	120	15
Total	15	525	15

and actual parts, obtain real numbers from engineering for those items and substitute them for the "dummy" numbers in the original plan.

8. *Validate/adjust lead times and resources as required.* Over time, as more information becomes available, the original estimates for lead times and resource requirements will need to be validated and, where appropriate, adjusted. The software system can then be used to recalibrate the entire project.

9. *Reprioritize materials and events.* This is where a scheduling and network system can be of the greatest use. If all engineering and manufacturing activities are driven by a common master schedule, each event will be in line with the others to ensure continuity with the entire schedule.

Prices and Promises to Keep

The schedule developed through the steps listed above has three uses in ETO and new-product introduction situations:

1. To determine a delivery date for the sales force or for the customer. In new-product introductions, as in the Lotus Development anecdote cited earlier in this chapter, it is important to be able to tell sales representatives, dealers, and customers when the product will be available. They need this information for their planning purposes, and woe be unto the manufacturer that fails to deliver on its promises. Delivery dates are also critical to the negotiating process between company and customer on engineer-to-order products.

2. In cases for which a delivery date requirement has already been determined, the bill-of-events product schedule allows the company to "backward schedule" to obtain all the event start and required completion dates that will make the delivery date feasible. These become the "start and due dates" for all individual tasks.

3. In the absence of bills-of-material, the schedule and bills-of-events just described form a basis upon which the company can estimate its costs in time and materials on an ETO product or new-product introduction. These costs are an important element in pricing the forthcoming product, which is generally required in competitive bidding situations for ETO products.[2]

[2] American and European firms have tended to determine product price on the basis of their manufacturing and development costs. Japanese firms generally have adopted a "target price" approach, first determining a price that will allow their new products to penetrate or create a market, and then work back through manufacturing and materials to design and engineer the product with a cost structure that allows them to meet that price objective profitably.

What Can Go Wrong

The ETO and new-product schedule can be upset by a number of unforeseen problems. In fact, the longer the planning horizon, the greater the potential for these problems to manifest themselves. Among the sources of scheduling problems are the following:

- *New or unknown processes and technologies*. Since the company is dealing with a new product, it is possible that the processes necessary to produce it may also be new. Of course, the same can be said for the technology needed to bring the product to the marketplace.
- *Lack of product specifications, at least initially*. It is not unusual in this environment for engineering to release to manufacturing an incomplete set of specifications.
- *Frequent design and engineering changes*. For example, in scheduling the introduction of a complex new product, a period of many months may elapse between the point at which certain materials are specified within the design and the date at which materials are actually scheduled for purchase. During this time, and unknown to the manufacturer, the supplier of that material may have gone out of business or switched to a different material, which may not be compatible with the design. This adversely affects the schedule.[3] This would not happen if the supplier was part of the team.

[3] For a very complete description of the problems of product development management, with emphasis on the worldwide auto industry, see Kim B. Clark and Takahiro Fujimoto, *Product Development Performance* (Boston, MA: Harvard Business School Press, 1991). Other research performed by the Ford Motor Company in 1986 indicated that the typical U.S. automaker accelerated the frequency of its engineering changes up to the time of the first production run, and even continued those engineering changes at a high pace several months into the production phase of the new-model introduction. The result was surely much confusion, delays, and poor-quality automobiles until such time as the level of changes stabilized. The same Ford study indicated that engineering changes for Japanese auto firms peaked out sixteen to twenty months *before* the first production run; very few changes were made in the months just prior to initial production, and virtually none once production was in full swing.

What typically happens in development projects is seen in Figure 10.5. This shows planned activities and their schedule along a time line from project inception in January to manufacturing and shipping in late August. The first part of the figure is what was planned; the second part shows what can happen: Here engineering has consumed more time than planned, and since the activities are sequential, all the remaining activities must be squeezed into a shortened time frame if commitments to customers are to be met. Product quality usually suffers and people frustrations mount as a result.

Figure 10.5 Effects of Schedule Delays

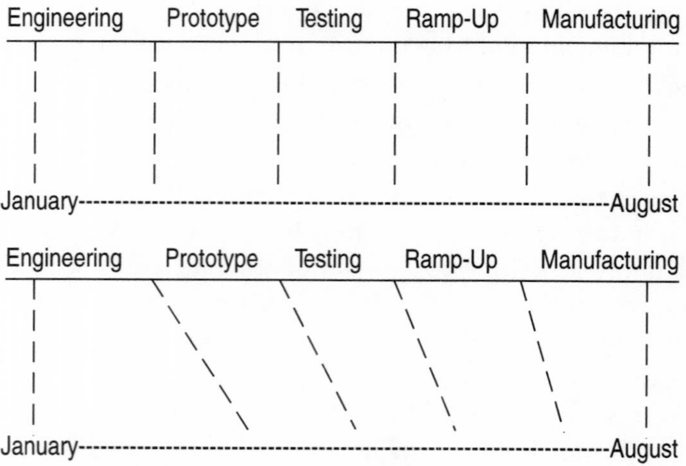

Integrating Engineering and Manufacturing Activities

Engineering and manufacturing schedules must be integrated so that all energy in the company is focused on a common goal—satisfying customer needs. In companies that produce highly engineered products, and in companies for which new-product development is a major strategic thrust, engineering and related functions make up a significant portion of schedule time and costs. These engineering activities precede manufacturing activities, and they do not stop with new-product design and release, but continue in the form of ongoing engineering support.

Even though it is easy to see why engineering and manufacturing activities should be integrated, they are not always integrated in practice. This is because engineering and product development schedules typically are not derived from manufacturing and procurement schedules that trace their origins back through the master schedule to sales plans and customer commitments.

Figure 10.6 illustrates the relationship between engineering/design

Figure 10.6 Engineering and Manufacturing Dependent Relationships

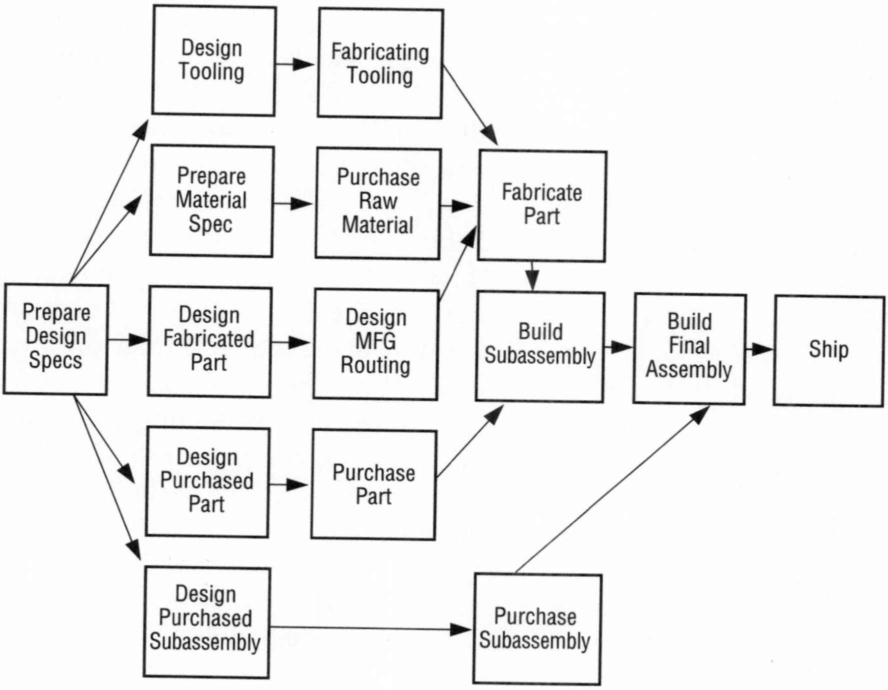

and manufacturing activities in moving from the early stages of a project to a delivered project. This relationship goes beyond parts engineering to tool design and process flow design.

Many companies fail to integrate engineering activities with manufacturing activities or drive them with a common master schedule. This is a typical source of trouble. It does very little good to be ready to perform a manufacturing operation on time when the product design is not yet complete; nor does it help company efficiency when different design projects converge on a design resource bottleneck at the same time.

The solution to the problem of engineering-manufacturing integration is to drive all requirements—whether engineering, sales, marketing, or manufacturing—with a common master schedule (see Figure 10.7).

A common master schedule ensures that a company's total resource requirements are aligned with the goal of satisfying customer needs. It is tied directly to the output of the sales and operations planning process. By generating need dates through MRP II, engineering personnel are informed of required dates for its "products" (drawings, specifications, process instructions, etc.). These required dates can be passed upstream until all activities and priorities are scheduled.

For years, manufacturing companies have used a combination of the master schedule, routings, and work center resource data to plan and control capacities. To do the same for engineering resources, process templates that define tasks for each engineering job need to be created. These templates identify the sequence of tasks, where work will be done (e.g., in the design department), and the time estimated to complete each task. With the templates in hand, a resource capacity plan can be generated for engineering and manufacturing work centers. Tasks that require common resources (e.g., checking) are highlighted as potential impediments to the scheduled completion of engineering requirements.

This process is known as Engineering Resource Planning (ERP). It is a methodology that integrates engineering and manufacturing requirements by means of a common master schedule.

Figure 10.7 Engineering and Manufacturing Resource Planning Using a Common Master Schedule

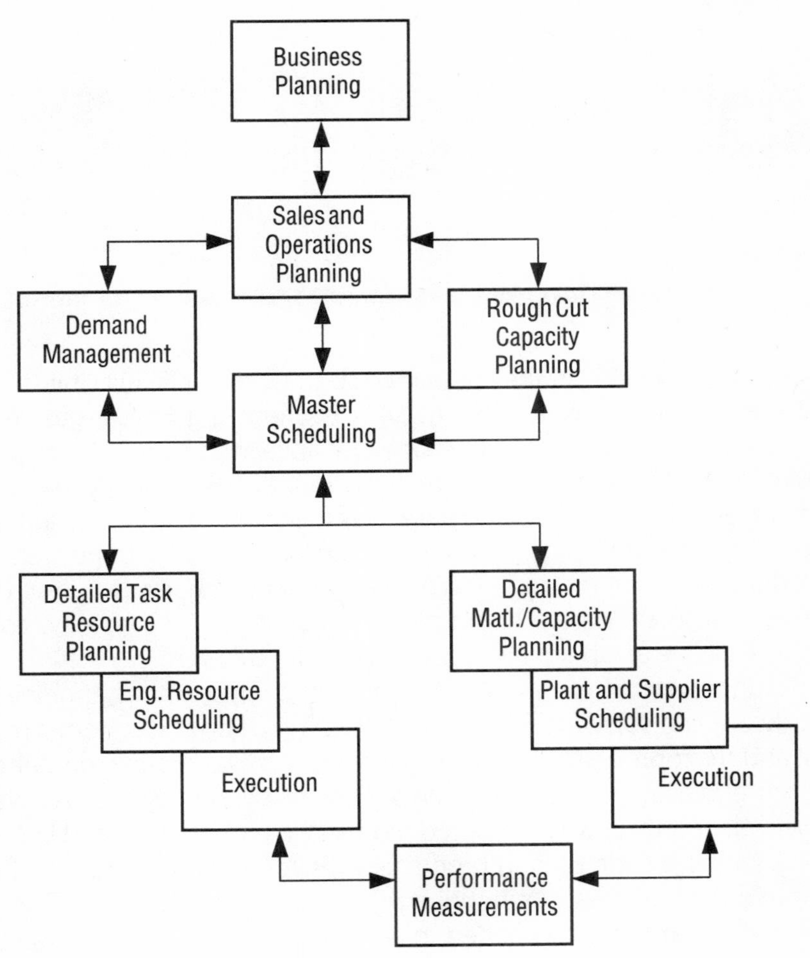

Capacity-Driven Environments

Just a few weeks on the job was enough to convince Bill Childs that he was dealing with a different set of scheduling challenges. As a master scheduler with ten years of experience in the automotive-parts industry, Childs was used to situations in which scheduling the flow and assembly of materials and parts was the foremost concern. Indeed, ensuring the smooth movement of materials into the finishing stage of production for alternators, starter motors, and other auto parts had defined his previous work. But at Testing Systems, Inc., his new company, Childs was up against something quite different.

Testing Systems was a high-technology company that engineered hardware and software for diagnostic testing of both electromechanical and microprocessor-based equipment. This was an environment in which engineers and programmers were many and assemblers were few, where output was measured more in circuitry designs and lines of programming code than in products shipped, and it required a different approach to master scheduling.

Childs found that he needed to change his thinking about many of the basics of scheduling that had served him well in the auto-parts industry. Instead of working back from end product demand through traditional bills-of-material, this environment required a focus on getting the most out of the company's cadre of highly paid, highly educated "knowledge workers." It was, after all, their capacity to design and program exotic electronic equipment that was Testing System's "product"; manufacturing and assembly were not where value was added and were, in fact, generally subcontracted to other firms.

Bill Childs's situation is no longer unique in modern industry and actually represents a growing segment of the master scheduling craft. The real growth industries of the past quarter century—software, microprocessers, medical-technology, biotechnology, and aerospace—present situations in which traditional manufacturing and assembly are often the tail of the value-adding process, and design, engineering, and development are the dog that wags that tail. Thus, schedulers have had to learn to measure and manage capacities similar to those presented above, and this learning will undoubtedly continue into the foreseeable future. These are capacity-driven environments, and they represent a departure from the material-driven environment typical of those represented elsewhere in this book.

To understand the difference between the material-driven and the capacity-driven environments, consider Figure 10.8, where the unique concerns of the two are contrasted.

This figure makes it clear that the focus of the master scheduler's attention in the capacity-driven environment is on the key resources of the company, and every opportunity is sought for getting the most from those resources. In a job shop, the internal resources might be metal machining equipment; in a law firm they might be billable hours; in a software-development company, they might be the capacity to create lines of programming code; in a plate glass–making

Figure 10.8 Two Different Scheduling Environments

Material-driven	Capacity-driven
• Schedule to meet demand • Schedule fewest number of items • Back schedule from end item or option • Schedule materials, then balance capacity • Customer demand is the controlling variables	• Schedule to utilize resources • Schedule bottlenecks • Forward schedule after bottleneck; back schedule before bottleneck • Schedule capacity, then balance materials • Capacity resources are the controlling variables

facility that utilizes multimillion-dollar continuous-process equipment, they might be machine hours.

What to Master Schedule

Unlike make-to-stock companies, such as a pencil producer, capacity-driven companies focus their scheduling not on the final product but the capacity that produces it. When the question What should I master schedule? is asked, the pencil company invariably answers finished pencils. The capacity-driven company, such as a machine-tooling company, might focus on machine-hour capacity. Consider just such a machine-tooling company and the situation described in Figure 10.9. This company has three items on its schedule, Items 121, 122, and 123. The master scheduler has learned through experience the amount of drilling-machine time required for each of these items. By multiplying the machine hours per hundred items by the quantity of expected demand (in hundreds), the total capacity requirements for each item can be determined.

Figure 10.9 Capacity Matrix

Item	Machine Hours Required per 100
#121	1.00
#122	1.25
#123	1.40

Like all demand, machine time has both a quantity and time dimension; i.e., the customer wants an item in a certain quantity and by, or at, a certain time. Figure 10.10 is the master scheduling matrix that matches demand and supply for the drilling operation. Here the master schedule lists demand not in terms of the number of items booked, but by the machine hours required for booked items. Available-to-promise and the master schedule lines are likewise expressed in machine-hour terms. Reviewing the MPS matrix for the

Figure 10.10 Master Schedule Matrix for Drilling

	1	2	3	4	5	6
Actual Demand	240	254	182	140	70	0
Available-to-Promise	0	−14	58	140	210	280
MPS (Capacity)	240	240	240	280	280	280

drilling operation, the master scheduler sees that he or she is sold out through period 2. In fact, period 2 shows that the company is overbooked by 14 hours. As with scheduling in other environments, the shortfall could be eliminated through the simple expedients of either 14 hours of overtime, off-loading some of the demand to another drilling work center, or subcontracting the work to an outside source. As in the materials-driven environment, the ATP line is a handy guide to determining whether new demand can be accepted and when. Beginning with period 3, for example, the master scheduler notices a positive ATP, signifying that drilling capacity is available to commit and sell.

The MPS matrix can help a capacity-driven company commit to customer deliveries without overselling its capacity. Figure 10.11 shows four customer orders in which the required capacity has been calculated.

Figure 10.11 Matrix Showing Required Capacities

Item	Machine Hours Required per 100	Order Quantity (100s)	Total Required Machine Hours
#121	1.00	50	50.0
#122	1.25	10	12.5
#123	1.40	12	16.8
#121	1.00	120	120.0

If these orders are to be sequenced in the order shown, when can the master scheduler commit each without further planning overtime, and so forth? (This example assumes that the master scheduler has decided to work overtime to satisfy the 14 hours overbooked in period 2. However, no more overtime will be planned.) The first order for #121 requires 50 hours; it can be committed for a period-3 delivery, which leaves 8 hours in period 3's ATP (58−50). The next order (#122) will use the remaining 8 hours of ATP in period 3 plus 4.5 hours of period 4's ATP, leaving 135.5 hours available-to-promise in period 4.

The next order, for item #123, requires 16.8 hours. It, too, can be promised in period 4, leaving an ATP of 118.7 hours of capacity. The last order in the example is again for item #121, which requires 1.00 hours of capacity per 100 units. The request is for 12,000 units, which will require 120 hours of capacity. The numbers tell us that period 5 should be the promise date (only 118.7 hours of capacity in period 4 being available-to-promise), but the experienced master scheduler, hoping to satisfy the customer and use company resources most effectively, may commit a period-4 delivery. Even though the rules are not to plan any extra capacity, the person working with capacity numbers must remember that capacity is aggregated planning and not an exact science. Of course, the specified jobs may also take longer than estimated! Knowing what to do in this instance is part of the "art" of master scheduling.

Capacity Master Schedules

In the capacity-driven environment, the focus tends to be on bottlenecks in the operation. Like the hourglass-shaped situations faced by many assemble-to-order manufacturers of option-laddened products, many capacity-driven companies have pinch points in their operations, and these are the critical scheduling points. By developing routings, or bills-of-events, such as those shown in this chapter, master schedulers can work backward to determine the latest start date required for each operation that passes through the bottleneck. Likewise, they can determine the earliest expected finish date by doing the same for all events and processes that occur beyond the bottleneck.

Make-to-Contract Environments

In the custom-products environments, many companies do little or nothing until they have a contract in hand for a particular product or project. At that point, development work begins, as do the other tasks that lead toward the completed job. This was not the case at Hyster Company when Larry Wilson, an Oliver Wight Principal, was the master scheduler. Hyster had an engineer-to-order product that was master scheduled with pseudos that contained total hours required on their major shops, an estimate of capacity for key suppliers and typical people-weeks required in engineering, etc. The pseudo was used to master schedule eighteen months into the future and was replaced with the actual bill-of-material upon receiving a customer's letter of intent. The process was then managed as described in this chapter.

The make-to-contract (MTC) world is very similar to the engineer-to-order world, however, in the make-to-contract environment, the company may very well have completed the design work; there may already be a working prototype. This is very much the situation in the aerospace industry, in which an aircraft producer may have to approach the U.S. Department of Defense with an operating prototype of the new fighter plane it hopes to sell. At this point, the company has no orders, but it has already invested billions in design, new-materials development, tooling, and flight testing. This is often the price of admission to the formal competition for the megabillion-dollar-contract award for the next generation of fighter aircraft.

In other cases, the producer may already have an established product that it is selling to a new customer. In winning a contract, it is only building the same product to the quantity and time specification of that customer—perhaps with some minor design changes.

Make-to-contract jobs, especially with the government, very often have strong inducements for on-time delivery—namely, late penalties. Thus, the master scheduler has a critical role to play not only in the completion of the project but in its profitability to the company.

These contracts sometimes feature partial-completion payouts to the contractor, in which the company is paid for materials and other expenses *as incurred;* this is quite different than being paid for the job on delivery dates and has an effect on the scheduling policy of the producer.

The Need for Standards

"The Aerospace/Defense Industry is characterized by change in high volume often at rates that seem beyond human responsiveness," according to Paul Hemmen, an Oliver Wight Principal.[4]

> The application of the computer to the manufacturing environment, in which precise processes are used to produce exacting designs subject to change, offered a solution for maintaining control and responsiveness to change. Using the computer to crunch the numbers as often as necessary to keep essential data current is also required.
>
> Manufacturing resource planning system components—the computer, planning software, and knowledgeable people—have provided the so often sought-after control potential for the commercial industry for two decades. MRP systems are ideally suited for the Aerospace/ Defense Industry as well. In fact, the basic logic of how MRP works was born in the industry during the 1950s on submarine programs.
>
> So much progress has been made since then, especially adapted by commercial users, that it may seem as though the A&D Industry stood still in updating their management systems. It is probably more correct to say that A&D systems have become nearly as sophisticated as the weapons systems being produced. Commercial users, having found the secret to controls in manufacturing, have on the other hand simplified their systems in applying Just-in-Time/Total Quality Control (JIT/ TQC) concepts in the factories that are driven by excellent planning

[4] Paul G. Hemmen, "The Standard for Master Production Schedules," APICS A&D SIG Digest, Edition II, April 1991.

and control processes, such as MRP II. Hence the need for standards that provide a coherent, simple means for applying MRP/MRP II systems in the A&D Industry.

The Standards

Early in 1987, the fate of MRP systems for the A&D Industry was essentially on hold awaiting application criteria and guidance. Government and industry worked as a team and reached agreement, which provided the ten Key Elements subsequently promulgated as Standards in application DFAR sections Sub part 242.72. The ad hoc committee selected the widely known and proven quality standards for successful use of MRP systems as they would be applied for materials management and accounting systems.

Standard Number 2 states in part: "Assure that costs of purchased and fabricated material charged or allocated to a contract are based on valid time-phased requirements as impacted by minimum/economic order quantity restrictions. A 98% bill of material accuracy and 95% master production schedule accuracy are desirable as a goal in order to assure that requirements are both valid and appropriately time-phased."

When these accuracy levels are not evident, the contractor is burdened with proving the relevant cost significance to the government. Of the Standards, this one is the meat-and-potatoes issue!

Some divergence of views and debate remains, however, about this key element, as to whether it means 95 percent accuracy or performance. MRP II users have established by overwhelming precedent of proof testing and pain in the manufacturing environment the realities and benefits of this goal.

As early users discovered, MRP II without an initial MPS step in the process produced no more than computerized order launching. The essence of the MPS is to inject a clearly distinguishable management step in the process to achieve balance, stability, and validity for requirements and schedules.

The master schedule is management's "anticipated build schedule" and as such must pass the test of doability regarding capacity resources and materials availability on a continuing basis. It is not a static parameter containing a snapshot of the contract requirements. Rather, the MPS is dynamic data representing product configuration and flow, forward-looking supply planning, and performance feedback, within the constraints of reasonable capability and expectation for the company.

The master schedule is management's steering control over all planned activity as it portrays supply versus demand. Continuous feedback (closed-loop in the MRP process) and performance reporting are essential to progress toward the goal of 95 percent MPS. What makes the MPS and BOM the meat and potatoes of MRP II is that they answer three of the four fundamental questions in the manufacturing equation:

What are we going to make? MPS
What does it take to make it? BOM
What do we need and when? MPS

Coupled with Standard Number 5, which sets the quality level for inventory record accuracy (IRA) at 95 percent, and the activity in manufacturing can be bracketed. The equation is solved.

What do we already have? IRA

The essence of the master schedule is to inject a clearly distinguishable management step in the process to achieve balance, stability, and validity for requirements and schedules.

Satisfying the Customer and the Standard

Figure 10.12 is the master schedule for an aerospace company that holds a contract to make and deliver air-to-ground missiles. *The contract is the demand* in this MTC situation, and here the actual demand line indicates the contract delivery dates (20 missiles in period 4 followed by 20 missiles in period 8). *The master schedule line is the supply.* Late penalties are part of this particular contract.

The level-loaded master schedule in Figure 10.12 works out just fine in terms of the dates and quantities required by the contract, but in its fear of encountering an unanticipated delay that might cause it to miss the delivery dates—and thus incur a financial penalty—the missile producer may sometimes decide to build ahead of the contract, as shown in Figure 10.13. Here the producer is leaving some

Figure 10.12 MTC Master Schedule, Missiles, Level-Loaded

	Past Due	1	2	3	4	5	6	7	8
Actual Demand					20				20
Projected Available Balance	0	5	10	15	0	5	10	15	0
Master Schedule		5	5	5	5	5	5	5	5

Figure 10.13 MTC Master Schedule, Missiles, Build Ahead

	Past Due	1	2	3	4	5	6	7	8
Actual Demand					20				20
Projected Available Balance	0	6	12	18	2	7	12	17	0
Master Schedule		6	6	6	4	5	5	5	3

slack in certain periods—slack that could be used to catch up if any delays occur.

In building slack into the schedule, the missile producer knows that if there is a delay in periods 1 through 3 or periods 5 through 7, time could be made up in periods 4 and 8. If that time is not needed, the production lines might be scheduled for some other work or for maintenance.

Building unnecessary inventory is generally avoided by MTC companies, but here the extra inventory might be viewed as a prudent safety stock against a possible financial penalty, and it may be that the government is paying the missile company for materials and other expenses as work is completed, not on delivery, in which case inventory has minimal carrying cost to the company. However, someone pays for early inventory; it's not free!

This same missile producer may have a design change to phase-in or have another contract for a different missile design that requires that work begins in period 9. In this situation, the company determines that it must close down its line for all of period 8 to make the changeover to begin building the new missile. Since the contract terms for the first missile remain unchanged, the company would have to schedule periods 1 through 7 differently. Figure 10.14 shows just one of the many possibilities.

Figure 10.14 MTC Master Schedule, Missiles, Line Closing (Period 8)

	Past Due	1	2	3	4	5	6	7	8
Actual Demand					20				20
Projected Available Balance	0	6	12	18	4	10	16	20	0
Master Schedule		6	6	6	6	6	6	4	0

Variations of these scheduling approaches are applicable to accommodate short weeks due to holidays, slow ramp-up to full production of a new product, slow ramp-down to phase-out one product and introduce another, etc. The possibilities are many. The only constant is that the contract defines the obligation to deliver in terms of product, specifications, quantities, and dates. The supply schedule need not be the same as the contract delivery.

When Supply Can't Satisfy Demand

Despite what many defense contractors believe, that "the customer won't let us change the master schedule," the company can and should do what it believes is valid and necessary with the master schedule as long as customer specifications, quality, costs, delivery dates, and quantities are satisfied. The misguided notion that the contract controls the supply schedule leads to all manner of dysfunctional behavior among companies. It is not atypical, for example, for a defense contractor to fall behind schedule, to the point that delivery dates cannot *possibly* be met, and yet refuse to do the rescheduling of materials, capacity, and assembly that will bring the process back under rational control. The excuse for not rescheduling is that "the customer won't let us change the master schedule." Perhaps the customer will not let the company change the committed *delivery date*, but changing the supply schedule should be under the company's control.

Producers must control the master schedule, and when the facts dictate that delivery dates cannot be met, the schedule must be adjusted to the new reality. A past-due master schedule *cannot* be made on time no matter how hard the company may try. If today is the fifth of February, the product scheduled for completion on the fourth of February will not be on time. Leaving the schedule completion date as the fourth of February sends invalid information throughout the system. So why not work to *valid* schedules, ones that can be made for which people can be held accountable?

Interplant Integration

Minuteman Electronics Company (MEC) is a manufacturer of a new line of laptop computers sold throughout the Western Hemisphere. Its finished production is done at three facilities in the United States: Boston, Massachusetts (in a plant adjoining its corporate headquarters); Raleigh, North Carolina; and Birmingham, Alabama. These finishing plants ship completed goods to one of three warehouses, which are located in Boston (at the plant); Chicago, Illinois; and San Francisco, California.

MEC's finishing plants are supported by component plants (located in Durham, North Carolina, and Waco, Texas); these, in turn, are supported by two subcomponent plants located in Durham and Pomona, California. The subcomponent plants both produce printed circuit boards used in the component plants' circuit board assemblies.

In the world of modern manufacturing, in which a vertically integrated company may have several finishing plants for different product lines, and several component and subcomponent plants serving these and outside customers, the level of complexity increases dramatically for the master scheduler.

Figure 10.15 describes just such a situation. Here the company operates three levels of production facilities: finishing plants, component plants, and subcomponent plants. Customers and company-owned distribution centers provide demand to the finishing plants and, in turn, the finishing plants create demand for components and

Figure 10.15 Interplant Supply and Demand

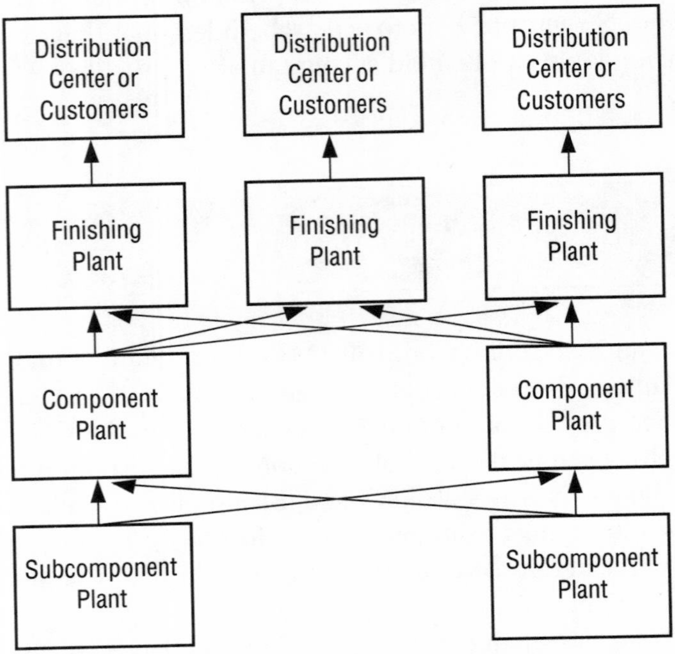

subcomponents. This demand is placed on the various plants through a series of iterations using the master scheduling and material requirements planning systems. Some view this situation as another form of make-to-contract.

Where should the master scheduling function be located in this interplant situation? In a centralized planning approach, it would be located at the finishing plant level. Demand would come down from the customers and distribution centers, the supply to satisfy that demand would be master scheduled, and an MRP system would reach down through the underlying layers of component and subcomponent facilities to schedule and order all necessary materials and capacity for those facilities. But this approach to being overly managed, still the norm in many industries, has severe negative side effects, as any plant managers at the bottom of the system will confirm.

What happens in this system is that changes in demand at the top (finishing plants) cascade downward through the MRP system, creating a "whipsaw effect" at lower levels. The component and subcomponent plants, which must respond mindlessly to order changes from above, are burdened with constant requests to increase or decrease supply. They cannot decouple themselves from demand at the finishing plant level; they cannot refuse an order that is beyond their capacities; they cannot—in a sense—control their destinies. The result is often chaos on all production floors involved.

Figure 10.16 on the following page diagrams this situation. On the left side of the figure is the traditional method just described, by which demand is accommodated through master scheduling at the finishing plant level; the MRP system is activated through the finishing plant to the component plant to the subcomponent plant. Any change in demand at the top races through this system. If the finishing plant moves in a supply order, all lower-level plants are sent directives to reschedule-in the required components. Never in this situation is the lower-level plant asked if they can do the reschedule.

A better way to operate is shown on the right side of Figure 10.16. This is the recommended method. Here, demand from customers and distribution centers is accommodated through master scheduling at the finishing plant and that plant's MRP system. The required

Figure 10.16 Interplant Master Schedule and Material Requirement Planning

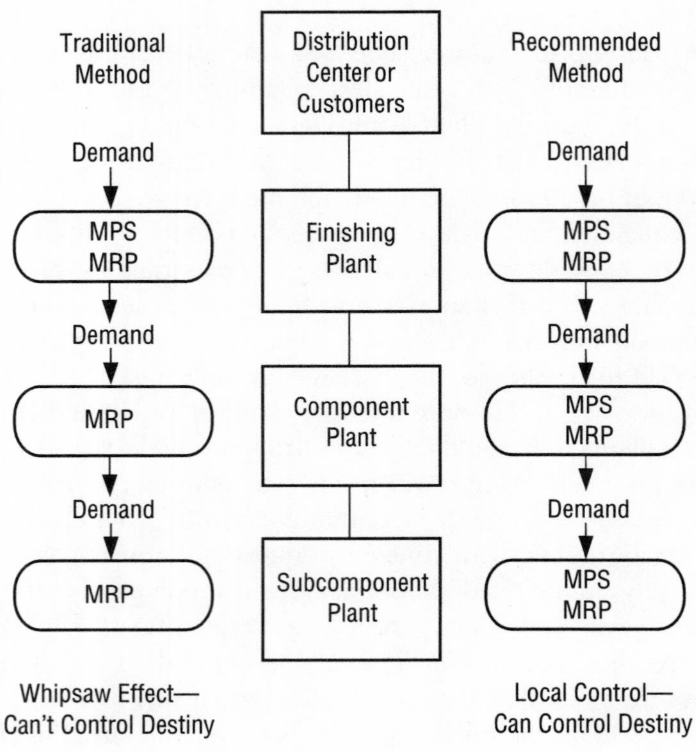

materials produced by the component plant's (printed circuit board assemblies in the MEC example) requirements become demand, which is entered into the MPS system at the component plant level. This demand is reviewed and analyzed before the master scheduler adjusts the MPS to support it. Only when the master scheduler believes that demand can be met is it put into the schedule. This leads to a very important principle: People should be held accountable only for those things they can control. If the finishing plants continue moving finishing schedules around, the component and subcomponent plants may automatically be set up for failure, either by missing schedules or by building and carrying incredible and unnecessary levels of inventory.

The component and subcomponent plants are in business to support upstream plants. They want to satisfy them as customers. But they need a chance to do it right. What is needed is a way to see the demand, but not let that demand automatically drive reschedules into the component and subcomponent manufacturing facilities. That can be done by using the planning time fence and firm planned order capability. By driving the finishing plant's demand into the master schedule at the lower-level plants, demand is decoupled from supply. This gives the supply plant the opportunity to say yes or no to the demand. If the supply plant cannot satisfy demand, then that information needs to be communicated up the chain, giving the finishing plants a chance to find another source of supply or replan appropriately.

This same process is continued from the component plants down to the subcomponent plants. In this case, the component's master schedule drives lower-level requirements through its MRP system, generating demand for printed circuit boards. This demand enters the master schedule of the subcomponent plant.

The benefit of this recommended method is that it gives greater control to managers at each level—these are the managers with the greatest knowledge of local capabilities and constraints. A production line may be closed because of a breakdown or scheduled maintenance; problems with a supplier may be constraining the availability of parts. Under the traditional method, schedulers who instigate change at high levels may be oblivious to these lower-level production problems.

Up to this point, we have concentrated our efforts on master scheduling and the planning of materials and resources to build products and satisfy customer needs. The next challenge is to schedule production by communicating these real customer needs to manufacturing. The formal communication lines are supported by various techniques, some of which the next chapter on finishing addresses.

11

Finishing Schedules

Rolling delivery promises gather no reorders.

Up to this point, the focus has been on bringing together the material and the capacities to build products that customers will eventually order. At some point the manufacturing floor must be told what to produce, in what quantities, and in what configurations. This communication is accomplished through the finishing (or final assembly) process. The finishing process converts the master schedule from a plan into manufacturing action.

The finishing schedule establishes work authorization—i.e., approval to perform work on defined products, using specified capacity and materials—according to a schedule that identifies the sequence in which the work is to be performed. The finishing schedule sets priorities for finishing, assembly, filling, testing, packaging, and so forth. This communication has a variety of labels: work orders, production orders, shop orders, factory orders, job orders, campaigns, production or line schedules, scheduling boards, run rates, and kanbans.

Manufacturing Strategy and Finishing Schedules

The manufacturing strategy of the company has an impact on how and when orders should be released to finishing. Is the company pursuing a make-to-stock (MTS) or engineer-to-order (ETO) strategy? Or is it something in between, like make-to-order (MTO)? To understand why strategy matters, look at Figure 11.1. On the left, the make-to-stock company has a typically short backlog of customer orders because the product is delivered off-the-shelf. Over the remainder of the time periods, it must schedule against forecasted demand. In a make-to-order environment—on the right side of the figure—the backlog is much longer and the company does not need to schedule against forecasted demand to nearly the same extent. This is because in the make-to-order environment, the customer places the order and typically expects to wait for delivery. The important point here is that the time allotted to the finishing process may be less than the sum of the backlog. In a make-to-stock company, the time allotted to finish the product is often greater than the sum of the customer backlog.

Figure 11.1 Finishing Schedules in Make-to-Stock and Make-to-Order Environments

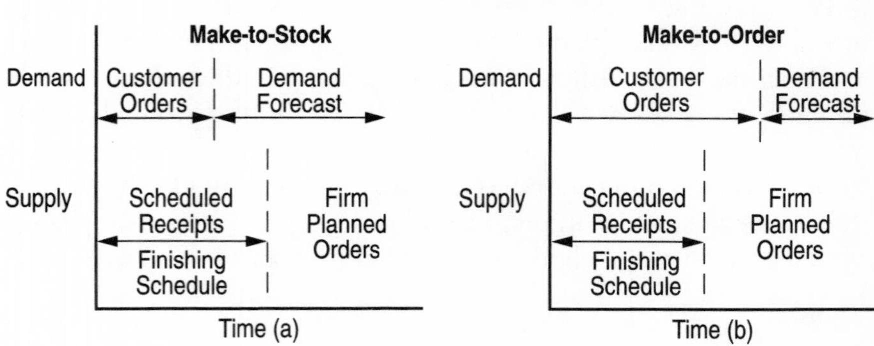

Satisfying these two different demand patterns requires different scheduling patterns. In a make-to-stock environment, the product must be on the shelf prior to receipt of the customer order. Therefore, released schedules must be created prior to receiving the customer orders, and the scheduler must key the finishing schedule to the demand forecast. In contrast, the make-to-order environment is one in which the final product is not built until the customer order is in hand, with all option requirements specified. Here, the customer expects to wait while the factory releases and executes the finishing schedule.

Although the company's selected manufacturing strategy impacts how and when to release orders into the finishing process, other variables also need to be addressed. Questions to be asked are:

- Is the manufacturing environment set up as a job shop or does it operate as a flow shop?
- What is the volume of product moving down the line?
- How about the product mix?
- Are lead times short or long?

The answers to these questions can affect how best to schedule, sequence, and communicate what needs to be done.[1]

Manufacturing Approaches

Having a manufacturing strategy is just part of what a company needs; beneath the level of strategy must be some chosen tactic, or approach to fulfilling the strategy. For most companies, the approach will be

[1] See John Dougherty and John Proud, "From Master Schedules to Finishing Schedules in the 1990s." APICS 33rd International Conference Proceedings, New Orleans, October 1990, page 368.

either the job shop or the flow shop. Both are represented graphically in Figure 11.2.

Job Shop

The left side of Figure 11.2 represents a job shop. In the job shop work centers and resources are grouped by like functions (saws together, presses together, etc.), so work flows to the various work centers in the sequence of steps needed to be performed. Here, the manufacturing process begins with material in a stock location. Material leaves this location to enter a queue at work center 1, where it awaits processing. When that job becomes the priority, work commences. From work center 1, the partially processed material is moved to either an intermediate stock location or into the queue for work center 2. And so it goes until each step of the manufacturing process has been completed and the transformed material enters the finished-goods inventory. Assembled products built in batches, engineer-to-order, and low-volume MTO products and others characterized by high-product variation are generally manufactured in this way.

Flow Shop

The right side of Figure 11.2 represents the flow shop. In the flow shop work centers and resources are grouped in the normal sequence

Figure 11.2 Job Shop and Flow Shop

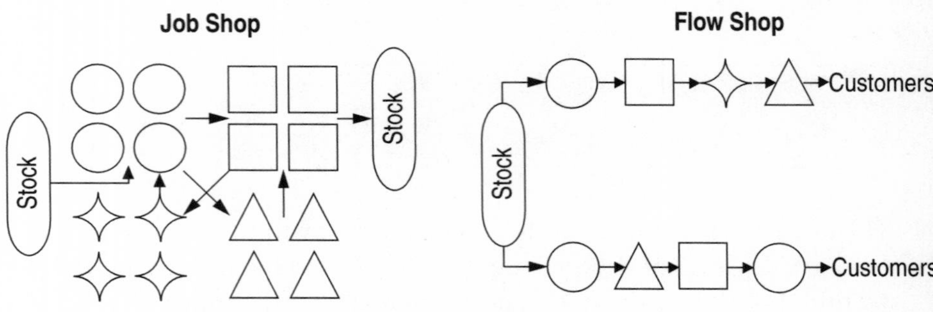

that work is performed. Here, material starts at the beginning of the line and is subject to processing operations and/or added materials as it literally "flows" down the line. Other materials flow into the line as required. A good example of a flow shop is found in plate-glass manufacturing, a continuous process in which raw materials are added to one end of a furnace tank, and molten glass pours out of the other, forming a continuous ribbon of glass. This ribbon is subjected to continuous forming, annealing, and cutting operations at various points on the production line. Make-to-stock, and high-volume make-to-order products with minimal product variation—particularly non-assembled products like glass, nylon, and so forth—are most frequently manufactured by this approach.

Mixed Approaches

Job shop and flow shop approaches to manufacturing are not mutually exclusive. It is quite common to have a job shop feeding a flow shop, a flow shop feeding a job shop, a flow shop feeding another flow shop, or one job shop feeding another job shop. The combination of approaches used, and their order, is determined by the requirements of the business and by the state of its process technology.[2]

Other Manufacturing Issues

Finishing schedules need to consider issues other than the manner in which manufacturing will take place. These are volume, the level of product variability in the product mix, and required completion lead times.

[2] These issues are addressed in James M. Utterback, *Mastering the Dynamics of Innovation* (Boston, MA: Harvard Business School Press, 1994). Utterback points out how the interaction of product and process innovation has often transformed traditional job shop operations into, first, traditional job shop routines interspersed by "islands of automation," and eventually continuous-flow manufacturing.

Volume

The finishing schedule for inexpensive ballpoint pens, a high-volume operation, is much different than that of a commercial aircraft manufacturer or other producers of high-cost, low-volume products. In the high-volume operation, completed products come off the line at hundreds per minute—e.g., 50,000 pens per shift. To ask manufacturing to report unit completions to a work order would be overwhelming and counterproductive. In the low-volume shop, however, using a work order to collect data about each operation is not overwhelming.

Variability in the Product Mix

The amount of variability in the product mix not only influences the choice of job shop versus flow shop, it also impacts the finishing schedule. High-product variability often causes a company to utilize the planning bill concept and pseudo items, which need to be pulled together in the finishing process to correctly communicate what the customer has ordered.

Completion Lead Time

Does it take a long time to actually produce the product, or is the manufacturing cycle short? The answer to this question may impact how the finishing schedule is communicated to the factory floor. If a long completion lead time is required, the master scheduler might lean toward the use of a work order. But if the company's business is producing sewing needles by the hundreds of thousands, or if its product takes just a few seconds to manufacture, then a work order may not make as much sense and some form of line schedule may be appropriate. A line schedule (sometimes supported by a schedule board) announces what will be run: by type, quantity, part number, sequence, and so forth.

Sequencing

During the creation of the master schedule, specific manufacturing sequences of products are generally not considered. What mattered then was what needed to be produced in what period to satisfy demand. Specific sequencing takes on critical importance in the finishing process, and for several different reasons. A printer, for example, may need to run the light colors first, then run the sheets again, this time with the darker colors.

Traditional Means of Communicating the Schedule

One traditional way master schedulers communicate to the manufacturing floor is by means of the production order (also commonly called a "shop order" or "work order"). Generally, software systems support this form of schedule communications fairly well. A production order is a document or group of documents, conveying authority for the manufacture of specified parts or products in specified quantities. It generally includes a bill-of-material for manufacturing the product, a list of operations or steps required by work center, and various other documents specifying tooling, equipment settings, inspection, and testing requirements. It may include documents to be used as "turn-around" forms to report material consumption, manufacturing activity, or completion of particular steps in the process.

Data contained on separate bills-of-material and routing documents can be combined into a single document with additional information. To do this, each component within the bill-of-material must

Do We Really Need These Computers?

One of the most interesting scheduling boards seen by the author was located in the plant of a Japanese rubber belt manufacturer (see Figure 11.3). It was not merely a scheduling board, but an inventory-control system as well. Each item was represented by a vertical tube into which wooden blocks of varying thickness (pot size) could be placed, representing the current inventory level (height of the blocks in each tube) and the required level for the current time frame (pieces of string attached by pins *across* each tube that could be moved up and down as demand for the item changed).

As work was completed, the block of wood representing the inventory was placed in the tube and the physical material was placed in an outbound stocking location. The operator would then remove the next-in-line block of wood from the "out" tube. This block was his or her authorization to begin work on the next item (identified by the block of wood). This simple board served as inventory control, demand driver, work authorization, and priority system. It was simple, and it seemed to work without benefit of electricity, computer chips, or megadollar software.

Figure 11.3 Manual Scheduling Board

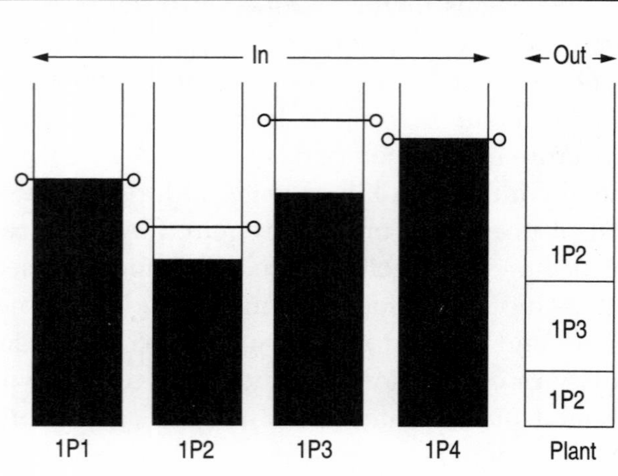

be identified to the operation or manufacturing step where it is needed. Additionally, the manufacturing location where material is to be delivered must be identified. With this information, a finishing document can be created.

Another way to communicate finishing schedules is by means of work-center schedules. Many job shops use these as final authorizations and to set priorities.

Yet another means of finishing-schedule communication is by means of a line schedule, which is most applicable in a flow-shop environment. When it comes to process, repetitive, or Just-in-Time environments, companies may find it beneficial to simply use line schedules without work orders. A line schedule can be a very simple directive, as in "run four lines and two shifts." Or it can be more definitive, as in "run product 123 on line 1 at 2,000 per shift"; or "run product 345 on line 2 at 6,000 per day for 3 days." Line schedules can be displayed on manually maintained schedule boards or electronic computer scoreboards. These boards notify personnel which job to run next, along with date and quantity requirements.

The Kanban System

The "kanban," the Japanese term for *signal*, is another popular method of communicating to the factory floor. The signal itself can be a card attached to a bin, a square painted on the floor, or a simple container holding assembly components. Japanese manufacturers originally created kanbans as a means for indicating when some action was to take place.

The entire kanban process is set in motion by a "demand pull" originating with a customer order. An order creates requirements for products which in turn "pull" materials through the entire system of suppliers and production. In the idealized kanban system, nothing moves until an order is taken, but when the order does appear, every level of the production system becomes the customer of the next lower level of production. As manufacturing depletes components from a kanban bin, the empty bin becomes an order to refill—a source of demand pulling more of the same components through the production process. When the bin is full, that sector of the production system stops.

The kanban system was designed as a simple but elegant way to tightly link production with demand, thereby eliminating the need for costly inventory and finished goods for which there might be no demand.[3] Materials and components are delivered by suppliers only as they are needed—i.e., Just-in-Time—and are brought to the factory floor only as needed. The manufacturing floor builds products only to fill orders. When demand is slack, workers perform maintenance, discuss improvements, and so forth. This system, which operates more on the basis of actual demand than on forecasted demand, has many obvious merits but also some serious weaknesses, especially insofar as products with long lead times and fluctuating demand are concerned. In a sense, kanban firms have adopted a make-to-order strategy in competitive environments where others would be make-to-stock. At the same time, they have corrected some of the lead-time problems normally associated with this strategy by pioneering new methods of rapid line changing, shorter cycle times, and Just-in-Time delivery of materials from suppliers.

Product-Dependent Kanban

There are two types of demand pull systems—product-dependent and product-independent. With product-dependent kanbans, the

[3] The kanban method is based upon the waste-reduction methodology that motivated Japan's postwar industrialists. Devastated by the war, and short on capital and materials, they viewed American production methods of the 1950s and 1960s as creating profligate levels of inventory for which orders might or might not appear. Far better, they thought, to only order materials and build things for which there were orders.

kanban itself is identified to a material. The product-dependent kanban is labeled with the item number, description, and kanban quantity. These kanbans are the visible records needed to set the system in motion. Think of the manufacturing floor and refer to Figure 11.4. Imagine that each work center has an outbound stocking location. These outbound stocking locations are identified to a product. In the example, work center B has three locations for 1S1, two for 1S2, and one for 1S3.

For work center A, there are five outbound stocking locations. The inbound stocking location for A might be the warehouse. The way product-dependent kanban works is as follows: If the kanban is empty, fill it. If the kanban is full, stop production. If all kanbans are full, the line is shut down. Now let's assume all kanbans are full, the line is full, and a customer needs a 1S1. That customer can be a customer from outside the plant or the next operation (each work center has cus-

Figure 11.4 Product-Dependent Kanban Example

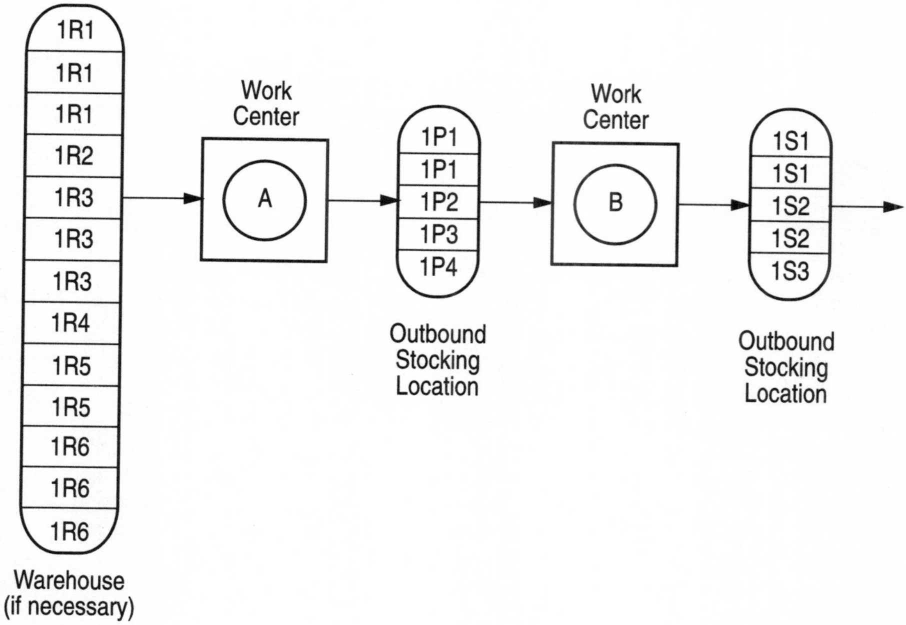

tomers and suppliers). Referring to Figure 11.5, we see that satisfying this demand leaves an empty kanban square formerly occupied by 1S1—which authorizes work center B to produce a 1S1.

Assume that it takes a 1P1 and 1P3 to manufacture the 1S1. Work center B would go get a 1P1 and 1P3 from work center A's outbound stocking location, move those two items to work center B, and commence the operations necessary to produce the 1S1. What this action does is free up two more kanbans—the 1P1 and 1P3. That now authorizes work center A to fill those two kanbans. Assume that it takes a 1R5 to make a 1P1. Work center A would go get a 1R5 from the warehouse and commence working on the 1P1. When finished, work center A would place the 1P1 in its outbound stocking location designated for 1P1, and would still know that it has a 1P3 to build, which takes a 1R3. Work center A would go get a 1R3 from the warehouse, build the 1P3, and place it in the outbound stocking location labeled 1P3. This action would free up the warehouse space for 1R5 followed by 1R3, which are replenished in the same manner as the work center's outbound stocking locations.

Figure 11.5 Product-Dependent Kanban System

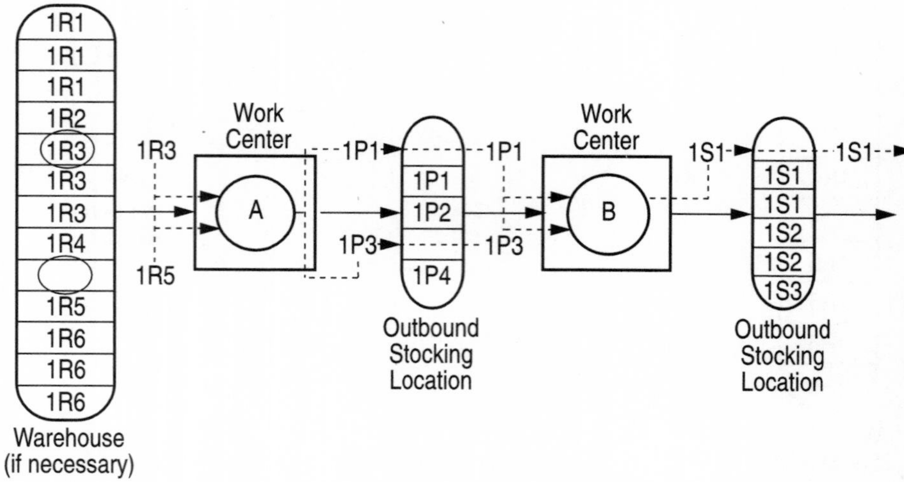

Product-Independent Kanbans

This system uses unlabeled outbound stocking locations (see Figure 11.6). Assume that the production line is full. A demand pull for the 1S1 sets the line in motion. The outbound stocking location for work center B is now empty, which authorizes work center B to produce another product.

The work center B operator looks back and pulls the 1S2 forward into his or her work space (may use additional materials from other feeder lines) and commences work center B's operations by taking the 1S2 (semicompleted item) and doing what's necessary to complete the product. When finished, work center B would move the 1S2 to its outbound stocking location. The initial pull action also puts work center A into action since its outbound stocking location has been freed up. The next question is, What does work center A start to work on? The decision is made by using the master schedule or finishing schedule. In the example the finishing schedule states that a 1S1 is the next desired item. Therefore, the gateway work center will commence building a 1S1.

Figure 11.6 Product-Independent Kanban System

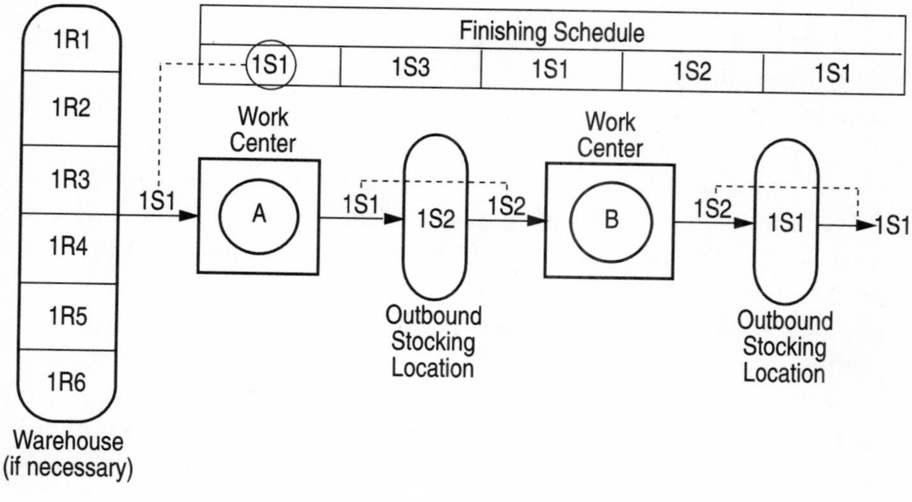

Tying It All Together

The Soft Seat example used in chapters 7 and 8 dealt with a conference center chair product family. In chapter 7 we discussed the process of restructuring the conference center chair's bill-of-material into a series of pseudo or planning bills. This was done to facilitate forecasting, bill-of-material database maintenance, master scheduling, and option overplanning. Let's return to the Soft Seat chair example and see how these pseudos and the overall planning bill concept is used during the finishing or final assembly process.

When the conference center chair planning bill was structured (refer to Figure 11.7 for a review), five options were identified: seat assembly, chair back splat assembly (although a purchased assembly in the example), left leg assembly, hardware kit, and right leg assembly. The seat and back splat assemblies were color sensitive, so we took the seat and back splat assemblies and put them into a color-sensitive option bill. This meant that a selection of the red option required the red seat assembly and the red back splat assembly. The other three items or parts (right leg assembly, left leg assembly, and hardware kit) were common to all conference center chairs. Therefore, these items were structured into a common parts bill. This structuring was done assuming that the marketplace was permitting a two-period (or week) delivery time. The use of the time-phased bill-of-material as well as knowing where the company desires or needs to meet the customer are very important when determining the best way to structure the planning bills. How would the following scenarios impact the planning bill structure? What if, by compressing the manufacturing and procurement lead times, we could remain competitive and not stock completed colored chair seat assemblies? Alternatively, what if the competition began quoting longer lead times so that we didn't have to stock completed colored chair seat assemblies? If we didn't have to stock completed chair seat assemblies, then the

Figure 11.7 Time-Phased BOM Meeting the Customer Before Chair Seat Assembly Work Is Commenced

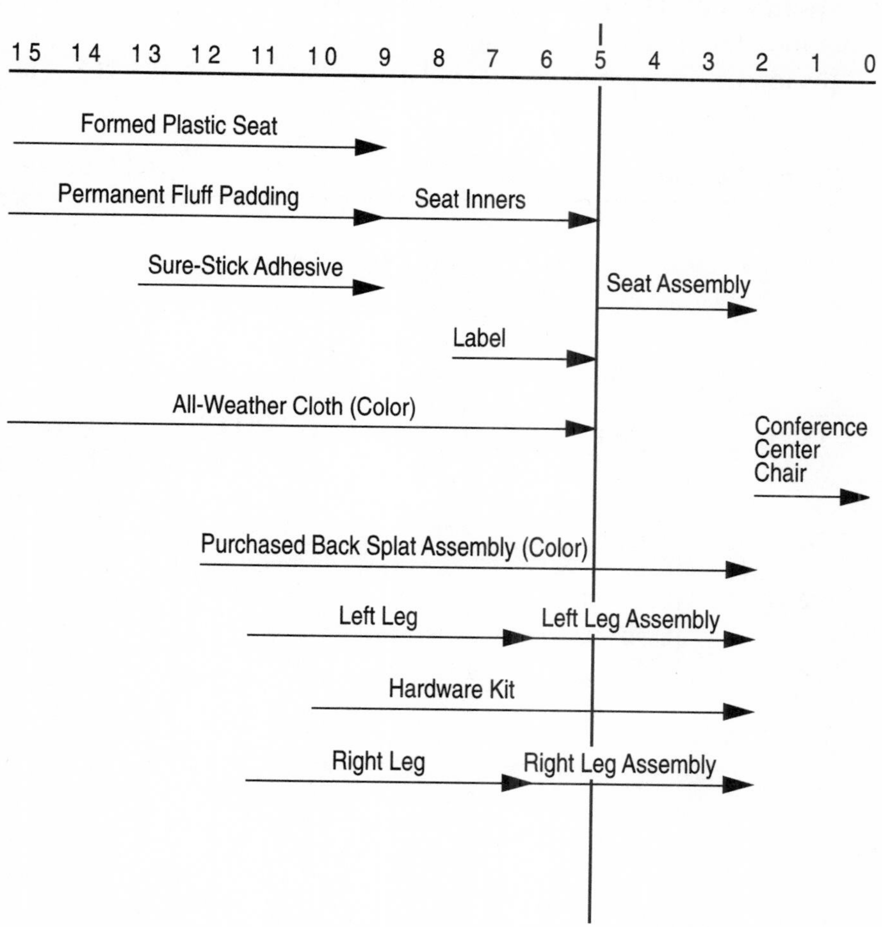

color sensitive items become the colored all-weather cloth and the colored chair back splat assembly—the seat inners and the label contained in the chair seat assembly become common parts (see Figure 11.7).

The new or restructured planning bill looks like Figure 11.8 on page 324. As you can see, the common parts bill now contains the label, seat inners, hardware kit, right leg assembly, and left leg assembly. The red option bill contains the red all-weather cloth and the red back splat assembly. Besides the planning bill structure, the master scheduler may desire to put other useful and meaningful data on each item in the pseudo bill. This data may include delivery point of usage, parent operation number, and lead-time offset.

Review the red option pseudo bill at the bottom of Figure 11.8. The

Figure 11.8 Planning Bills When Colored Chair Seats Are Not Stocked

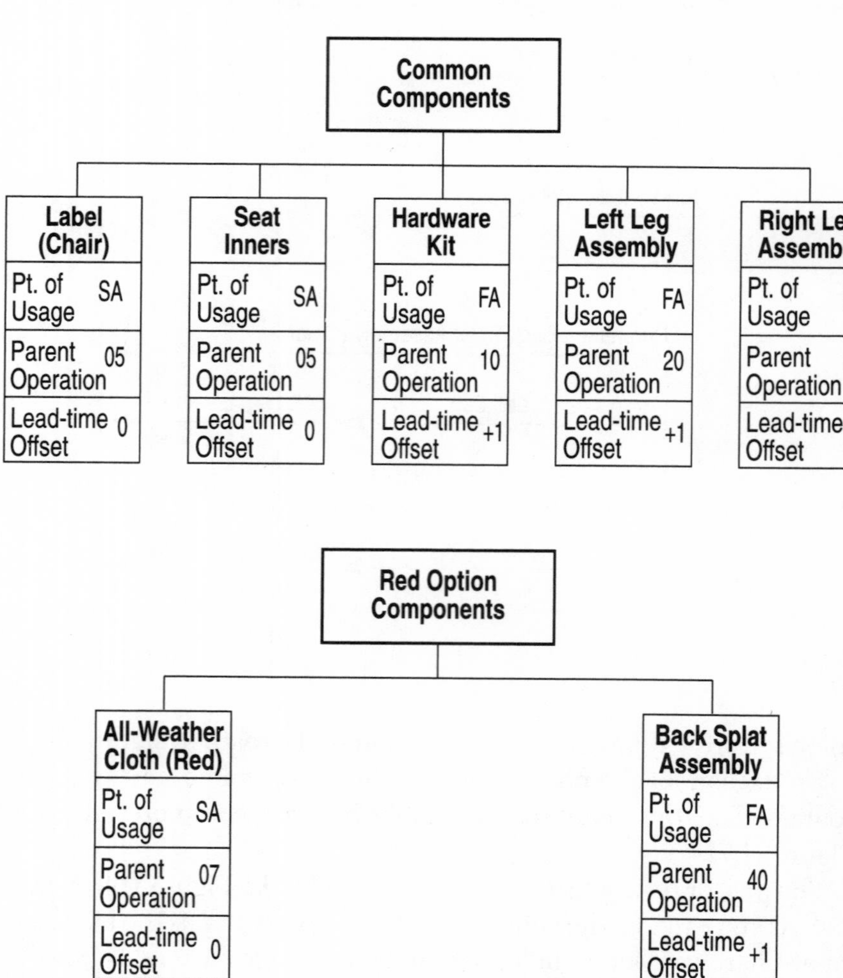

seat cloth and chair back splat assembly are the items in this bill. Notice that the cloth is required for operation 07, which is done in work center "SA." This tells us that the seat cloth will need to be delivered to location SA when operation 07 is started. The all-weather seat cloth item (as Figure 11.8 states) has a lead-time offset equal to 0. In other words, the cloth is needed when the manufacturing work for the conference center chair commences.

If we review the chair back splat assembly, it can be seen that the back splat assembly is needed for operation 40 and is to be delivered to location "FA," its point of usage. The lead-time offset for the chair back is +1, which means that the chair back splat assembly is required to be on the line one period after the assembly of the chair commences. The conference center chair's planning lead time is used to offset all parts in the option as well as all parts in the common parts bills. Next, the lead-time offset serves to adjust or add back in time the identified lead-time offset. By using this technique, all items in the conference center chair can be time-phased to the time required on the line. In addition, these materials can be delivered directly to their usage points. This technique and capability are very important when a company commences flattening their bills-of-material, expanding the use of common parts bills, and moving toward the flow-line concept.

Final Assembly or Process Routings

Prior to flattening the planning bills for the conference center chair product family (chapter 7), the red seat assembly was built and put into stock. During this chapter's discussion of the chair's planning bill, we have flattened the chair's bill and no longer plan to stock red seat assemblies. This means that we also need to flatten the associated routings or process instructions.

A routing is defined as the sequence of events necessary to build or produce a product. Figure 11.9 identifies two routings: one for the final assembly of the conference center chair (top half of the figure) and one for the subassembly of the seat assembly (bottom half of the figure).

However, we no longer plan to build and stock the seat assembly—it has been removed from the planning bill structure (see Figure 11.8). But we know the manufacturer still needs to build the chair seat if we are to prouce a conference center chair. The red chair seat is composed of seat inners, a label, and red all-weather cloth (see Figures 11.7 (page 323) and 11.9—subassembly routing). Since we no longer have a seat assembly in the planning bill to attach the required operations documentation, we have resequenced the operations of the subassembly work (operation 10, which states to attach the label to the seat inners, has become operation 05, and operation 20, which states to attach the colored all-weather cloth, has become operation 07). These two operations are now the first two operations in the conference center chair's build sequence. The six-step process (two for the seat work and four for the final chair work) is now one

Figure 11.9 Final Assembly and Subassembly Routings for Red Conference Center Chair

Operation	Final Assembly Routing	Point of Usage
10	Lay out hardware kit per instructions	FA
20	Assemble left leg assembly to seat assembly using provided hardware	FA
30	Assemble right leg assembly to seat assembly using provided hardware	FA
40	Attach back splat assembly	FA
	Subassembly Routing	
10 → 05	Attach *label* to *seat inners*	SA
20 → 07	Attach *all-weather cloth* to seat inners	SA

complete routing for the final chair assembly (see Figure 11.10). This complete routing is attached to the common parts' parent item as it will be required for all conference center chairs that need to be built, the same requirement that is placed on the common parts.

The routing for the conference center chair has also taken on the characteristics of a generic or common chair. Look at operation 07 in Figure 11.10. It states that the all-weather cloth will be the color stated on the customer order. The same is true for operation 40. By adding these instructions, this final assembly routing can be used to communicate to the manufacturing floor the events that must take place in order to produce a customer's desired colored chair, be it red or black.

Continuing to look at Figure 11.10, we see the component's operation number and point of usage that were attached to the planning bill. Look at operation 05 again. It states that the label needs to be attached to the seat inners. This tells the master scheduler that the label and seat inners are needed to support operation 05. Since operation 05 is done in location SA, that's where the label and seat inners need to be delivered (point of usage). If we look at operation 10, we see that the hardware kit is required in location FA. The routing states that operations 05 and 07 will be started in location SA

Figure 11.10 General Final Assembly Routing Attached to Common Parts (required for each chair sold)

Operation	Description	Point of Usage
05	Attach label to seat inners	SA
07	Attach all-weather cloth to seat inners *(color per customer order)*	SA
10	Lay out hardware kit per instructions	FA
20	Assemble left leg assembly to seat assembly using provided hardware	FA
30	Assemble right leg assembly to seat assembly using provided hardware	FA
40	Attach back splat assembly *(color per customer order)*	FA

one period prior to operations 10 through 40, which are done in location FA. This is the reason behind the lead-time offset of +1 for all items required in work center FA versus work center SA.

Configuring and Building to a Customer Order

We now have in place the database necessary to respond to a customer request and order. If the demand management (see chapter 14 for a discussion on this subject), master scheduling, material management, and manufacturing process works, the materials required to support a customer request for delivery in two to five periods (equates to where the company has decided to meet the customer) and the resources necessary to produce the final configuration should be in place. The next step is to book an order, commit to a delivery date (assuming the materials and capacity are available), and produce the desired product.

Figure 11.11 identifies what's needed to produce a red conference center chair. This figure shows that in order to produce a red chair, one set of common parts (which are composed of a label, seat inners assembly, hardware kit, left leg assembly, right leg assembly) and one set of red option items (which are the red cloth and the red back splat) are needed. Using this data, a material list for the real component items such as the label, left leg assembly, right leg assembly, back splat, etc., can be generated. So, if a customer should order a red conference center chair, we can use the planning bills and specific configuration desired to identify all the engineered items required (see Figure 11.12).

Reviewing the figure, you can see the component, description, quantity needed (dependent upon the customer order—the example shows that 5 red conference center chairs have been ordered), point

Figure 11.11 Red Conference Center Chair Bill-of-Material

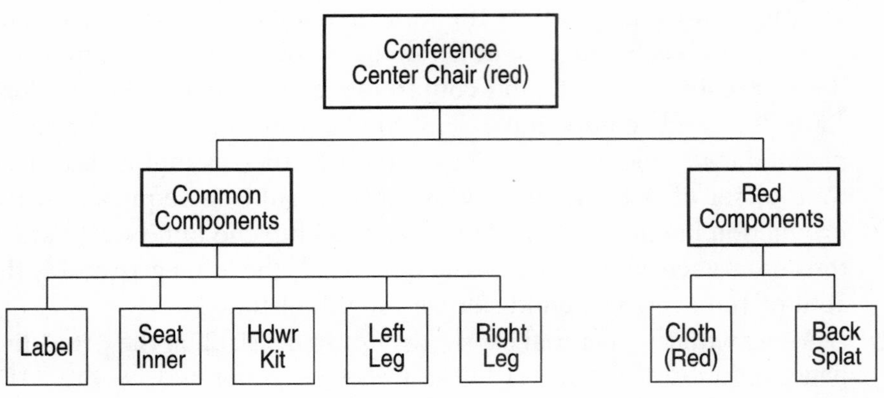

Figure 11.12 Finishing Materials for Red Conference Center Chair

Materials List **Finish Order #F1234**

Component #	Description	Qty.	Pt. of Usage	Date
125	Chair label	5	SA	6/9/XX
666	Seat Inners	5	SA	6/9/XX
780	All-weather Cloth	5	SA	6/9/XX
861	Hardware Kit	5	FA	6/16/XX
122	Left Leg Assembly	5	FA	6/16/XX
128	Right Leg Assembly	5	FA	6/16/XX
880	Back Splat Assembly	5	FA	6/16/XX

of usage (location to deliver the items), and date required. The date required for each component is calculated by the MPS system using the customer's due date and conference center chair's planned lead time plus each component's lead-time offset (say the chair has a planned lead time of two periods and the left leg assembly has a lead time offset of +1, the left leg assembly would be required on the production line in location FA one period after the build start date of the conference center chair—example needs the left leg assembly the 16th of June versus a build start of the 9th of June.)

Along with the material list shown in Figure 11.12 on the preceding page, a routing (Figure 11.13) can also be generated by the MPS system. Remember, the routing was attached to the common parts item, which is also needed to build conference center chairs. When the customer order is taken and a due date is committed, this routing can be used to determine when each operation needs to be done. This is done either by backward scheduling from the due date to identify the latest possible start date, or by forward scheduling from the first operation to identify the earliest expected completion date. In most cases the choice should be to backward schedule from the customer's need and promise date.

Figure 11.13 Finishing Routing for Conference Center Chair

Operations List **Finish Order #F1234**

Sequence	Description	Work Center	Date
05	Attach label to seat inners	SA	6/10/XX
07	Attach all-weather cloth to seat inners *(color per customer order)*	SA	6/16/XX
10	Lay out hardware kit per instructions	FA	6/17/XX
20	Assemble left leg assembly to seat assembly using provided hardware	FA	6/19/XX
30	Assemble right leg assembly to seat assembly using provided hardware	FA	6/21/XX
40	Attach back splat assembly *(color per customer order)*	FA	6/23/XX

Finishing Combined Materials and Operations List

At this point we have successfully used the planning bill and the generic routing to create a materials list and to identify all the operations that must be performed in order to produce the customer's requested product—5 red conference center chairs. Since we know the operation and when the material is needed, a combined materials and operations list can be created on one screen, as shown in Figure 11.14.

Figure 11.14 Finishing Combined Materials and Operations List

Operation	Material	Description	Qty	W/C	Date
05		Attach label to seat inners	5	SA	6/10/XX
	125	Chair label	5		6/9/XX
	666	Seat inners	5		6/9/XX
07		Attach all-weather cloth to seat inners *(per customer order)*	5	SA	6/16/XX
	780	All-weather cloth	5		6/9/XX
10		Lay out hardware kit per instructions	5	FA	6/17/XX
	861	Hardware kit	5		6/16/XX
20		Assemble left leg assembly to seat assembly using provided hardware	5	FA	6/19/XX
	122	Left leg assembly	5		6/16/XX
30		Assemble right leg assembly to seat assembly using provided hardware	5	FA	6/21/XX
	128	Right leg assembly	5		6/16/XX
40		Attach back splat assembly *(per customer order)*	5	FA	6/23/XX
	880	Back splat assembly	5	FA	6/16/XX

This screen shows the first event is operation 05. In this operation the manufacturing floor is being instructed to attach the label to the seat inners. In order to do this, labels and seat inners are needed on the 9th of June in location SA. The attaching of the labels to the seat inners will be done five times and all the work is to be completed by the 10th of June. The next event in sequence is operation 07, where the all-weather seat cloth (color per customer order) is attached to the seat inner assembly. In order to complete this operation, five pieces of cloth (color identified) must be delivered to SA by the 9th of June. When this work is done we will have an all-weather colored seat. This seat is then flowed to location FA where the next operation (10) will be done.

During operation 10, the hardware kit is made ready for use in final assembly. This means that the hardware kit is needed to be delivered to FA by the 16th of June. Operation 10 is scheduled to be completed by the 17th of June, which was determined by backward scheduling from the customer order commit date.

This process continues until all the operations have been completed and the total customer order is finished. During the process, the manufacturing floor can report progress by each operation, milestone, checkpoint operations, or completed chairs. This choice is dependent upon the environment, manufacturing strategy chosen, product lead times, product volumes, and desired or needed information.

Choosing the Most Effective Approach

There is no one *right* approach to communicating the schedule to the floor. The key to making the *best* choice is keeping the ultimate purpose of the finishing schedule in mind: the simple and clear communication of work authorization, specifications, and priority.

The best choice is also a function of previously discussed environmental issues. While no iron-clad rules are possible, some approaches to finishing schedules are used more often in certain environments. In a business with a job shop organization, low volumes, high-potential product mix, long lead times, and high need for proper sequencing, it is normal to see individual work orders and bills-of-material traveling with the job to communicate work authorization and specifications.

Conversely, in environments with a flow shop organization, high volumes, few product variations, and short lead times, manual or electronic-generated line schedules such as schedule boards communicate end-product priorities. Kanbans are used to trigger work authorization and signal priorities for all feeder lines and departments that supply the finishing line.

Most manufacturing environments are somewhere between these two ends of the spectrum. The influence of continuous improvement programs is pushing more of the discrete job shop environments toward the flow shop scenario. It is also pushing high-volume flow shops toward shorter, quicker runs that can be better supported by the vigorous use of kanbans in all upstream-process steps. Thus, there is something of a convergence of the two extreme models of manufacturing.

Finishing Schedules Versus Master Schedules

The master schedule is a tool to schedule and prioritize material and capacity in anticipation of delivering final products to customers. It is typically organized into weekly periods. In the finishing process, however, the manufacturing schedule may be stated in daily or hourly periods. This difference in the required precision of planning periods is not the only difference between finishing and master schedules. The master schedule is driven by the sales and operations planning process through the demand and production plans, while the finishing process is driven by actual stock replenishment and customer orders.

This naturally results in quite different time horizons—the cumulative lead time being the minimum planning horizon for the master schedule, and the finishing lead time for the finishing schedule.

When the master schedule is put together, the actual build sequence is generally not considered; only the date when the product is expected to be needed is identified. This is not true when looking at the finishing schedule. It is very important to analyze the situation and define the best sequence to produce the various products scheduled. Take an athletic sock manufacturer—it would not be smart to dye the blue socks before the yellow socks. If this is done, a complete clean-out or wash-down would be needed before the lighter dye could be used.

The master schedule's function is to ensure that the material and adequate capacity will be available when it is needed to produce the product. The finishing schedule's function is to drive the finishing process using the materials and capacities the master scheduler has preplanned. In other words, the finishing or final assembly schedule relieves the master schedule. Once the finishing process commences, the job of the master scheduling function basically comes to an end and the completion process is managed under the eyes of the finishing or final assembly process.

Master scheduling and finishing are keys to a successful MRP II implementation. If a company's master scheduling effort fails, it is going to be very difficult for that company to reach Class A standards. The same can be said for the finishing process. To ensure an orderly and smooth master scheduling and finishing implementation, a defined process has been developed. This defined process and the various elements necessary to effectively implement master scheduling into a company is the subject of the next four chapters covering integration and implementation.

12

Sales and Operations Planning

There are three types of people: those who make things happen, those who watch things happen, and those who wonder what happened.

In business, as in war, failures often stem from lack of coordination between essential functions. On the battlefield, armies that fail to coordinate the movement of infantry with support from artillery, air, and armor typically are defeated by opponents whose main force and support functions operate as one. In business, the company whose sales force is out booking orders and promising delivery dates without the concurrence of finance, engineering, and manufacturing are likewise imperiled.

While coordination among business functions is obviously essential, it does not just happen, but needs a formal mechanism to ensure that it occurs. For most companies, that mechanism is "Sales and Operations Planning" (S&OP). Sales and operations planning is a formal process for managing change related to product demand. As described by George Palmatier and Joseph Shull:

> S&OP is the process whereby the management of the company provides direction, resolves conflicts, and manages the operations of the business. It is the tool that links the business plan to the more specific objectives of the organization . . . [ensuring] that all the divisions, departments, and other organizations within the company are pulling in the same direction at the same time toward the same goals.[1]

Sales and operations planning is an ongoing process, characterized by monthly review and continually adjusted to match company plans in light of fluctuating customer demand and the company's available resources. The process generates a number of other high-level plans. Figure 12.1 enumerates the inputs and the outputs of this planning process.

Figure 12.1 Sales and Operatons Planning Inputs and Outputs

Inputs

- Statement of anticipated demand (from Marketing and Sales)
- Indication of capabilities and capacities (from Manufacturing)
- Estimate of financial resources required (from Finance)
- Conformation of new-product design availability (from Engineering)

Outputs

- Sales plan (accountability— Marketing and Sales)
- Backlog projection (accountability—General Manager)
- Production plan (accountability—Manufacturing)
- Financial plan (accountability—Finance)
- Engineering/new-product development plan (accountability—Engineering)
- Inventory projection (accountability—General Manager)

[1] George E. Palmatier and Joseph S. Shull, *The Marketing Edge* (Essex Junction, VT: Oliver Wight Publications, Inc., 1989), p. 26.

The key functions of the organization are all involved in the S&OP process. Each provides input and develops its respective plans on understandings reached in the process. The S&OP process ensures that individual plans are in sync with each other. Thus, the production plan is coordinated with the sales plan; the financial plan is reconciled with the production, sales, and business plans; and so forth. In addition to serving as a means of generating other plans, S&OP is a process for developing a "budget" for the master schedule.

Sales and operations planning generally has a planning horizon of one year or more (the average is 18 months), and deals with sales and production volumes at the product family level. Unlike the overall business plan of the company, which is stated in financial terms, S&OP speaks in the language of sales and production: bookings, demand, supply, standard hours, units, tonnages, etc.

Workable, Adjustable Plans

One of the principal benefits of the S&OP process is its focus on "workable" plans. Natural optimism and business units planning in isolation are factors that lead to plans that cannot be fulfilled. Workable plans can be created only by systems that have built-in reality checks. The S&OP process offers those checks by starting at the top and providing verification at lower levels. The participation of all major functions is mandated by the process, and the feasibility of each function's plans is scrutinized by the others. Feedback loops ensure that plans are adjusted to the capabilities of related functions. Thus, an optimistic sales plan put forth by marketing is critiqued by manufacturing, which may not have nearly the capacity to deliver product at the requested level, assuming planned sales volume is reached. Figure 12.2 on the following page indicates where S&OP fits into the scheme of other company activities and the points where feedback can and should take place. Here, S&OP serves as a link between the highest-level business planning (and strategy) and operations. S&OP ties the company's high-level business and strategic plans to the operations of each department. The feedback loops in Figure 12.2 indicate how each department participates in the process. All major functions of the company are involved, ensuring that plans are attainable from the top down. The absence of this linkage creates the potential for loss of control and for significant miscommunication within the organization. For example, production operations might be working from one set of numbers while sales is planning on something quite different. The potential for confusion and failure in such a case is obviously great, and S&OP can eliminate its occurrence.

Customers cancel firm orders; unexpected new orders miraculously appear; manufacturing capacity slips as unanticipated breakdowns occur. British Prime Minister Benjamin Disraeli once said that "what we anticipate seldom occurs, what we least expect generally happens." This statement applies equally to politics, war, and busi-

Figure 12.2 Sales and Operations Planning and Other Company Functions

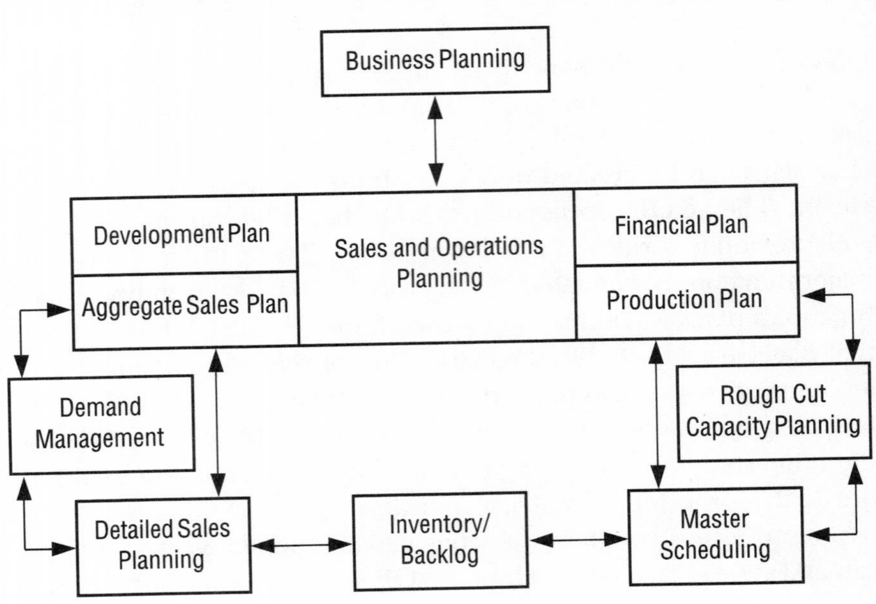

ness. The events we plan often unfold in ways we do not expect. Even well-coordinated plans can lead us into failure if they are carved in stone. To be successful, we need plans that are sufficiently flexible, or "robust," to accommodate the contingencies that naturally occur. Fortunately, the S&OP process, with its regular monitoring and inputs from many sources, provides an opportunity for planning adjustments as needed. As a result, it is an exceptional process for managing change. All the information needed to make adjustments ends up on the table, and each of the parties whose agreement to those adjustments is critical has a seat at the table. Moreover, because S&OP links high-level plans together while the MRP II system links high- and low-level plans, changes made at the S&OP level are formally communicated down into detailed plans. This channel of information enables different functions in the company to seize opportunities and avoid potential disasters.[2]

S&OP also allows companies to better manage finished-goods inventories and backlog. The right people come together to make decisions in a structured planning process that reflects top management's expectations. And finally, S&OP provides a basis for measuring performance, which is critical to any organization that is serious about continuous improvement.

S&OP and the Master Schedule

The past few pages painted a picture of S&OP in very broad strokes, demonstrating its benefits to the company as a whole. From the prospective of the master scheduler, smaller strokes are needed. The business plan must be converted into a production plan specifying production rates that, in turn, must be converted to a detail product-

[2] For a more complete review of sales and operations planning, see Richard Ling and Walter Goddard, *Orchestrating Success* (Essex Junction, VT: Oliver Wight Publications, Inc., 1988).

mix plan. To understand how this conversion takes place, we will eavesdrop on an S&OP meeting and observe the interaction among sales, marketing, manufacturing, engineering, and finance.

THE CASE OF S&OP AT AUTOTEK

Members from all key departments arrived at the monthly sales and operations planning meeting of AutoTek Corporation, a manufacturer of automotive parts and a subsidiary of the industrial giant Execor Industries. After exchanging pleasantries, they settled down to business. The meeting began with a discussion of special items, the most important being a report from AutoTek's general manager, Jack Saunders, about the recent budget meeting at Execor's corporate headquarters. Saunders cleared his throat and began:

"Good third-quarter news: It looks like we'll see a significant upturn in AutoTek sales—the new sales promotion has really grabbed the marketplace. We think that the business could grow by 15 percent over the next six months . . . maybe by 20 percent if our most optimistic projections come true."

Cheers rang out and several at the table raised the *V* sign triumphantly.

"Yeah, and what's the *bad* news?" snickered old Dave "Razor Tongue" Wilcox, vice president of finance.

Hisses and groans filled the room. "Will somebody tell Dave to send his wet blanket to the Laundromat," someone called out from the other side of the room.

"Okay, people, let's settle down," said Saunders. "Unfortunately, Dave's right, there is some bad news—or should I say a 'window of opportunity.' Because of our success at turning our division around, corporate has asked us to be responsible for 5 percent more of overall corporate profits."

More groans. Saunders raised both hands, as if to hold back a wave of protest. "Folks, let's not stew about that. Let's get down to work and figure out how we're going to hit those targets."

For the next ten minutes, the S&OP team reviewed the company's aggregate performance in comparison to the business plan. They talked about how they had performed with respect to sales, production, and inventory projections. The team also examined the backlog and shipment projections. Next, they reviewed their assumptions for the coming period, which included the hiring and training of ten new people in the next sixty days. This added personnel was expected to help AutoTek increase production rates if necessary. In addition, the company directors speculated about their major competitors. Jelco was facing a general strike, and JDR Enterprises was threatened by acquisition by Murco & Watts. Everyone agreed that there was both opportunity and danger for AutoTek in these developments.

The master scheduler had been following the discussion with interest. But his adrenaline really began to flow when the general manager announced that it was time to conduct the regular review of each product family. This was the main course for the master scheduler.

Saunders turned the meeting over to Sally Lattimer, the vice president of sales, who made an announcement. "Before we get into the product family review," she said, "please note that this is a landmark day for the S&OP team—we're now going high-tech! Instead of working from printed reports, we will be projecting output from the computer onto the screen through a link to an overhead projector. Ted Glass of marketing has loaded the usual S&OP data into the new database, and as we make changes, we will see the results right on the screen."

"Big deal," snorted Wilcox.

Saunders flashed Wilcox a warning glance, then nodded to Lattimer to proceed with her sales review of the product families, the first of which was the stocked muffler family (see Figure 12.3 on page 342). "We now have ninety days of history, beginning in February," Lattimer explained. "We had anticipated selling 32,000 units per month. But as you can see, we actually booked 36,000 units in February, 34,000 in March, and 37,000 in April. The third line on the screen shows the monthly differences between planned sales and actual sales; the fourth line shows cumulative differences by month, which increased to 11,000 units in April. On the whole, we're pretty pleased with our performance," said Lattimer. "Not only are we selling over the plan, we're within 10 percent of what we said we would do."

Figure 12.3 Sales and Production Plans, Stocked Muffler Family

Stocked Muffler Family		History			Plan	Future Planning				
Sales Plan		FEB	MAR	APR		MAY	JUN	JUL	AUG	SEP
Planned		32000	32000	32000	Orig.	32000	32000	32000	32000	32000
Actual		36000	34000	37000	New	36000	36000	36000	36000	36000
Monthly Diff.	90% Perf.	+4000	+2000	+5000						
Cum. Diff.	0	+4000	+6000	+11000						
Production Plan		FEB	MAR	APR		MAY	JUN	JUL	AUG	SEP
Planned		35000	35000	35000	Orig.	35000	30000	30000	25000	25000
Actual		34000	33000	33000	New	35000	35000	37000	37000	37000
Monthly Diff.	95% Perf.	–1000	–2000	–2000						
Cum. Diff.	0	–1000	–3000	–5000						
Finished Goods Inventory		FEB	MAR	APR		MAY	JUN	JUL	AUG	SEP
Planned		23000	26000	29000	Orig.	32000	30000	28000	21000	14000
Actual	Starting Bal. 20000	18000	17000	13000	New	12000	11000	12000	13000	14000
Difference	45% Perf.	–5000	–9000	–16000						

Applause rang out. Even Razor Tongue Wilcox nodded his approval.

Next, Bill Weston, vice president of manufacturing, stepped to the head of the table to begin discussion of the production plan. "We had a planned production rate of 35,000 mufflers for February, March, and April, but we fell short by 1,000 in February, 2,000 in March, and another 2,000 in April, making us short by 5,000 overall. Still, our performance over these ninety days was 95 percent of plan—not bad over the aggregate period."

"Not great either," Wilcox muttered. "Your group is *always* under plan."

A suggestion by Weston that constant overselling by Lattimer's group was creating a problem for production set off a heated debate.

Saunders motioned that it was time to move on to the inventory position on mufflers, one of his areas of responsibility. "As you can see from the data, we entered February with a starting balance of 20,000 units and planned to boost that level to 29,000 units by the end of April to meet the expected growth in our business. But the higher than expected sales and lower than planned production have resulted in a net depletion of our muffler inventory—just the opposite of our plan."

The master scheduler studied the information, noting how every month's pattern of higher than planned sales, and lower than planned production had progressively reduced inventory. That was good in the sense that AutoTek had less inventory to finance during those three months, but it was abundantly clear that unless this pattern was reversed, demand would very quickly outpace the company's supply (from production and from inventory), resulting in angry customers, missed sales, and opportunities for competitors to expand market share at AutoTek's expense.

He wondered how management planned to deal with this problem, knowing that the decision would affect him directly. He wanted to know how production rates would be adjusted; these, he knew, would be driven by whatever sales projections the sales and marketing people assumed for the coming periods.

Sally Lattimer pointed to the information on the screen. "The plan that we all agreed to last month called for sales of 32,000 units each month. We've been doing some analysis since the last meeting, and we are prepared to boost the forecast by 4,000 units per month through September. We believe the demand is very real, and that our overselling the plan in each of the past three months is not a fluke. What does everyone else think?"

"I like that number," said Jack Saunders. "It looks realistic to me, and it correlates with other information I am getting from the field."

From the master scheduler's prospective, this was a critical point in the meeting. He needed to know the projected production rate—something that could not be determined without considering future sales.

Discussion ensued as the S&OP team members debated how they could achieve the plan. First, they looked back at the previous month's inventory plan, noting its shortfalls. To satisfy the expected demand

and to provide some demand protection for variation to plan, Saunders had authorized raising inventory levels to a maximum of 32,000 units in May, then gradually reducing it to 14,000 units in September. The current inventory position was planned to be at 29,000 units; however, due to the situation described above, muffler inventory had fallen to 13,000 units.

"How are we ever going to get back on plan?" Wilcox asked.

The new sales projections and shortfall in inventory demanded a workable response from production. Bill Weston offered this manufacturing prospective: "It sounds like we need to ramp-up production to meet the increased sales plan. But I can't do it instantly. I need to hire and train a few more people and bring in some new equipment, and that will take time."

"How much time?" Saunders asked.

"Probably sixty days or so," Weston responded. "I am confident that we will be able to sustain a run rate of 35,000 for the next two months while we are getting prepared for the increased production rate. We have had problems coming up to 35,000 units in the past, but I think those problems are now behind us. The way I figure it, our inventory position will be at 11,000 units in sixty days if we produce at a rate of 35,000 per month and sell at a rate of 36,000 per month. In principle, I believe that we can meet the higher sales projection, but I want to figure out a way to meet it and still run the plant at a reasonable and level rate of production."

Weston wanted to keep the production plan level because shifts in production rates were expensive due to changeovers, adding and laying off personnel, etc. Therefore, he computed a level production plan as follows:

- Sum the forecast or sales plan, then add or subtract the expected or desired change in the inventory levels
- Divide the result by the number of months in the planning period

For July, August, and September, Weston began with total demand of 108,000 units (36,000 per month). To compute the desired change in inventory levels stipulated by Saunders, he looked at the target for the last period, September, which was 14,000, then subtracted the expected beginning inventory for July of 11,000 units. Thus, ending inventory needed to increase by 3,000 units. It made sense to just add this requirement to projected customer demand of 108,000 to get a total demand for July through September of 111,000 units, or 37,000 per month (or 111,000 for 3 months).

Would this approach satisfy the plan? To find out, the new sales and production figures were entered into the system and a new inventory projection was calculated (Figure 12.4). In July, August, and September, the company would produce 1,000 more units than it planned to sell and

Figure 12.4 Recalculation of Sales, Production, and Inventory

Stocked Muffler Family		History			Plan	Future Planning				
Sales Plan		FEB	MAR	APR		MAY	JUN	JUL	AUG	SEP
Planned		32000	32000	32000	Orig.	32000	32000	32000	32000	32000
Actual		36000	34000	37000	New	36000	36000	36000	36000	36000
Monthly Diff.	90% Perf.	+4000	+2000	+5000	Hi	38000	38000	38000	38000	38000
Cum. Diff.	0	+4000	+6000	+11000	Lo	30000	30000	30000	30000	30000
Production Plan		FEB	MAR	APR		MAY	JUN	JUL	AUG	SEP
Planned		35000	35000	35000	Orig.	35000	30000	30000	25000	25000
Actual		34000	33000	33000	New	35000	35000	37000	37000	37000
Monthly Diff.	95% Perf.	−1000	−2000	−2000						
Cum. Diff.	0	−1000	−3000	−5000						
Finished Goods Inventory		FEB	MAR	APR		MAY	JUN	JUL	AUG	SEP
Planned		23000	26000	29000	Orig.	32000	30000	28000	21000	14000
Actual	Starting Bal. 20000	18000	17000	13000	New	12000	11000	12000	13000	14000
Difference	45% Perf.	−5000	−9000	−16000	Hi	10000	7000	6000	5000	4000
					Lo	18000	23000	30000	37000	44000

ship. That surplus production would increase AutoTek's inventory. The ending September inventory figure would be 14,000 units—just what Saunders had asked for. Before pronouncing the new plan as workable, however, the group needed to check plant capacity as well as its key suppliers. (Assume for now that the plan has been checked for realism and the group is ready to move on with its analysis of the customized muffler product family). A detailed discussion of how to "sanity check" the proposed production plan against capacity and key resources follows in chapter 13 on rough cut capacity planning.

Even though the S&OP team had determined that the plan was realistic, questions remained. "What's the high watermark?" Weston asked the sales vice president. "How high could sales really go?"

Lattimer shuffled through her papers and responded: "We could possibly hit 38,000 from May through September."

"And if you bomb out?" asked Dave Wilcox.

"Worst-case scenario, 30,000," she shot back before Wilcox could open his mouth. "We've already studied that possibility."

With the best- and worst-case scenarios numerically defined, the group was then able to project inventory levels for either case (Figure 12.4). If sales succeeded on the high side, inventory would drop to a low of 4,000 units in September; if sales were poor, AutoTek would find itself with 44,000 units on the shelf at the end of that month. Saunders noticed Dave Wilcox grow pale as that figure passed his eyes.

"Now that we know what the opportunities and risks are, is everyone still breathing?" Saunders asked. "Can we can meet the plan?" All nodded in agreement. "Okay. Let's get on with it. Sally, go get those orders. Bill, you've told us that you can get up to 37,000 units in sixty days. Go make it happen. Dave, you need to be ready to support both Sally and Bill with additional financing, if needed. Now, unless there is further discussion, let's move on to the manifold product family."

The new production plan is the budget that will be used by the master scheduler when constructing the master schedule for the product family individual members. It's not enough for the master scheduler to just create the master schedule; he must also ensure that when aggregated by product family, it equals the production plan by volume.

The S&OP team went through the same routine with manifolds, adjusting and testing the plan in terms of sales, production, and inventory, carrying out a validity check at each step. When they finished with all make-to-stock families, Jack Saunders suggested a five-minute break before switching over to make-to-order products, which included customized mufflers and spoilers. The make-to-order items represented a smaller, but higher-margin, part of the business.

After the break, Ted Glass from marketing displayed the data for the customized muffler family (see Figure 12.5), and at Jack Saunders's suggestion, Sally Lattimer again kicked off the discussion. The format was basically the same as the one used for the make-to-stock products, with the sales plan on top, followed by the production plan. The make-to-stock planning screens displayed finished-goods inventory, the

Figure 12.5 Sales and Production Plans, Customized Muffler Family

Customized Muffler Family		History			Plan	Future Planning				
Sales Plan		FEB	MAR	APR		MAY	JUN	JUL	AUG	SEP
Planned		800	800	800	Orig.	800	800	800	800	800
Actual		840	860	880	New	850	850	900	900	1000
Monthly Diff.	107.5% Perf.	+40	+60	+80						
Cum. Diff.	0	+40	+100	+180						
Production Plan		FEB	MAR	APR		MAY	JUN	JUL	AUG	SEP
Planned		850	850	850	Orig.	850	800	800	800	800
Actual		820	830	820	New	850	850	977	977	977
Monthly Diff.	97% Perf.	–30	–20	–30						
Cum. Diff.	0	–30	–50	–80						
Backlog		FEB	MAR	APR		MAY	JUN	JUL	AUG	SEP
Planned		970	920	870	Orig.	820	820	820	820	820
Actual	Starting B/L 1020	1040	1070	1130	New	1130	1130	1053	976	999
Monthly Diff.	130% Perf.	+70	+150	+260						

make-to-order plan focused on backlog—not to be confused with "backorders," which are past-due customer orders. Generally, backlog refers to orders promised to customers, but not shipped. In the make-to-order business, orders are generally accepted for future deliveries. A company in Portland, Oregon, appropriately labeled these customer orders "future history."

Sally Lattimer began with the sales plan, showing the actual versus planned lines, explaining the difference (180 over plan for the last three months). She noted that her department's performance to the sales plan was right at 107.5 percent (see Figure 12.5 on the preceding page). Once again, applause greeted the conclusion of her report.

As with the make-to-stock muffler example, Lattimer proposed that the company would experience an increase in sales, from 800 to 850 in May and June, from 800 to 900 in July and August, and from 900 to 1,000 in September.

When she finished, Jack Saunders suggested moving on to the company's backlog position, shown on the bottom of the matrix. "Ninety days ago we had 1,020 units in the backlog. We wanted to take that 1,020 and work it down to 820 by the end of September. The 820 units represented approximately one month's production. What has happened is that as we look back over the last three months, the actual backlog went from 1,020 to 1,130. That means that we're looking at about 1⅓ months of backlog, based on the original plans. This is not the direction in which we want the backlog to go."

Next, Bill Weston of manufacturing stepped up to the projector. "We came in a tad low," he confessed, "but we're nevertheless 97 percent performance to plan. The problem is that the backlog simply isn't decreasing because sales is booking at a higher rate than plan and we are producing slightly below the plan. If we are sitting on 1⅓ months of backlog, we should be quoting lead times of 1⅓ months—assuming, of course, that the customers requested delivery as early as possible [the shape of this backlog curve is important to know since it affects the lead times used to quote and promise customer deliveries]. We need to change something if we are to achieve Jack's plan. If backlog and lead time are to be reduced to under one month, we'll have to create a production plan that works off part of the backlog over the next few months.

"As we evaluate the plan, let's bear in mind that ramping-up production in May and June will be difficult," Weston cautioned. "But with the training discussed earlier today, I believe we'll achieve our planned production of 850 units in May and June. In July, we can increase production to satisfy the increase in demand and begin to work down that backlog."

Weston agreed that at the end of June, he could increase production to 977 units.[3] For the months of July, August, and September, a level production plan was computed by taking the beginning backlog (1,130 in June) and subtracting the desired ending backlog (1,000 units, which equals the new sales plan for September). That left a desired change of 130 units. Adding that to the 2,800 expected bookings in the sales plan for the planning period July through September (900 + 900 + 1,000) yielded 2,930 units that needed to be shipped if the company was to hit its goal by the end of September. The 2,930 units divided by 3 months gave a level production rate of 977 units per month. If both Weston and Lattimer achieved their respective plans, Saunders's target of a one-month backlog would be realized. The next step was to do a "sanity check" of the proposed plan by running it through rough cut capacity planning (see chapter 13).

Once everyone agreed that these two plans were reasonable and realistic, the next step was to combine the make-to-stock and make-to-order muffler families on the same S&OP matrix (Figure 12.6 on page 350). This required computing an aggregate sales plan, production plan, inventory projection, backlog projection, and shipment projection derived by summing the make-to-stock (MTS) and make-to-order (MTO) data.

In May, for example, the new MTS sales plan calls for 36,000 units (Figure 12.3 on page 342), while the new MTO sales plan calls for 850 units (Figure 12.5 on page 347), summing to 36,850 units (Figure 12.6). The process of aggregating the sales plans is continued for each month through completion. The same logic is used to aggregate the production plan, using the MTS production plan and the MTO production plan figures.

[3] Weston reached the figure of 977 by summing the new sales plan numbers over July through September, adding to this the desired change in backlog, and then dividing the total by the number of months in the planning period.

Figure 12.6 Sales and Production Plans, Including Inventory, Backlog, and Shipment Projections

Combined Muffler Family		History			Plan	Future Planning				
Sales Plan		FEB	MAR	APR		MAY	JUN	JUL	AUG	SEP
Planned		32800	32800	32800	Orig.	32800	32800	32800	32800	32800
Actual		36840	34860	37880	New	36850	36850	36900	36900	37000
Monthly Diff.		+4040	+2060	+5080						
Cum. Diff.	0	+4040	+6100	+11180						
Production Plan		FEB	MAR	APR		MAY	JUN	JUL	AUG	SEP
Planned		35850	35850	35850	Orig.	35850	30800	30800	25800	25800
Actual		34820	33830	33820	New	35850	35850	37977	37977	37977
Monthly Diff.		–1030	–2020	–2030						
Cum. Diff.	0	–1030	–3050	–5080						
Inventory/Backlog		FEB	MAR	APR		MAY	JUN	JUL	AUG	SEP
Inventory	Starting Bal. 20000	18000	17000	13000	New	12000	11000	12000	13000	14000
Backlog	Starting B/L 1020	1040	1070	1130	New	1130	1130	1053	976	999
Shipments		36820	34830	37820	New	36850	36850	36977	36977	36977

The next step is to look at the inventory, backlog, and shipment projections. The muffler family inventory is a result of make-to-stock planning, while the backlog position is the result of make-to-order planning. Therefore, the projected muffler family inventory at the end of May (Figure 12.6) is equal to the MTS muffler inventory at the end of May (Figure 12.3, page 342). The projected muffler family backlog at the end of May (Figure 12.6) is equal to the MTO muffler backlog at the end of May (Figure 12.5, page 347).

The last thing that needs to be determined are the projected shipments. Here the group takes the sales plan (bookings and expected shipments) from the muffler make-to-stock family (in MTS companies, products are generally shipped as orders are received and booked) and adds these totals to the muffler make-to-order production plan (in MTO companies, products are shipped as they are built; they do not go to stock). The result is an aggregate shipping projection for the muffler product family. If we again look at May, Figure 12.3 shows expected shipments of 36,000 units (sales plan) for the stocked muffler family. Figure 12.5 shows expected shipments of 850 units (production plan) for the customized muffler family. Therefore, the total expected shipments are 36,850 units (Figure 12.6).

Once everyone at the AutoTek sales and operations planning meeting had agreed to the basic numbers, the group generated a rough cut capacity plan for the entire muffler family to ensure that the resources and capacity were, or would be, available when needed. This was done during the meeting using the S&OP data and the computer. Team members then watched as the computer software changed unit numbers into dollars, making it possible to compare the total sales and operations plans to the business plan. This was yet another check, determining if the business plan could be fulfilled if Lattimer, Weston, Wilcox, and Saunders accomplished their stated plans with respect to sales, production, inventory, backlog, shipments, and finances.

With the main business settled, the group briefly discussed new products and their possible impact on future business. This was an important area of concern to the master scheduler since he needed to gather data relevant to each new-product introduction.

The main business over, team members began glancing at their watches and thinking about the work that awaited them in their respective departments. Jack Saunders asked if anyone had any questions or further issues for discussion. There being no takers, he started the "critique process," which entailed his asking each person at the meeting for input on how future meetings and the S&OP process could be improved. This opportunity for each member of the team to suggest improvements had—over time—proven to be effective in AutoTek's efforts to make the meeting and the entire process more productive.

From the master scheduler's prospective, this meeting has provided the numerical ingredients of sales, production, inventory, backlog, and shipments that will guide his activities between this point and the end of the next scheduled S&OP meeting. He knows that the numbers will not hold up in the absolute sense, but they have the benefit of reflecting the best judgment of a roomful of people who have intimate knowledge of the company's operations. Further, the production plan he will work with has been subject to a reality check called "rough cut capacity planning," which compares the production plan to the internal capabilities of the company. Just how that reality check is accomplished is the subject of the next chapter.

13

Rough Cut Capacity Planning

It is forgivable to be defeated, but never to be surprised.

Imagine that your job is hauling stacks of crates from Los Angeles to San Diego on a flatbed truck. You have decided to take Interstate 5, a highway that you know travels beneath several underpasses. Along the way you discover that your cargo is loaded 15-feet high, but the underpasses have only 14 feet of clearance. How can you continue your journey? Here are some possibilities:

- Crash on through, knowing that your top crates will wind up as two-dimensional displays on the pavement.
- Unload just enough crates to allow the truck to pass under each overpass; then reload the truck on the other side.
- Let some air out of the tires to lower the truck's height.
- Take an exit or back the truck up the on-ramp and take a detour.
- Reconstruct the underpasses.

None of these options are either practical or acceptable. You should have planned ahead, loading the truck with respect to the height of the underpasses. This could mean stacking the boxes to a compatible height or picking a route that allows for safe passage of your cargo. Perhaps other constraints force you to stack the boxes to a certain height, making clearance under two of the underpasses impossible. In that case, you might take I-5, but seek other roads as you approach the two low underpasses. Either way, as the old saying goes, the best time to make an escape plan is before you need one.

Know Before You Go

The overloaded truck has a direct analogy in manufacturing. Managers cannot just take a production plan and a master schedule and toss them onto the shop floor and hope for the best. Chances are that this approach will bump into some low underpasses: a work center with too few people to assemble the product as called for in the production plan or MPS, too little lead time in another work center, not enough space on the manufacturing floor that month, no design engineers available to start the process, the sole supplier of a critical part unable to deliver on time.

To avoid being caught by such unpleasant surprises, managers and master schedulers need a manufacturing road map called "rough cut capacity planning" (RCCP). Rough cut capacity planning answers one question: Do we have a chance of meeting the production plan and master schedule as currently written? Rough cut capacity planning helps to identify the material and personnel shortages, the lead-time constraints, and the capacity issues that make it possible to create a production plan and master schedule that can be executed with every expectation of success. It also suggests possible options for navigating around bottlenecks. In short, rough cut capacity planning makes it possible: 1) to test the validity of a production plan and master schedule before doing any detailed material or capacity planning, and 2) to be able to initiate action for making mid- to long-range capacity adjustments.

One way or another, everyone does some form of rough cut capacity planning. It might be as simple as saying, "My plan calls for shipping $3 million worth of product this month and we've always been able to ship $4 million per month. Therefore, we have the proven capacity to meet the plan." Alternately, one might say, "Management wants to ship $7 million a month during the summer season. We have no precedent for being able to do that. Therefore, management's new plan appears to be unrealistic at this time." At the other extreme, a formal rough cut capacity plan might be carried out that evaluates all key resources and determines the feasibility of fulfilling the S&OP plan.

This chapter focuses on the formal approach and covers all of the essential elements and techniques needed to make rough cut capacity planning understandable and workable.

Rough Cut Revealed

Simply put, rough cut capacity planning attempts to identify 80 to 90 percent of the issues or potential problems that may occur on the manufacturing floor *before* detailed production schedules and capacity plans are either developed or contemplated. The other 10 to 20 percent typically surface in the course of material and capacity requirements planning. These problems might be related to space or machinery. Then there are the ever-present bottlenecks that ultimately limit output. Similarly, a gateway work center where the entire production process begins may be a potential problem. Perhaps limited storage tank space will cause a problem. Because every manufacturing process has potential limitations to output, the list could go on for pages and would be unique to each company.

With RCCP, managers and master schedulers can quickly identify obstacles to the plan without wading through all the detail. This is done by focusing on the "key resources" in the company. These key resources may include labor, equipment, materials, floor space, suppliers' capabilities, and, in some cases, money.

The Rough Cut Process

To do rough cut capacity planning in a company with simple products and bills-of-material, a clip board, a pencil, and a simple hand-held calculator may suffice. If a company has products of average complexity and more extensive BOMs, a personal computer with a spreadsheet program is very helpful. For very complex planning operations, master scheduling software that includes a rough cut capacity planning module may be necessary. These programs run on mini- or mainframe computers. Whatever the situation, rough cut capacity planning tools must be interactive with the user.

As a starting point, we need to understand these key terms:

Required capacity. The capacity needed to meet the production plan and/or master schedule. This is derived by taking the production plan and/or master schedule and extending it by the run time and setup time necessary to produce the product.

Available capacity. The capacity that a work center would have if it operated at a 100 percent productivity level (based on present staffing, equipment, and number of shifts worked).

Demonstrated capacity. The "proven" or historical capacity of a key resource or work center calculated on the basis of actual output performance.

Planned capacity. Demonstrated capacity plus anticipated adjustments to that capacity in the future. Adjustments might include the addition of equipment or people, or reductions in machines or staff.

Maximum capacity. The highest level of capacity at which a production system is able to operate without additional capital expenditures.

With these basic definitions understood, we can consider the rough cut process itself, which entails three basic steps:

1. Calculate the capacity required to meet the proposed production plan and master schedule.
2. Compare the required capacity to the planned capacity.
3. If necessary, adjust the required and/or planned capacity so that the two are in balance.

As Figure 13.1 indicates, the validation process begins when data from the production plan or master schedule is entered into the rough cut capacity planning system. Data from two other sources is then drawn upon: the resource or load profile database, which contains information about the company's use of key resources to build products; and the work center database, which has information about the *available* as well as the *demonstrated* and planned capacity of each key work center used to manufacture the products in question.

Figure 13.1 Rough Cut Capacity Planning Process

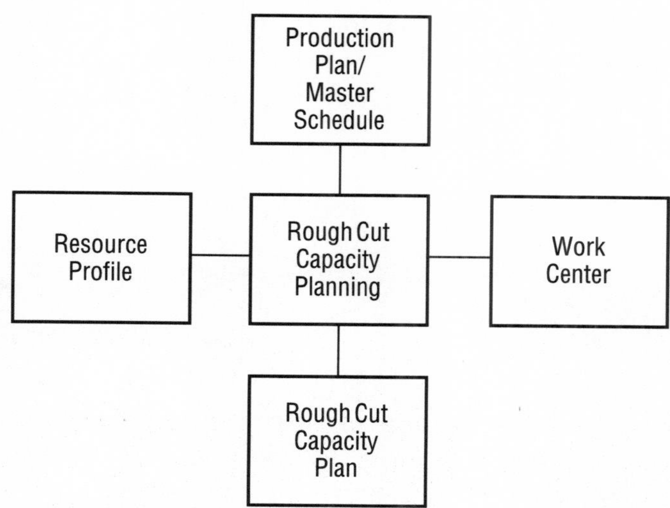

Combining information from the production plan and the resource profile, the rough cut capacity planning software module determines the *required capacity* necessary to meet the production plan. This required capacity is then compared to the work center's *planned capacity* to determine if adequate capacity exists. If the work center's planned capacity is adequate, the production plan is deemed realistic and is used to create both the master schedule and detailed material and capacity plans. If rough cut capacity planning determines that the work center's planned capacity cannot support the plan, that information is given to management, which then must either alter the production plan or increase the work center's capacity.

Essentially, management must balance the production plan's required capacity against a work center's planned capacity by asking these questions:

- What is the required capacity by time period?
- What is the planned capacity?
- What is the difference between the two?

These questions make it possible to identify potential problem areas and to make adjustments before moving on to any detailed material or capacity planning.

The next two sections explain the creation of resource profiles and work center capacity data. Be aware that this activity involves both science and art, resulting in a "refined guess," albeit one with high predictive value.

Creating Resource Profiles

A resource profile is a statement of the key resources needed to build the product being evaluated by RCCP. It is created through the following process:

IDENTIFY THE KEY WORK CENTERS AND CRITICAL RESOURCES NEEDED TO SUPPORT THE PRODUCTION PLAN. This is done by a quaint but effective method: asking people on the manufacturing floor, in purchasing, in design, and in engineering. Those who deal with the engineering and production process every day know what the key resources and bottlenecks are for any particular product normally run through the plant. Typical responses will be influenced by the following elements:

- Constraining or bottleneck work centers.
- One-of-a-kind or special tooling needed at a particular work center.
- Processes that are difficult to subcontract because they require special skills or equipment.
- High "mix sensitivity" where large numbers of options exist.
- Physical properties of the product make it easy for the production process to get out of control, causing yields to vary.

To be systematic in identifying all the key resources, the person chartered with identifying the key resources and creating the resource profiles may find it helpful to use a matrix like the one in Figure 13.2 on the following page. On the left side, the key resources required to support the production plan and/or master schedule are listed. Across the top, the reasons these resources may pose obstacles to achieving the plan are listed. For example, assembly, drilling, mixing, and fabricating, among others, could be listed down the left column. Across the top such obstacles as bottlenecks, not easy to off-load, special skills, or single-source suppliers may be listed.

Once the matrix is complete, determine if any of the resources identified can be combined. For example, three drill presses might be grouped into the "drilling department"; a drilling and milling machine might be grouped into "fabrication." Keep the resource profile as simple as possible and with as few entries as absolutely necessary,

Figure 13.2 Key Resources Worksheet

Key Resources	Reasons							
	Bottleneck	Not Easy to Off-Load	Mix Sensitivity	Physical Properties	Can't Change Over Quickly	Costly to Underutilize	Special Skills Required	Travel Distance
Tooling (Dies)	X	X				X		
Packing Operations	X	X			X			
Semifinished Operations			X	X				
Assm/Test						X	X	
Design Engineering		X				X	X	
Plating				X				X
Press 1	X	X						
Press 2	X				X	X		
Random, Inc. (Special Material)		X		X				X
Fabrication		X	X			X	X	

remembering that the purpose of RCCP is to answer the question, Do we have a *chance* of meeting this production plan or master schedule as currently written?

Determine the times and standards associated with each of the key resources. "Times" and "standards" refer to setup time and run time (processing time required), as opposed to queue time, waiting time, and move time (interoperational times). In traditional manufacturing, setup and run times impact the workload on a work center because they actually tie up the resource. In contrast, the queue, wait, and move times impact the time it takes to move work through the work center, but do not affect the load at the work center, which is the real consideration when it comes to testing the validity of the production plan.

Here is a four-step method for deriving the resource profile's processing time:

1. Select the product family for which the resource profile is being created.
2. Explode the product family using the entire bill-of-material.
3. Search each of the associated detail routings to determine whether a previously identified key resource is involved in the manufacture of the product family.
4. For each identified key resource, determine its profile time. This can be time consuming, but is readily done using one of the following methods:
    - *Choose a typical or representative part*, one that most ideally represents the entire product line—perhaps one or more from a similar product family—and use it as a proxy for the planned item.
    - *Compute an arithmetic average for the resource*. Add up the time spent on all items within the family that pass through the key resource and divide that time by the number of items processed.
    - *Compute a weighted average*. This requires that a weight, which correlates to the anticipated product demand mix, is applied to the individual item's time. The weighted times are then summed to create a weighted average for the resource.
    - *Estimate the time it takes for the planned product to pass through a work center*. Ask people on the floor how long it takes for an average lot size to go through the key work center and extrapolate the time for the planned product from this.

These methods will yield estimated times that are useful for developing predictive resource profiles. If detailed routing and process sheets are available with engineering standards, the resource profile times created using one of the above methods can be quite accurate.

Once they are estimated, enter the times for each resource in a matrix that breaks out each key resource by family, as shown in Figure 13.3. This matrix constitutes a "resource profile by product family."

We also need to determine what is called the "lead-time offset." The lead-time offset is the time between the *need* for the resource and the date that the order has been *promised*. The application of lead-time offset is necessary if a product has longer lead times—generally more than a month. In that case, you may have to use the offset so that the need for the resource can be identified in the proper period in the rough cut capacity plan.

Figure 13.4 shows a simple two-level bill-of-material for a customized pen, detailed routings for the pen and body assembly, and a time

Figure 13.3 Resource Profile by Product Family (Per 1000)

Key Resources	Unit of Measure	SOP Family A	SOP Family B	SOP Family C	SOP Family D	SOP Family E
Filling Lines 1 & 2	Machine Hours	1.1	1.8		0.8	1.5
Filling Line 3	Machine Hours	0.8	2.0		2.2	2.25
Filling Line 4	Machine Hours	1.0		4.0		
Finishing Line	Workers Hours	15.0	28.0	48.0	24.0	26.0
In-Process Storage	Lbs.	15000				
Processing Department	Equipment Hours	265.0		22.0	33.0	20.0
Incoming Test	Worker Hours	13.0		8.0	26.0	6.0
Supplier 100	Lbs.	450		215	335	
Supplier 200	Cases	250		1000		

Figure 13.4 Two-Level Bill-of-Material and Time Line Illustrations Lead-Time Offsets, Pen Product

A. Bill-of-Material

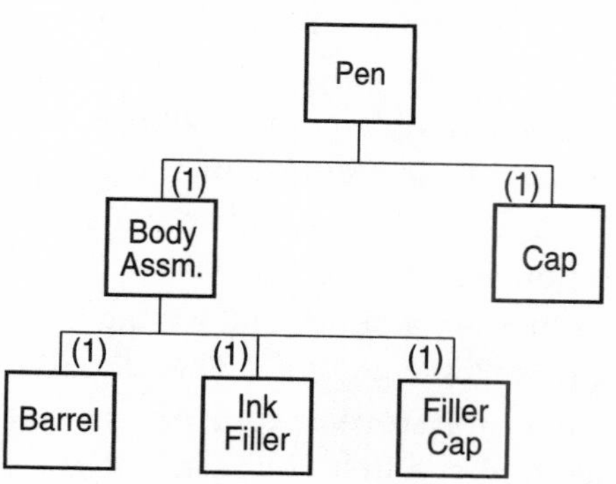

B. Routing

Pen

Operation Number	Operation Description	Work Center	Setup Time	Run Time
10	Silk Screen	100	1.2	1.0
20	Drying	650	.5	—
30	Assembly	250	—	.2
40	Inspection	900	1.5	.1
50	Monogram	400	—	.2
60	Inspection	900	.6	.1

Body Assm.

Operation Number	Operation Description	Work Center	Setup Time	Run Time
10	Assembly	200	1.6	1.2
20	Assembly	250	.4	.3
30	Test	800	.3	.6
40	Inspection	900	.75	.2

C. Custom-Monogramed Assembled Pen

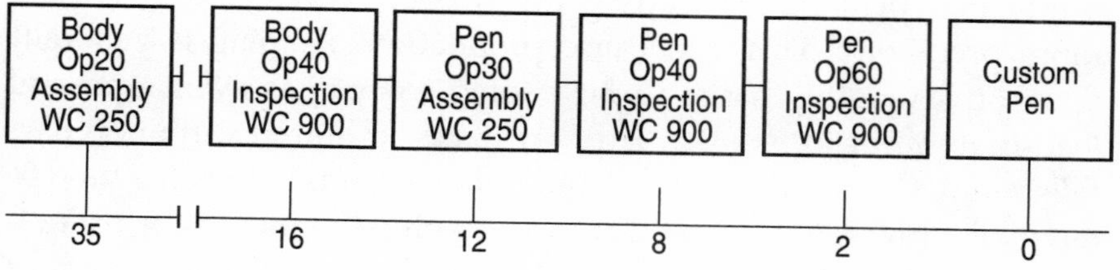

line for the pen product. A review of the bill-of-material (Figure 13.4A on the preceding page) indicates that the pen is composed of one body assembly and one cap. The body assembly in turn is an assembly made up of one barrel, one ink filler, and one filler cap. The expected ship date or promised date for delivery of the product is identified with the completed pen. But body assemblies must be manufactured or assembled before pens can be produced.

For purposes of discussion, assume that we have identified two key resources, work centers 250 and 900. The detail routing (Figure 13.4B) for the body assembly reveals four operations. As we look at the routing, we notice that the first key resource encountered in the body assembly is operation 20, which takes place at work center 250. On the time line shown at the bottom (Figure 13.4C), operation 20 in work center 250 for body assemblies is required 35 days prior to the due date assigned for the product pen. Therefore, this resource has a lead-time offset of 35 days.

The next key resource encountered is operation 40, which is to be performed in work center 900. In this case, the resource is required 16 days prior to the completion of the pen and is assigned a lead-time offset of 16 days. The customized pen's routing is shown at the top of Figure 13.4B; it also contains the two key resources—one pass through work center 250, and two passes through work center 900. As the time line shows, the lead-time offsets assigned are 12 days, 8 days, and 2 days respectively from the pen's planned completion date.

By definition, *every* key resource has a lead-time offset. But in practice, if the offset is less than 30 days, it does not need to be entered into your calculations when evaluating the validity of the production plan (rough cutting the master schedule may require more precision). This is because production planning is generally done on a monthly basis. In fact, some companies even represent lead-time offset in months. Every resource required within 30 days falls within the month that the order is due. Offsets between 30 and 60 days fall in the month immediately preceding the month the order is due, and so forth. The choice is arbitrary and one that a company must make prior to implementing rough cut capacity planning.

This arbitrary choice might compromise overall accuracy. But it doesn't really matter—with rough cut capacity planning, the goal is to balance simplicity and speed with accuracy, and to determine if the production plan is realistic. The manager or master scheduler is not trying to match the precision of a space shuttle launch. Rough cut is applied common sense, not hard science, and should be considered only a general guideline. If a resource has an offset of 35 days and production planning is done in months, the extra five days will not make much of a difference in determining whether the production plan is realistic. The lead time of a resource with a 120-day offset, on the other hand, must be taken into account if the rough cut capacity plan of its production plan is to have any predictive value.

Finalizing the Resource Profile

At this point it is possible to take all of the concepts presented and demonstrate how resource profile computations are actually made for key resources. The computations are simple if you understand the fundamental principles involved.

Profile Times

When using detail routings to create the resource profile, use the following equation to determine the profile times:

(Run Time × BOM quantity) + (Setup Time ÷ Order Quantity)

This yields the time required for the resource in question. Refer to Figure 13.4 on page 363. For pens there are two key resources: an assembly operation (work center 250) and an inspection operation (work center 900). Each operation has a setup and run time that can be used in the profile time equation.

At this point, the resource profile is complete and the master scheduler can move on to the other input for the rough cut capacity planning system: planned capacity, which must be compared against the required capacity.

Capacity Inputs

The sales and operations planning process yields a production plan, establishing volume requirements by product family item. An example of such a plan is shown in Figure 13.5.

This particular plan covers five product families with three future months worth of data. Here we will see what happens when the production plan is exploded through the resource profile. The production plan calls for 30,000 units of family A in July. Referring back to the resource profile for family A (see Figure 13.3 on page 362), the required time for the first key resource, filling lines 1 and 2, is 1.1 hours per 1,000 units. That means 30,000 units will require 33 hours on the 1 and 2 lines—(30,000 × 1.1)/1,000 = 33. For family B, the resource profile indicates that 1.8 hours per 1,000 units are required on the 1 and 2 lines. Since the production plan for family B calls for 10,000 units in July, the required capacity will be 18 hours—(10,000 × 1.8)/ 1,000 = 18.

Figure 13.5 Production Plan

Month		Family A	Family B	Family C	Family D	Family E
July		30000	10000	4000	3000	3000
August		25000	5000	4000	3000	3000
September		25000	5000	5000	4000	3000
Total		80000	20000	13000	10000	9000

Continuing this simple calculation for each family in the production plan, the required capacity for the entire plan can be determined. Figure 13.6 shows this required capacity for the production plan shown in Figure 13.5 using the resource profile developed in Figure 13.3.

Figure 13.6 Rough Cut Required Capacity

Key Resource	Unit of Measure	Month	Family A	Family B	Family C	Family D	Family E	Required Capacity
Filling Lines 1 & 2	Machine Hours	July	33.0	18		2.4	4.5	58
		August	27.5	9		2.4	4.5	44
		September	27.5	9		3.2	4.5	44
		Total	88.0	36		8.0	13.5	146
Filling Line 3	Machine Hours	July	24	20		6.6	6.75	57
		August	20	10		6.6	6.75	43
		September	20	10		8.8	6.75	46
		Total	64	40		22.0	20.25	146
Filling Line 4	Machine Hours	July	30		16			46
		August	25		16			41
		September	25		20			45
		Total	80		52			132
Finishing Line	Worker Hours	July	450	280	192	72	78	1,072
		August	375	140	192	72	78	857
		September	375	140	240	96	78	929
		Total	1,200	560	624	240	234	2,858
In-process Storage	Lbs.	July	450,000					450,000
		August	375,000					375,000
		September	375,000					375,000
		Total	1,200,000					1,200,000
Processing Department	Equipment Hours	July	7,950		88	99	60	8,197
		August	6,625		88	99	60	6,872
		September	6,625		110	132	60	6, 927
		Total	21,200		286	330	180	21,996
Incoming Test	Worker Hours	July	390		32	78	18	518
		August	325		32	78	18	453
		September	325		40	104	18	487
		Total	1,040		104	260	54	1,458
Supplier 100	Lbs.	July	13,500		860	1,005		15,365
		August	11,250		860	1,005		13,115
		September	11,250		1,075	1,340		13,665
		Total	36,000		2,795	3,350		42,145
Supplier 200	Cases	July	7,500		4,000			11,500
		August	6,250		4,000			10,250
		September	6,250		5,000			11,250
		Total	20,000		13,000			33,000

Once the production plan's required capacity has been calculated by the rough cut method, the next step is to compare that required capacity to the actual capacity at the master scheduler's disposal. The comparison determines whether adjustments need to be made to available resources or the production plan. A company's capacity really consists of several types of capacities, two of which are described in further detail in the following sections.

Demonstrated capacity. This was earlier shown to be the "proven" or historical capacity of a key resource or work center. To illustrate demonstrated capacity, consider a racing car. Imagine that you've been working for the past five years to design a very fast vehicle. During the design process, you have determined that the car should be able to achieve a speed of 200 miles per hour. Actual time trials, however, reveal that the car never exceeds 180 mph. No matter what your engineers do, the car never exceeds 180 mph. So, what is the demonstrated speed of the vehicle? Obviously, it is 180 mph or less, and it would be foolish to enter the vehicle in a race that requires 200 mph.

The same mechanism applies in manufacturing. It is foolish to adopt a plan that loads a factory or a key resource with 200 units of work per month when past experience indicates that 180 units of work per month is the best that has been achieved. More than a few manufacturing companies do just that. While this "can do" attitude may appear admirable, attempts to exceed demonstrated capacity are invariably doomed to failure and should not receive support.

Adequate demonstrated capacity in itself, however, is not sufficient to make the decision to adopt the production plan—demonstrated capacity could potentially change if resources are added or if operations are altered. Planned adjustments to capacity must be considered before making an evaluation of the production plan.

Planned capacity. This is demonstrated capacity plus or minus anticipated changes or adjustments to the product-flow process. To understand this better, let us return to the racing car analogy for a moment. Perhaps later tests determine that by installing an exotic, special-purpose air blower, your car can achieve 200 mph. The air blower manufacturer indicated that it can deliver the new part at the end of five weeks. This means the car can be expected to clock at 180 mph for the next five weeks and at 200 mph in the sixth. Now you have a decision to make: Should you adjust your racing strategy in week six? Here you need to analyze the possibility of really being able to compete at 200 mph in the future. If you are confident that the design is good, that production will deliver as promised, and that you will be able to achieve 200 mph six weeks out, then it seems reasonable to adjust your planned racing speed for the car.

Likewise, if a manufacturing unit has regularly demonstrated its ability to produce 180 units per month, an upward adjustment to 200 units per month beginning sometime in the future might be reasonable if operators are scheduled for special training or additional equipment is expected to be available.

With this sort of knowledge in hand, the management team and master scheduler can begin to make a valid comparison of the required capacity and the planned capacity (refer to Figure 13.7 on the following page).

In some cases, there are underloads (i.e., less capacity is required than is planned to be available), while in other cases there may be overloads. For example, in the finishing operation shown in Figure 13.7 (fourth row), a total of 857 hours are required in August, yet current plans have only 600 available. Do such potential overloads truly indicate that the production plan cannot be met? Not necessarily. Management might be able to increase the capacity at selected work centers. This prompts our next subject: maximum capacity.

Maximum capacity. By definition, this is the heaviest load a resource can handle under any reasonable set of circumstances and without capital expenditures. It can be achieved through a number of means. In the case of personnel, the use of overtime, including added shifts and weekends, or outright staff additions can increase the resource. In the case of a critical supplier, some work might be offloaded to another supplier, the company could agree to pay extra for supply priority, or premium freight methods could be used to expe-

Figure 13.7 Required Capacity Versus Planned Capacity

Key Resource	Unit of Measure	Month	Required Capacity	Net Difference	Planned Capacity	Maximum Capacity
Filling Lines 1 & 2	Machine Hours	July	58	56	114	152
		August	44	16	60	80
		September	44	100	144	192
		Total	146	172	318	424
Filling Line 3	Machine Hours	July	57	76	133	171
		August	43	27	70	90
		September	46	122	168	216
		Total	146	225	371	477
Filling Line 4	Machine Hours	July	46	49	95	114
		August	41	9	50	60
		September	45	75	120	144
		Total	132	133	265	318
Finishing Line	Worker Hours	July	1,072	68	1,140	1,596
		August	857	–257	600	840
		September	929	511	1,440	2,016
		Total	2,858	322	3,180	4,452
In-process Storage	Lbs.	July	450,000	690,000	1,140,000	1,140,000
		August	375,000	225,000	600,000	600,000
		September	375,000	1,065,000	1,440,000	1,440,000
		Total	1,200,000	1,980,000	3,180,000	3,180,000
Processing Department	Equipment Hours	July	8,197	2253	10,450	12,350
		August	6,872	–1372	5,500	6,500
		September	6,927	6273	13,200	15,600
		Total	21,996	7,154	29,150	34,450
Incoming Test	Worker Hours	July	518	14	532	551
		August	453	–173	280	320
		September	487	185	672	768
		Total	1,458	26	1,484	1,639
Supplier 100	Lbs.	July	15,365	29,635	45,000	45,000
		August	13,115	31,885	45,000	45,000
		September	13,665	31,335	45,000	45,000
		Total	42,145	92,855	135,000	135,000
Supplier 200	Cases	July	11,500	7500	19,000	23,000
		August	10,250	–250	10,000	12,000
		September	11,250	12,750	24,000	29,000
		Total	33,000	20,000	53,000	64,000

dite material delivery. In the case of machine time, an extra shift might be added. Attempts to operate a production system beyond its maximum capacity generally lead to confusion on the manufacturing floor, and almost always lead to a failure to achieve planned production quantities.

Evaluating the Plan

Clearly, "flexing" capacity up or down or using any other approaches to boost or lower capacity may have a cost impact, and must therefore be carefully evaluated by management. Rough cut capacity planning answers questions about critical capacity and material requirements in terms of numbers. It points out where potential problems are likely to occur and reveals what happens when alternatives (e.g., maximum capacity) are applied. The rough cut capacity plan provides an opportunity for people to exercise skill, knowledge, and creativity in balancing demand for product with the supply of resources. It makes it possible to "manage by the numbers" and to evaluate whether a production plan or master schedule is achievable or merely an unrealistic gleam in someone's eyes.

Rough cut capacity planning can also determine where the energies of management should be focused. If product family A is an "elephant" (refer to Figure 13.6 on page 367) compared to the other product families—i.e., it has by far the largest need for capacity and creates the biggest problems—management can focus its efforts on that family.

Rough Cut at the MPS Level

Figure 13.8 on page 372 recaps the relationship between sales and operations planning, the master schedule, and rough cut capacity planning. Here, the production plan is developed in the sales and operations planning process. Next, the production plan is checked for validity through the rough cut capacity planning process and adjusted as necessary. Once top management determines that a realistic plan exists, the production plan becomes the driver and constraint in the master scheduling process, which translates the production plan into

Figure 13.8 Rough Cut Capacity Planning and Operational Relationships

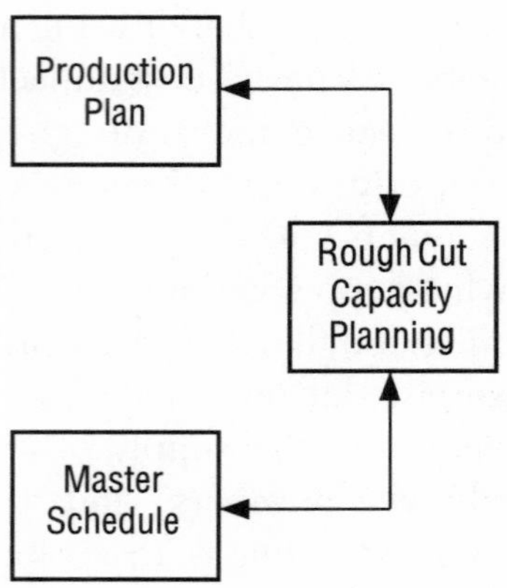

discrete part numbers, quantities, and due dates. This accomplished, the master schedule drives the material and capacity planning processes.

While all companies need to do rough cut capacity planning at the production planning level, many manufacturing environments require a second pass through the rough cut analysis, this time at the master schedule level. Companies with highly varied mixes of product are among these. This section covers techniques for carrying out rough cut capacity planning for complex product mixes.

Rough cut capacity planning at the MPS level uses the same principles as rough cut at the production plan level, but extends the calculations down to the MPS level. This is done by exploding the master schedule, instead of the production plan, through an item resource profile to generate the required capacity to meet the master schedule. As Figure 13.9 indicates, each S&OP family may be divided into constituent items. Family A, for example, consists of items A1, A2, A3, and A4.

The key resources are listed on the left side of the resource profile, along with the associated times and standards. In addition, the resource profile contains the predicted mix probability for each item. In the case of family A, for example, each product is indicated as having a

Figure 13.9 Resource Profile by MPS Item (Per 1000)

S&OP Family		A					B			C			D			E		
Key Resource	Unit of Measure	A1	A2	A3	A4	Average	B1 B2 B3	B11 B12 B13	Average	C1	C2	Average	D1	D2	Average	E1	E2	Average
Typical Mix %		25%	25%	25%	25%	100%	60%	40%	100%	50%	50%	100%	33%	67%	100%	50%	50%	100%
Lines 1 &2	Hours	2.0	2.4			1.1	3.0		1.8				2.4		0.8	3.0		1.5
Line 3	Hours			3.2		0.8		5.0	2.0					3.3	2.2		4.5	2.25
Line 4	Hours				4.0	1.0				3.0	5.0	4.0						
Finishing Department	Hours	12.0	12.5	16.7	20.0	15.0	18	45	28	36	60	48	19	26	24	24	27	26
In-Process Storage	Lbs	10000	10000	20000	20000	15000												
Processing Department	Hours	160.0	260.0	320.0	320.0	265.0				15.0	29.0	22.0	24.0	45.0	38.0	13.0	27.0	20.0
Incoming Test	Hours	8.0	12.0	16.0	16.0	13.0				7.0	9.0	8.0	18.0	30.0	26.0	5.0	7.0	6.0
Supplier 100	Lbs		1800			450				150	280	215	225	390	335			
Supplier 200	Cases				1000	250				1000	1000	1000						

25 percent probability; i.e., there is a 25 percent probability that sales of an A will be as an A1, A2, A3, and as an A4.[1] This product mix percentage is very important at the master schedule level, because it yields a much more detailed estimate of how the various key resources will be deployed for each item within the family. Consider family D, which has just two items, the first of which (D1) constitutes 33 percent of the mix. That means when you need a product D, one third of the time you would expect to need a D1, and two thirds of the time you would need a D2.

Jump back to the B product family. This is different. Three of the items (B1, B2, and B3) are very much alike and use the same key resources. The same is true for items B11, B12, and B13. Therefore, two groups are formed and resource profiles are created to cover the two groupings. As shown in Figure 13.9 on the preceding page, when a product of the B family is needed, 60 percent of the time we expect it to be a B1, B2, or B3. The remaining 40 percent of the time we expect to need a B11, B12, or B13.

In addition to this breakout by individual items within a family, the MPS item rough cut resource profile also shows the average resource times developed for the aggregate family (see Figure 13.9, average columns). Now take a close look at filling lines 1 and 2 for the S&OP family A. In the resource profile for product family A, we learned that lines 1 and 2 required 1.1 hours per 1,000 units. Using the master schedule resource load profile by item, we review the computation of this weighted average for lines 1 and 2.

Item A1 requires 2.0 hours per 1,000 units.

Item A2 requires 2.4 hours per 1,000 units.

Items A3 and A4 do not use lines 1 and 2.

Since all items are 25 percent of the mix, the times for each unit would be

[1] These probabilities are established by management as part of the S&OP process.

A1 = 2.0 × 25 percent = 0.5

A2 = 2.4 × 25 percent = 0.6

A3 = 0.0 × 25 percent = 0.0

A4 = 0.0 × 25 percent = 0.0

Weighted average = 1.1 hours

The same calculation is performed for each key resource in the resource profile for each family. Once average hours or standards have been computed for each key resource, rough cut capacity planning can be used to evaluate the capacity for each resource on a month-by-month basis using the production plan and on a week-by-week basis using the master schedule. This process has already been examined at the production plan level. Now we examine the process at the master schedule level.

The example shown in Figure 13.10 provides the quantities scheduled for each master schedule item. Note that the totals for these master schedule items are identical to those stipulated in the production plan (see Figure 13.5, page 366). What's different is that the item quantities have been broken out as components of the production

Figure 13.10 Master Schedule for July

Family	A	B	C	D	E	Total
July Week 1		B1 4000 B2 4000 B3 2000				10000
Week 2	A1 6000		C1 1000	D1 2000 D2 1000	E1 3000	13000
Week 3	A3 2000 A4 10000		C2 1000			13000
Week 4	A4 12000		C2 2000			14000
Total	30000	10000	4000	3000	3000	50000

plan totals. These item quantities are the result of the master scheduler's taking the production plan and translating it into discrete items, quantities, and weekly due dates based on the predicted mix and inventories available. In other words, firm planned orders have been created by the master scheduler for the items as shown in the figure.

During the rough cut capacity planning process, the quantities for each MPS item are multiplied by the time requirements in the resource profile. This results in a week-by-week summary of total required capacity. The total required capacity is then compared to the planned and maximum capacities for each master schedule item (see Figure 13.11).

Again, note that the production plan quantities by family (Figures 13.5 and 13.10) equal the totals of the master schedule quantities within each family. But the master schedule rough cut capacity plan clearly yields more detailed information, since it is at the item level. This additional detailed information allows us to assess whether the MPS is valid given the planned and maximum capacity. As we begin

Figure 13.11 Rough Cut Capacity Plan by MPS Item

Family		A	B	C	D	E	Required Capacity	Net Difference	Planned Capacity	Maximum Capacity
Lines 1 & 2	Week 1		30				30	−6	24	32
	Week 2	12			5	9	26	4	30	40
	Week 3						0	30	30	40
	Week 4						0	30	30	40
	Total	12	30	0	5	9	56	58	114	152
Line 3	Week 1						0	28	28	36
	Week 2				3		3	32	35	45
	Week 3	6					6	29	35	45
	Week 4						0	35	35	45
	Total	6	0	0	3	0	9	124	133	171
Line 4	Week 1						0	20	20	24
	Week 2			3			3	22	25	30
	Week 3	40		5			45	−20	25	30
	Week 4	48		10			58	−33	25	30
	Total	88	0	18	0	0	106	−11	95	114

looking at specific master schedule line items, a couple of guidelines (that the author has used for years) may be useful.

If the required capacity is:

- No more than 10 percent greater than the planned capacity, the master schedule seems to be realistic and more detail should be pursued (detailed material and capacity requirements planning).

- More than 20 percent greater than the planned capacity, the master schedule seems to be unrealistic and a corrective action plan should be derived before proceeding.

- Between 10 and 20 percent greater than the planned capacity, the master schedule is in the gray area, and prior work center behavior must determine what is to be done (what do we know about the resource in question).

At this point we can apply the general guidelines to an analysis of the weekly rough cut capacity requirements in July for lines 1 through 4 (refer to Figure 13.11). Whereas the aggregate plan revealed an underload for lines 1 and 2, at the MPS level, we observe an expected overload in the first week of July (required capacity versus planned capacity) and underloads in the third and fourth weeks. Is the overload a reason for changing the MPS? Maybe not, because it is within the 20-percent guideline. Besides, the maximum capacity is 32 hours. Remember, you only want to know if we have a chance to achieve the master schedule, not if we will be able to accomplish it in every detail.

For line 3, significant underloads are indicated in each week, and for line 4, an underloaded condition appears in weeks 1 and 2, and overloads in excess of 20 percent in weeks 3 and 4. In fact, required capacity in weeks 3 and 4 greatly exceeds maximum capacity.

Handling Under- and Overloads

Several options exist for dealing with under- and overloads. First, for lines 1 and 2, it might be possible to move some of the load from week 1 of July into June or into weeks 3 and 4 of July, where underloads are projected. By looking back at the MPS (Figure 13.10, page 376), B1,

B2, and B3 are the candidates for load shifting since they are the only units planned to run during the first week in July. Each 1,000-unit run requires 3 hours. Therefore, if we want to balance required and planned capacity, we must either shift 2,000 units of B1, B2, or B3 into another time period or increase the planned capacity. Of course, any discussion of moving out an MPS item requires consideration of the impact of that move on the ability to meet the customer promise dates.

Analysis of weeks 3 and 4 in July for line 4 indicates a significant potential overload. What is causing this potential problem, and what can be done about it? To determine the cause of the overload, look back at Figure 13.10 to see which MPS items are scheduled to run in weeks 3 and 4. There we note that A3, A4, and C2 are scheduled for production. Items A3 and C2, however, do not use line 4 (see Figure 13.9 on page 373). Therefore, we need concern ourselves only with the 10,000 units of A4 scheduled in week 3 and the 12,000 units of A4 scheduled in week 4. What started out to be a potential problem that we may not have even recognized has been reduced to a single MPS item over a two-week period, further illustrating another payback of rough cut capacity planning. Now, the master scheduler must determine if load shifting from weeks 3 and 4 to weeks 1 and 2 can be accomplished within the framework of the master schedule.

When dealing with the underloaded condition in weeks 3 and 4 in July for lines 1 and 2, the master scheduler may decide to allow the equipment on these lines to sit idle in weeks 3 and 4 and do preventive maintenance. Another possibility is to plan to move people from work center to work center. The people who work on lines 1 through 4 may be people with the same skills, or they could all be people who work on various filling lines and therefore possess similar skills. Perhaps these workers could be moved to line 4 in weeks 3 and 4, along with a group of operators from line 3, who will be virtually without activities for the entire month.

By using rough cut capacity planning to validate the master schedule, it is possible to validate whether the production plan derived during the S&OP process can be met at the product mix level. This validity check brings us full circle in the rough cut capacity planning process.

Working the Rough Cut Capacity Plan

Now that the method and use of rough cut capacity planning at both the production plan and master schedule level has been explained, it is time to look more deeply into the evaluation process. Continuing with the rough cut capacity planning example already developed in this chapter (refer to Figure 13.7 on page 370), a review of the necessary capacity shows that for lines 1 and 2, the potential problem is a projected underload in July (58 hours required versus 114 planned), August (44 hours required versus 60 planned), and September (44 hours required versus 144 planned). This indicates that the plan is realistic in terms of having *sufficient* resources to satisfy demand, at least at the aggregate level. The same appears to be true for lines 3 and 4.

So far so good. Now consider the next key resource, finishing. Here the situation is tight—1,072 required hours versus 1,140 planned hours in the month of July. If everything goes smoothly, the plan should work. But if anything goes astray or unexpected orders roll in the door, the situation could quickly shift from an acceptable condition to an overload situation. There is definite trouble in August—an overload of 257 hours, which represents a potential overload of approximately 30 percent. In September the finishing work center appears to have sufficient capacity.

Up to this point, only one of four key resources has a potential problem—finishing, in August. As you can see, this analysis has narrowed down the key resources that are potential obstacles to meeting the production plan.

Move down the list of key resources in Figure 13.7 and compare required and planned capacities. Here the capacity planner finds that in-process storage contains no problem for any of the three months. The processing department, however, contains a potential overload, again in August; but adequate capacity in July and September for this resource suggests that some load shift may alleviate the problem.

For the incoming test resource, capacity is marginally adequate for

July, but August is overloaded by 50 percent. September appears to be in good shape. Material from supplier 100 is more than adequate in all three months, and for supplier 200, material is sufficient for July and September, but marginal for August.

In effect, this exercise has reduced the potential obstacles to meeting the production plan from nine to four. Within those four problematic resources, only three—finishing, processing, and incoming test—represent significant issues, and then only in the month of August. Knowing the locations and depth of these problems makes the search for solutions possible. The example also points out the importance of evaluating resources on at least a monthly basis. Look at the three-month totals. From a quarterly, aggregate perspective, sufficient resources are available for all key resources. But the month of August is clearly problematic now, since three resources and one key supplier will be overloaded during that month. The process thus entails moving from the aggregate to the pegged-detail level as you determine that more information is necessary to answer the question, Do we have a chance of meeting the production plan and master schedule as currently written?

Taking Action

Once the problem resources have been identified and analyzed as much as possible, the next step is to evaluate potential solutions. First, determine whether action really needs to be taken in August for each of the key resources identified. Recall the general action guidelines stated earlier—the challenge is to have the required capacity equal the planned capacity *within the tolerances* established by such guidelines.

In an out-of-balance situation, there are only three choices of action: 1) modify the production plan so that required capacity equals planned capacity; 2) adjust the planned capacity to equal required capacity; and 3) do a combination of the two actions just noted. The second option is generally preferable. Let us see how this might be achieved to resolve the problems anticipated for August.

Overloads

Several actions may be taken in order to adjust the planned capacity for each overloaded resource:

1. Work overtime or extra shifts.
2. Transfer people from underloaded work centers to boost the resources in the overloaded work centers.
3. Reroute some of the work to an alternate work center if one is available.
4. Subcontract all or a portion of the work.
5. Hire temporary workers.
6. Install more equipment.
7. Build a new facility.

Underloads

As the example in Figure 13.7 on page 370 demonstrates, a number of underload situations exist (lines 1 through 4). These are not necessarily undesirable situations, as they present opportunities to:

1. Deploy workers on other lines.
2. Conduct training.
3. Do preventive maintenance on idle equipment and housekeeping in idle work centers
4. Reduce shifts and/or overtime.
5. Assign line workers to other departments like design or engineering. The workers can then learn what these departments have in mind as they develop a product. The line workers can

give engineers ideas of manufacturing-related problems that appear on the plant floor.

6. Run a promotion to increase demand and thereby increase required capacity.
7. Establish a task force to reduce setup times.

And the list goes on. Clearly, dealing with underloads, like overloads, requires good communication among marketing, sales, finance, engineering, manufacturing, purchasing, and human resources.

Each option must be examined in light of the capacity needed as well as the maximum capacity available. In the case of the finishing resource, for example, we see that the most capacity that can be expected is 840 hours (maximum capacity). But the required capacity is 857 hours. Therefore, even bringing the finishing resource up to its maximum capacity of 840 hours by moving people from lines 3 and 4 would not alleviate an overloaded condition. Moreover, the movement of workers from one work center to another might create negative impacts elsewhere. There generally is no "free lunch." The key question is whether the action alleviates the original problem or creates a new one.

Finessing the Situation with Customers

In addition to looking for possible move-ins and move-outs on the factory floor, marketing and sales may find customers willing to receive their orders early or late. Financial incentive may be cost-effective in getting them to accept rescheduled deliveries. For example, Multitek, Inc., may be happy to take delivery of a commercial vehicle a month sooner if it is offered an added option or engine upgrade at no additional cost. Turbo Brothers might be willing to take early delivery of a vehicle from the manufacturer's current inventory without all the features it originally ordered if a special warrantee package is offered. In cases like these, the production plan and master schedule can be modified by moving some orders forward in the schedule and others back.

Lot Splitting

Another alternative is to do a "lot split." For example, an August run of 10,000 might be split into a run of 5,000 in July and 5,000 in August, thus alleviating a predicted capacity shortage. The master scheduler could also plan to ship the product early (if the customer agrees) or hold the early build and ship the entire lot as planned and continue to honor any promises made to the customer.

When Capacity Cannot Be Adjusted

If the planned capacity for the finishing line cannot be adjusted in August, it may become necessary to modify the production plan and master schedule. This requires asking what the plan hoped to achieve in the first place. If the plan was trying to build product to satisfy firm customer orders, marketing and sales must decide which customer orders, if any, can get moved out of the problem period. If the plan was devised to satisfy a combination of customer orders and replenish some warehouses, marketing and sales must again decide whether the customer or the warehouses take priority. Perhaps the demand includes one very large order from a new customer. This order may be a candidate for splitting or moving in or out.

"What If" Analysis and Rough Cut Capacity Planning

Sales and marketing have just notified the master scheduler that because of an unexpected strike at a competitor's plant several key changes will take place in the production plan for product family C (see Figure 13.12). For family C, the anticipated demand in July and August will increase from 4,000 to 6,000 units per month. In September, the old plan called for 5,000 units, while the new plan calls for 10,000. What will be the impact on the identified key resources over and beyond the problems we have already examined?

The new capacity requirements are shown in Figure 13.13. As can be seen, the same four key resources that were identified as potential problems are affected by this change, but the predicted capacity overloads in August are more severe. In addition, the underloads for finishing and incoming tests in July have now vanished, and an overloaded condition is predicted. Also, remember we were thinking of shifting workers from lines 3 and 4 to the finishing line to alleviate the overload condition, but the change indicates a greater load on line 4, making that shift questionable.

Rough cut capacity planning makes it possible for management to see the impact of the proposed changes very clearly. Additionally, the "what if" capability built into rough cut capacity planning software makes it possible for management to juggle the numbers—shifting workers, rescheduling-in and -out, splitting lots, and so forth—until the production plan becomes realistic and achievable.

Figure 13.12 Modified Production Plan, Product Family C

Month	Family A	Family B	Family C	Family D	Family E
July	30000	10000	6000	3000	3000
August	25000	5000	6000	3000	3000
September	25000	5000	10000	4000	3000
Total	80000	20000	22000	10000	9000

Figure 13.13 Revised Rough Cut Capacity Plan

Key Resource	Unit of Measure	Month		Family C		Required Capacity	Net Difference	Planned Capacity	Maximum Capacity
Filling Lines 1 & 2	Machine Hours	July				58	56	114	152
		August	...		...	44	16	60	80
		September				44	100	144	192
		Total				146	172	318	424
Filling Line 3	Machine Hours	July				57	76	133	171
		August				43	27	70	90
		September				46	122	168	216
		Total				146	225	371	477
Filling Line 4	Machine Hours	July		24		54	41	95	114
		August		24		49	1	50	60
		September		40		65	55	120	144
		Total		88		168	97	265	318
Finishing Line	Worker Hours	July		288		1,164	–24	1,140	1,596
		August		288		953	–353	600	840
		September		480		1,169	271	1,440	2,016
		Total		1,056		3,286	–106	3,180	4,452
In-process Storage	Lbs.	July				450,000	690,000	1,140,000	1,140,000
		August				375,000	225,000	600,000	600,000
		September	...		...	375,000	1,065,000	1,440,000	1,440,000
		Total				1,200,000	1,980,000	3,180,000	3,180,000
Processing Department	Equipment Hours	July		132		8,241	2,209	10,450	12,350
		August		132		6,916	–1,416	5,500	6,500
		September		220		7,037	6,163	13,200	15,600
		Total		484		22,194	6,956	29,150	34,450
Incoming Test	Worker Hours	July		48		534	–2	532	551
		August		48		469	–189	280	320
		September		80		527	145	672	768
		Total		176		1,530	–46	1,484	1,639
Supplier 100	Lbs.	July		1,290		15,795	29,205	45,000	45,000
		August		1,290		13,545	31,455	45,000	45,000
		September		2,150		14,740	30,260	45,000	45,000
		Total		4,730		44,080	90,920	135,000	135,000
Supplier 200	Cases	July		6,000		13,500	5,500	19,000	23,000
		August	...	6,000	...	12,250	–2,250	10,000	12,000
		September		10,000		16,250	7,750	24,000	29,000
		Total		22,000		42,000	11,000	53,000	64,000

Screen and Report Formats

There are several screen and report formats among current off-the-shelf planning systems. The choice is a matter of preference. A few of the more commonly used formats are discussed here.

Information Displayed Horizontally

In this screen format, the units of time are displayed across the top (e.g., July, August, September). The left side displays the maximum, planned, and required capacities, followed by the period and cumulative variances (see Figure 13.14). In some software, this arrangement is reversed to display units of time vertically.

Combined Tabular/Graphic Report

A variant of the horizontal and vertical screens includes a graphic representation of the capacity situation. In the sample screen shown in Figure 13.15, an additional column has been included. This provides a graphic view of the required capacity versus the planned capacity for the key resource.

Exception Screen

The exception screen shows only the problematic work centers (see Figure 13.16 on page 388). It is useful for highlighting underloads and overloads. The middle of the screen lists the key resources that have an exception to parameters entered by the user. This means that the user defines an underload or overload condition in its own terms. This is done by setting target levels for underloads (e.g., 60 percent) and overloads (e.g., 120 percent).

The left side of the screen shows the potential underloads, represented by periods of time (months, quarters, etc.). When a load ratio is shown in any column, it indicates that the required capacity is less

Figure 13.14 Horizontal Format, Rough Cut Capacity Plan Screen

KEY RESOURCE: FINISHING (HOURS)

	July	August	September	Total
Maximum Capacity	1596	840	2016	4452
Planned Capacity	1140	600	1440	3180
Required Capacity	1164	953	1169	3286
Difference	–24	–353	271	–106
Cum. Difference	–24	–377	–106	–106

Figure 13.15 Combined Tabular and Graphic Screen

KEY RESOURCE: FINISHING (HOURS)

	Required Capacity	Planned Capacity	Period Difference	Cum. Difference	Maximum Capacity
July	1164	1140	–24	–24	1596
August	953	600	–353	–377	840
September	1169	1440	271	–106	2016
Total	3286	3180	–106	–106	4452

	Required to Planned Ratio 0% 50% 100% 150%	Load Percent
July	XXXXXXXXXXXXXXXXXXXXX	102
August	XXXXXXXXXXXXXXXXXXXXXXXXXXXXXXX	159
September	XXXXXXXXXXXXXX	81
Total	XXXXXXXXXXXXXXXXXXXXXX	103

Figure 13.16 Rough Cut Capacity Plan Exception Screen

Underload Indicators Percent: 60				Underload Indicators Percent: 120		
July	August	September	Key Resource	July	August	September
51		31	Lines 1 & 2			
43		27	Line 3			
57		54	Line 4			
			Finishing Line		159	
39		26	In-Process Storage			
		53	Processing Dept.		126	
			Incoming Test		168	
35	30	33	Supplier 100			
			Supplier 200		123	

than 60 percent (the target level of the minimum capacity chosen for this example). Again, the target percentages are determined by the user.

Overloads are represented on the right side of the screen. When a load ratio is shown in any column, the key resource is projected to be overloaded in excess of 120 percent. (Again, the 120 percent was arbitrarily chosen for this example.)

The Limitations and Benefits of Rough Cut Capacity Planning

Like all tools, rough cut capacity planning provides benefits to the user in particular situations. But, again like all tools, its very design limits those situations for which it is appropriate.

Limitations

It is important to bear in mind that resource profiles are based on representative products for an entire family. Incoming orders, however, may not exactly fit the predicted mix, causing discrepancies between aggregate and detail planning. Also, the manner in which setup time is handled may affect load predictions in various ways. For instance, suppose that a particular machine requires 8 hours for setup, and the rough cut resource profile assumes runs of 10,000 pieces. If it turns out that only 100 units of one product line are actually run, the rough cut assessment may be invalid. The reason for this is that the setup time (say 8 hours) either is assumed to be required for any run quantity, or it has been divided by the expected run quantity to establish the setup time per unit. Thus, suppose you plan to run 100 units. What's the setup time required? Is it 4.8 minutes (8 hours × 60 minutes × 100 units divided by the 10,000 unit lot size), or is it 8 hours (the setup time per lot)? Someone must make a decision.

Another limitation of rough cut is that it ignores work-in-process and work completed. This negates its value as a short-term planning tool—where these balances matter—and limits it to an intermediate- and long-range planning tool. To understand this fully, let us review the logic of rough cut capacity planning. The logic starts by exploding the production plan or master schedule through the resource profile to determine the required capacity. The results of this explosion are compared to the planned capacity, and from this comparison an action plan is created. At no time during this process does rough cut capacity planning look at the work-in-process (WIP) or at what work was completed. This WIP netting does not take place until material requirements planning, capacity requirements planning, and shop floor control systems are run (refer to chapter 2, closed-loop MRP II). Thus, RCCP data is often invalid in the short term. It is not useful in planning for this week's production; its eyes are on the future.

Finally, rough cut capacity planning is limited by the fact that it considers only *key* or *critical* resources. Actual building of a product, however, requires the resources in *all* work centers. It is in this sense that rough cut capacity planning is limited to answering the questions: Do we have a *chance* to meet the production plan? and Do we have a *chance* to meet the master schedule? Thus, execution of the production plan and master schedule is always vulnerable to contingencies not highlighted during the rough cut process.

Benefits

One of the major benefits of rough cut capacity planning is that master schedulers do not need a detail routing for every item in the plan. This is what makes rough cut capacity planning a simple and quick tool to use. In contrast, detail capacity requirements planning (CRP) requires master scheduling, material requirements planning, inventory control, bills-of-material, detail routings, and shop floor control. In addition, CRP requires a high degree of accuracy in bills-of-material, detail routings and inventory records. Only then can accurate detail capacity planning be done.

On the average, rough cut capacity planning can be productively used in as little as thirty to ninety days after implementing a rough cut capacity system. In the standard implementation scheme, detail capacity requirements planning (CRP) is not generally effective until twelve to fifteen months after the MRP II implementation is commenced.

A related benefit is that rough cut can be run as often as needed prior to execution of the production plan and master schedule. Because it requires minimal computer time (relative to CRP), it is a better simulation tool than CRP, though its output is more of a shadow of reality, owing to its use of only key resources. Simulations such as: What is the effect of changing the mix of expected demand, the booking of a large order, or the shifting of replenishment orders either in or out? are possible with RCCP. Since rough cut capacity planning is a simple simulation tool, you can use it to test the impact of proposed actions before putting the actions into practice. Rough cut capacity planning also allows the master scheduler to test the proposed master schedule if necessary before obtaining more detail via

Figure 13.17 Differences Between Rough Cut Capacity Planning and Capacity Requirements Planning

	RCCP	CRP
What	Projected Gross Capacity Requirements for Key Resources	Project Net Capacity Requirements for Each Work Center
How	Explode Production Plan or Master Schedule Through Resource Profiles	Explode MPS & MRP Planned Orders Through Detailed Routings: Combine With Current WIP Status from Shop Floor Control
When	As Required for Simulation	Annual & Quarterly Budget Development; Weekly, Monthly
Why	1. Pre-MRP Evaluation of Production Plan &/or MPS 2. Intermediate- to Long-Range Planning	1. Post-MRP Detailed Analysis 2. Periodic Check of All Work Centers
Precision	Aggregate or Gross—Key Resources Only	Detailed—Considers Inventory, Lot Sizing, WIP Completions, Work Center Lead Times—Voluminous Data
Complexity	Much Less Than CRP	Usually Exceeds MRP
Planning Horizon	Production Plan Limits	MRP Horizon Less Lead-Time Offsetting
Implementation	Short (Manual or PC/Spread Sheet at First)	Requires Work Centers, Routing, MPS, MRP, and WIP Status of SFC

MRP and CRP. Figure 13.17 illustrates the differences between rough cut capacity planning (RCCP) and detailed capacity requirements planning (CRP).[2]

[2] For a detailed discussion on capacity requirements planning, see James G. Conell and Norris W. Edson, *Gaining Control: Capacity Management and Scheduling* (Essex Junction, VT: Oliver Wight Publications Inc., 1990).

Implementing the Rough Cut Process

Unlike most other manufacturing systems, rough cut capacity planning does not generally require lengthy cost justification, a large budget, a full project team, or a major educational effort. As mentioned earlier, for products with simple bills-of-materials and steady mixes, a number-2 pencil, a piece of paper, and the steps outlined in this chapter will do. Those steps are summarized as follows:

1. Identify the key resources using the resource matrix.
2. Develop resource profiles for the key resources using the best times and standards available.
3. Get production plan numbers from the S&OP process and the master schedule from the master scheduler.
4. Calculate the required capacity by exploding the production plan and/or the master schedule through the appropriate resource profiles.
5. Compare required capacity and planned capacity.
6. Identify the potential over- and underloads by time period.
7. If necessary, identify alternatives that balance required capacity and the planned capacity.
8. Determine the best course of action and implement solutions by either increasing/decreasing the planned capacity or increasing/decreasing the production plan or master schedule.

The payback from following these steps can be immense in terms of better schedules and a more refined planning process.

Final Thoughts

Remember the time-honored expression: KISS! (Keep It Simple, Stupid!) This should be our motto when designing a rough cut capacity planning system and deciding what to rough cut. Every company should rough cut at the production plan before converting that plan into a master schedule. But is this enough to proceed with detail material and capacity planning? The answer is simple: If you do not require rough cut capacity planning beyond the production plan, do not do it. There is no reason to rough cut at a detail level just to put numbers on a screen or paper. A general guideline when using rough cut capacity planning is expressed with one word: *Simplify*. Remember, the idea is to look only for information necessary to making quick, informed decisions.

Pareto's Law tells us that 80 percent of our results typically come from just 20 percent of our efforts. This is a rule of thumb that has proven its value in many fields. With respect to capacity planning, Pareto's Law explains why a small number of key resources can be used to predict large-scale outcomes, and it is used to reduce the number of constraints in a production system to just a small number of problems.

If a key work center represents a problem, you need to take another step—identify what makes it a problem. Perhaps there are six reasons for a particular work center's being a production bottleneck—the equipment, the suppliers, the operators, and so forth. Now ask which of the six reasons would yield the highest benefit if it were eliminated. Equipment overheating might represent 80 percent of the problem in this particular work center; eliminating overheating as a problem through preventive maintenance would represent the most efficient course to take. Using the Pareto technique in this way helps managers and master schedulers to refine their analysis of key resources and to improve the predictive value of the rough cut system.

Since MRP II requires a realistic production plan as a starting point, Class A MRP II companies use rough cut capacity planning simulation tools to assist in creating valid production plans. Since the manufacturing part of MRP II begins with the production plan, that plan must be realistic. Rough cut capacity planning allows companies to check their production plans as well as their master schedules and, consequently, get the very most out of MRP II.

Production plans, master schedules, and manufacturing schedules are only half of the equation—the supply half. In order for MRP II and master scheduling to work well in a company, the other side of the equation must also be addressed.

The next chapter will give the reader a flavor of demand planning and demand management as viewed through the perspective of master scheduling. Since MRP II is a demand-driven process, the master scheduling process is very dependent upon demand management activity. The better it is done, the better the master scheduling process will be.

14

Demand Management

Customers can order anything they want as long as it agrees with the forecast.

In the final analysis, virtually all of us show up at work on Monday morning for one reason: to either create or satisfy demand for our employers' products or services. Customer demand is the spark that ignites our entire economic system, and it serves as the controlling factor in all productive activities. While product supply can sometimes get out of balance and the imbalance appears as unsold inventory or poor customer service, the clear signal of customer demand eventually brings production back into equilibrium.

The master scheduler's role in this dynamic process has already been discussed: to harmonize the "when" and "how much" of production with actual and forecasted customer demand. If forecasted demand was always reliable, this would be a simpler job. But as we will see shortly, nothing is simple in predicting the future of customer orders.

What Is Demand Management?

The idea of "supply management" is easy enough to understand: It implies controlling the production process to specified levels of output. Since production facilities and labor are under the thumb of the company's management, these ideas seem straightforward.

The concept of "demand management" requires more explanation. Demand generally comes from outside the company and is, thus, beyond the full control of management, prompting many to ask, What's to manage? To a sales representative living and working a thousand miles away from the company's production facility, the idea of managing demand seems unimportant. All he or she may be interested in is managing the order book—getting as many orders booked as quickly as possible. More orders mean more commissions, and more compliments from the boss. If February's orders are twice those of January's, that is an unqualified achievement. If everyone doubled his or her orders, however, the production floor could be thrown into chaos, and only about half of those orders would be filled on time.

Because demand is largely external to the company, it would be convenient to proceed with the notion that demand should be left to rise and fall of its own accord, with all of management's attention directed toward supply. This notion fails on several counts:

- Few production facilities are so flexible with respect to volume that they can operate efficiently with low output in one period and high output in the next. This violates the basic principle of load-leveling.

- Not all demand is external to the company—at least in the larger sense. Much of modern production simply creates components for use in final products manufactured by the same company or its subsidiaries. In 1992, for example, General Motors Corporation "in-sourced" for 70 percent of its components and subassemblies. Thus, even though the final customer decision is external, demand is not entirely created from outside of the company.

• Demand can be created or its timing shifted through marketing. Thus, the idea of managing demand is reasonable and necessary if sales and the company's capabilities are to be kept in balance.[1] Demand management has four fundamental requirements:

1. *Prediction*. Maintaining a balance of supply and demand requires some ability to know the level of incoming orders *in advance*, especially in assemble-to-order and make-to-stock environments.

2. *Communications*. Infantry units have traditionally set out listening posts to detect and give early warning of approaching enemy forces. Successful companies know that they will have a chance of preparing for incoming demand if they maintain their own listening posts near the customers. Typically this is done through the field sales force, which visits customer facilities, talks with purchasing managers, and otherwise tries to gauge the level and timing of future orders.

3. *Influence*. Communications leads to knowledge and knowledge leads to influence. As described earlier, production works to level the load on the factory; it abhors a situation where it works at 100 percent of capacity in odd-numbered months, and at 50 percent during even-numbered months. Ideally, the plant manager would like work scheduled at 75 percent of capacity *every* month. The master scheduler uses his or her influence with sales and marketing to negotiate, where necessary, the shifting of customer demand to produce a better situation on the manufacturing floor—one that makes better use of fixed assets and human resources. This might take the form of a phone call to marketing or to the sales representative asking, Do you really need this big order in October? Would it be helpful to you if we shipped a third in September and two-thirds in October? Or would it be a problem for you if we shipped half in October and half in November?

[1] For a very complete treatment of demand management and forecasting, see George E. Palmatier and Joseph S. Shull, *The Marketing Edge* (Essex Junction, VT: Oliver Wight Publications, Inc., 1989).

Marketing can also influence demand, both its quantity and timing, through the use of advertising, pricing, and incentives to dealers, sales representatives, and customers.

4. *Prioritization and Allocation*. The idea behind demand management and master scheduling is to satisfy all customer demand. However, if a situation presents itself that not enough product exists as requested, or that the materials and resources needed to produce the required product are not available, then a decision must be made as to which customers get their orders filled as requested and which need to wait. This decision is the responsibility of sales and marketing.

Allocation is the process used when the company cannot produce enough product to cover the demand, whereas prioritization is the process used to determine which customer gets its order filled first. If a company cannot produce enough product, then some business may have to be turned away. In this case, the available product needs to be allocated so that the company does not oversell and overcommit its ability to produce.

Thus, the idea of "managing demand" is reasonable and has plenty of precedents.

THE ROLE OF FORECASTING IN THE COMPANY: THE CASE OF HASTINGS & BROWN

Richard Phillips sat in front of his computer, checking all the numbers he had just entered into an elaborate spreadsheet. The first column listed each of the company's fifty key products, which collectively accounted for almost 95 percent of company revenues. Arrayed across the top were the company's forty-two sales territories. The number he entered into each cell represented a sales forecast by product as determined by a field representative, based upon contacts with customers who were just then beginning the lengthy process of making purchase decisions.

Phillips was assistant sales director for Hastings & Brown, a publisher of college textbooks with revenues of $38 million. H&B's customers were college professors scattered across North America who determined which textbooks their students would be required to use during the next fall semester. Their purchase decisions were generally made between April 15 and June 15.

Each April, Phillips had to prepare a sales forecast for July through September, the period during which fall semester books would be ordered. Although this was his third experience at handling the fall forecast, this year would be more difficult than ever. Many new editions of H&B texts were just now being published, and their acceptance by the marketplace would be one large question mark until actual orders came in from the field. The competition had been active in both new publications and its promotions. Forecasting fall sales this year would clearly be more difficult than in any of the past few years.

In H&B's industry, every new book was an experiment. Many, in fact, joked that "the first printing is our market research." Some of the books published in the spring would catch on and be ordered in large numbers for the fall and for subsequent semesters; most, however, would be used by just a few schools and would disappear from the marketplace in a year or two. Determining the winners and losers at this point was the tough part.

Many in H&B management needed the forecast and would rely on it for a variety of purposes. Phillips's boss needed it for his report to the president. He would also comb through it for evidence of "big winners" to be touted to the sales force to spur them on to even larger sales.

The production manager would use the forecast to plan reprints. Since the first printing of a new title was, indeed, a form of market research, initial printings were deliberately kept small. Once the winners were identified by the field sales force, planning for second printings had to be made; the same had to be done for other, older publications.

The company's financial manager also had a keen interest in the forecast, as he would have to finance production and budget further expenses. Finally, H&B's president would be making his quarterly trek to New York, where he was expected to report to the parent company's board of directors on the plans and progress of the subsidiary company he managed. The fall sales forecast would be his primary resource in preparing for that important meeting.

All forecasted sales figures were submitted directly by the field sales representatives, who were (or were suppose to be) in regular contact with their customers. As a former field representative who knew most of the field staff, Phillips was suspicious of many of their forecasts. The Nashville representative, Rhett Farnsworthy, he remembered as a self-defined big shot. Farnsworthy's forecasts were always higher than just about everyone else's, yet his optimism was never supported by actual sales. Joan Sommerville of Seattle, on the other hand, was a high-performing sales representative who invariably turned in a low forecast.

Phillips liked to think that the overly optimistic and overly pessimistic figures submitted by individual field representatives would naturally cancel themselves out when the figures were aggregated into a final forecast. But he had neither the time nor a method to empirically evaluate that theory.

Some field representatives he suspected of simply pulling numbers out of a hat. Because the forecast played no part in establishing sales quotas for their territories, and since no rewards or penalties were ever assessed for accurate or inaccurate forecasts, the largely unsupervised field representatives had no particular incentive to take the forecasting job seriously. To many, it was an annual chore that took away from their selling time. H&B management had never emphasized the importance of good sales forecasting to the overall workings of the company, nor had it provided them with a methodology for doing the job systematically.

One who did take the forecasting job seriously was Arthur Petersen, of the Wisconsin territory. Petersen had a reputation for being diligent in developing his territory forecast for each major project. He kept careful records of past order quantities, called his customers frequently about their plans, and used early order patterns to project future orders. This attention to detail paid off in booking orders and in more accurate forecasts for the Wisconsin territory. But Petersen was an exception to the rule.

Phillips continued the tedious business of compiling the forecast figures, and as he did so he determined that he would ask Petersen to develop a short training program on sales forecasting for the other sales representatives. But not until next year.

This story of sales forecasting at Hastings & Brown is not meant to be typical, but to indicate the good and the bad of forecasting methods and how forecasts are used by different parties in a company.

Problems with Forecasting

Virtually every industry employs individuals to forecast future levels of business activity; in the H&B case, this task was done by unsupervised field sales representatives. Other companies use more formal processes. The many sectors of the energy industry, for example, attempt to predict demand for coal, natural gas, and petroleum so that production, distribution, and financing can be arranged in an orderly fashion. Large individual companies like money center banks, auto producers, and chemical giants have traditionally employed individuals with specialized training to develop proprietary forecasts of future business activity. Whichever way demand forecasting is conducted, one thing can be said with some certainty: **The forecast is never 100 percent accurate.**

Economist John Kenneth Galbraith once remarked, "We have two classes of forecasters: Those who don't know, and those who don't know they don't know." Predicting the behavior of thousands if not millions of individual decision makers is by nature a questionable business, no matter how scientifically done. The result is that forecasts are invariably inaccurate to some degree. Economic and stock market forecasters are often held up for special ridicule; indeed, many joke that economic seers exist solely for the purpose of making astrologers look good.

Coping with Forecast Inaccuracies

Even though demand forecasts are imperfect, they are necessary and companies have developed a number of ways to make the most of the situation. Over the years, the author has observed how different companies cope with the inherent inaccuracies of demand forecasting. Here are the twelve most popular techniques used in today's environment, listed alphabetically:

Accountability	Lead-time reduction
Communications	Manufacturing flexibility
Customer/supplier linking	Performance measurement
Demand management	Reserve capacity
Forecasting systems	S&OP and MPS policies
Inventory management	Safety stocks/overplanning

It's About Quantities

To be useful to the master scheduler, forecasts must be expressed as items (or product families), quantities, and dates. A forecast of $10 million in sales revenue is of little value to the multiproduct company when it needs to schedule its production. A forecast of 1,000 A, 2,000 B, and 1,500 C is more useful. Getting from a useless to a useful demand forecast is a challenging activity in which both sales and manufacturing can participate for mutual benefit.

Breaking Down the Forecast

For the company with multiple product lines, the forecast may be developed in the aggregate but must then be broken down into manufacturable segments. Consider an office furniture manufacturer with a very simple offering of two products whose forecast for a period looks like Figure 14.1.

If these products were made in one style and color, this forecast would be directly usable by the master scheduler. There would be two discrete products to be built in specified quantities, and each of these would have a specific bill-of-materials. But business is rarely that simple, and each of these chairs is actually a product family that comes in three colors: black, gray, and burgundy.

In a make-to-order environment in which the color variety can be made as part of the finishing process, master scheduling can be done to the point where the color items are added. But assuming that this is not the way the chairs are built, or if the finishing stage is to be scheduled, then marketing needs to break down its forecast into color-specific categories for each period, as in Figure 14.2.

Figure 14.1 Demand Forecast for Two-Product Company

Product Line	Forecast (in units)
Deskmate Secretarial Chairs	5000
Executive Chairs	1000

Figure 14.2 Deskmate Secretarial Chair Family

Color	Estimated Percent	Forecasted Units
Black	20	1000
Gray	50	2500
Burgundy	30	1500
Total	100	5000

This is a "product mix forecast" for just one of the company's two product families, and for just one time period. Here, the sales department estimated how, as percentages, orders would be distributed among the product options within the family. In most cases, breaking down an aggregate forecast is not this simple as there are usually many more product items, colors, and options.

It's About Time

Knowing the "what" of the forecast is just half of what is needed by the master scheduler. The other half is "when" those items are needed.

Book Date and Demand Date

Since most forecasts are made by marketing personnel, the forecasted date is typically expressed by booking (or "order") date—i.e., when the order is to be received. This is the red-letter day for marketing, as getting orders is the reason for its existence. But master scheduling is concerned with satisfying demand with a complete product, so it needs to know the demand (or customer's desired "shipping") date. The degree to which booking and demand dates differ depends upon the nature of the business and its manufacturing strategy. In a make-to-stock business, for example, the two dates may be separated by just a few hours or a day—just long enough to pack, invoice, and ship the items from finished goods. In a make-to-order business, a greater gap typically exists because the items are in some incomplete stage of production when the orders are booked. Here, a lead time is added to the booking date to get the true demand date. Figure 14.3 illustrates the difference for make-to-stock and make-to-order environments. For general learning purposes, an MTO situation in which a single blanket order with multiple shipments is also shown.

The master scheduler's focus on the demand date pays off partic-

Figure 14.3 Bookings Versus Demand

Period	1	2	3	4	5
MTS					
Bookings	100	150	125	150	
Demand	100	150	125	150	
MTO (1 period-lead time)					
Bookings	100	150	125	150	
Demand		100	150	125	150
MTO—Scheduled shipments, blanket order (1-period lead time)					
Bookings	1000				
Demand		250	250	250	250

ularly well when the customer is focused on the same date. Consider a candy company whose big seasons are Easter and Halloween. Customers may give the candy company's sales representative an order for chocolate Easter eggs in January, but they have a definite delivery date in mind—not January (the booking date), but sometime just before Easter.

Spreading the Forecast by Time Period

Forecasts are typically made for large blocks of time: "The current year's sales forecast is 3.2 million units." That may be helpful information to the board of directors, but down in the trenches the figure is

Small Numbers and the Master Schedule

While the Law of Large Numbers is a useful tool in a number of statistical applications, small numbers frequently confront the unwary master scheduler.

Consider a situation in which the product mix demand is being determined. The sales department states that one particular option of a product family will account for 6 percent of its total demand, which is figured as follows, using master scheduling software:

Period	1	2	3	4	5	6
Forecast	10	10	10	10	10	10
6% Option	0.6	0.6	0.6	0.6	0.6	0.6
Demand (rounded)	1	1	1	1	1	1

Because some software rounds less than whole numbers, demand for this option is not 6 percent of the product family, but 10 percent (6/60).

Virtually all MPS software includes this troublesome feature. One way the problem can be eliminated is by entering fractional

not that useful. Since master scheduling needs information to established ship dates, a call goes over to marketing:

"Can you give me some shipping dates for next month?" the scheduler asks.

The sales director checks his computer. "No dates, but we've forecasted 12,000 units of product number 73. Does that help you?"

"Yes," the master scheduler says with suppressed sarcasm, "that information is of tremendous help."

If sales and marketing do not know when forecasted customer orders will need to be shipped during November, it is certain that the "remainders" as artificial inventory that is carried over from period to period. When this artificial inventory reaches a value equal to or greater than the demand, it is accommodated in the demand line. (The answer is rounded down and the faction is reduced by the amount needed.)

This is a way of keeping the fractional values in the system and making the mathematics work correctly. To see how this works, consider the same example, but with remainders carried over.

Period	1	2	3	4	5	6
Forecast	10	10	10	10	10	10
6% Option	0.6	0.6	0.6	0.6	0.6	0.6
Demand (rounded)	1	1	0	1	0	1
Cumulative Remainder	0.4	0.8	0.2	0.6	0	0.4

In this situation, demand has totaled to 4, which is 6 percent of the total forecasts for the six periods (4/60).

master scheduler does not know either. A first approach to scheduling 12,000 units would be to look at the record of actual shipments of product number 73 during November of the previous two or three years. Is there a pattern? In a seasonal business, like a producer of chocolate Easter eggs or ski apparel, a strong pattern may exist.[2]

[2] WARNING: If the pattern shows past November orders skewed toward the end of the month, do not automatically assume that this is when the customers wanted the product. It may merely indicate the company's tendency to play the "end-of-the-month nightmare" described in chapter 1.

If no strong pattern exists, the company may simply spread the 12,000 forecasted units evenly over the days or weeks in the month. With this many units forecasted, the Law of Large Numbers favors this even distribution. The Law of Large Numbers holds that, barring some internal bias, outcomes will be evenly distributed around the mean (average). Thus, the shipping dates for the 12,000 units should be scattered evenly through November, and the master scheduler can earmark them for production in this fashion. If the company's products are something like furniture, in which just 100 to 150 units were forecasted for November, no such assumption of even distribution can be made; half of them might be part of a single large order, due for shipping on one particular date. Sales should be asked directly if these units are expected to come in many small orders or from one or two large customers.

A monthly forecast can be broken down, based upon the number of working days in a given week, taking into account holidays and plant maintenance shutdowns. This could also take into account the fact that the month in question may begin and end in the middle of a week. Here forecasts from different months need to be blended within weekly periods. For example, Monday and Tuesday might be part of October and Wednesday through Sunday would then be part of November.

Demand and Forecast Adjustment

In addition to the discussion of how the forecast is developed, it is also necessary to understand how to use it in the master scheduling process. Consider Figure 14.4, which contains a one-month forecast of 400 units. This demand came from the S&OP process described in chapter 12; the breakdown of this aggregate figure of 400 into weekly periods was accomplished through collaboration between production and marketing. Thus, weeks (periods) 1 through 4 are each forecasted at 100 units, which both parties deemed reasonable in terms of past

Figure 14.4 Aggregate Forecast of 400 Spread Over Time

	1	2	3	4
Product Forecast	100	100	100	100
Abnormal Demand				
Actual Demand	85	0	90	50
Total Demand				

order patterns and future expectations. The figure contains lines for actual demand, abnormal demand, and one for total demand, all of which will be addressed soon.

Actual Demand

The third line of the example in Figure 14.4 represents actual demand, i.e., the quantity of product for which the company has firm customer commitments. In the figure, each week has less actual demand than what had been forecasted. The actual demand line is updated as confirmed orders are received.[3] These quantities remain in this line, however, until those items are produced and shipped.

Forecast Consumption

As actual demand appears and is entered into the matrix, that demand "consumes" part of the forecast. Thus, in Figure 14.5 on the following page, the 85 units of actual demand in period 1 consume that same amount of the forecast, leaving 15 units remaining. The 90 units of actual demand in period 3 consume all but 10 units of that period's forecast, and half of the original forecast of 100 in period 4 are consumed by actual demand in that period. Notice, however, that

[3] Updating of actual demand may be accomplished automatically through the company's order-entry system.

Figure 14.5 Consumption of the Forecast

	1	2	3	4
Unconsumed Forecast	15	100	10	50
Abnormal Demand				
Actual Demand	85	0	90	50
Total Demand	100	100	100	100

total demand remains the same as the original forecast of 100 per week. Here an assumption has been made that the actual demand represents demand already anticipated during the development of the forecast.

Timing Versus Demand Problems

Time passes, and as the end of week 1 is reached, the forecasting system automatically drops that column and shifts the remaining 3 weeks to the left. But if no new orders came in to consume the remaining 15 units of the original forecast, what would we do with those 15 units? This question highlights a perennial problem for supply and demand managers: determining whether the forecast was inaccurate in quantity—and those orders will never appear—or whether the forecasted orders are simply delayed. Here, two options are available:

1. Assume that orders for the 15 units will *never* come in, and drop them entirely
2. Assume that the orders for the 15 units are merely delayed and carry them over as part of the unconsumed forecast

The first option involves a change in the forecast—from 400 to 385—which may require consultation with other parties in the company (marketing and finance in particular). Many forecasting and master scheduling software systems will automatically drop the 15 unsold units as they update the records with the passage of time. This may not be prudent, however, and the demand manager and/or master scheduler would be advised to check with sales about any variance between actual demand and the forecast before the period is closed out.

If the second option is chosen—i.e., the missing 15-unit order is merely delayed—no change to the overall forecast of 400 units is made, and the unsold 15 are "rolled" forward. But how? There are many possible approaches to this problem, and Figure 14.6 shows just a few:

In the first option, the entire 15 units are "front loaded" into the next period; subsequent options spread the 15 in other ways. Master schedulers should know that there is no "best way" of rolling the forecast that fits all companies and all situations. Ultimately, they must exercise judgment based upon demand patterns experienced by their own companies and the input of knowledgeable and affected parties.

Figure 14.6 Rolling the Forecast

	Past Due	1	2	3
Original Forecast	100	100	100	100
Unconsumed Forecast	15	100	100	100
New Forecast (Option 1)		115	100	100
(Option 2)		110	105	100
(Option 3)		105	105	105
(Option 4)		100	100	115
etc.		etc.		

One general decision rule that bears following, however, is: **Orders that fail to materialize in an aggregate forecasting period should not be automatically rolled into the next forecasting period**. For example, the situation in Figure 14.6 on the preceding page represents an aggregate forecasting period—4 weeks; 400 units of demand are anticipated during that period. The 15 units that failed to materialize in the past-due week might be rolled forward into new weeks 1, 2, and 3 by any means viewed as reasonable. However, a new aggregate forecasting period would take effect in weeks 5 through 8, and it should not be burdened by any inaccuracies that manifested themselves in the previous forecasting period. Prudence dictates

Computer Alert

One peril of almost all master scheduling software is the fact that it looks at the forecast and the actual demand for each period and takes the *greater of the two* as total demand. On the surface this seems to make sense: If actual demand outstrips the forecast, the master scheduler needs to build to that level. If the forecast exceeds actual demand, we might assume that the orders are late.

Look at the situation below. Sales forecasts the need for 400 units over 4 periods. But the software logic has automatically taken the greater of the forecast and actual demand, thus increasing the forecast by 20 units, to 420.

Period	1	2	3	4	Total
Product Forecast	100	100	100	100	400
Abnormal Demand					
Actual Demand	100	80	110	110	400
Total Demand	100	100	110	110	420

that—barring reliable information to the contrary—demand that fails to materialize in weeks 1 through 4 could be assumed to be lost, and therefore not rolled forward into weeks 5 through 8. Instead, it could be dropped. If that demand were still lurking in the market, one would expect that the new forecast would have picked it up. The best way to handle this situation is to have someone in marketing and demand management review the prior period's forecast and make a determination as to whether the unconsumed forecast should be rolled forward or dropped. By doing this, the accountability for forecast accuracy is not lost.

Now consider what happens when a customer calls to request a rescheduling of an order, so that 40 units of actual demand are shifted from period 2 to period 3. Remember, this is not an *increase* in demand, just a reschedule. As shown below, the software logic does its thing, taking the greater of forecast and actual demand in determining total demand, and in so doing increases total demand by 40 units (from 420 to 460) out of thin air!

Period	1	2	3	4	Total
Product Forecast	100	100	100	100	400
Abnormal Demand					
Actual Demand	100	40	150	110	400
Total Demand	100	100	150	110	460

Tracking Cumulative Demand

In the case described in Figure 14.5 on page 410, a shortage of actual demand in the first period would most likely be rolled over. Demand managers and master schedulers would not be losing any sleep at this point, knowing that the forecast is always inaccurate to some degree, and that the division of the 400 units into four discrete demand periods was, after all, based more on intuition than on science. Besides, there are three more weeks available in the planning horizon.

As the days and the weeks slip by, however, variances between actual demand and the forecast have fewer and fewer opportunities to come into balance. How can we deal with variances as time passes?

One useful approach to dealing with deviations from the forecast over periods of time is through the tracking of demand on a cumulative basis—i.e., by comparing the *total* of actual demand over a period of time to the *total* forecasted for that same elapsed period. This technique filters out the effects of timing problems from inaccuracies in the forecast quantity. Figure 14.7 applies this technique to the example we have been following. Here a range using high and low indicators is established to accommodate the inevitable inaccuracy of the forecast. This range is the sum for both the expected timing errors and the expected forecast errors. Any values that fall outside of these high and low boundaries are signals to management to investigate. Another line

Figure 14.7 Tracking Cumulative Demand

	1	2	3	4
Low	40	100	200	320
Forecast	100	200	300	400
High	160	300	400	480
Deviation from Forecast	60%	50%	33%	20%

is added to indicate the deviation of actual demand from forecasted demand, expressed as a percentage of forecasted demand. Over time, this deviation should decrease.

Since the first period is less likely—percentagewise—to correspond to the forecast than would the four weeks taken as a whole, the spread between the high and low boundaries is greatest. But this spread should narrow progressively over time. Why? Simply because the passing of time allows the timing problems to work themselves out, leaving only the inaccuracies of the forecast quantity as the source of deviation. The result, in a normal situation, should look something like Figure 14.8.

How does demand management use these tracking signals? If the actual demand in period 1 is fewer than 40 units, a signal is sent (flags up) to watch this product through the coming weeks because the forecast could be biased high. If the actual demand at the end of period 1 is greater than 160 units, a signal is sent to demand management that the forecast may be biased low or some unexpected demand may have appeared. This situation could result in the forecast's being understated. Incremental demand not anticipated is known as "abnormal demand" and must be recognized if demand planning and master scheduling are to work effectively.

Figure 14.8 Converging Deviation from Forecast Over Time

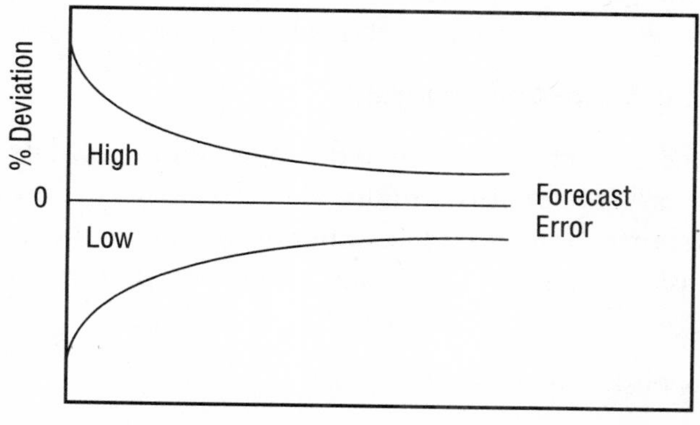

The Problem of Abnormal Demand

Our discussion of forecast consumption began with an assumption that orders being entered into actual demand were all part of the original forecast. This assumption, however, rarely holds up in a dynamic marketplace. Unanticipated bookings are made as sales representatives locate new customers and obtain orders; marketing's efforts at trade shows and with direct mail sometimes result in huge new accounts.

These unanticipated orders, or "abnormal demand," are every salesperson's dream, but they can be every master scheduler's nightmare. If these orders enter the system as actual demand and consume the forecast, big overbooking problems can result when the forecasted orders do appear. In fact, it can be stated that a master scheduling system *will not work* effectively if normal and abnormal demand cannot be differentiated. Without this ability, total demand cannot be determined with sufficient accuracy to produce a reliable projected available balance line of the MPS matrix. And it is from this line that the master scheduling system generates the all-important action messages. If the projected available balance line cannot be calculated correctly, the generated action, or exception, messages could be misleading and could cause the master scheduler to make bad decisions.

Identifying Abnormal Demand

To enjoy the benefits of abnormal demand and to avoid its problems, it is necessary to identify abnormal orders *before* they enter the system or shortly thereafter. Customer orders should be analyzed and classified as "normal" or "abnormal" at order-entry time. Some of the tell-tale signs of abnormal demand are:

- A new customer account
- The seasonal pattern is wrong

- A one-time order
- A larger than normal order
- An order that comes through a nontraditional distribution channel

Marketing and sales personnel should be encouraged to help in this process, and demand managers and master schedulers should communicate with these individuals when in doubt about any suspicious orders.

Accommodating Abnormal Demand

Once abnormal demand is properly identified, working it into the forecast and master schedule is straightforward. Figure 14.9 demonstrates a situation in which a one-time order is submitted in period 3 as a result of attendance by marketing at an industry trade show. The customer is a foreign company that wants to buy 150 units on an experimental basis. Only time will tell if this company becomes a regular customer.

Notice here that these 150 units of abnormal demand are added to the unconsumed forecast of 10, and the actual demand of 90 to obtain a total demand of 250 units. The original forecast is unchanged,

Figure 14.9 Treatment of Abnormal Demand

	1	2	3	4
Unconsumed Forecast	15	100	10	50
Abnormal Demand			150	
Actual Demand	85	0	90	50
Total Demand	100	100	250	100

as is the unconsumed forecast. What is changed is the total demand, which shows an incremental amount equal to the abnormal demand.

Customer Linking

The difficulty of determining customer demand has already been explained. Difficult and imprecise as it is, forecasting is nevertheless a requirement of modern business. But what if we could get the customers to do the forecasting? Who, after all, could possibly know their needs with greater certainty? A number of companies do, in fact, have such a forecasting system, which is generally known as customer connectivity or "linking."[4] They are most prevalent and applicable when the customer is an "upstream" producer, distributor, or retailer for whom the company acts as a supplier.

Customer linking uses the logic of manufacturing resource planning (MRP II) and distribution resource planning (DRP) to create demand plans at the manufacturing plant and master schedule level (see Figure 14.10).

These planning systems take the customer's product forecast, booked demand, inventories, open purchase orders, open manufacturing orders, and bills-of-distribution to create planned receipts of products needed in order to prevent stockout conditions.

Once a customer determines replenishment requirements for its various products, these demands are communicated to the supplier. This has long been done using traditional purchase orders. But why use the purchase order? Why not send the supplier the expected demand directly in the form of a shipment schedule? This can be done by having the customer's MRP or DRP system determine the

[4] For a very complete treatment of distribution resource planning and customer connectivity, see Andre J. Martin, *Distribution Resource Planning* (Essex Junction, VT: Oliver Wight Publications, Inc. 1990).

Figure 14.10 Distribution Resource Planning

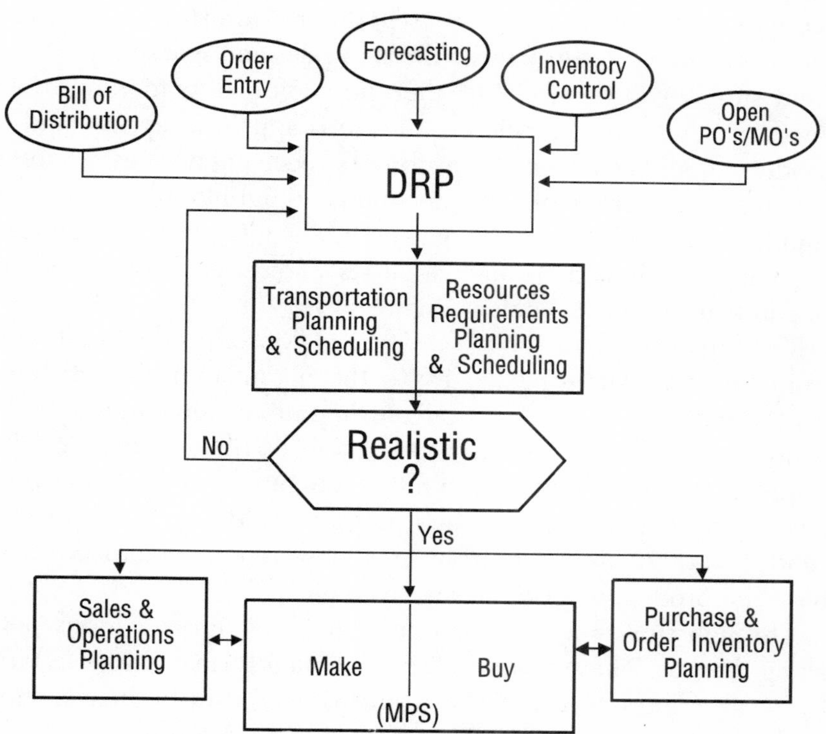

(Reprinted from *Distribution Resource Planning* by Andre J. Martin, Oliver Wight Publications, Inc., with permission of the publisher.)

plant's required shipping date by offsetting the transportation time necessary to move the product from the supplier to the customer's delivery point.

This demand along with other customer demands is aggregated and used by sales and operations planning to plan "make" items, it is used by procurement to plan "buy" items, and it is used by the master scheduler to plan both make and buy items. This same customer demand data is also used to do transportation and resource requirements planning and scheduling.

While customer linking solves many of the problems associated with demand, the master scheduler must still analyze the expected supply to see if the demand can be satisfied. If it cannot be satisfied, it is the responsibility of the master scheduler to inform the customer of the problem, either directly or through sales and marketing. If sufficient supply will be available, then no additional communication is necessary and the principle of "silence is approval" applies and the product should arrive on the customer's receiving dock as requested.

Once customer linking is understood and put into place, the entire supply/demand chain can be connected. The ultimate vision is to have the customer linked through a series of events directly with the manufacturing plant. Look at Figure 14.11.

The top of the figure shows the typical flow of product as it moves from the manufacturing facility to the manufacturer's distribution center or to its customer's manufacturing site. From here the product continues its journey possibly to a retail distribution center, which sends it to a retail store, which ultimately puts it in the hands of the customer. Of course, a manufacturing site could produce its product, send it to other manufacturing sites or warehouses, and eventually have the product wind up at the customer.

Through this process, inventories are built up at various points along the way. These inventories and demands (many times affected by lot sizes and safety stocks) are quite often out-of-balance as shown in the center of the figure. The bottom of the figure is where we all would like to be, a smooth flow with pockets of reduced inventories that are balanced with the feeding operations (suppliers) and the needing operations (customers). The challenge is to link all these operations together and balance the flow.

Getting Pipeline Control

Customer and supplier linking offers many opportunities for the manufacturing company using master scheduling. We have already discussed how forecasting can be improved by connecting up to the

Figure 14.11 Typical and Improved Pipelines

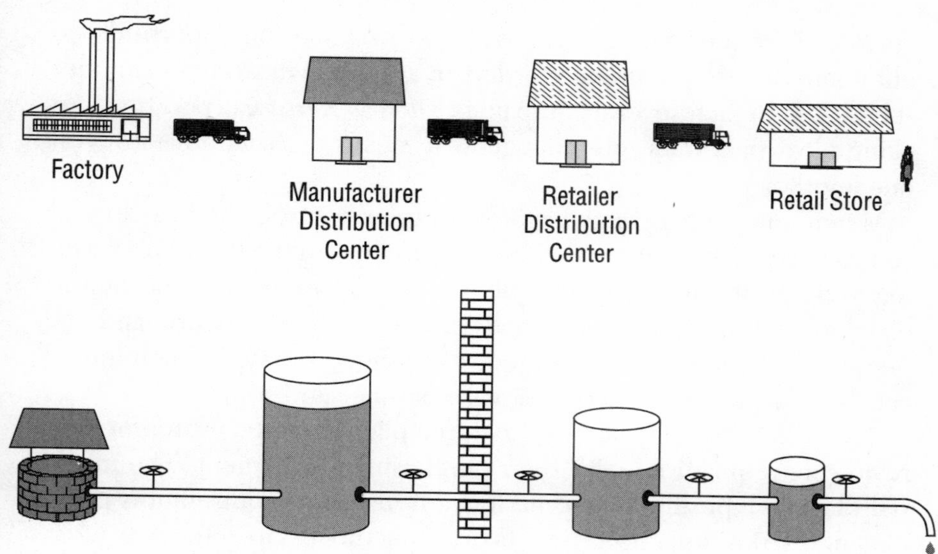

Traditional Product Flow with Unbalanced Inventories

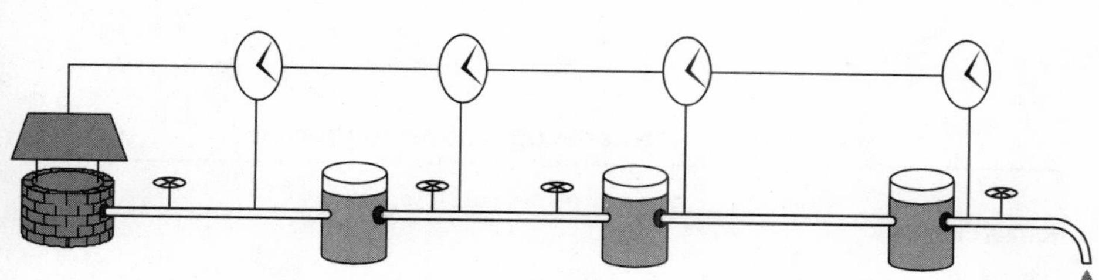

Customer-Linked Product Flows with Balanced Inventories

(Reprinted from *Distribution Resource Planning* by Andre J. Martin, Oliver Wight Publications, Inc., with permission of the publisher.)

customer's requirements. We have also discussed the opportunity to eliminate the use of purchase orders by using the customer's supplier schedules. In fact, several companies, such as Xerox Corporation, are using electronic data interchange as a means to communicate with one another.

When companies get the pipeline under control, the next logical step is to remove *all* waste that may be resident in the flow. This waste may exist in the form of multiple stocking locations, transportation, obsolete materials, damaged goods, unnecessary paperwork, and unnecessary communications. Figure 14.12 shows the typical communication links between the traditional customer and supplier.

The traditional flow shows a material planner at the customer site, reviewing requisitions with their purchasing department. The material planner typically uses some form of material requirements planning or distribution requirements planning process to determine what needs to be ordered and when. Purchasing then communicates with the supplier's sales department, who places the order (demand or request for product) into the order-entry system. This demand is

Figure 14.12 Customer/Supplier Information Flow

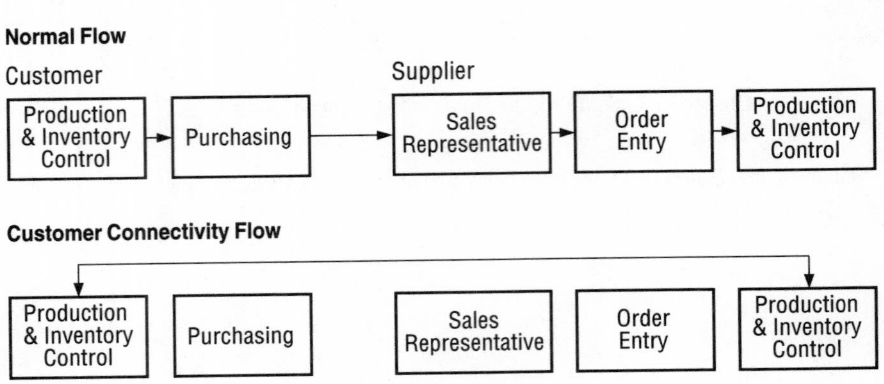

(Reprinted from *Distribution Resource Planning* by Andre J. Martin, Oliver Wight Publications, Inc., with permission of the publisher.)

communicated to the scheduling department of the supplier, who further communicates it to the manufacturing function. Looks like a lot of stress filled with wasted motions.

What if the company could get its purchasing department to work out a volume agreement with the supplier's sales department that covers a defined planning horizon? If this could be arranged and an agreement drawn up, then why not have the customer's production and inventory control department talk and make releases directly to the supplier's production and inventory control department? These people speak the same language. Think of all the communication and miscommunication problems we could avoid. And what about the time factor? Customer connectivity is a win-win situation.

By doing this (which resembles the supplier-linking process, but from the other side), the sales force is focused on what it's good at—selling. It removes huge amounts of administrative time requirements that are generally needed to place multiple orders and releases. And most companies that implement customer and supplier linking are finding that they do less expediting. That alone makes it worth looking into the concept.

Distribution Resource/Requirements Planning

In military operations, logistics personnel attempt to site all foreseeable manpower, supply, and material requirements as close to battlefield operations as practical. This is its method for ensuring the availability of critical resources. In Operation Desert Storm, for example, a six-month supply of equipment and materials was shipped to Saudi Arabia before any major engagements were undertaken. The military, of course, does not have shareholders screaming about excess inventories! Many manufacturers follow a similar model—

though tempered by concerns for inventory cost—shipping finished goods out to regional distribution points where they are more readily available to the customer. This strategy has three purposes:

1. *To reduce lead time.* If shipping from a manufacturing plant in North Carolina to a customer in Utah normally requires four days by overland truck, at least three of those days can be eliminated by sitting inventory in Utah itself. This reduction in lead time may be an important element of customer service (for both products and spares) and increase the company's competitive position.

2. *Reduce transportation cost.* Distributed inventories are sometimes motivated by greater transportation cost efficiencies. For example, in the case just given, shipping individual orders on demand by truck from North Carolina to customers in Utah would be much more costly than would planned, full truckload shipments to a Utah distribution center. This latter approach might also eliminate the need for periodic air-freight shipments to satisfy special customer needs.

3. *Control the market channel.* For many common consumer and industrial goods, a true market presence can sometimes be established only when a local inventory and distribution system is in place. Controlling shelf space in the supermarkets of Salt Lake City, for example, could not be established or maintained by a potato chip maker in Pennsylvania unless it had a distribution center in that metropolitan area. Effective shelf-stocking at supermarkets and convenience stores could not possibly be accomplished from Pennsylvania in a cost-effective way.

Distributed inventory is not a panacea for every business problem. Distribution centers are cost centers and must ultimately be judged in terms of the value their costs add to the company and its customers.

The Mechanics of DRP

Minuteman Electronics Company (MEC), the laptop computer manufacturer, was introduced earlier. As noted, MEC produces the finished computers in Boston, Raleigh, and Birmingham. These manufacturing plants ship finished products to distribution centers located in Boston, Chicago, and San Francisco. Figure 14.13 illustrates the MEC distribution scheme and—on the left of the figure—the planning tools used to build and move products through it.

From the master scheduler's perspective, MEC products are built according to the master schedule supported by an MPS system at the company's main plant, a system that reaches down to material and capacity requirement levels using MRP. This same MPS system is driven by demand from three sources: direct sales to customers, and orders placed by the warehouses located in Chicago and San Francisco—each of which is viewed as a "customer." For direct customer sales—those filled from the plant warehouse—demand is forecasted by MEC's local sales team. Sales to Midwestern and West Coast customers, however, are forecasted by the sales organizations based in Chicago and San Francisco respectively.

Figure 14.13 Distribution Scheme and Planning Tools, MEC

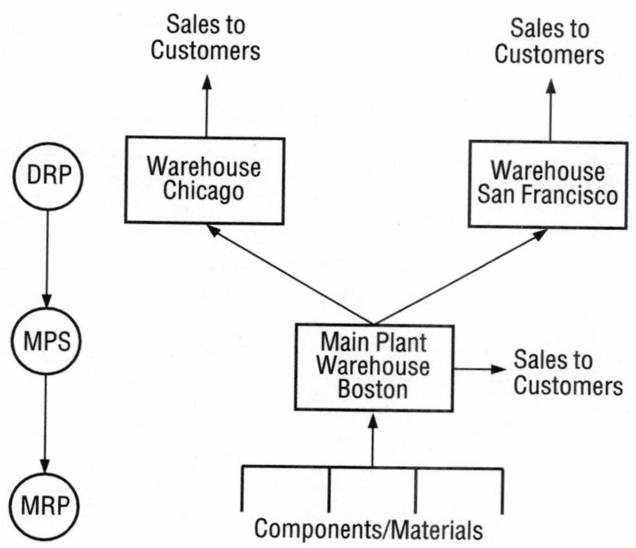

Figure 14.14 provides a more detailed look at the linkage between the manufacturing plant and the two MEC distribution centers with respect to just one product: Item 247. As the figure makes clear, each of the distribution centers has an on-hand balance, specific order quantity, transit lead time, and safety stock defined for this item. The Chicago facility, for example, begins the current period with an on-hand balance of 500, has a order quantity of 400, a safety stock of 200 (one week's worth of demand), and a lead-time requirement of 1 week.

How activities at the distribution centers signal activities at the manufacturing plant becomes clear as we examine several periods in Figure 14.14. Here, the Chicago distribution center's first-period forecast of 200 is expected to use all but 300 of the on-hand balance of Item 247—leaving 300 as a projected available balance at the end of period 1. The second week's demand is also 200, which will leave 100

Figure 14.14 Distribution Resource Planning Linkages, Item 247

Chicago DC

O/H: 500
O/Q: 400
L/T: 1 WK
S/S: 1 WK

		Period							
		1	2	3	4	5	6	7	8
Sales Forecast		200	200	200	200	200	200	200	200
In Transit									
Projected Available Balance	500	300	500	300	500	300	500	300	500
Planned Order Release		400		400		400		400	

San Francisco DC

O/H: 350
O/Q: 300
L/T: 2 WK
S/S: 300

		Period							
		1	2	3	4	5	6	7	8
Sales Forecast		150	150	150	150	150	150	150	150
In Transit		300							
Projected Available Balance	350	500	350	500	350	500	350	500	350
Planned Order Release		300		300		300		300	

Boston Plant/Warehouse

O/H: 1300
O/Q: 1000
L/T: 2 WK
S/S: 400

		Period							
		1	2	3	4	5	6	7	8
Sales Forecast (BOS)		100	100	100	100	100	100	100	100
Warehouse Requirements (CHI)		400		400		400		400	
Warehouse Requirements (SF)		300		300		300		300	
Total Demand		800	100	800	100	800	100	800	100
Projected Available Balance	1300	500	1400	600	500	700	600	800	700
Master Schedule			1000			1000		1000	

units (300−200) projected available balance at the end of period 2. Since that number is below the safety stock requirement, a planned order release is made for 400 units—the specified order quantity. That order is required to be received in week 2 but must be shipped from the Boston manufacturing plant in week 1 (transportation lead time is one period). When the plant acknowledges or ships the order, the planned order release will be changed into a scheduled receipt and show up on the "in transit" line by its due date, which is week 2. This process would continue through the Chicago distribution center's horizon. As the reader can see, a series of planned orders is being created for the Boston manufacturing plant.

A similar set of events is going on at the San Francisco distribution center, though an "in transit" shipment is expected to arrive during week 1, obviously due to a planned order released earlier (two weeks earlier, given the expected in-transit lead time to move the product to that facility). Again, a series of planning orders is being placed on the Boston manufacturing plant.

The Impact of Distribution Center Orders on the Plant

The manufacturing facility that receives distribution center orders views them as another source of demand. In the current example, the MPS system at the Boston plant indicates three sources of demand: its own sales forecast of regional sales (100 per week), Chicago's warehouse requirements of 400 every other week, and San Francisco's warehouse requirements of 300 every other week. In week 1 of the example, these warehouse requirements total 800: 100 from Boston, 400 from Chicago, and 300 from San Francisco. Together, the warehouse requirements from each location and for each week in the planning horizon constitute total demand to which the master scheduler must respond. In addition to understanding the total demand, the master scheduler must also know where the demand comes from. This requirement is supported by the "pegging" capability in the MPS system. "Pegging" informs the master scheduler which warehouse caused the demand. The reader should understand some of the reasons for this requirement: assigning priorities, if necessary, and effective shipping to name just two.

Distribution Requirements Planning Versus Distribution Resources Planning

The information system that makes distribution *requirements* planning possible also makes distribution *resources* planning feasible. This extends a company's ability from simply building and shipping items to the ability to maximize the total resources of the company. As an example, MEC's information system enables the master scheduler to intelligently manage supply and demand throughout the company and its distribution system; in addition, this same information system very likely has enough stored data to develop a shipping routine that minimizes costs and balances transportation loads. In Figure 14.15, Item 247 is shown to be just one of four for which quantity, space, and weight have been calculated to facilitate balanced shipping in weeks 1 and 2.

Based upon this information, the master scheduler or transportation planner can reserve an appropriate level of transportation capabilities to move combined orders at the most effective cost from the Boston plant to the Chicago distribution center.

The next question must be, If we can get the distribution centers to

Figure 14.15 Transportation Plan, Chicago Distribution Center

	Week 1				Week 2			
Item No.	**Qty (Ea)**	**Space (Ft^3)**	**Weight (Lbs)**	**Notes (*)**	**Qty (Ea)**	**Space (Ft^3)**	**Weight (Lbs)**	**Notes (*)**
141	250	27	1250		250	27	1250	
223	100	16	824					
247	400	36	2000					
288	200	20	1700		200	20	1700	
Etc.	....	....	....		....	....	....	
Total	2900	312	16974		1370	135	6650	

communicate their planned requirements, why can't we get the customers to communicate their planned requirements? It's the next logical step and is similar to the interplant environment, described earlier for Minuteman Electronics Company.[5] And it impacts a subject of fundamental importance to the manufacturer—load-leveling.

Expected Results

Companies that use DRP continue to experience improved customer service with reduced inventories. This is being done with less reliance on sales forecasting and improved sales productivity by keeping the sales representatives doing what they are paid to do, which is to sell. Periodic demand monitoring and transportation planning, coupled with the other DRP processes, can lead to increased product pipeline velocity and reduced lead times from supplier to customer. And let's not forget the reduction of distribution and manufacturing costs associated with the benefits already stated. Overall, the customer-linking process can give a company the opportunity to eliminate all unnecessary activities. This is a continuous-improvement program expanding to include the distribution and logistics network.

The notion of DRP and linking outside or within companies is not without its problems, risks, and opportunities as the following material makes clear.

MULTIPLANT COMMUNICATIONS

Larger companies generally support production through a number of production plants. The automobile industry, whose finished products contain upwards of forty-five hundred parts, are a case in point. Final assembly and finishing are supported by separate production facilities for engines, interiors, metal stamping, and so forth.

[5] Both the manufacturer and its customers must be Class A companies for this to be feasible.

Consider a simpler example: a company with three finishing plants and two component plants.

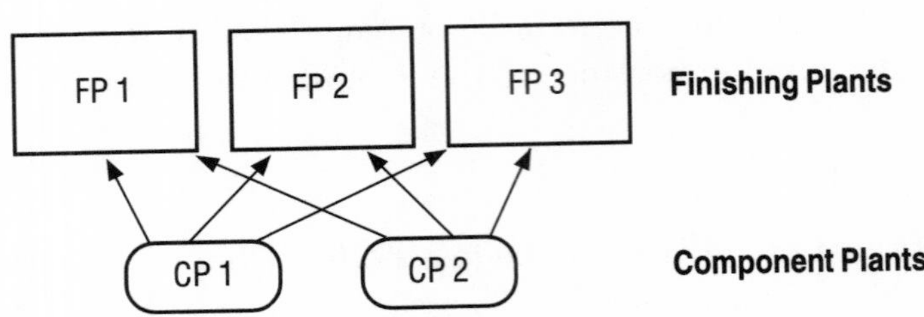

The component plants may be total captives of the finishing plants—serving their needs exclusively. They may, on the other hand, have some outside customers to whom they sell part of their output. In either case, good communications among plants is an important element in successful manufacturing. The finishing plants establish demand for the component plants, which, in turn, attempt to produce an adequate supply. When finishing and component plants fail to communicate and fail to work together, manufacturing productivity and output suffer.

Scheduling practitioners recognize one problem of multiplant communications that stands out above all others: Lower-level plants have trouble controlling their own schedules, and are often whipsawed by the changing demand situation at the upper-level plants they serve. Unlike the independent company, which has a "right of refusal" with respect to customer demand, the lower-level plant as part of the larger corporate machinery typically cannot just say no to demand from a finishing plant or corporate office. Nor does it have much latitude in shifting or splitting orders, or in outsourcing the work. Overloading of the master schedule at lower-level plants is the typical result.

Management Issues

When a finishing plant passes down an order to a component plant, its knowledge of the scheduling and manufacturing situation at the component plant is often imperfect. Lack of communications and general lack of insight into production problems at the lower-level plant provoke a number of management concerns, one going directly to the heart of how people should be managed.

Most management practitioners acknowledge that an individual should never be held responsible for the results of operations over which he or she lacks control. Yet, this hallowed principle is routinely violated by a great number of manufacturers whose corporate schedulers control the master schedules of their component plants. General managers of component plants are held accountable for stabilizing production, controlling costs, and meeting supply demands from finishing plants, even though the strings that control schedules on their own plant floors are often pulled by someone else, perhaps by a lower-level staffer located in corporate offices thousands of miles away. "We could be having equipment problems, materials shortages, whatever, and this would not be reflected in the schedule we're expected to follow," is a common complaint. "Just tell us what you want, and when, and let us figure out the best way to schedule the work."

Managers of lower-level plants, in the author's experience, would generally prefer a multiplant system in which they have greater autonomy in meeting the requirements of higher-level plants—their *best customers.* That greater autonomy would give them control of their own master schedules, the ability to negotiate movement and splitting of orders, the right to refuse an order—in effect, the same autonomy enjoyed by independent companies that must adhere to the sharp discipline of the marketplace if they hope to survive and prosper.

Corporate staffers are often uncomfortable with this notion of component plant independence and their own loss of control. In cases observed by the author, that discomfort stems from a lack of confidence in the scheduling capabilities of lower-level managers. But experience indicates that good things usually happen when decision-making responsibility is pushed down to the lowest possible level. This has been one of the important lessons of the quality movement and the practice of continuous improvement in manufacturing. Here, control is maintained through accountability for performance and through incentives that naturally align the interest of the component plant manager with those of the corporation.

Tell Us What You Want, and We'll Do the Rest, Sir

One of the lessons from America's military experience in Vietnam was that command and control cannot be exercised effectively from afar. To the great frustration of U.S. field commanders, much of the war was run directly from the Pentagon. Analysts and staffers working and living in the comfortable environments of Washington, D.C., plotted campaigns for corps commanders and selected targets for bomber pilots stationed half a world away. Lacking a feel for local resources and circumstances, many of their directives were either ineffective or outright damaging to U.S. war efforts. While overall strategy was logically the domain of the White House, high-echelon military officers, and their staffs, the business of effecting that strategy should have been left to the discretion of local commanders who had a better grasp of conditions on the ground.

This important lesson from Vietnam was not lost on the captains and majors who, twenty years later, filled the general officer ranks of the U.S. armed forces during the Gulf War. As the new generation of U.S. commanders, they defined the broader strategy of driving Iraqi forces from Kuwait, but they gave local commanders broad discretion in implementing the strategy. And it worked exceedingly well.

Multiplant scheduling problems affect just about everyone, so solving them is in everyone's interest. Marketing and sales have a problem when orders are not shipped on time because the component plant fails to deliver due to overscheduling. Manufacturing managers and production supervisors at component plants often see some of their own problems as the result of scheduling failures higher up ("they just dump all of their scheduling and forecasting mistakes onto us"). Finance wonders where all the profits are going—reschedules, expediting, overtime, etc., cost money. In the long run, accountability is lost and overall performance suffers.

Available-to-Promise

A promise made is a debt unpaid! This little sentence ought to be posted prominently wherever demand managers and master schedulers work as it articulates one of the primary responsibilities of their function.

When a customer requests a product, the demand manager, customer service, or the master scheduler must respond to that request and commit to a date for shipment. This constitutes an explicit promise to the customer, and the available-to-promise (ATP) data of the master schedule is an important tool in making good on promises. In this sense it is an important element of demand management.

The available-to-promise line of the master schedule matrix indicates the portion of scheduled production that is "unconsumed" after all other commitments are covered and tells demand management, customer service, order entry, and master scheduling what is available to fill new requests. While the mechanics of ATP were briefly touched on in chapters 3 and 8, a little refresher is appropriate here. Consider the following example of a ballpoint pen manufacturer (Figure 14.16 on page 434). This producer, which begins the current period with an on-hand balance of 150 cases of pens, has a demand forecast of 100 cases per week over an eight-week horizon. Given that forecast, the master scheduler has placed three firm planned orders of 300 cases each in periods 2, 5, and 8.

Given the on-hand balance, total demand, and existing master scheduled orders, the master scheduling system can calculate the projected available balance for all future periods as shown in the figure.

In determining the quantities available-to-promise, the master scheduler's first concern is in protecting commitments already made—namely, actual demand.

The master scheduler's second concern is in protecting those com-

Figure 14.16 Available-to-Promise, Pen Manufacturer

	Past Due	1	2	3	4	5	6	7	8
Product Forecast		100	100	100	100	100	100	100	100
Option Forecast									
Actual Demand									
Total Demand		100	100	100	100	100	100	100	100
Projected Available Balance	150	50	250	150	50	250	150	50	150
Available-to-Promise									
Master Schedule			300			300			300

mitments in the most efficient manner; here, this means protecting demand with the closest MPS lot that immediately precedes it. Thus, if an actual order for a period-8 delivery is received and accepted, it would be more efficient to protect that commitment from supply expected to be generated as near to period 8 as possible. In the situation given here, for example, an experienced demand manager or master scheduler would never protect a period-8 demand with on-hand inventory when a source of supply is anticipated in period 8.

To deal with these two concerns, the master scheduling system calculates ATP from right to left—here moving from period 8 to period 1. An available-to-promise is calculated for all MPS supply orders, the ones scheduled in periods 8, 5, and 2, plus period 1 since there are pens on hand and they are available to sell or promise. Since ATP is the master scheduled quantity less actual demand, the ATP for period 8 is 300 − 0 = 300 (see Figure 14.17). There are at least 300 cases of pens available-to-promise to any customer that needs delivery in that period. However, this calculation is only for the period and does not take into account previous periods' ATP.

Figure 14.17 Available-to-Promise, Pen Manufacturer

	Past Due	1	2	3	4	5	6	7	8
Product Forecast		100	100	100	100	100	100	100	100
Option Forecast									
Actual Demand		90	100	60	50	60			
Total Demand		100	100	100	100	100	100	100	100
Projected Available Balance	150	50	250	150	50	250	150	50	150
Available-to-Promise		60 60	90 150	150	150	240 390	390	390	300 690
Master Schedule			300			300			300

Moving to period 5, the next period in which supply is scheduled, the calculation is again straightforward: 300 firm planned orders −60 actual demand = 240 ATP. Period 2 is more complicated. A demand of 100 cases of pens is committed in this period, but there is also demand in periods 3 and 4. With no other supply anticipated to intervene until period 5, all of that demand must be protected by the firm planned order of 300 cases scheduled for completion in period 2. Thus, the ATP for period 2 is 300 − (100 + 60 + 50) or 300 − 210 = 90.

Period 1 has 90 units of actual demand, and that is covered by the 150 cases on hand. The ATP for period 1 then is 150 − 90 = 60. Once the ATP by period is known, the master scheduling system can calculate the cumulative ATP (bottom row of numbers) as shown in Figure 14.17. This cumulative result is calculated by adding each period's ATP in the horizon to the prior period's cumulative ATP value. Available-to-promise logic is generally used to support the make-to-order environment more than the make-to-stock environment since customer-committed backlog reaches farther into the future in MTO companies than it does in MTS companies.

ATP with Two Demand Streams

So far, we have looked at the classical available-to-promise calculation and use. This classical approach is valid and works for most companies as they commit product for customer delivery. However, as in most manufacturing situations, there are incidents or events that cause the standard logic to falter. This is the case when a company has multiple demand streams, such as one source of demand being from production and another source of demand being from service or spare parts. Refer to Figure 14.18 during the discussion of this expanded ATP logic.

Figure 14.18 Available-to-Promise with Two Demand Streams

	Past Due	1	2	3	4	5	6	7	8
Service Forecast		2	2	2	2	2	2	2	2
Production Forecast				4	4	4	4	4	4
Actual Demand		5	4						
Total Demand		7	6	6	6	6	6	6	6
Projected Available Balance	20	13	7	1	20	14	8	2	21
Available-to-Promise (Normal)		11			25				25
Available-to-Promise (Spares)		7			9				9
Available-to-Promise (Production)		5			17				17
Master Schedule					25				25

The available-to-promise (ATP Normal) has been calculated as described earlier for periods 1, 4, and 8 (noncumulative values). As you can see, the ATP in period 1 is 11. Let's say that production calls the person committing inventory and requests that all the items available be sent to the floor no later than period 3. To satisfy this request and to ensure that other promises are protected, the person doing the committing reviews the ATP in period 1, sees that 11 are available-to-promise, and makes the commitment.

The next event that occurs is a phone call from the service parts organization requesting the 2 items that they forecasted in period 1. What does the person tell them? "Oops! Don't have them!" What about period 2? "Oops! Don't have them!" What about period 3? "Oops! Don't have them!" Okay, three strikes and you're out. The next time the service parts organization orders, it will likely order hundreds, thousands, millions, etc. Here is a case when the forecaster tried to do what's right; tell the master scheduler what he or she really thinks will be needed. However, it didn't work, so it's back to the old way of doing business.

If a company has the two-demand-stream situation, the logic of calculating ATP must be changed in order to protect the forecast. In the case being addressed in Figure 14.18, three ATP lines are shown: one for the aggregate ATP (normal), one for production, and one for service. To calculate the ATP for production, the MPS system will use the standard logic (on hand, which equals 20 plus the master schedule of 0 minus the actual demand of 9) resulting in 11 available-to-promise. Taking this result, the MPS system will now subtract the service forecast of 6 (2 each in periods 1, 2, and 3) leaving an ATP for production equal to 5 (20 + 0 − 9 − 6).

Turning our attention to the service ATP, the system takes the on hand of 20 plus the master schedule of 0 minus the actual demand of 9 minus the remaining production forecast of 4, leaving 7 available-to-promise for service (20 + 0 − 9 − 4). As the demand manager and master scheduler review the numbers, it is easy to see that the summation of 5 ATP for production and 7 ATP for service does *not* equal the 11 total available-to-promise (there are only 11 available-to-promise). There is 1 unit up for grabs. First come, first served! When the first request for the extra unit is satisfied, the ATP will be recalculated and adjusted to take this into account (refer to Figure 14.19).

Let's go back to production's phone call—production needs as many as there are available by period 3. The answer to that question is now 5, not 11. So, let's take the order and commit delivery in period 3. When this is done, the production forecast in period 3 is consumed and reduced to 0.

The new ATP for production is the on hand of 20 plus the master schedule of 0 minus the actual demand of 14 (5 + 4 + 5) minus the service parts forecast of 6 equaling 0 (20 − 14 − 6). The new ATP for service is the on hand of 20 plus the master schedule of 0 minus the actual demand of 14 minus the production forecast of 0 equaling 6 (20 − 14 − 0). As you can see, the extra unit has been committed, the

Figure 14.19 Available-to-Promise with Two Demand Streams After Accepting Production Order for 5 Units in Period 3

	Past Due	1	2	3	4	5	6	7	8
Service Forecast		2	2	2	2	2	2	2	2
Production Forecast					4	4	4	4	4
Actual Demand		5	4	5					
Total Demand		7	6	7	6	6	6	6	6
Projected Available Balance	20	13	7	0	19	13	7	1	20
Available-to-Promise (Normal)		6			25				25
Available-to-Promise (Spares)		6			9				9
Available-to-Promise (Production)		0			17				17
Master Schedule					25				25

production commitments have been acknowledged and protected, and the service forecast has likewise been protected.

This example has shown the need to modify the standard ATP logic in order to deal with the more complex, multiple-demand-stream environment. It should not be expected by the reader that standard master scheduling software will support this logic; most of the time the master scheduling software system must be modified in order to protect forecast as well as actual demand. What's important is that the logic of the MPS system be such that it supports the people making the decisions. In order to do this, the information presented must be accurate, timely, and factual.

Should Companies Have Demand Managers?

Hopefully, this chapter has made clear the importance of good demand management to the manufacturing organization. Without it, the production function is at the mercy of external forces over which it has little or no control.

Over the years, manufacturing companies have seen the wisdom of having an individual (or more than one individual) dedicated to the job of managing its manufacturing schedules: that is the master scheduler. Class A companies give the same attention to demand management. In many ways, these are parallel functions. A demand manager position (usually reporting to a marketing function) is not universally present in manufacturing companies, but it is highly recommended. Figure 14.20 on the following page presents a process diagram of how a demand manager interacts with the demand side of the business and how that same function is linked with the master scheduling function, which benefits directly from more accurate and robust information about demand.

Sales and marketing play important roles in demand management, and their active involvement leads to improved master schedul-

Figure 14.20 The Role of the Demand Manager

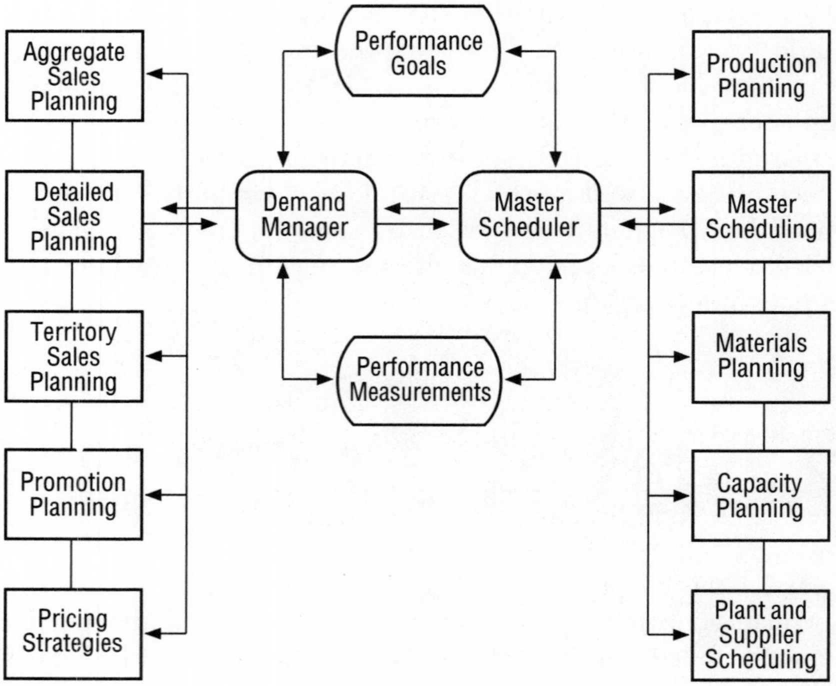

Aggregate Sales Planning
Detailed Sales Planning
Territory Sales Planning
Promotion Planning
Pricing Strategies
Performance Goals
Demand Manager
Master Scheduler
Performance Measurements
Production Planning
Master Scheduling
Materials Planning
Capacity Planning
Plant and Supplier Scheduling

ing. These organizations are responsible for developing and maintaining sales plans, both aggregate and disaggregated. Sales and marketing must take responsibility for predicting the product family mix, customer order promising, and identification of abnormal demands.

Additionally, as members of management, sales and marketing must have a role in formulating company policies with respect to lead-time definitions, rescheduling time zones, safety stocks, overplanning, inventory levels, and customer service levels. As participants in the sales and operations planning process, sales and marketing groups have inputs to development of the production plan. Finally, they should consult with the master scheduler on supply-and-demand problems.

To assist in the function of managing demand, the demand management position is responsible for the following activities:

- Facilitate sales and operations planning through the gathering and presentation of appropriate data
- Provide assistance in sales planning and generation of the product family mix forecast
- Communicate detailed demand to the master scheduler and provide input with respect to rescheduling and reprioritizing decisions

Overall, the demand manager is to sales and marketing what the master scheduler is to manufacturing.

The last fourteen chapters have discussed the "whys," "whats," and "hows" of master scheduling. Much of this discussion has been in the format of what the master scheduler must do in order to become an effective scheduler. The last three chapters have addressed the master scheduling integration issues. The final chapter in this book is designed to provide the reader with a proven methodology to implement master scheduling and achieve Class A operating results.

15

Effective Implementation

If you always do what you've always done, you will always get what you've always gotten.

Over the past quarter century, thousands of companies have taken steps in the direction of greater effectiveness, quality, and customer service. Perhaps at no time since the early years of the Industrial Revolution has the impulse toward self-improvement been so widespread. In North America, the motive for that impulse is not difficult to understand: intense competition of foreign competitors—primarily Asian corporations—threatens both the profitability and survival of companies in a wide range of industries.

An important set of tools used by companies in their drive toward improvement in manufacturing has been MRP II, Manufacturing Resource Planning. Thousands of companies in a variety of industries have turned to this important tool as a means of improving customer service, shortening delivery times, increasing productivity, and reducing inventory costs. Of these companies, hundreds have reached the coveted status of Class A.

In 1976 the late Oliver Wight, who did so much to develop and popularize this powerful tool, asked his colleague Darryl Landvater to investigate and document the critical activities and steps taken by companies that had been successful in adopting MRP II and making it their operating philosophy. The purpose of this investigation was to provide implementation guidelines that others might follow—what the Oliver Wight Companies would call "The Proven Path." Not surprisingly, Landvater found that successful implementation of MRP II does not happen by chance, luck, or sorcery, but through thoughtful planning and teamwork. Today, the most current version of the Proven Path is fully documented in a book by Thomas F. Wallace, which spells out in detail the steps and activities needed to successfully implement MRP II.[1]

Master scheduling is a subsystem of MRP II, and the process of implementing master scheduling has many parallels to the implementation of MRP II. In that sense, it is worth taking just a few moments to review some of those processes.

The Proven Path to Successful MRP II Implementation

Research by the Oliver Wight Companies has found that those who pursue a course of implementing MRP II spend between twelve and twenty-four months in a series of activities that involve the participation of managers and technical workers from the top to the lower levels of the organization. Typically, these activities are similar to those represented in Figure 15.1.

The process begins with an *Audit/Assessment* of the company's current situation—its operations, problems, strategies, and opportunities—and its readiness to adopt MRP II. This exercise not only

[1] Thomas F. Wallace, *MRP II: Making It Happen*, 2nd edition (Essex Junction, VT: Oliver Wight Publications, Inc., 1990).

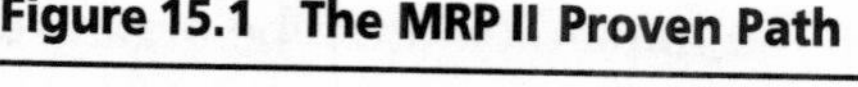

Figure 15.1 The MRP II Proven Path

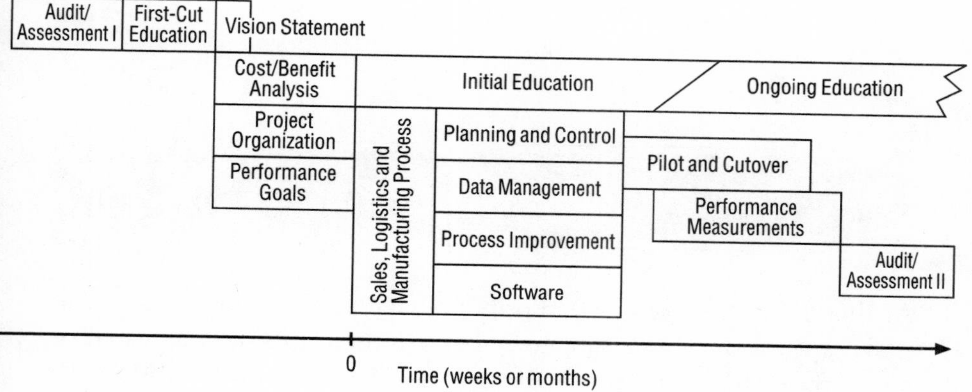

forces managers to take a hard look at existing practices but forms a valuable baseline against which future programs will eventually be measured.

The next step is *First-Cut Education*, in which both senior managers and operating managers learn about MRP II, what it is and how it operates, and what it takes to implement it properly. This group must also determine whether MRP II makes sense for their particular business.

Assuming that this step has a positive outcome, the same set of managers must then develop a *Vision Statement*, a written document that describes the company and its competitive capabilities once MRP II is adopted and integrated company-wide. Concurrent with the beginning of the vision statement process are three critically important activities, which are performed in parallel: *Cost/Benefit Analysis, Project Organization*, and the development of *Performance Goals*.

Cost/benefit analysis results, again, in a formal written document that articulates all the anticipated costs and benefits that will accrue to the company if MRP II is adopted and implemented. Project organization and performance goals are developed in parallel to the cost/benefit analysis. In effect, they consider two issues: If MRP II is adopted, how will the implementation be organized within the company? And what levels of performance would be expected in areas touched by the MRP II implementation?

The Decision Point

At this point, the company and its management are in a position to make an informed decision to either continue business as usual or adopt the MRP II approach. If their decision is to go with MRP II, they will face a one- to two-year period of implementation activities—some of which are sequential while others are approached in parallel.

The first set of these activities is the preparation for converting the company's entire process over to the MRP II approach. This crossover may include the implementation of a new software system or a reimplementation of the system already installed. Prior to the full cutover, a series of pilots are performed to minimize the risk of failure and to increase the overall chances of achieving Class A results. These preparation activities include:

- Creation of a detailed implementation plan
- Education and training of key and affected employees
- Development of sales, logistic, and manufacturing processes as they will take place under MRP II
- Writing of company policies and procedures with respect to planning and control
- Development of an accurate database for inventory records, bills-of-material, routings, and manufacturing centers
- Search for process improvement that will make the entire system work more efficiently

- Acquisition, installation, and maintenance of the software needed to support MRP II and related activities
- Identification of performance measurements and methods of tracking them

Going on the Air

Once these activities have been successfully completed (recognizing that education is *never* completed), the company is ready to "go on the air," to use an Oliver Wight term. There the policies, procedures, disciplines, work flows, and computer systems developed earlier around conference room tables are tested in a series of measured experiments. Generally, this is done with a small set of parts or products, so that if the new system fails or contains bugs, operations within the company will not be jeopardized. Pilot operations also provide opportunities for personnel to learn to operate the system in measured steps.

Satisfactory pilot operations then lead to a full cutover to the MRP II system—again, in measured steps. At this point data on performance is collected for comparison to the performance goals set earlier.

The Path to MPS Implementation

Presentation of the essential activities on the MRP II Proven Path to successful implementation is appropriate here because so many MPS issues must be addressed by the aspiring MRP II company if it hopes to progress successfully along the Path. In fact, an MRP II system will not work if master scheduling is not in place and operating correctly; quantities driven down through the MRP system will be too many, too few, too early, or too late if there is no master schedule to connect production supply and market demand in an intelligent fashion.

Master scheduling issues appear frequently on the Proven Path. For example, in First-Cut Education, the importance of master scheduling to the smooth functioning of MRP II is made clear, often for the first time, to many participants. Again, in the development of performance goals, goals for master scheduling are as relevant and important as are those for inventory record accuracy, quality, and management of the MRP II system. Perhaps, the importance of master scheduling to MRP II is nowhere greater than in the planning and control area, where the defined methodology to balance supply and demand at the item mix level is implemented. If a company cannot effectively manage this balance, it will have trouble planning and controlling materials and capacities, and creation of a valid master schedule will be difficult.

The implementation of a solid master scheduling system has a path of its own; one that shares many of the characteristics of its MRP II cousin, but also with several unique characteristics. These are schematically described in Figure 15.2.

Implementation of master scheduling takes place within three broad stages:

- *Stage 1* is an evaluation and learning period in which key personnel in the company gain a general knowledge about master scheduling, determine where they currently stand with respect to the practice of master scheduling, analyze the costs and benefits of a state-of-the-art MPS system to their company, and decide what will have to happen to get it up and running. At the end of this stage, a decision is made to either move forward with MPS, reject it, or go on hold.

- *Stage 2* is devoted to the organizational issues required to launch and sustain a successful master scheduling process. This is a period of

Figure 15.2 The Path to Effectively Implementing Master Scheduling

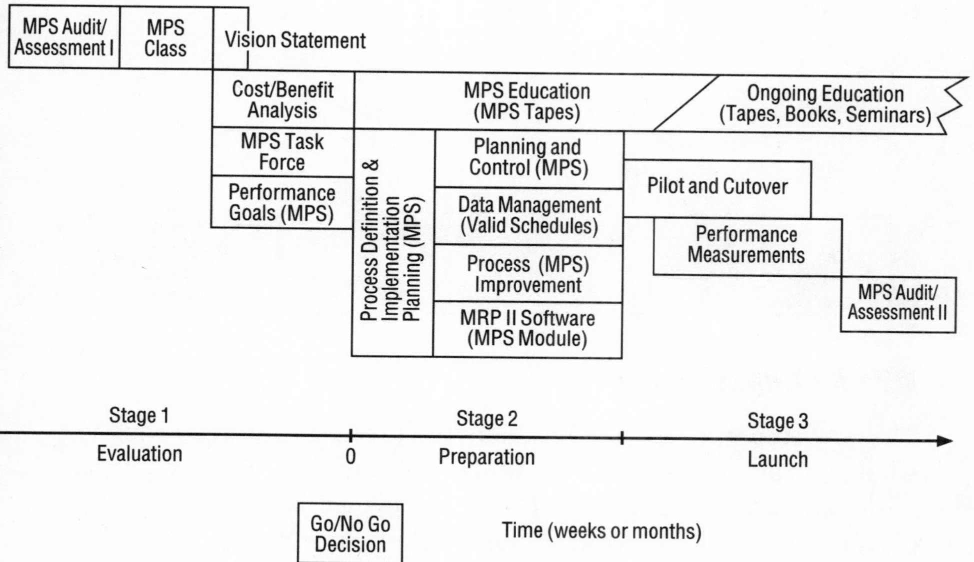

preparation. Like the previous stage, this one features more education. It features regular meetings by the personnel charged with implementing and operating the system and, to a lesser extent, others in the company who will be touched by master scheduling in important ways. Master scheduling task force personnel must iron out the details with respect to demand management, sales and operations planning, and the other features of MPS discussed in earlier chapters. When this stage is over, it should be clear what is to be done, who will do it, and when.

• *Stage 3* is launch. This is when the company takes its first deliberate steps toward putting the processes in place and bringing the master scheduling computer software system on line. Because newly developed processes may not be fully understood and the chance that software bugs may be present in a newly adopted system, introduction is conducted in small steps. Eventually, as the processes become familiar and all bugs are found and corrected, and as personnel learn more about using their new set of tools, the master scheduling system goes company-wide.

Stage 1: Evaluation

MPS Audit/Assessment I

The first step in preparing for a lengthy journey is to determine just where you are and the distance to the destination. This is the purpose of the audit/assessment step. The company needs to understand the current state of its scheduling capabilities—systems, practices, and the skill of its operating personnel. It needs to rate itself against some standard of good practice and, if the evaluation stage results in the decision to go forward with the master scheduling implementation, a baseline of performance against which future progress can be measured must be established.

The Oliver Wight ABCD Checklist for Operational Excellence is a list of comprehensive questions that companies can use to rate themselves on critical points in strategic planning, people and teams, new-product development, total quality management, planning and control, and continuous improvement. This is the rating system that defines Class A, B, C, and D companies.[2] While this publication was written to address the larger concerns of modern manufacturing, it does contain a section on master scheduling and its related disciplines. The questions in that section can be used to determine where the company stands in terms of Class A master scheduling perfor-

[2] *The Oliver Wight ABCD Checklist for Operational Excellence*, 4th edition (Essex Junction, VT: Oliver Wight Publications, Inc., 1993).

mance. (See the Appendix, page 485.) The findings of this initial audit/assessment need to be systematically recorded for comparison against future progress.

Master Scheduling Education

In the MRP II Proven Path, top and middle managers receive about two to six hours of classroom-based education on master scheduling as part of the overall MRP II first-cut education program. In a program to implement master scheduling specifically, several people from manufacturing and other disciplines need more education and should take a concentrated course on master scheduling.[3]

Vision Statement

Once the core group has received a solid base of education about master scheduling, the group needs to think deeply about what their company would be like if Class A master scheduling was thoroughly integrated into its operations. From this thinking the group should develop a master scheduling vision that describes the ways in which the company would be different or improved.

Since the typical company already has some form of vision and mission statement, or is following a defined strategy that features an all-embracing focus for its business future, the vision statement that emerges from the master scheduling implementation process should logically address the central tenets of that primary mission or strategy. For example, if customer service is the strategic thrust of the company, the master scheduling vision may describe how customer service will be improved by the adoption of Class A master scheduling: e.g., on-time delivery and reduced lead times.

3 Ideally, this group would include master schedulers, MRP planners, demand managers, production control supervisors, materials managers, manufacturing supervisors, managers from engineering and finance, and systems analysts.

Master Scheduling Vision Statement (A Sample)

The manufacturing environment will be more even-paced and less chaotic. Month-end backlogs and reliance on expediters will be essentially eliminated as production dates and customer requirement dates become the same. The manufacturing floor will run at a level pace, leaving adequate time for line changeovers, repairs, and preventive maintenance.

The company will be in a more competitive position as its ability to deliver on promises to customers with respect to product specifications, quantities, and delivery dates reaches and exceeds 95 percent. This will result in improved financial results for shareholders and employees. Sales personnel will spend more time selling and earning commissions, and less time apologizing for late deliveries; manufacturing personnel will gain the satisfaction of producing orders on-time, with a margin of time available for quality and process improvements; and production bonuses will increase. Management will benefit from improved financial results and will have more time to dedicate to planning, training, and process improvements.

While it may seem premature to develop a vision at this early stage, the core MPS group will have learned enough in the education process to understand how MPS can improve operations, and optimism about that prospect is the normal result. The steps that follow are filled with hard work and constant reminders about the difficulties of fully integrating master scheduling into company operations. The unencumbered optimism of a vision is needed during those difficult stages to remind everyone of the future value of their efforts.

Cost/Benefit Analysis

Implementing a master scheduling system takes plenty of time, spent by dozen of individuals in meetings, in doing analysis, in writing reports. And that time costs the company. There are other direct costs as well—costs for computer hardware and software, education and training, achieving inventory record accuracy, getting the bills-of-material and routings accurate, systems analysis, policy and procedure creation, programming, and consulting. The costs in time, effort, and direct outlays for implementing any new operating system are usually obvious to everyone. Less obvious are the benefits.

To win support for implementing a new or enhancing the current master scheduling process and system, leaders need to do a careful and unbiased analysis of the costs and benefits, which must be communicated to all parties concerned. There is no easier way to lose support for a good program than to fail to justify its costs to those who pay the bills and to those who do the work. The master scheduling task force also needs cost/benefit data to make informed decisions with respect to completing the implementation process.

Every company has its own set of implementation costs and benefits, and these need to be determined on an individual basis. In all cases, however, the categories of cost are *people, data, and computers*. Benefits invariably accrue to *sales* and various aspects of *material* and *labor costs*. Figure 15.3 on page 454 itemizes the general categories of costs and benefits that implementers should include in their analysis.

The best source of costs and benefits are the individuals closest to the facts. For example, the sales vice president is in the best position to know what incremental increase in sales would result if the company could deliver as promised and on time. The manufacturing vice president is in the best position to identify expected productivity improvements that would result from valid, level-loaded schedules. The stockroom manager knows better than anyone the costs associated with bringing inventory record accuracy up to the Class A level needed to support a master scheduling system. The engineering department has the means to estimate the cost of improving the bills-of-material it develops. Using these individuals as sources for cost/

Figure 15.3 MPS Cost/Benefit Analysis

	Costs		
People	Steering committee	$xxxx	
	Spin-off task forces	xxxx	
	Project team	xxxxxx	
	Education	xxxxxxx	
	Consulting	xxxxxx	
Data-related	Inventory record accuracy	xxxxxx	
	Routing accuracy	xxxx	
	BOM accuracy/structure	xxxxx	
	Work center accuracy	xx	
Computer	Hardware & software	xxxxxxxxx	
	Systems & Programming	xxxxxxxx	
Total Cost			$xxxxxxxxx
	Benefits		
Revenues	Increased sales	$xxxxxxxx	
People	Increased productivity	xxxxxxx	
	Overtime reduction	xxxxx	
	Expediting cost reduction	xxxxxx	
Materials	Purchase cost reduction	xxxxxxx	
	Inventory reduction	xxxxxxx	
	Fewer premium charges		
Plant Utilization	Better utilization rate	xxxxxxxxxxx	
	Level-loading, less scrap	xxxxxxx	
Freight	More complete loads	xxxxx	
	Fewer rush shipments	xxx	
Total Benefits			$xxxxxxxxxx

(Adapted from Thomas F. Wallace, *MRP II: Making It Happen*, Oliver Wight Publications, Inc.)

benefit figures is also a way of enlisting their *commitment* to those costs and benefits when the program is fully implemented.

The MPS Task Force

The business of master scheduling, as the preceding chapters have made clear, involves a broad set of disciplines, routines, policies, and procedures: demand management, sales and operations planning, bills-of-material, routings, inventory records, computers and software, rough cut capacity planning, and linkages to other parts of the business, to name only the most obvious. As part of the implementation process, each of these tasks must be planned, staffed, and given a set of operational guidelines. The computer requirements for MPS, for example, do not just appear. Someone must determine what capabilities are needed and how they would be used on the manufacturing floor.

Good implementation results when these assorted master scheduling disciplines, routines, procedures, and policies are thought out by a number of task force members. The task force itself is staffed in part by members of the core group that is dedicated to the implementation process, and in part by personnel likely to be involved in an up-and-running system.

The task force is not immediately charged with developing the operational details required of a fully implemented MPS system. That would be premature, since the decision to go ahead with implementation has not yet been made. Instead, their job is to determine *what would have to be done and what resources would be required.* In terms of computers and software, as just one example, the task force would determine the dimensions of the requirements, who should be assigned to the job, and how much time would be required to get the computer software system into operation. Once questions like these have been answered by the task force members, their findings should be compiled for the implementation group that is charged with the "go/no-go" decision. (These findings are useful later if a "go" decision is made; at that point they become the basis for operation planning in the next stage.)

MPS Performance Goals

The last step of the evaluation stage is for the core implementation group to consider what performance goals would be appropriate if a full MPS implementation were made. Manufacturing resource planning has many performance goals, and some key ones pertain directly to master scheduling: customer service as well as master schedule and manufacturing schedule performance should be 95 percent or better (Class A). Production planning performance should be ± 2 percent to the plan. Lead time reduction, inventory reduction, and throughput velocity improvement are other appropriate goals. Another important goal is to stabilize the master schedule; to do so requires discipline and a process to minimize unnecessary schedule changes.

At this point management has the information it needs to make an informed decision with respect to fully implementing a master scheduling system. The core group of decision makers has been educated on the subject; it has made an assessment of the company with respect to Class A master scheduling performance; and it has formed a vision of how the company would look and how its ability to satisfy customers would be altered if it reached the heights of Class A performance. A number of concrete facts would be laid alongside that mental image of the new company: cost/benefit analysis, task force reports and a list of the resources and efforts necessary for full implementation, and a set of performance goals that would be the new company's yardstick for future performance. With this information, management decides to either back off or go forward.

The decision to go forward must be articulated in a way that identifies the following:

- This is where the company now stands with respect to its master scheduling practices (from the audit/assessment).
- This is where the company can go (from the vision statement).
- Moving forward with full MPS implementation will result in measurable benefits supported by defined costs (from cost/benefit analysis).

- To move from the company's current practices to a Class A master scheduling environment will require this amount of time and this amount of staffing resources (from the project organization recommendations).
- This is a checklist of important tasks that will need to be performed to reach full implementation—planning bills, inventory accuracy, computer system, etc. (from the MPS task force investigation).
- These are the kinds of performance achievements that would be expected under Class A master scheduling (from the performance goal and measurement definitions).

Stage 2: Preparation

The decision to go for full MPS implementation commits the company and many of its personnel to a long but rewarding process. Organizationally, the effort will be managed by a spin-off task force manager or leader and many of the operational responsibilities will be doled out to other specialized task forces. The first part of that effort is to prepare the company and its personnel for the job of starting and operating a first-rate MPS system. This might be called the preparation stage, and its objective is to work out all the operational details that the MPS task force in Stage 1 merely enumerated. There the task was to determine what would have to be done and what it would require. Here a full-blown operational blueprint is developed. This blueprint will take the form of a detailed *master scheduling implementation plan*.

As in the previous stage, education is an important part of that process. Members of the master scheduling task force of Stage 1 continue the education process begun earlier. The Oliver Wight Companies videotape library contains material on master scheduling that is valuable for this purpose. At this stage, accelerated learning is critical, and so members of the task force along with other members of the implementation team should convene every day or every other day for a series of highly structured two-hour meetings that reviews current progress, provides education on specific master scheduling techniques, and features discussion on how those techniques can be implemented within the company. Discussion should account for fully half of the business meeting. A sample of a typical meeting agenda is shown on the facing page.

The end result of each such meeting should be a list of "action items" that individuals must do in order to implement the activities discussed. Responsibility for these items should be allocated to specific individuals with specific dates for resolution. Progress on these action items should be discussed at future meetings, and their successful resolution should be rolled into the detailed MPS implementation plan.

Education at this stage must also be extended to personnel outside of the core implementation group, to those individuals who will be dealing either directly or indirectly with the fully implemented MPS system. These sessions are more spread out and include discussion of the overall vision.

While this MPS education process continues, other implementation activities take place in parallel. Before considering these, however, we should look at how the core implementation group helps to define the company's new environment.

Process Definition and Implementation Planning

Meetings of task force members provide more than learning for a core group of employees—they also serve as a format in which the important details of the company's emerging MPS system begins to emerge. These details, as mentioned previously, must be captured in an implementation plan that defines the entire MPS process for the company. Here the MPS system is transformed from the "what the system *should* look like" of Stage 1, to "what the system *will* look like" in the near future. Central to this definition of the MPS process are manufacturing strategy and processes, material flows, customer order

Business Meeting Agenda
(A Sample)

Topic: Master Scheduling Time Zones
Meeting Agenda (2 hours):

- Review action items list (15 minutes)
- Fact transfer of master scheduling methodology (30 minutes)
- Discuss how to implement methodology (60 minutes)
- Create action items and assign responsibility (15 minutes)

Key Items to Be Addressed and Resolved:

- People versus computer behavior and control
- Approval policy needed for people behavior

Applications:

- A policy is required defining who needs to approve changes by zone
- The approvals required will be based on timing and cost impact

Action Items for MPS Implementation Plan:

- Write rescheduling approval policy
- Circulate for comments
- Secure approval
- Release and implement policy

promising, establishing the schedule, policies, procedures, and the assignment of responsibility.

A good example of an important policy that must be determined at this point is the question of manufacturing strategy, or "Where will we meet the customer?" Will the company follow a strategy of make-to-order, with minimal inventory, and moderate levels of customer delivery service or will it pursue a strategy of make-to-stock, characterized by aggressive levels of customer service and ample inventories to service demand? Or will yet another strategy be followed? This is a management issue of the first magnitude, and it requires input from all core functions of the company. As we will see shortly, the impact of which manufacturing strategy is accepted will spill over to the procedures area of MPS implementation. For example, a make-to-stock strategy generally uses a different bill-of-materials scheme than does make-to-order than does engineer-to-order (e.g., engineering bills versus planning bills versus configuration bills versus activity bills).

Figure 15.4 considers primary areas within which policies and procedures must be developed and modified as well as the individuals typically assigned responsibility for them.

In essence, Figure 15.4 is a "rough cut" of what needs to be done. The level of detail in the development of policies and procedures, and in the assigning of responsibility, is specified. The MPS implementation plan requirements are at a much higher level of detail. For example, the procedure for making changes to the master schedule—to pick just one area—requires full development of an approval process, naming those individuals authorized to approve changes, and describing the situations (by time period) in which they have that authority. For multiproduct companies, this may require an elaborate set of approvals. Figure 15.5 on page 462 suggests how such a set of approvals might appear. (This is a more specific set of guidelines than the discussion of time zones in chapter 4.)

Policy: Changes to the master schedule can be requested by sales, marketing, finance, production, purchasing, quality, engineering, design, and distribution. All changes to the master schedule within an item's cumulative lead time will be approved by the person(s) identified.

Figure 15.4 Areas That Require Policies and Procedures

Policy and Procedure	Functions Involved
Manufacturing Strategy	President VP Sales & Marketing VP Manufacturing Controller
Service Levels	VP Sales & Marketing VP Manufacturing
Backlog/Order Promising	VP Sales & Marketing VP Manufacturing
Sales & Operations Planning	President VP Sales & Marketing VP Manufacturing VP Engineering VP Finance VP Quality
Production Plan	VP Sales & Marketing VP Manufacturing VP Industrial Relations Materials Manager Manufacturing Manager Controller
MPS (Overplanning, time fences, past dues)	VP Manufacturing Materials Manager Master Scheduler Controller
Lead Times	VP Sales & Marketing VP Manufacturing Materials Manager
Lot Sizes	VP Manufacturing Materials Manager Purchasing Manager
Processes to Be Improved	VP Manufacturing Manufacturing Managers Manufacturing Personnel
Inventory Levels	VP Sales and Marketing VP Manufacturing Materials Manager Controller

Figure 15.5 Approval Policy for Master Schedule Changes

	0–2 weeks	2–4 weeks	4–6 weeks	6–8 weeks
Product A	President General Manager	VP Sales VP Manufacturing	Sales Director Mfg. Director	Sales Director Mfg. Manager
Product B	General Manager	General Manager	VP Sales Mfg. Manager	VP Sales Mfg. Manager
Product C	VP Sales Mfg. Director	Sales Director Mfg. Director	Sales Manager Mfg. Director	Master Scheduler

Process: Changing the Master Schedule.
Initiator: Sends the master scheduler a written request for the change.
Master Scheduler: Has a maximum of two working days to respond to the initiator with one of three answers:

1. Yes, the change can be made and is being implemented.

2. The change can be accommodated but the following schedules are affected. What is your recommendation?

3. The change cannot be made for the following reason(s). Best alternative is ______________________________.

The definition of the MPS process and its implementation planning having been completed, it is then time to move directly into the functional areas where the detailed blueprint for its daily operation must be drawn up and executed. These are planning and control, data management, process improvement, and software—all of which have been treated to some degree in previous chapters of this book.

Planning and Control

The previous activity of process definition created an inclusive set of policies and procedures for all the master scheduling activities. Here the policies are flushed out in operational detail. An analogy to these two different levels of detail is found in the federal government, where Congress passes legislation that establishes a set of rules. Once signed by the president, those rules are handed over to the appropriate agency, whose technical staff creates a much more detailed set of operational statutes, complete with dates, amounts, and so forth, all developed to reflect the "intent of Congress." Here the "intent" of the higher-level policy makers is specified through written policies and implemented through written procedures.

Planning and control must concentrate on demand management, rough cut capacity planning, sales and operations planning, and master scheduling. A demand management procedure needs to be drawn up in detail, focusing on the role of the demand manager (if there is one), sales and marketing personnel, and rules governing order promising. Here, many of the master scheduling procedures described earlier have to be spelled out clearly: Exactly where will planning time fences be placed? What safety stock policy will be followed? Who has authority to make a change, and when?

Sales and operations planning has to be institutionalized in company operations, with a regular schedule of meetings, a slate of attendees, and general agenda. The Oliver Wight Companies recommends that regular S&OP meetings begin several months prior to full implementation of MRP II, and the same advice applies here. This gives everyone a chance to develop the skills needed to hand the master scheduler a credible set of aggregate demand requirements and supply constraints.

Policies and procedures for MPS must be developed and disseminated to all who come into contact with the system. The following is just one example of a formal set of policies and procedures. The sample policies deal with a valid master schedule while the sample procedure deals with treatment of action messages.

Master Scheduling Policy
(A Sample)

Manufacturing, supported by a valid master schedule, will maintain a performance level of 95 percent or better on meeting schedules' completion dates.

Rough cut capacity planning will be used to check that critical resource capacity is available to satisfy the written master schedule before the master schedule is released for action.

The master schedule will be firmed up through the planning time fence using a combination of scheduled receipts, released orders, and firm planned orders.

Master Schedule Procedure
Action Message Review
(A Sample)

Purpose: To establish a process that the master scheduler will follow to evaluate and initiate action as necessary after each MPS run.

Scope: This procedure affects sales, marketing, manufacturing, material control, production control, purchasing, inventory control, and engineering.

Definition: An action or exception message is an action that the MPS software system recommends that the master scheduler execute in order to correct an imbalance in supply and demand. Action messages may also be generated because of a past-due condition.

Reference:
1. Master scheduler's position description
2. Master schedule policy covering valid schedules
3. Reschedule time zone policy

Exhibits:
1. Master schedule time-phased screen/report
2. Master schedule action screen/report

Procedure:

Responsibility	*Action*
Master Scheduler	1. Receives the latest MPS computer output (exhibit 1).
	2. Reviews action messages (exhibit 2).
	3. Determines which action messages require action.
	4. Asks the 5 questions to determine material, capacity, and cost impact (reference 1).
	5. Determines appropriate changes to MPS within production plan guidelines (reference 2).
	6. Forwards change recommendations to approval authorities (reference 3).
Sales VP	7. Determines if changes will satisfy customer requirements.
	8. Forwards change recommendations to Manufacturing VP
Manufacturing VP	9. Analyzes recommended changes to master schedule and supporting documentation.
	10. Approves or disapproves changes.
Master Scheduler	11. Forwards change decisions to master scheduler. 12. Receives decision; takes appropriate action.
	13. Informs appropriate parties when action is completed and what expected results will be.

The sample procedure provided is not intended to be complete, but merely to provide an example.

Data Management

Like MRP II, master scheduling will not be successful in the absence of data, or in the absence of *accurate* data. For MRP II purposes, data can be divided into two categories: "forgiving" data, and "unforgiving" data. Forgiving data need not be extremely accurate; some margin for error is possible. From the master scheduling perspective, this includes lead times, safety stocks, order quantities, maximum capacities, and—of course—the demand forecast.

The "unforgiving" data can trip up MRP II and MPS without exception. This includes on-hand inventory balances, scheduled receipts, allocations (components reserved for scheduled receipts), bills-of-material, and actual customer orders. Certainly, not all of these are the responsibility of the master scheduler, but without accuracy near 100 percent, the integrity of the company's game plan will come apart at the seams.

This is the point in the MPS implementation process where a number of activities must be spelled out in detail:

- The items to be master scheduled are identified. If the inventory records for these items are not up to Class A standard, the process of making them so must be begun. The same applies to bills-of-material for the MPS items.

- The structuring of Class A planning bills is now begun.

- The key resources needed for the engineering and manufacturing job ahead are identified so that resource profiles and rough cut capacity planning can be effectively done.

- The company's approach to forecasting demand must be examined and steps outlined to improve its accuracy.

- The work center database, including capacities of the key resources, must be defined and accuracy achieved.

Process Improvement

Back in the process definition box, where policy was developed, areas for process improvement were identified. At this point, detailed plans for making improvements in those areas are developed and assigned to individuals. For example, the use of kanbans may have been articulated in the process definition box as a company policy and procedure to be followed. Here, the means to execute that policy must be spelled out in detail. A policy dictating a kanban system would naturally require far-reaching process improvement on the manufacturing floor. Changeover times, a matter of concern for the master scheduler, would need to be dramatically reduced. This would not happen by itself, but would succeed only in the face of a detailed plan for which some individual was made accountable.

Software

An effective master scheduling process requires software for four purposes: the master scheduling process itself, sales and operations planning, rough cut capacity planning, and customer order management. Some software packages can handle all four purposes. Some can do one, but not the others. In certain operations, S&OP may be handled on a personal computer using off-the-shelf spreadsheet software, while the master schedule and rough cut capacity planning jobs are handled on the company's mainframe computer.

The first step in implementing the software requirements of an MPS system is to actually determine those requirements. This may require the hiring of outside expertise. Once the right software is acquired, a period of training for operational personnel is required, as is a "shake out" period in which the software is de-bugged and any needed customization takes place.

Who's in Control of the Software?

Many off-the-shelf software packages for both MRP II and master scheduling offer a maintenance service that provides for the "care and feeding" of the current system with periodic enhancements as the software. This practice is commonplace in most sectors of the software industry and is provided at an additional charge.

While it is reassuring to know that the expensive software being purchased today is insured against obsolescence by such an offer, and that the company will be able to convert to the newer versions as they become available, a caution should be observed. *Reliance on an outside vendor for so important a tool as manufacturing software is unwise*. Thomas Wallace makes this warning for MRP II software, and the same caution applies to MPS software. The dangers of this reliance are threefold:

1. In the fast-paced world of software development, your vendor may not be in business tomorrow, leaving your company with a dead-end product.

2. Software firms may be committed to upgrading their products with new versions, but the timing of these improvements will be on their schedule, not yours. Thus, allowing an outside firm to control one of the most important management tools of your business is to allow an outsider to control the pace of your own continuous improvement. Management should never accede to that lose of control.

3. You cannot fully appreciate the capabilities, the limits, and the quirks of a software system if you do not fully understand how to alter and maintain it.

Stage 3: Launch

A friend of mine tells the story of how he spent the better part of one Sunday connecting a new shower in his basement. First, he turned off the main water line, then cut into nearby hot and cold feeder lines and, using a dozen or so copper elbows and "Ts" and straight pipe, joined his new shower to the house water system. By 6 P.M. he soldered in the last connection using his very last piece of flux, then proudly surveyed all the bright new copper and the professional-looking fittings and angles that he—a mere amateur—had put together. After inspecting all the soldering work he called his wife from upstairs to observe the ceremony of turning on the new shower. He proudly turned on the main water value and watched in disgust as fine streams of water sprayed out of at least half of his pipe fittings. The last of soldering flux being used up, and the hardware store being closed for the day, my friend shut off the main water valve. He would call a plumber in the morning. The family would have no running water until then.

My friend had done everything according to plan; he even double-checked all of his fittings. Everything had seemed ready to go. But the only way to be sure was to actually turn on the water!

A company with fixed payroll expenses, customer promises to keep, and millions invested in plant and equipment cannot take a chance that its new operating system will spring a leak. Prudence dictates that any new system brought onto line in a complex business cannot be adopted "cold turkey" but must go through a trial period in which the system is de-bugged and proven out. To fully cutover to the new system without this trial period would endanger the entire operation. This applies equally to a new telephone system, information system, MRP II system, or master scheduling system. Stage 3 concerns itself with the final step in the implementation process—the switching on of the new policies and procedures of master scheduling.

Pilot and Cutover

There are three methods for switching on the new MRP II system, and these apply as well to master scheduling. They are:

1. *The cold turkey approach*. Here, the old system is switched off and the new system is switched on. This is like jumping out of an airplane with a parachute packed by several unknown people—not recommended.

2. *The parallel approach*. Here, the new system is operated "off line," and its results and recommendations are compared to those of the existing system, which continues in operation. When the new system can consistently provide essentially the same information as the old system, the old system is shut down and the new one continues "on line."

Problems with respect to the parallel approach are (1) that it is difficult to maintain and staff two different systems, and (2) the two systems should not be expected to be comparable in results—the old system is being phased out because its output is inadequate. If we're upgrading our system, why would we ever want to duplicate the output of the system we plan to retire?

3. *The pilot approach*. This is the application of the cold turkey approach to a small part of the system, ideally in a highly controlled environment. Here, the new MPS system can be tried out and monitored closely without too much risk of damage to the overall operations of the business. If a company manufactured all sorts of writing instruments—ballpoint pens, felt tip pens, mechanical lead pencils, traditional wooden pencils, etc.—it might use its new MPS system strictly in the wooden pencil operations, where a failure would not throw a monkey wrench into the other parts of the business. The pilot approach accomplishes a number of things:

- Policies and procedures developed earlier can be tried in a "real time" live exercise (or "live pilot")
- Personnel can learn to operate the system using company data

- The hardware/software system can be tested and stressed in a live exercise (or "live pilot")
- Problems can be identified and resolved
- The organization has an opportunity to gain confidence in the new system

Of these approaches, the pilot approach is recommended for reasons that should be obvious. Once a pilot testing of the new MPS system has been made in one area of the total manufacturing operation, the next step is to a cutover, in which the new system totally displaces the old.

A crossover can be accomplished in one stroke or by degrees. In a small operation, or one in which the results of a small pilot have been an overwhelming success, a total cutover may be feasible, but caution normally dictates a crossover *by degrees*—i.e., the extension of the pilot to other operations.[4]

Performance Measurements

As early as the evaluation stage, the implementation team for master scheduling develops a set of ideas about the kinds of goals that the new system should hold out for itself. But goals by themselves are not helpful unless they can be rendered into specific measurements. No one can tell how they are doing—and certainly cannot measure progress—unless performance can be measured.

In developing a set of performance measures, a number of questions must be addressed:

- What is being measured?
- What is the purpose of the measurement?
- Who does the measurement affect?
- Who is responsible for the measurement?

[4] Of course, the cutover plans of the MRP II system implementation really dictate when the master schedule portion of the system will be activated.

- What are the targets?
- How is performance calculated?
- How is the measurement data secured?

Once measurements have been established, operators must know what constitutes good and bad performance. This is accomplished by setting "performance targets." For example, master schedule performance may be defined as:

- Minimum acceptable performance = 92 percent
- Satisfactory performance = 95 percent
- Outstanding performance = 98 percent or better

But percent of what? Here tolerances must be determined. For example, we could say that if manufacturing produced items within certain tolerances, that would be a success. Thus, production of the master scheduled item ±2 days of scheduled completion date and ±4 percent of the scheduled quantities would be considered a hit. Production completions falling outside those specified ranges would be considered a miss. If performance to the master schedule is 95 percent or better, the company would be operating at a satisfactory or Class A level of performance. A recommended master schedule performance measurement definition is shown in Figure 15.6.

A good system of performance measurement carries with it requirements that trigger action any time that performance falls below specified levels. For example, any time the MPS performance slips below minimum, the person with responsibility for master schedule performance would submit a written explanation of what went wrong and the corrective action taken; that explanation would be due on a manager's desk within, say forty-eight hours.

Figure 15.6 Master Schedule Performance Measurements

Master Schedule

Purpose (Purpose of the Measurement)

To ensure that the company is maintaining a Class A level of performance to the defined master schedule.

Scope (Whom Does It Affect?)

The master schedule performance measurement affects manufacturing, capacity planning, material planning, engineering, inventory control, and master scheduling.

Definition (If Necessary)

The anticipated build plan by specific configuration, quantity, and due dates.

Responsibility

Name: (Plant Input—Materials & Capacity	Name: (Plant Output—Product
Title: (Master Scheduler)	Title: (Manufacturing Manager)
Signature: ______	Signature: ______

Target Performance

Minimum	*Satisfactory*	*Outstanding*
92%	95%	98%

Calculation

$$\frac{\text{Actual Completions (within tolerance)} \times 100}{\text{Planned Completions (for week or month)}} = \%$$

Source

Numerator: Manufacturing Completed Orders by Date (Weekly)
Denominator: Master Schedule (Released Plus Firm Planned Orders)

Tolerance

Date: (?) Days (e.g., 2 days early, no days late)
Quantity: (?) Pieces (e.g., 25 pieces more, 10 pieces less than scheduled quantity).

This level of detail with respect to performance needs to be developed before the pilot and cutover take place—back in the process definition phase. But it should be revisited here even as the pilot and cutover are taking place. Performance to the master schedule notifies management just how well the pilot is performing and where corrective interventions may be required. As cutover to the new MPS system is completed, performance measures become matters of ongoing importance to the operation and continuous improvement of the master scheduling process.

Audit/Assessment II

Once the MPS system is up an running, the company and its management team need to determine what is working and what is not. Compare the performance results to the expected performance goals that were established in Audit/Assessment I. Ask the questions: "Are we better off?" and "Where do we go from here?" Typical answers are "Onto the path of continuous improvement" and "Let's do more!" Several senior managers believe that this is the most important part in the entire process. For sure, it is a very important ingredient for success.

MPS Education Never Quits

The final element of the launch stage is ongoing education. Just as the modern manufacturer understands that the road to success is paved with continuous process improvements, individuals close to the field of master scheduling understand that knowledge and operational competence are among those important processes. The Class A master scheduling company maintains an ongoing education program that continues to develop more master scheduling organizational expertise. This is done through outside classes, business meeting education, books, seminars, certification programs, and general master scheduling meetings. And it never stops.

Deterrents to Successful Implementation of MPS

Not every attempt to implement master scheduling will be successful. Fewer still will succeed in reaching Class A status. The typical problems that get in the way are:

• *Ignorance*. People do not know how to do things right because they do not understand the principles and the details of master scheduling. The antidote? *Educate key people*.

• *Not all of the important people are on-board*. It is easy to believe that master scheduling is only a production issue. But if sales and marketing people do not understand the issues involved, and if they do not participate in the demand management and sales and operations planning process, problems with demand, plant overloading, overpromising, and so forth will persist. Solution: *Get marketing and sales involved*.

• *Do sales and operations planning early*. This is where senior management gets into the game. MPS is absolutely reliant upon early sales and operations planning, and the early involvement of senior management in this process sends a clear signal to the rest of the company that it means business. Recommendation: *You cannot start soon enough*.

• *Improve rough cut capacity planning*. This is a quick sanity check on the production plan and prevents an unrealistic master schedule from getting onto the floor. *Start RCCP on Monday*.

• *Unload the overloaded master schedule*. If a friend asked your advice about learning how to swim, you would not suggest that he start by putting on a ten-pound weight belt and jumping into a fast-moving river. This would only lead to disaster. Your friend would do better to start with the least encumbrance and in a calm pool. Nevertheless, many MPS implementation programs start with schedules that are so overloaded and overpromised that they quickly sink and never come up for air. Word to the wise: *Give your new system every opportunity for success by starting with a clean slate.*

- *Clarify organizational responsibilities.* Many failures can be traced to the simple problem of key people not understanding their responsibilities. *Be sure that everyone understands the goal and his or her part in reaching it.*

- *Document policies and procedures.* Each policy, procedure, and instruction should be written; the implementation of these should be followed and enforced. Needed: *A list of required policies and procedures, assignments, expected completion dates, and execution.*

- *Measure performance.* Performance measurement is one key to success. The measurements themselves must be clearly defined so that everyone understands them. Advice: *Use MPS performance measurements as an improvement tool, not as a report card.*

The Master Scheduler's Job

It is only fitting that this chapter on effective implementation (indeed, the entire book) should end with some discussion of the individual at the center of the process: the master scheduler. In the end, he or she must implement the policies and procedures that the president, various vice presidents, controller, sales director, and others had a hand in crafting. It is the master scheduler who must be the artful manager, responsible on a daily basis for the fine balance between what the customers have ordered and what the company can deliver. If the responsibilities of this position were distilled into a job description, they would appear as follows:

Master Scheduler Position Description

Objective

Create and maintain a valid master schedule for material and capacities by effectively balancing supply and demand for product. A valid master schedule is one in which priority due dates equal need dates, and planned capacity equal required capacity.

Responsibilities

Develop a working knowledge of the company's products and processes to ensure optimal master schedule stability, order creation, rescheduling, load-leveling, etc.

Analyze the demand and supply balance at the product family and master schedule levels, determining out-of-balance conditions, identifying alternatives, and recommending action for approval.

Work with sales, marketing, and manufacturing to better understand competitive lead times for master scheduled items. Seek ways to reduce internal lead times as well as lead times to the customer.

Challenge current manufacturing strategies for all product lines to be sure that the best and most customer-oriented strategy is being used. Look for ways to move the company to make-to-order manufacturing.

Conduct rough cut capacity planning prior to publishing a master schedule in which significant changes have occurred.

Summarize daily and weekly master schedules for released and firm planned orders and compare these to the production plan to ensure that the master schedule is within S&OP policy.

Work within policy guidelines pertaining to master scheduling. Observe and follow all stated master scheduling procedures.

(*continued*)

Respond in a timely manner to significant action messages generated by the master scheduling software.

Act as internal educator and consultant on master scheduling issues, providing education and training throughout the company to improve company-wide understanding of MPS functions.

Identify, negotiate, and resolve conflicts with respect to material and capacity availability and order-promising integrity.

Maintain a master schedule following the company policy of permitting no MPS item to have a released or firm planned order date less than the current date (no past dues at the master schedule level).

Create a monthly financial summary of overplanned stock to ensure that it is within budget. Integrate master scheduling with other company functions.

Maintain planned lead times, lot sizes, safety stocks, delivery times, and order file data for all MPS items.

Review each master scheduled item at least weekly.

Create a master schedule that satisfies customer demand with optimum inventory levels and resource utilization as dictated by company policy.

Ensure that a common master schedule is used to drive all company priorities in manufacturing, marketing, sales, engineering, and finance.

Create a master schedule that can be used for detailed material and capacity planning as well as financial planning. Master scheduling operational data should be the basis of a single set of books.

Establish a working line of communication with all company functions.

Assist demand management in setting priorities when demand outstrips the company's supply of products or the resources necessary to build the requested product.

Maintain planning bill structures, however *not* be responsible for mix factors, which belong to marketing and sales.

Inform management when demand cannot be met and recommend alternatives on how the requested demand could be satisfied.

Create a master schedule that levels work being released to manufacturing and at the same time satisfies customer demand.

It takes an extraordinary person to meet the requirements of this job description, but these challenging duties merely underscore the importance of effective master scheduling to the business success of a manufacturing organization.

Epilogue

Order from Chaos

This book began with a parable about a manufacturing company whose production floor on the last business day of the month was out of control. Partially completed products waited on skids for delayed parts. Frustration and frayed nerves were commonplace among managers and employees. Customers were calling to complain about late shipments. Expediters ran around the plant with hot sheets. Instead of channeling its energies into problem resolution and customer-oriented production, the company's energy was being dissipated through finger-pointing and internal conflict.

"Is this the manufacturer from hell?" some might ask. Hardly. It is symptomatic of too many manufacturing situations today. Hopefully, this nightmarish parable will become a quaint fairy tale, an artifact of the industrial past as master scheduling practices become more professional and as those practices diffuse through the industry. In the case of our fictional company, we can hypothesize that change will eventually come because the company could not survival and prosper if it did not.

The Place:	The plant manager's office of a typical North American manufacturing company
The Time:	9:00 A.M.
The Date:	The first day of a new month
Those Present:	The plant manager, the sales director, and the manufacturing vice president

"I've had enough of this! And I hope that you've had enough of it, too. I am sick and tired of what we just went through the other day. What we have on our hands is a situation in which we are incurring higher costs, production disruptions, and frayed nerves." The others in the room nodded their agreement. "Worse, there seems to be no winners for all this trouble on our manufacturing floor. Everyone is the loser!"

"It's starting to hurt us in the field, too," the sales director interjected. "I got a call from one of our better Florida accounts warning me that one more late shipment and they'll find a new supplier."

"I agree," said the manufacturing vice president. "Something has to change. Our people on the line are tired of every week and every month being a race against the clock, of stealing parts from one order to take care of another. It's getting hard to hold on to our best people and harder to motivate the rest."

"Then change is the thing, isn't it?" said the plant manager. "Something has to change. Something fundamental. I want to see a change in the way our plant looks and acts. No more queues, no more hot lists, no more stockouts or late deliveries."

Few companies undertake fundamental change as a natural step in the road to progress. It usually takes some extraordinary event, such as the threat of failure, to motivate the leadership to undertake a serious campaign of change. Ford Motor Company and Xerox Corporation underwent a course of internally generated change in the period 1978–1983 because both sensed that they were in a serious downward trajectory in their respective industries. General Motors, IBM, and DEC are facing the same stage of awareness and change as we approach the mid-1990s. Our fictional company appears to have reached that point where something like a "deathbed conversion" is taking place with respect to its manufacturing.

If we were to "fast-forward" in time, we might see this company entering that period of self-assessment that leads to the effective implementation of a master scheduling program, as laid out in this book. Over a period of six to twelve months, the company would develop the internal competencies and sets of guidelines that make a full changeover to master scheduling possible. From that point, through a period of adjustment and improvement, the company would experience steady incremental increases in manufacturing efficiency as measured by the absence of production-floor disruptions, delayed shipments, hot lists, "past dues," the dreaded end-of-the-month crunch, and the other ills that motivated the plant manager to recommend a course of change.

The ills of the past would eventually be replaced by the rewards that accrue to a Class A manufacturing company, the foremost of these being measurable improvements in profits and employee morale and high levels of customer satisfaction.

Appendix

Class A Master Scheduling Performance Checklist*

The Oliver Wight ABCD Checklist for Operational Excellence was published to help companies become the best they can be. Being the best of the best is what Class A is all about. Many companies take pride in achieving Class A and the results that come along with this lofty accomplishment. Most companies that attain Class A status tend not to be completely satisfied. In fact, they tend to become more aggressive in pushing forward, knowing they can do even better. "Yes, we are good and probably better than our competition, but we all know that we can be even better with just a little more effort," is a comment commonly heard from Class A companies.

While the *ABCD Checklist* was written to address the larger concern of modern manufacturing, it does contain a section on master scheduling and its related disciplines. The questions in that section can be pulled together and answered to determine where a company stands in terms of Class A master scheduling performance. The questions addressing master scheduling are shown in this appendix.

* Reprinted from *The Oliver Wight ABCD Checklist for Operational Excellence*, 4th ed. (Essex Junction, VT: Oliver Wight Publications, Inc., 1993), pp. 87–90.

Master Scheduling

The master scheduling process is perpetually managed in order to ensure a balance of stability and responsiveness. The master production schedule is reconciled with the production plan resulting from the sales and operations planning process.

a) Accountability for maintaining the master schedule is clear. The importance of master scheduling is reflected in the organization and reporting relationship of the master scheduling function.

b) The master scheduler understands the product, manufacturing process, manufacturing planning and control system, and the needs of the marketplace.

c) The master scheduler participates in and provides important detail information to the sales and operations planning process.

d) The master scheduler responds to feedback that identifies master schedule impacting material and/or capacity availability problems by initiating the problem-resolution process.

e) Planning bills-of-material (if used) are maintained jointly by the master scheduler and sales and marketing.

f) A written master schedule policy is followed to monitor stability and responsiveness; goals are established and measured.

g) The master schedule is "firmed up" over a sufficient horizon to enable stability of operations. Guidelines for this firmed horizon include:

   1. cumulative material lead time
   2. lead time to planned capacity
   3. lead time to cover customer order backlog (order book)

h) Master schedule changes within the "firm zone" (closest time fence) are managed; they are authorized by the appropriate people, measured, and reviewed for cause.

i) Policy governs the use of safety stock and/or option overplanning used to increase responsiveness and compensate for inconsistent supply and/or demand variations.

j) The master schedule is summarized appropriately and reconciled with the agreed to production rate (production plan) from the sales and operations planning process.

k) All levels of master scheduled items are identified and master scheduled.

l) The master schedule is in weekly, daily, or smaller periods, may be rate-based, and replanned at least weekly.

m) The structure of the bills-of-material supports the master scheduling/forecasting process.

n) Forecast consumption processes are used to prevent planning nervousness.

o) The alternative approaches used with planning bills-of-material to develop production forecasts for master scheduled items are well understood and an appropriate process is used.

p) Rough cut capacity planning, or its equivalent, is used to evaluate the impact of significant master schedule changes on critical resources. Demonstrated capacity is measured and compared to required capacity.

q) A finishing/final assembly mechanism or kanban approach is coordinated with the master schedule to schedule customer orders to completion or replenish finished goods.

r) Where applicable, mixed-model master scheduling is being used.

s) A weekly master schedule communications meeting exists and is attended by all using functions.

t) The linearity of output is measured; the graphic illustration of results should reflect daily performance to a planned linear output; reasons for deviations are highlighted with appropriate analysis.

Glossary

Any body of knowledge, be it Accounting, Engineering, Law, or Medicine, acquires a vocabulary of its own. Manufacturing resource planning, Just-in-Time, and master scheduling are no exceptions. Jargon and acronyms not withstanding, the need to use specific terminology remains. Hence, this glossary is provided to help you with terms that may not be totally familiar.*

ABCD Classification A method of categorizing items based on dollar volume or other criteria. The "A" items are those with the greatest dollar impact, and hence receive the most attention in terms of control. "B" items have less dollar impact and receive less control effort, and the "C" items have the least impact of all. *See:* Pareto's Law

Abnormal Demand Demands that are not part of the forecast. Typically abnormal demands are large, one-time orders.

Action Message An output of a master scheduling system that identifies the need for and the type of action to be taken to correct a current potential problem. Examples of action messages are "Release Order," "Reschedule-out," "Cancel," etc. *Syn:* exception message

Actual Demand Customer orders (and often allocations of items/ingredients/raw materials to production or distribution). It nets against, or "consumes," forecast, depending on rules chosen over a time horizon. For example, actual demand totally replaces forecast inside the "sold out" zone and partially replaces the forecast between the "sold out" and "no order" zone (known as the "partially sold out" zone).

* Many of these definitions are taken directly from the *Dictionary of the American Production and Inventory Control Society* (APICS), 7th edition, Dr. James F. Cox III, CFPIM; Dr. John H. Blackstone, CFPIM; and Michael S. Spencer, CFPIM; editors.

Actual Volume Actual output expressed as a volume of capacity. It is used in the calculation of variances when compared to demonstrated capacity (practical capacity) or budgeted capacity.

Aggregate Forecast An estimate of sales, often time phased, for a grouping of products or product families produced by a manufacturing facility or firm. Stated in terms of units or dollars or both, the aggregate forecast is used for sales and aggregate planning purposes.

Aggregate Planning The process of comparing the sales forecast to the production capabilities to develop a business strategy. The sales forecast and production capabilities are compared and a business strategy that includes a production plan, budgets and financial statements, and supporting plans for purchasing, work force, engineering, etc., are developed. The production plan is the result of the aggregate planning process.

Anticipated Delay Report A report, normally issued by both manufacturing and purchasing to the material planning function, regarding jobs or purchase orders that will not be completed on time, the reasons why, and when they will be completed. This is an essential ingredient of a closed-loop MRP and MPS system.

APICS Acronym for the American Production and Inventory Control Society.

Assemble-to-Order A make-to-order product for which key components (bulk, semifinished, intermediate, sub-assembly, fabricated, purchased, packaging, etc.) used in the assembly or finishing process are planned and stocked in anticipation of a customer order. Receipt of an order initiates assembly of the finished product. This is quite useful where a large number of finished products can be assembled from common components. *Syn:* finish-to-order

Assembly Attachment A choice or feature offered to customers for customizing the end product. In many companies, this term means that the choice, although not mandatory, must be selected before the final assembly schedule. In other companies, however, the choice need not be made at that time.

Automatic Rescheduling Rescheduling done by the computer to automatically change due dates on scheduled receipts when it detects that the due dates and need dates are out of phase. *Ant:* manual rescheduling

Available Inventory The on-hand balance minus allocations, reservations, backorders, and (usually) quantities held for quality problems. Often called "beginning available balance." *Syn:* net inventory

Available-to-Promise (ATP) The uncommitted portion of a company's inventory and planned production, maintained in the master schedule to support customer order promising. The ATP quantity is the uncommited inventory balance in the first period and is normally calculated for each period in which an MPS receipt is scheduled. In the first period, ATP equals on-hand inventory less customer orders that are due and overdue. In any period containing MPS scheduled receipts, ATP equals the MPS less customer orders in this period and all subsequent periods before the next MPS scheduled receipt. A negative ATP generally reduces prior period(s) ATP.

Backlog All of the customer orders received but not yet shipped. Sometimes referred to as "open orders" or the "order book." *Syn:* order backlog

Backorder An unfilled customer order or commitment. It is an immediate (or past-due) demand against an item whose inventory is insufficient to satisfy the demand.

Back Scheduling A technique for calculating operation start and due dates. The schedule is computed starting with the due date for the order and working backward to determine the required start date and/or due dates for each operation.

Baseline Measures A set of measurements (or metrics) that seek to establish the current or starting level of performance of a process, function, product, firm, etc. Baseline measures are usually established before the implementation of improvement activities and programs.

Bill-of-Material (BOM) A listing of all the subassemblies, intermediates, parts, raw materials, etc., that go into a parent item, showing the quantity of each component required. May also be called "formula," "recipe," "ingredients list" in certain industries.

Bill-of-Resources A listing of the required capacity and key resources needed to manufacture one unit of a selected item or family. The resource requirements are further defined by a lead time offset so as to predict the impact of the item/family scheduled on the load of the key resource by time period. Rough cut capacity planning uses these bills to calculate the approximate capacity requirements of the master schedule. Resource planning may use a form of this bill to calculate long-range resource requirements from the production plan. *Syn:* product load profile, bill of capacity, resource profile.

Blow-Through The computer technique for passing requirements through pseudo and phantom bill-of-material items. This process creates requirements for the component materials needed to manufacture higher-level items.

Bottleneck A facility, function, department, or resource whose capacity is equal to or less than the demand placed upon it. For example, a bottleneck machine or work center exists where jobs are processed at a slower rate than they are demanded.

Bottom-up Replanning In MRP, the process of using pegging data to solve material availability and/or problems. This process is accomplished by the planner (not the computer system), who evaluates the effects of possible solutions. Potential solutions include compressing lead time, cutting order quantity, substituting material, and changing the master schedule.

Bucketed System An MRP, DRP, or other time-phased system in which all time-phased data is accumulated into time periods, or "buckets." If the period of accumulation were one week, then the system would be said to have weekly buckets.

Bucketless System An MRP, DRP, or other time-phased system in which all time-phased data is processed, stored, and displayed using dated records rather than defined time periods, or "buckets."

Business Plan A statement of long-range strategy and revenue cost, and profit objectives usually accompanied by budgets, a projected balance sheet, and a cash flow (source and application of funds) statement. It is usually stated in terms of dollars and grouped by product family. The business plan and the sales and operations plan, although frequently stated in different terms, should be in agreement with each other.

Capacity The capability of a worker, machine, work center, plant, or organization to produce output per time period. Capacity required represents the capability needed to make a given product mix (assuming technology, product specification, etc.). As a planning function, both capacity available and capacity required can be measured in the short-term (capacity requirements planning), intermediate-term (rough cut capacity plan), and long-term (resource plan). Capacity control is the execution through the I/O control report of the short-term plan. Capacity can be classified as theoretical, rated, demonstrated, planned, protective, productive, dedicated, budgeted, standing, or maximum.

Capacity Available The capability of a system or resource to produce a quantity of output in a particular time period.

Capacity Management The function of establishing, measuring, monitoring, and adjusting limits or levels of capacity in order to execute all manufacturing schedules; i.e., the production plan, master schedule, material requirements plan, and dispatch list. Capacity management is executed at four levels: resource planning, rough cut capacity planning, capacity requirements planning, and input/output control.

Cellular Manufacturing A manufacturing process that produces families of parts within a single line or cell of machines operated by machinists who work only within the line or cell.

Common Parts Bill (of Material) A type of planning bill that groups common components for a product or family or products into one bill-of-material, structured to a pseudo parent item number.

Configuration The arrangements of components as specified to produce an assembly.

Constraint Any element or factor that prevents a system from achieving a higher level of performance with respect to its goal. Constraints can be physical, such as a machine center or lack of material, but they can also be managerial, such as a policy or procedure.

Consuming the Forecast The process of reducing the forecast by customer orders or other types of actual demands as they are received. The adjustments yield the value of the remaining forecast for each period.

Cumulative Lead Time The longest planned length of time involved to accomplish the activity in question. For any item planned through MRP, it is found by reviewing the lead time for each bill-of-material path below the item; whichever path adds up to the greatest number defines cumulative lead time. *Syn:* aggregate lead time; combined lead time; composite lead time; critical path lead time; stacked lead time

Cumulative Manufacturing Lead Time The cumulative planned lead time when all purchased items are assumed to be in stock. *Syn:* composite manufacturing lead time

Customer Connectivity The process of "linking" customers and suppliers. This is often made possible by tools such as Distribution Resource Planning and Supplier Scheduling. Frequently Electronic Data Interchange (EDI) is used as the communications medium.

Customer Order An order from a customer for a particular product or a number of products. It is often referred to as an "actual demand" to distinguish it from a forecasted demand.

Customer Sevice Ability of a company to address the needs, inquiries, and requests from customers. A measure of the delivery of a product to the customer at the time the customer specified.

Cycle Time In industrial engineering, the time between completion of two discrete units of production. For example, cycle time of motors assembled at a rate of 120 per hour would be 30 seconds. In materials management, it refers to the length of time from when material enters a production facility until it exits. *Syn:* throughput time

Database A data processing file management approach designed to establish the independence of computer programs from data files. Redundancy is minimized and data elements can be added to, or deleted from, the file designs without necessitating changes to existing computer programs.

Delivery Lead Time The time from the receipt of a customer order to the delivery of the product. *Syn:* delivery cycle

Demand A need for a particular product or component. The demand could come from any number of sources, e.g., customer order or forecast, or an interplant requirement or a request from a branch warehouse for a service part or for manufacturing another product. At the finished-goods level, "demand data" is usually different from "sales data" because demand does not necessarily result in sales; i.e., if there is no stock, there will be no sale.

Demand Management The function of recognizing and managing all of the demands for products to ensure that the master scheduler is aware of them. It encompasses the activities of forecasting, order entry, order promising, branch warehouse requirements, interplant orders, and service parts requirements.

Demand Pull The triggering of material movement to a work center only when that work center is out of work and/or ready to begin the next job. It in effect eliminates the queue from in front of a work center, but it can cause a queue at the end of a previous work center.

Demand Rate A statement of requirements in terms of quantity per unit of time (hour, day, week, month, etc.).

Demonstrated Capacity Proven capacity calculated from actual output performance data, usually expressed as the average number of items produced multiplied by the standard hours per item.

Dependent Demand Demand that is directly related to or derived from the bill-of-material structure for other items or end products. Such demands are therefore calculated and need not and should not be forecast. A given inventory item may have both dependent and independent demand at any given time. For example, a part may simultaneously be the component of an assembly and also sold as a service part.

Derived Demand Demand for industrial products that arises from the demand for final design products. For example, the demand for steel is derived from the demand for automobiles.

Design for Manufacturability (DFM) A rigorous, structured method of new-product design and introduction that intensively involves people from manufacturing, marketing, and suppliers in the development process. DFM, done effectively, can dramatically enhance a company's ability to bring new products to market quickly, at lower costs, and with fewer downstream engineering changes.

Dispatch List A listing of manufacturing orders in priority sequence. The dispatch list is usually communicated to the manufacturing floor via hard copy or CRT display, and contains detailed information on priority, location, quantity, and the capacity requirements of the manufacturing order by operation. Dispatch lists are normally generated daily and oriented by work center.

Distribution Center A warehouse with finished goods and/or service items. A company, for example, might have a manufacturing facility in Philadelphia and distribution centers in Atlanta, Dallas, Los Angeles, San Francisco, and Chicago. Distribution center is synonymous with the term "branch warehouse," although the former has become more commonly used recently. When there is a warehouse that serves a group of satellite warehouses, it is usually called a regional distribution center. *Syn:* field warehouse

Distribution Requirements Planning The function of determining the needs to replenish inventory at branch warehouses. A time-phased order-point approach is used where the planned orders at the branch warehouse level are "exploded" via MRP logic to become gross requirements on the supplying source. In the case of multilevel distribution networks, this explosion process can continue down through the various levels of regional warehouses, master warehouse, factory warehouse, etc., and become input to the master schedule. Demand on the supplying source(s) is recognized as dependent, and standard MRP logic applies.

Distribution Resource Planning (DRP) The extension of distribution requirements planning into the planning of the key resources contained in a distribution system: warehouse space, work force, money, trucks, freight cars, etc.

Documentation The process of collecting and organizing documents or the information recorded in documents. The term usually refers to the development of material specifying inputs, operations, and outputs of a computer system.

Due Date The date when purchased material or production material is due to be available for use. *Syn:* arrival date; expected receipt date

End Item A product sold as a completed item or repair part; any item subject to a customer order or sales forecast. *Syn:* end product; finished good; finished product

Engineering Change A revision to a blueprint or design released by engineering to modify or correct a part. The request for the change can be from a customer or from production, quality control, or another department.

Engineer-to-Order Product whose customer specifications require unique engineering design or significant customization. Each customer order results in a unique set of part numbers, bills-of-material, and routings.

Exception Message *Syn:* action message

Expedite To "rush" or "chase" production or purchase orders that are needed in less than the normal lead time; to take extraordinary action because of an increase in relative priority.

Expeditor A production control person whose primary duties are expediting.

Families A group of end items whose similarity of design and manufacture facilitates being planned in aggregate, whose sales performance is monitored together, and occasionally, whose cost is aggregated at this level.

Feedback The flow of information back into the control system so that actual performance can be compared with planned performance.

Final Assembly Schedule (FAS) A schedule of end items to finish the product for specific customer orders in a make-to-order or assemble-to-order environment. It is also referred to as the "finishing schedule" because it may involve operations other than just the final assembly; also, it may not involve "assembly," but simply final mixing, cutting, packaging, etc. The FAS is prepared after receipt of a customer order as constrained by the availability of material and capacity, and it schedules the operations required to complete the product from the level where it is stocked (or master scheduled) to the end level.

Finishing Lead Time The time that is necessary to finish manufacturing a product after receipt of a customer order. The time allowed for completing the product based on the final assembly schedule.

Finish-to-Order *Syn:* assemble-to-order

Firm Planned Order (FPO) A planned order that can be frozen in quantity and time. The computer is not allowed to automatically change it; this is the responsibility of the scheduler in charge of the item that is being planned. This technique can aid schedulers working with master scheduling systems to respond to material and capacity problems by firming up selected planned orders. Firm planned orders are the normal method of stating the master schedule.

Fixed Order Quantity A lot-sizing technique in MRP or inventory management that will always cause planned or actual orders to be generated for a predetermined fixed quantity, or multiples thereof, if net requirements for the period exceed the fixed order quantity.

Flexible Capacity The ability to operate manufacturing equipment at different production rates by varying staffing levels and operating hours or starting and stopping at will.

Flow Order An order filled not by moving material through production as an integral lot but by production made over time and checked by cumulative count until the flow-order quantity is complete.

Flow Shop A form of manufacturing organization in which machines and operators handle a standard, usually uninterrupted, material flow. The operators generally perform the same operations for each production run. A flow shop is often referred to as a mass production shop, or is said to have a continuous manufacturing layout. The plant layout (arrangement of machines, benches, assembly lines, etc.) is designed to facilitate a product "flow." Some process industries (chemicals, oil, paint, etc.) are extreme examples of flow shops. Each product, though variable in material specifications, uses the same flow pattern through the shop. Production is set at a given rate, and the products are generally manufactured in bulk.

Forecast An estimate of future demand. A forecast can be determined by mathematical means using historical data; it can be created subjectively by using estimates from informal sources; or it can represent a combination of both techniques. The sum of the unconsumed forecast and the booked customer orders should remain constant unless an intentional change to the forecast is desired. Abnormal demands should not consume the forecast.

Forecast Error The difference between actual demand and forecast demand, stated as an absolute value or as a percentage.

Forward Scheduling A scheduling technique where the scheduler proceeds from a known start date and computes the completion date for an order, usually proceeding from the first operation to the last. Dates generated by this technique are generally the earliest start dates (ESD) for operations. *Ant:* backward scheduling

Gross Requirements The total of independent and dependent demand for a part or an assembly prior to the netting of on-hand inventory and scheduled receipts.

Hedge In master scheduling, a quantity of stock used to protect against uncertainty in demand. The hedge is similar to safety stock, except that a hedge has the dimension of timing as well as amount. In purchasing, any purchase or sale transaction intended to eliminate the negative aspects of price fluctuations.

Horizontal Display A method of displaying output from a master scheduling or other time-phased systems in which requirements, scheduled receipts, projected balance, etc., are displayed across the document. Horizontal displays routinely summarize data into time periods or buckets.

Indented Bill-of-Material A form of multilevel bill-of-material. It exhibits the highest level parents closest to the left side margin and all the components going into these parents are shown indented to the right of the margin. All subsequent levels of components are indented further to the right. If a component is used in more than one parent within a given product structure, it will appear more than once, under every subassembly in which it is used.

Independent Demand Demand for an item that is unrelated to the demand for other items. Demand for finished goods, parts required for destructive testing, and service parts requirements are examples of independent demand.

Interplant Demand Items to be shipped to another plant or division within the corporation. Although it is not a customer order, it is usually handled by the master scheduling system in a similar manner. *Syn:* interplant transfer

Inventory Those stocks or items used to support production (raw materials and work-in-process items), supporting activities (maintenance, repair, and operating supplies), and customer service (finished goods and spare parts). Demand for inventory is dependent and independent. Inventory functions are anticipation, hedge, cycle (lot size), fluctuation (safety, buffer, or reserve), transportation (pipeline), and service parts.

Item Record The "Master" record for an item. Typically it contains identifying and descriptive data and control values (lead times, lot sizes, etc.), and many contain data on inventory status, requirements, planned orders, and costs. Item records are linked together by bill-of-material records (or product structure records), thus identifying the bill-of-material. *Syn:* item master record; part master record; part record

Job Order *Syn:* manufacturing order

Job Shop A functional organization whose departments or work centers are organized around particular types of equipment or operations, such as drilling, forging, spinning, mixing, compressing, blending, etc. Products move through departments by individual work orders. *See:* flow shop

Just-in-Time (JIT) A philosophy of manufacturing based on planned elimination of all waste and continuous improvement of productivity. It encompasses the successful execution of all manufacturing activities required to produce a final product, from design engineering to delivery and including all stages of conversion from raw material onward. The primary elements of zero inventories are to have only the required inventory when needed; to improve quality to zero defects; to reduce lead times by reducing setup times, queue lengths, and lot sizes; to incrementally revise the operations themselves; and to accomplish these things at minimum cost. In the broad sense it applies to all forms of manufacturing, job shop and process as well as repetitive. *Syn:* short-cycle manufacturing; stockless production; zero inventories

Kaizen The Japanese term for improvement; continuing improvement involving everyone—managers and workers. In manufacturing, kaizen relates to finding and eliminating waste in machinery, labor, or production methods. *Syn:* continuous process improvement

Kanban A method of Just-in-Time production that uses standard containers or lot sizes with a single card attached to each. It is a pull system in which work centers signal with a card that they wish to withdraw parts from feeding operations or suppliers. Kanban, in Japanese, loosely translated means "card," "billboard," or "sign." The term is often used synonymously for the specific scheduling system developed and used by the Toyota Corporation in Japan.

Latest Start Date The latest date at which an operation order can be started in order to meet the due date of the order.

Lead Time The span of time required to perform an activity. In a logistics context, the activity in question is normally the procurement of materials and/or products either from an outside supplier or from one's own manufacturing facility. The individual components of any given lead time can include some or all of the following: order preparation time, queue time, set up time, production time, move or transportation time, receiving and inspection time.

Lead-Time Offset A technique used in MRP where a planned order receipt in one time period will require the release of that order in an earlier time period based on the lead time for the item. *Syn:* offsetting

Level Every part or assembly in a product structure is assigned a level code signifying the relative level in which that part or assembly is used within the product structure. Normally the end items are assigned level 0 with the components/subassemblies going into it assigned to level 1 and so on. The

MRP explosion process starts from level 0 and proceeds downward one level at a time.

Level-Loading *Syn:* level schedule; load-leveling

Level Schedule A schedule that has distributions of material requirements and labor requirements that are as even as possible. In JIT, a level schedule ideally means scheduling a day's worth of demand on production each day.

Line A specific physical space for manufacture of a product that in a flow plant layout is represented by a straight line. This may be in actuality a series of pieces of equipment connected by piping or conveyor systems.

Line Balancing The balancing of the assignment of the elemental tasks of an assembly line to workstations to minimize the number of workstations and to minimize the total amount of idle time at all stations for a given output level. In balancing these tasks, the specified time requirement per unit of product for each task and its sequential relationship with the other tasks must be considered.

Line Loading The loading of a production line by multiplying the total pieces by the rate per piece for each item to come up with a finished schedule for the line.

Load The amount of planned work scheduled and actual work released for a facility, work center, or operation for a specific span of time. Usually expressed in terms of standard hours of work or, when items consume similar resources at the same rate, units of production.

Load-Leveling Spreading orders out in time or rescheduling operations so that the amount of work to be done in sequential time periods tends to be distributed evenly and is achievable.

Lot A quantity produced together and sharing the same production costs and resultant specifications.

Lot-for-Lot A lot-sizing technique that generates planned orders in quantities equal to the net requirements in each period. *Syn:* discrete order quantity

Lot Size The amount of a particular item that is ordered from the plant or a supplier. *Syn:* order quantity

Make-to-Order Product A product that is finished after receipt of a customer's order. The final product is usually a combination of standard items and items custom designed to meet the special needs of the customer. Frequently long lead time components are planned prior to the order arriving in order to reduce the delivery time to the customer. Where operations of other subassemblies are stocked prior to customer orders arriving, the term "assemble-to-order" is frequently used.

Make-to-Stock Product A product that is shipped from finished goods, "off the shelf," and therefore is finished prior to a customer order arriving. The master scheduling and final assembly scheduling are conducted at the finished-goods level.

Manufacturability A measure of the design of a product or process in terms of its ability to be produced easily, consistently, and with high quality.

Manufacturing Cycle The length of time between the release of an order to the shop and the shipment to the final customer or receipt into finished stores: *Syn:* manufacturing lead time; production cycle

Manufacturing Environment The framework in which manufacturing strategy is developed and implemented. Elements of the manufacturing environment include external environmental forces, corporate strategy, business unit strategy, other functional strategies (marketing, engineering, finance, etc.), product selection, product/process design, product/process technology, and management competencies.

Manufacturing Lead Time The total time required to manufacture an item, exclusive of lower-level purchasing lead time. Included here are order preparation time, queue time, setup time, run time, move time, inspection time, and put--away time. *Syn:* manufacturing cycle

Manufacturing Order A document, group of documents, or schedule conveying authority for the manufacture of specified parts of products in specified quantities. *Syn:* batch card; job order; production order; work order; shop order

Manufacturing Resource Planning (MRP II) A method for the effective planning of all resources of a manufacturing company. Ideally, it addresses operational planning in units, financial planning in dollars, and has simulation capability to answer "what if" questions. It is made up of a variety of functions, each linked together: business planning, sales and operations planning, master scheduling, material requirements planning, capacity requirements planning, and the execution support systems for capacity and material. Output from these systems is integrated with financial reports such as the business plan, purchase commitment report, shipping budget, inventory projections in dollars, etc. Manufacturing resource planning is a direct outgrowth and extension of closed-loop MRP.

Manufacturing Strategy A collective pattern of decisions that act upon the formulation and deployment of manufacturing resources. To be most effective, the manufacturing strategy should act in support of the overall strategic direction of the business and provide for competitive advantages.

Manufacturing Volume Strategies An element of manufacturing strategy that includes a series of assumptions and predictions about long-term market, technology, and competitive behavior in the following areas: 1) the predicted growth and variability of demand, 2) the costs of building and operating different-sized plants, 3) the rate and direction of technological improvement, 4) the likely behavior of competitors, and 5) the anticipated impact of international competitors, markets, and sources of supply. It is the sequence of specific volume decisions over time that determines an organization's long-term manufacturing volume strategy.

Market Demand The total need for a product or product line.

Master Planning A classification scheme that includes the following activities: forecasting and order servicing (which together constitute demand management); production and resource planning; and master scheduling (which includes the final assembly schedule, the master schedule, and the rough cut capacity plan).

Master Schedule (MPS) The anticipated build schedule for those items assigned to the master scheduler. The master scheduler maintains the schedule and, in turn, it becomes a set of planning numbers that drives material requirements planning. It represents what the company plans to produce expressed in specific configurations, quantities, and dates. The master schedule is not a sales forecast that represents a statement of demand. The master schedule must take into account the forecast, the production plan, and other important considerations such as backlog, availability of material, availability of capacity, management policies and goals, etc.

Master Schedule Item An item number selected to be planned by the master scheduler. The item is deemed critical in terms of its impact on lower-level components and/or resources such as skilled labor, key machines, dollars, etc. Therefore, the master scheduler, not the computer, maintains the plan for these items. A master schedule item may be an end item, a component, a pseudo number, or an event.

Master Schedule Process A time-phased planning activity using firm and planned quantities of demand, supply, and inventory balances for each item. Its primary use is to help in developing the master schedule, and it contains lines for forecast and customer order demands, the MPS supply, and the available-to-promise and projected available inventory balances. Most computer systems use logic to assist the master scheduler in establishing MPS quantities and due dates that meet lead time, safety stock, and lot-size policies established for the item.

Master Scheduler The job title of the person who manages the master schedule. This person should have substantial knowledge of the company's products, processes, and people.

Material Requirements Planning (MRP) A set of techniques that uses bills-of-material, inventory data, and the master schedule to calculate requirements for materials. It makes recommendations to release replenishment orders for materials. Further, since it is time-phased, it makes recommendations to reschedule open orders when due dates and need dates are not in phase. Time-phased MRP begins with the items listed on the MPS and determines the quantity of all components and materials required to fabricate those items and the date that the components and material are required. Time-phased MRP is accomplished by exploding the bills-of-materials, adjusting for inventory quantities on hand or on order, and offsetting the net requirements by the appropriate lead times.

Materials Management The grouping of management functions supporting the complete cycle of material flow, from the purchase and internal control of production materials to the planning and control of work-in-process to the warehousing, shipping, and distribution of the finished product.

Mixed-Model Master Schedule The technique of setting and maintaining the master schedule to support mixed-model production.

Mixed-Model Production Making several different parts of products in varying lot sizes so that a factory is making close to the same mix of products that will be sold that day. The mixed-model schedule governs the making and the delivery of component parts, including those provided by outside suppliers. The goal is to build every model, every day, according to daily demand.

Mix Forecast Forecast of the proportion of products that will be sold within a given product family, or the proportion of options offered within a product line. Product and option mix must be forecasted as well as aggregate product families. Even though the appropriate level of units is forecasted for a given product line, an inaccurate mix forecast can create material shortages and inventory problems.

Modular Bill of Material A type of planning bill that is arranged in product modules or options. It is often used in companies where the product has many optional features, e.g., eight-, six-, and four-cylinder engines; automatic versus manual transmissions, power steering versus manual; etc.

Move Card In Just-in-Time context, a card or other signal indicating that a specific number of units of a particular item are to be taken from a source (usually outbound stockpoint) and taken to the point of use (usually inbound stockpoint). It authorizes the movement of one part number between a single pair of work centers. The card circulates between the outbound stockpoint of the supplying work center and the inbound stockpoint of the using work center. *Syn:* move signal

Multilevel Bill-of-Material A display of all the components directly or indirectly used in a parent, together with the quantity required with each component. If a component is a subassembly, blend, intermediate, etc., all of its components will also be exhibited and all of their components, down to purchase parts and materials.

Multilevel Master Schedule A master scheduling technique that allows any level in an end item's bill-of-material to be master scheduled. To accomplish this, MPS items must receive requirements from independent and dependent demand sources.

Net Requirements In MRP, the net requirements for a part or an assembly are derived as a result of applying gross requirements and allocations against inventory on hand, scheduled receipts, and safety stock. Net requirements, lot sized and offset for lead time, become planned orders.

Netting The process of calculating net requirements.

On-Hand Balance The quantity shown in the inventory records as being physically in stock.

Operation Number A sequential number, usually two, three, or four digits (such as 010, 020, 030, etc.), that indicates the sequence in which operations are to be performed within an item's routing.

Option A choice or feature offered to customers for customizing the end product. In many companies the term "option" means a mandatory choice—the customer must select from one of the available choices. For example, in ordering a new car, the customer must specify the engine (option), but need not necessarily select an air conditioner (accessory).

Option Overplanning *Syn:* hedge

Order Entry The process of accepting and translating what a customer wants into terms used by the manufacturer or distributor. This can be as simple as creating shipping documents for a finished goods product line, or it might be a more complicated series of activities, including engineering efforts for make-to-order products.

Order Promising The process of making a delivery commitment, i.e., answering the question, When can you ship? For make-to-order products, this usually involves a check of uncommitted material and availability of capacity. *Syn:* customer order promising; order dating

Order Quantity The amount of an item to be ordered. *Syn:* lot size

Outbound Stockpoint Designated locations near the point of use on a plant floor to which material produced is taken until it is pulled to the next operation.

Pareto's Law A concept developed by Pareto, an Italian economist, that states that a small percentage of a group accounts for the largest fraction of the impact, value, etc. For example, 20 percent of the inventory items may constitute 80 percent of the inventory value. *Syn:* Pareto analysis

Pegging In MRP, the capability to identify for a given item the sources of its gross requirements and/or allocations. Pegging can be thought of as "live where-used" information.

Period Order Quantity A lot-sizing technique under which the lot size is equal to the net requirements for a given number of periods, e.g., a week into the future. *Syn:* fixed period ordering

Phantom Bill-of-Material A bill-of-material coding and structuring technique used primarily for transient (nonstocked) subassemblies. For the transient item, lead time is set to zero and the order quantity to lot-for-lot. This permits MRP logic to drive requirements straight through the phantom item to its components, but the MRP system usually retains its ability to net against any occasional inventories of the item. This technique also facilitates the use of common bills-of-material for engineering and manufacturing. *Syn:* blow-through; pseudo bill-of-material; transient bill-of material

Pipeline Stock Inventory to fill the transportation network and the distribution system, including the flow through intermediate stocking points. The flow time through the pipeline has a major effect on the amount of inventory required in the pipeline. Time factors involve order transmission, order processing, shipping, transportation, receiving, stocking, review time, etc. *Syn:* pipeline inventory; transportation inventory

Planned Order A suggested order quantity, release date, and due date created by MRP processing when it encounters net requirements. Planned orders are created for components at the next lower level. Planned orders, along with released orders, serve as input to capacity requirements planning to show the total capacity requirements by work center in future time periods.

Planning Bill-of-Material An artificial grouping of items and/or events in the bill-of-material format, used to facilitate master scheduling and/or material planning. It is sometimes called a pseudo bill-of-material.

Planning Fence *Syn:* planning time fence

Planning Horizon The amount of time the master schedule extends into the future. This is normally set to cover a minimum of cumulative lead time plus time for lot sizing low-level components and for capacity changes of primary work centers. *Syn:* horizon

Planning Time Fence A policy or guideline established to note where various restrictions or changes in operating procedures take place. For example, changes to the master schedule can be accomplished easily beyond the cumulative lead time, whereas changes inside the cumulative lead time become increasingly more difficult to a point where changes should be resisted. Planning time fences can be used to define these points.

Prediction An intuitive estimate of demand taking into account changes and new factors influencing the market, as opposed to a forecast, which is an objective projection of the past into the future.

Priority Planning The function of determining what material is needed and when. Master scheduling and material requirements planning are the elements used for the planning and replanning process in order to maintain proper due dates on required materials.

Probability Mathematically, a number between zero and one that estimates the number of experiments (if the same experiment were being repeated many times) in which a particular result would occur. This number can be either subjective or based upon the empirical results of experimentation. It can also be derived for a process to give the probable outcome of experimentation.

Procedures Definitions of approved methods used to accomplish tasks.

Process Plant *Syn:* flow shop

Production Plan The agreed upon plan that comes from the sales and operations planning function, specifically the overall level of manufacturing output planned to be produced, usually stated as a monthly rate for each product family (group of products, items, options, features, etc.). Various units of measure can be used to express the plan: units, tonnage, standard hours, number of workers, etc. The production plan is management's authorization for the master scheduler to convert it into a more detailed plan, that is, the master schedule.

Productivity An overall measure of the ability to produce a good or a service. It is the actual output of production compared to the actual input of resources. Productivity is a relative measure across time or against common entities. In the production literature, attempts have been made to define total productivity where the effects of labor and capital are combined and divided into the output. One example is a ratio that is calculated by adding the standard hours of labor actually produced plus the standard machine hours actually produced in a given time period divided by the actual hours available for both labor and machines in the time period.

Product Life Cycle The stages a new product idea goes through from beginning to end, i.e., the stages that a product passes through from introduction through growth, maturity, and decline. The time from initial research and development to the time at which sales and support of the product to customers are withdrawn. The period of time during which a product can be produced and marketed profitably.

Product Structure The sequence that components follow during their manufacturing into a product. A typical product structure would show raw material converted into fabricated components, components put together to make subassemblies, subassemblies going into assemblies, etc.

Projected Available Balance The inventory balance projected into the future. It is the running sum of on-hand inventory minus requirements plus scheduled receipts and planned orders.

Prototype A product model constructed for testing and evaluation to see how the product performs before releasing the product to manufacture.

Pseudo A grouping of components which is artificial in that it cannot be manufactured. "Pseudo" common parts groups and option groups are frequently found in modularized bills-of-materials. Pseudos are "blow-through" items.

Pull System (Production) The production of items only as demanded for use, or to replace those taken for use.

Push System (Production) The production of items at times required by a given schedule planned in advance.

Rate-Based Scheduling A method for scheduling and producing based on a periodic rate, e.g., daily, weekly, or monthly. Traditionally, this method has been applied to high-volume and process industries. The concept has been recently applied within job shops using cellular layouts and mixed-model level schedules where the production rate is matched to the selling rate.

Remanufacturing An industrial process in which worn-out products are restored to like-new condition. In contrast, a repaired or rebuilt product normally retains its identity, and only those parts that have failed or are badly worn are replaced or serviced.

Repetitive Manufacturing A form of manufacturing where various items with similar routings are made across the same process whenever production occurs. Products may be made in separate batches or continuously. Production in a repetitive environment is not a function of speed or volume.

Rescheduling The process of changing order or operation due dates, usually as a result of their being out of phase with when they are needed.

Rescheduling Assumption A fundamental piece of MRP logic that assumes that existing open orders can be rescheduled in nearer time periods far more easily than new orders can be released and received. As a result, planned order receipts are not created until all scheduled receipts have been applied to cover gross requirements.

Resource Anything that adds value to a product or service in its creation, production, and delivery.

Rough Cut Capacity Planning (RCCP) The process of converting the production plan and/or the master schedule into capacity needs for key resources: work force, machinery, warehouse space, suppliers' capabilities, and in some cases, money. Bills-of-resources are often used to accomplish this. Comparison of capacity required of items in the MPS to available capacity is usually done for each key resource. RCCP assists the master scheduler in establishing a feasible master schedule.

Routing A set of information detailing the method of manufacture of a particular item. It includes the operations to be performed, their sequence, the various work centers to be involved, and the standards for setup and run. In some companies, the routing also includes information on tooling, operator skill levels, inspection operations, testing requirements, etc. *Syn:* bill of operations; instruction sheet; manufacturing data sheet; operation chart; operation list; operation sheet; routing sheet

Safety Capacity The planned amount by which the available capacity exceeds current productive capacity. This capacity provides protection from planned activities such as resource contention, preventive maintenance, etc., and unplanned activities such as resource breakdown, poor quality, rework, lateness, etc. Safety capacity plus productive capacity plus idle or excess capacity is equal to 100 percent of capacity. *Syn:* protective capacity

Safety Lead Time An element of time added to normal lead time for the purpose of completing an order in advance of its real need date to protect against fluctuations in lead time. When used, the MRP system, in offsetting for lead time, will plan both order release and order completion for earlier dates than it would otherwise.

Safety Stock In general, a quantity of stock planned to be in inventory to protect against fluctuations in demand and/or supply. In the context of master scheduling, the additional inventory and/or capacity planned as protection against forecast errors and/or short-term changes in the backlog.

Safety Time *Syn:* safety lead time

Sales and Operations Planning The function of setting the overall level of manufacturing output (production plan) and other activities to best satisfy the current planned capabilities are compared and a business strategy that includes a sales plan, production plan, budgets, pro forma financial statements, and supporting plans for materials and work force requirements, etc., is developed. One of its primary purposes is to establish sales and production rates that will achieve management's objective of satisfying customer demand by maintaining, raising, or lowering inventories or backlogs, while usually attempting to keep the work force relatively stable. Because these plans affect many company functions, they are normally prepared with information from marketing and sales and coordinated with the functions of manufacturing, engineering, finance, materials, etc.

Sales Mix The proportion of individual product-type sales volumes that make up the total sales volume.

Sales Plan The overall level of sales expected to be achieved, usually stated as a monthly rate of sales for a product family (group of products, items, options, features, etc.). It needs to be expressed in units identical to the production plan (as well as dollars) for planning purposes. It represents sales and marketing managements' commitment to take all reasonable steps necessary to make the sales forecast (a prediction) accurately represent actual customer orders received.

Sales Representative Employee authorized to accept a customer's order for a product. Sales representatives usually go to the customer's location when industrial products are being marketed.

Scheduled Receipt Orders already released either to manufacturing (production, manufacturing, or shop orders) or to suppliers (purchase orders).

Scheduling The act of creating a schedule, such as a master schedule, shop schedule, maintenance schedule, supplier schedule, etc.

Scrap Factor A percentage factor in the product structure used to increase gross requirements to account for anticipated loss within the manufacture of a particular product. *Syn:* scrap rate

Sequencing Determining the order in which a manufacturirng facility is to process a number of different jobs in order to achieve certain objectives.

Service Parts Those modules, components, and elements that are planned to be used without modification to replace an original part during the performance of maintenance. *Syn:* repair parts

Service Parts Demand The need or requirement for a component to be sold by itself, as opposed to being used in production to make a higher-level product. *Syn:* repair parts demand

Setup Time The time required for a specific machine, resource, work center, or line to convert from the production of the last good piece of lot A to the first good piece of lot B.

Shelf Life The amount of time an item may be held in inventory before it becomes unusable.

Shipping Lead Time The number of working days in transit normally required for goods to move between a shipping and receiving point, plus acceptance time in days at the receiving point.

Shop Packet A package of documents used to plan and control the shop floor movement of an order. The packet may include a manufacturing order, operations sheets, engineering blueprints, picking lists, move tickets, inspection tickets, time tickets, and others.

Significant Part Number A part number that is intended to convey certain information, such as the source of the part, the material in the part, the shape of the part, etc. These usually make part numbers longer. *Ant:* nonsignificant part number

Simulation The technique of using representative or artificial data to reproduce in a model various conditions that are likely to occur in the actual performance of a system. It is frequently used to test the behavior of a system under different operating policies. Within MRP II, using the operational data to perform "what-if" evaluations of alternative plans to answer the question, Can we do it? If yes, the simulation can then be run in the financial mode to help answer the question, Do we really want to? *Syn:* what-if analysis

Split Lot A manufacturing order quantity that has been divided into two or more smaller quantities, usually after the order has been released. The quantities of a split lot may be worked on in parallel or a portion of the original quantity may be sent ahead to a subsequent operation to be worked on while work on the remainder of the quantity is being completed at the current operation. The purpose of splitting a lot is to reduce the lead time of part of the order.

Subcontract Sending production work outside to another manufacturer.

Super Bill of Material A type of planning bill, located at the top level in the structure, that ties together various modular bills (and possibly a common parts bill) to define an entire product or product family. The quantity per relationship of the super bill to its modules represents the forecasted percentage of demand of each module. The master scheduled quantities of the super bill explode to create requirements for the modules that also are master scheduled.

Supply The quantity of goods available for use. The actual or planned replenishment of a product or component. The replenishment quantities are created in response to a demand for the product or component or in anticipation of such a demand.

Synchronized Production A manufacturing management philosophy that includes a consistent set of principles, procedures, and techniques where every action is evaluated in terms of the global goal of the system. Both kanban, which is a part of the JIT philosophy, and drum-buffer-rope, which is a part of the theory of constraints philosophy, represent synchronized production control approaches. *Syn:* Just-in-Time; theory of constraints

Time Phasing The technique of expressing future demand, supply, and inventories by time period. Time phasing is one of the key elements of material requirements planning.

Total Employee Involvement (TEI) An empowerment program where employees are invited to participate in actions and decision making that were traditionally reserved for management.

Two-Level MPS A master scheduling approach for make-to-order products where an end-product type is master scheduled along with key options and common parts.

U-Lines Production lines shaped like the letter U. The shape allows workers to easily perform several different tasks without much walk time.

The number of workstations in a U-line is usually determined by line balancing. U-lines promote communication.

Vertical Display A method of displaying or printing output from a master scheduling system where requirements, scheduled receipts, projected balance, etc., are displayed vertically, i.e., down the page. Vertical displays are often used in conjunction with bucketless systems. *Ant:* horizontal display

Voice of the Customer Actual customer descriptions in words for the functions and features they desire for products and services. In the strict definition, as relates to quality function deployment (QFD), the term "customer" indicates the external customer to the supplying entity.

What-If Analysis The process of evaluating alternate strategies by answering the consequences of changes to forecasts, manufacturing plans, inventory levels, etc. *Syn:* simulation

Work Center A specific production facility, consisting of one or more people and/or machines with identical capabilities, that can be considered as one unit for purposes of capacity requirements planning and detailed scheduling. *Syn:* load center

Work-in-Process (WIP) A product or products in various stages of completion throughout the plant, including all material, from raw material that has been released for initial processing up to completely processed material awaiting final inspection and acceptance as finished product. Many accounting systems also include the value of semifinished stock and components in this category. *Syn:* in-process inventory

Work Order *Syn:* manufacturing order

Workplace Organization The arrangement of tools, equipment, materials, and supplies according to their frequency of use. Those items that are never used are removed from the workplace, and those items that are used frequently are located for fast, easy access and replacement. This concept is an extension of "a place for everything and everything in its place" idea.

Workstation The assigned location where a worker performs the job; it could be a machine or a work bench.

Yield The ratio of useable output from a process to its input.

Index